Date Due

THE COLLECTED WORKS OF
WALTER BAGEHOT

VOLUME TWO

THE COLLECTED WORKS OF

WALTER BAGEHOT

EDITED BY

Norman St John-Stevas

The Literary Essays
(in two volumes)

VOLUME TWO

HARVARD UNIVERSITY PRESS

CAMBRIDGE, MASSACHUSETTS

1965

The Collected Works of Walter Bagehot
First published 1965
This edition © *The Economist* 1965

PRINTED IN ENGLAND

THE COLLECTED WORKS OF
WALTER BAGEHOT

VOLUMES I & II · LITERARY ESSAYS
VOLUME III · HISTORICAL
VOLUMES IV & V · POLITICAL
VOLUMES VI & VII · ECONOMIC
VOLUME VIII · LETTERS & MISCELLANY

CONTENTS

Volume Two

Pierre Jean de Béranger
Introductory note

Pierre Jean de Béranger (1780–1857), (self-styled 'de') was neglected by his family and spent most of his youth working at an inn. In 1804 his verses were seen by Lucien Bonaparte, who arranged for him to receive a small pension. This enabled him to write *Chansons Morales et Autres*, 1815, containing *Le Roi d'Yvetot*, an already famous and genial mockery of Napoleon's despotism. Béranger's *Chansons*, 1821, satirised the abuses of the Restoration, for which he was dismissed from his post and imprisoned. His Bonaparte sympathies were too vigorously expressed in *Chansons Inédites*, 1828, and he was again imprisoned and heavily fined, but his popularity was increased by this severity and the fine was paid by public subscription. *Chansons Nouvelles et Dernières* appeared in 1833. During his lifetime Béranger was considered the national poet of France, and at his death was given a magnificent public funeral by Napoleon III.

Béranger[1]

THE invention of books has at least one great advantage. It has half-abolished one of the worst consequences of the diversity of languages. Literature enables nations to understand one another. Oral intercourse hardly does this. In English a distinguished foreigner says not what he thinks, but what he can. There is a certain intimate essence of national meaning which is as untranslatable as good poetry. Dry thoughts are cosmopolitan; but the delicate associations of language which express character, the traits of speech which mark the man, differ in every tongue, have not even cumbrous circumlocutions that are equivalent in another. National character is a deep thing—a shy thing; you cannot exhibit much of it to people who have a difficulty in understanding your language; you are in strange society, and you feel you will not be understood.

'Let an English gentleman,' writes Mr. Thackeray, 'who has dwelt two, four, or ten years in Paris, say at the end of any given period how much he knows of French society, how many French houses he has entered, and how many French friends he has made. Intimacy there is none; we see but the outsides of the people. Year by year we live in France, and grow grey and see no more. We play *écarté* with Monsieur de Trêfle every night; but what do we know of the heart of the man—of the inward ways, thoughts, and customs of Trêfle? We have danced with Countess Flicflac, Tuesdays and Thursdays, ever since the peace; and how far are we advanced in her acquaintance since we first twirled her round a room? We know her velvet gown and her diamonds; we know her smiles and her simpers and her rouge; but the real, rougeless, *intime* Flicflac we know not.'* Even if our words

---

[1] *Œuvres complètes de C.-J. de Béranger. Nouvelle édition revue par l'Auteur*, contenant *les Dix Chansons nouvelles, le facsimile d'une Lettre de Béranger; illustrée de cinquante-deux gravures sur acier, d'après Charlet, D'Aubigny, Johannot Grenier, De Lemud, Pauquet, Penguilly, Raffet, Sandoz, exécutées par les artistes les plus distingués, et d'un beau portrait d'après nature par Sandoz.* 2 vols. 8vo, 1855. This essay was first published in the *National Review* for October 1857, Volume V, pp. 411–39. (Béranger's initials should be P. J. not C.-J.—Ed.)

* We have been obliged to abridge the above extract, and in so doing have left out the humour of it.

did not stutter, as they do stutter on our tongue, she would not tell us what she is.

Literature has half mended this. Books are exportable; the essence of national character lies flat on a printed page. Men of genius with the impulses of solitude produce works of art, whose words can be read and re-read and partially taken in by foreigners to whom they could never be uttered, the very thought of whose unsympathising faces would freeze them on the surface of the mind. Alexander Smith has accused poetical reviewers of beginning as far as possible from their subject. It may seem to some, though it is not so really, that we are exemplifying this saying in commencing as we have commenced an article on Béranger.

There are two kinds of poetry, which one may call poems of this world, and poems not of this world. We see a certain society on the earth held together by certain relations, performing certain acts, exhibiting certain phenomena, calling forth certain emotions. The millions of human beings who compose it have their various thoughts, feelings, and desires. They hate, act, and live.[2] The social bond presses them closely together; and from their proximity new sentiments arise, which are half superficial and do not touch the inmost soul, but which nevertheless are unspeakably important in the actual constitution of human nature, and work out their effects for good and for evil on the characters of those who are subjected to their influence. These sentiments of the world, as one may speak, differ from the more primitive impulses and emotions of our inner nature as the superficial phenomena of the material universe from what we fancy is its real essence. Passing hues, transient changes have their course before our eyes; a multiplex diorama is for ever displayed; underneath it all we fancy— such is the inevitable constitution of our thinking faculty—a primitive immovable essence, which is modified into all the ever-changing phenomena we see, which is the grey granite whereon they lie, the primary substance whose *débris* they all are. Just so from the original and primitive emotions of man, society—the evolving capacity of combined action—brings out desires which seem new, in a sense are new, which have no existence out of the society itself, are coloured by its customs at the moment, change with the fashions of the age. Such a principle is what we may call social gaiety: the love of combined amusement which all men feel and variously express, and which is to

[2] Possibly this should be 'love' but the *National* has 'live'—p. 411.

the higher faculties of the soul what a gay running stream is to the everlasting mountain,—a light, altering element which beautifies while it modifies. Poetry does not shrink from expressing such feelings; on the contrary, their renovating cheerfulness blends appropriately with her inspiriting delight. Each age and each form of the stimulating imagination has a fashion of its own. Sir Walter sings in his modernised chivalry:

> Waken, lords and ladies gay,
> On the mountain dawns the day,
> All the jolly chase is here,
> With hawk, and horse, and hunting-spear!
> Hounds are in their couples yelling,
> Hawks are whistling, horns are knelling,
> Merrily, merrily, mingle they,
> 'Waken, lords and ladies gay.'
>
> Louder, louder, chant the lay,
> Waken, lords and ladies gay!
> Tell them youth, and mirth, and glee,
> Run a course as well as we;
> Time, stern huntsman! who can baulk,
> Staunch as hound, and fleet as hawk :
> Think of this, and rise with day,
> Gentle lords and ladies gay.

The poet of the people, '*vilain et très vilain*,' sings with the pauper Bohemian

> Voir c'est avoir. Allons courir!
> Vie errante
> Est chose enivrante.
> Voir c'est avoir. Allons courir!
> Car tout voir c'est tout conquérir.
>
> Nous n'avons donc, exempts d'orgueil,
> De lois vaines,
> De lourdes chaînes;
> Nous n'avons donc, exempts d'orgueil,
> Ni berceau, ni toit, ni cercueil.

13

Mais, croyez-en notre gaîeté,
Noble ou prêtre,
Valet ou maître;
Mais, croyez-en notre gaîeté,
Le bonheur c'est la liberté.

Oui, croyez-en notre gaîeté,
Noble ou prêtre,
Valet ou maître;
Oui, croyez-en notre gaîeté,
Le bonheur c'est la liberté.

The forms of these poems of social amusement are, in truth, as various as the social amusement itself. The variety of the world, singularly various as it everywhere is, is nowhere so various as in that. Men have more ways of amusing themselves than of doing anything else they do. But the essence—the characteristic—of these poems everywhere is, that they express more or less well the lighter desires of human nature;—those that have least of unspeakable depth, partake most of what is perishable and earthly, and least of the immortal soul. The objects of these desires are social accidents; excellent perhaps, essential possibly,—so is human nature made—in one form and variety or another, to the well-being of the soul, yet in themselves transitory, fleeting, and in other moods contemptible. The old saying was, that to endure solitude a man must either be a beast or a god. It is in the lighter play of social action, in that which is neither animal nor divine, which in its half-way character is so natural to man, that these poems of society, which we have called poems of amusement, have their place.

This species does not, however, exhaust the whole class. Society gives rise to another sort of poems, differing from this one as contemplation differs from desire. Society may be thought of as an object. The varied scene of men,—their hopes, fears, anxieties, maxims, actions,—present a sight more interesting to man than any other which has ever existed, or which can exist; and it may be viewed in all moods of mind, and with the change of inward emotion as the external object seems to change: not that it really does so, but that some sentiments are more favourable to clear-sightedness than others are; and some bring before us one aspect of the subject and fix our attention upon it, others a different one and bind our minds to that likewise.

Among the most remarkable of these varied views is the world's view of itself. The world, such as it is, has made up its mind what it is. Childishly deceivable by charlatans on every other subject,—imposed on by pedantry, by new and unfounded science, by ancient and unfounded reputation, a prey to pomposity, overrun with recondite fools, ignorant of all else,—society knows itself. The world knows a man of the world. A certain tradition pervades it; a *disciplina* of the market-place teaches what the collective society of men has ever been, and what, so long as the nature of man is the same, it cannot and will not cease to be. Literature, the written expression of human nature in every variety, takes up this variety likewise. Ancient literature exhibits it, from obvious causes, in a more simple manner than modern literature can. Those who are brought up in times like the present necessarily hear a different set of opinions, fall in with other words, are under the shadow of a higher creed. In consequence, they cannot have the simple *naïveté* of the old world; they cannot speak with easy equanimity of the fugitiveness of life, the necessity of death, of goodness as a mean, of sin as an extreme. The theory of the universe has ceased to be an open question. Still the spirit of Horace is alive, and as potent as that of any man. His tone is that of prime ministers; his easy philosophy is that of courts and parliaments; you may hear his words where no other foreign words are ever heard. He is but the extreme and perfect type of a whole class of writers, some of whom exist in every literary age, and who give an expression to what we may call the poetry of equanimity, that is, the world's view of itself; its self-satisfaction, its conviction that you must bear what comes, not hope for much, think *some* evil, never be excited, admire little, and then you will be at peace. This creed does not sound attractive in description. Nothing, it has been said, is so easy as to be 'religious on paper:' on the other hand, it is rather difficult to be worldly in speculation; the mind of man, when its daily maxims are put before it, revolts from any thing so stupid, so mean, so poor. It requires a consummate art to reconcile men in print to that moderate and insidious philosophy which creeps into all hearts, colours all speech, influences all action. We may not stiffen common sense into a creed; our very ambition forbids:

> It hears a voice within it tell:
> '*Calm's not life's crown, though calm is well,*'
> 'Tis all perhaps which man acquires,
> But 'tis not what our youth desires.

Oui, je voudrais qu'elle fût laide,
Mais laide, laide à faire peur.
Belle ainsi faut-il que je l'aime!
Dieu, reprends ce don éclatant;
Je le demande à l'enfer même:
Qu'elle soit laide et que je l'aime autant.

A ces mots m'apparaît le diable;
C'est le père de la laideur.
'Rendons-la,' dit-il, 'effroyable;
De tes rivaux trompons l'ardeur.
J'aime assez ces métamorphoses.
Ta belle ici vient en chantant:
Perles, tombez; fanez-vous, roses.
La voilà laide, et tu l'aimes autant.'

'Laide! moi?' dit-elle, étonnée.
Elle s'approche d'un miroir,
Doute d'abord, puis, consternée,
Tombe en un morne désespoir.
'Pour moi seul tu jurais de vivre,'
Lui dis-je, à ses pieds me jetant;
'A mon seul amour il te livre.
Plus laide encore, je t'aimerais autant.'

Ses yeux éteints fondent en larmes,
Alors sa douleur m'attendrit:
'Ah! rendez, rendez-lui ses charmes.'
'Soit!' répond Satan qui sourit.
Ainsi que naît la fraîche aurore,
Sa beauté renaît à l'instant.
Elle est, je crois, plus belle encore;
Elle est plus belle, et moi je l'aime autant.

Vite au miroir elle s'assure
Qu'on lui rend bien tous ses appas;
Des pleurs restent sur sa figure,
Qu'elle essuie en grondant tout bas.
Satan s'envole, et la cruelle
Fuit et s'écrie en me quittant:
'Jamais fille que Dieu fit belle
Ne doit aimer qui peut l'aimer autant.'

And this is even a more characteristic specimen:

La Mouche
Au bruit de notre gaîté folle,
Au bruit des verres, des chansons,
Quelle mouche murmure et vole,
Et revient quand nous la chassons? (*bis.*)
C'est quelque dieu, je le soupçonne,
Qu'un peu de bonheur rend jaloux.
Ne souffrons point qu'elle bourdonne, ⎤
Qu'elle bourdonne autour de nous.   ⎦ *bis.*)

Transformée en mouche hideuse,
Amis, oui, c'est, j'en suis certain,
La Raison, déité grondeuse,
Qu'irrite un si joyeux festin.
L'orage approche, le ciel tonne;
Voilà ce que dit son courroux.
Ne souffrons point qu'elle bourdonne,
Qu'elle bourdonne autour de nous.

C'est la Raison qui vient me dire:
'A ton âge on vit en reclus.
Ne bois plus tant, cesse de rire,
Cesse d'aimer, ne chante plus.'
Ainsi son beffroi toujours sonne
Aux lueurs des feux les plus doux.
Ne souffrons point qu'elle bourdonne,
Qu'elle bourdonne autour de nous.

C'est la Raison; gare à Lisette!
Son dard la menace toujours.
Dieux! il perce la collerette:
Le sang coule! accourez, Amours!
Amours, poursuivez la félonne;
Qu'elle expire enfin sous vos coups.
Ne souffrons point qu'elle bourdonne,
Qu'elle bourdonne autour de nous.

Victoire! amis, elle se noie
Dans l'aï que Lise a versé.
Victoire! et qu'aux mains de la Joie
Le sceptre enfin soit replacé.

Un souffle ébranle sa couronne;
Une mouche nous troublait tous.
Ne craignons plus qu'elle bourdonne,
Qu'elle bourdonne autour de nous.

To make poetry out of a fly is a difficult operation. It used to be said of the Lake school of criticism, in Mr. Wordsworth's early and more rigid days, that there was no such term as 'elegant' in its nomenclature. The reason is that, dealing, or attempting to deal, only with the essential aboriginal principals of human nature, that school had no room and no occasion for those minor contrivances of thought and language which are necessary to express the complex accumulation of little feelings, the secondary growth of human emotion. The underwood of nature is 'elegant'; the bare ascending forest tree despises what is so trivial,—it is grave and solemn. To[3] such verses, on the other hand, as have been quoted, 'elegance' is essential; the delicate finish of fleeting forms is the only excellence they can have.

The characteristic deficiencies of French literature have no room to show themselves in this class of art. 'Though France herself denies,' says a recent writer, 'yet all other nations with one voice proclaim her inferiority to her rivals in poetry and romance, and in all the other elevated fields of fiction. A French Dante, or Michael Angelo, or Cervantes, or Murillo, or Goethe, or Shakespeare, or Milton, we at once perceive to be a mere anomaly; a supposition which may, indeed, be proposed in terms, but which in reality is inconceivable and impossible.' In metaphysics, the reason seems to be that the French character is incapable of being mastered by an unseen idea, without being so tyrannised over by it as to be incapable of artistic development. Such a character as Robespierre's may explain what we mean. His entire nature was taken up and absorbed in certain ideas; he had almost a vanity in them; he was of them, and they were of him. But they appear in his mind, in his speeches, in his life, in their driest and barest form; they have no motion, life, or roundness. We are obliged to use many metaphors remotely and with difficulty to indicate the procedure of the imagination. In one of these metaphors we figure an idea of imagination as a living thing, a kind of growing plant, with a peculiar form, and ever preserving its identity, but absorbing from the earth and air all kindred, suitable, and, so to say, annexable materials. In a mind such as Robespierre's, in the type of the fanatic mind, there

---

[3] The *National Review* has 'Of' instead of 'To'.—p. 419.

is no such thing. The ideas seem a kind of dry hard capsules, never growing, never enlarging, never uniting. Development is denied them; they cannot expand, or ripen, or mellow. Dogma is a dry hard husk; poetry has the soft down of the real fruit. Ideas seize on the fanatic mind just as they do on the poetical; they have the same imperious ruling power. The difference is, that in the one the impelling force is immutable, iron, tyrannical; in the other the rule is expansive, growing, free, taking up from all around it moment by moment whatever is fit, as in the political world a great constitution arises through centuries, with a shape that does not vary, but with movement for its essence and the fluctuation of elements for its vitality. A thin poor mind like Robespierre's seems pressed and hampered by the bony fingers of a skeleton-hand; a poet's is expanded and warmed at the same time that it is impelled by a pure life-blood of imagination. The French, as we have said, are hardly capable of this. When great remote ideas seize upon them at all, they become fanatics. The wild, chimerical, revolutionary, mad Frenchman has the stiffest of human minds. He is under the law of his creed; he has not attained to the higher freedom of the impelling imagination. The prosing rhetoric of the French tragedy shows the same defect in another form. The ideas which should have become living realities, remain as lean abstractions. The characters are speaking officials, jets of attenuated oratory. But exactly on this very account the French mind has a genius for the poetry of society. Unable to remove itself into the higher region of imagined forms, it has the quickest detective insight into the exact relation of surrounding superficial phenomena. There are two ways of putting it: either, being fascinated by the present, they cannot rise to what is not present; or, being by defect of nature unable to rise to what is not present, they are concentrated and absorbed in that which is so. Of course there ought not to be, but there *is*, a world of *bonbons*, of *salons*, of *esprit*. Living in the present, they have the poetry of the present. The English genius is just the opposite. Our cumbrous intellect has no call to light artificialities. We do not excel in punctuated detail or nicely-squared elaboration. It puts us out of patience that others should. A respectable Englishman murmured in the *Café de Paris*, 'I wish I had a hunch of mutton.' He could not bear the secondary niceties with which he was surrounded. Our art has the same principle. We excel in strong, noble imagination, in solid stuff. Shakespeare is tough work; he has the play of the rising energy, the buoyant freedom of the unbounded mind; but no writer is so destitute of the simplifying dexterities of the manipulating intellect.

It is dangerous for a foreigner to give an opinion on *minutiæ* of style, especially on points affecting the characteristic excellences of national style. The French language is always neat; all French styles somehow seem good. But Béranger appears to have a peculiar neatness. He tells us that all his songs are the production of a painful effort. If so, the reader should be most grateful; *he* suffers no pain. The delicate elaboration of the writer has given a singular currency to the words. Difficult writing is rarely easy reading. It can never be so when the labour is spent in piecing together elements not joined by an insensible touch of imagination. The highest praise is due to a writer whose ideas are more delicately connected by unconscious genius than other men's are, and yet who spends labour and toil in giving the production a yet cunninger finish, a still smoother connection. The characteristic aloofness of the Gothic mind, its tendency to devote itself to what is not present, is represented in composition by a want of care in the pettinesses of style. A certain clumsiness pervades all tongues of German origin. Instead of the language having been sharpened and improved by the constant keenness of attentive minds, it has been habitually used obtusely and crudely. Light, loquacious Gaul has for ages been the contrast. If you take up a pen just used by a good writer, for a moment you seem to write rather well. A language long employed by a delicate and critical society is a treasure of dextrous felicities. It is not, according to the fine expression of Mr. Emerson, 'fossil poetry;' it is crystallised *esprit*.

A French critic has praised Béranger for having retained the *refrain*, or burden, *'la rime de l'air.'* as he calls it. Perhaps music is more necessary as an accompaniment to the poetry of society than it is to any other poetry. Without a sensuous reminder, we might forget that it was poetry; especially in a sparkling, glittering, attenuated language, we might be absorbed as in the defined elegancies of prose. In half trivial compositions we easily forget the little central fancy. The music prevents this: it gives oneness to the parts, pieces together the shavings of the intellect, makes audible the flow of imagination.

The poetry of society tends to the poetry of love. All poetry tends that way. By some very subtle links, which no metaphysician has skilfully tracked, the imagination, even in effects and employments which seem remote, is singularly so connected. One smiles to see the feeling

recur. Half the poets can scarcely keep away from it: in the high and
dry epic you may see the poet return to it. And perhaps this is not
unaccountable. The more delicate and stealing the sensuous element,
the more the mind is disposed to brood upon it; the more we dwell
on it in stillness, the more it influences the wandering, hovering
faculty[4] which we term imagination. The first constructive effort of
imagination is beyond the limit of consciousness; the faculty works
unseen. But we know that it works in a certain soft leisure only: and
this in ordinary minds is almost confined to, in the highest is most
commonly accompanied by, the subtlest emotion of reverie. So in-
sinuating is that feeling, that no poet is alive to all its influences; so
potent is it, that the words of a great poet, in our complex modern
time, are rarely ever free from its traces. The phrase 'stealing calm,'
which most naturally and graphically describes the state of soul in
which the imagination works, quite equally expresses, it is said, the
coming in and continuance of the not uncommon emotion. Passing,
however, from such metaphysics, there is no difficulty in believing
that the poetry of society will tend to the most romantic part of society,
—away from aunts and uncles, antiquaries and wigs, to younger and
pleasanter elements. The talk of society does so, probably its literature
will do so likewise. There are, nevertheless, some limiting considerations, which make this tendency less all-powerful than we might
expect it to be. In the first place, the poetry of society cannot deal with
passion. Its light touch is not competent to express eager, intense
emotion. Rather, we should say, the essential nature of the poetry of
amusement is inconsistent with those rugged, firm, aboriginal elements which passion brings to the surface. The volcano is inconsistent
with careless talk; you cannot comfortably associate with lava. Such
songs as those of Burns are the very antithesis to the levity of society.
A certain explicitness pervades them:

> Come, let me take thee to my breast,
> And pledge we ne'er shall sunder;
> And I shall spurn as vilest dust
> The warld's wealth and grandeur.

There is a story of his having addressed a lady in society, some time
after he came to Edinburgh, in this direct style, and being offended
that she took notice of it. The verses were in English, and were not

[4] The *National Review* omits 'faculty'.—p. 421.

intended to mean any thing particular, only to be an elegant attention; but you might as well ask a young lady to take brandy with you as compliment her in this intense manner. The eager peasant-poet was at fault in the polished refinements of the half-feeling drawing-room. Again, the poetry of society can scarcely deal with affection. No poetry, except in hints, and for moments, perhaps ever can. You might as well tell secrets to the town-crier. The essence of poetry somehow is publicity. It is very odd when one reads many of the sentiments which are expressed there,—the brooding thought, the delicate feelings, the high conception. What is the use of telling these to the mass of men? Will the grocer feel them?—will the greasy butcher in the blue coat feel them? Are there not some emphatic remarks by Lord Byron on Mr. Sanders ('the d—d saltfish-seller' of Venice), who could not appreciate *Don Juan*? Nevertheless, for some subtle reason or other, poets do crave, almost more than other men, the public approbation. To have a work of art in your imagination, and that no one else should know of it, is a great pain. But even this craving has its limits. Art can only deal with the universal. Characters, sentiments, actions must be described in what in the old language might be called their conceptual shape. There must always be an idea in them. If one compares a great character in fiction, say that of Hamlet, with a well-known character in life, we are struck almost at once by the typical and representative nature of the former. We seem to have a more *summary* conception of it, if the phrase may be allowed, than we have of the people we know best in reality. Indeed, our notion of the fictitious character rather resembles a notion of actual persons of whom we know a little, and but a little,—of a public man, suppose, of whom from his speeches and writings we know something, but with whom we never exchanged a word. We generalise a few traits; we do what the historian will have to do hereafter; we *make* a man, so to speak, resembling the real one, but more defined, more simple and comprehensible. The objects on which affection turns are exactly the opposite. In their essence they are individual, peculiar. Perhaps they become known under a kind of confidence; but even if not, nature has hallowed the details of near life by an inevitable secrecy. You cannot expect other persons to feel them; you cannot tell your own intellect what they are. An individuality lurks in our nature. Each soul (as the divines speak) clings to each soul. Poetry is impossible on such points as these: they seem too sacred, too essential. The most that it can do is, by hints and little marks in the interstices of a universalised delineation, to suggest that there is some-thing more than what is stated, and more inward and potent than what is stated. Affection as a settled subject is incompatible with art. And thus the poetry of society is limited on its romantic side in two ways: first, by the infinite, intense nature of passion, which forces the voice of art beyond the social tone; and by the confidential, incomprehen-sible nature of affection, which will not bear to be developed for the public by the fancy in any way.

Being so bounded within the ordinary sphere of their art, poets of this world have contrived or found a substitute. In every country there is a society which is no society. The French, which is the most worldly of literatures, has devoted itself to the delineation of this out-side world. There is no form, comic or serious, dramatic or lyrical, in which the subject has not been treated: the burden is—

> Lisette, ma Lisette,
> Tu m'as trompé toujours;
> Mais vive la grisette!
> Je veux, Lisette,
> Boire à nos amours.

There is obviously no need of affection in *this* society. The whole plot of the notorious novel, *La Dame aux Camélias*,—and a very remarkable one it is,—is founded on the incongruity of real feeling with this world, and the singular and inappropriate consequences which result if by any rare chance it does appear there. Passion is almost *à fortiori* out of the question. The depths of human nature have nothing to do with this life. On this account, perhaps, it is that it harmonises so little with the English literature and character. An Englishman can scarcely live on the surface; his passions are too strong, his power of *finesse* too little. Accordingly, since Defoe, who treated the subject with a coarse matter-of-factness, there has been nothing in our literature of this kind—nothing at least professedly devoted to it. How far this is due to real excellence, how far to the *bourgeois* and not very outspoken temper of our recent writers, we need not in this place discuss. There is no occasion to quote in this country the early poetry of Béranger, at least not the sentimental part of it. We may take, in preference, one of his poems written in old or rather in middle, age:

BÉRANGER

Cinquante Ans

Pourquoi ces fleurs? est-ce ma fête?
Non; ce bouquet vient m'annoncer
Qu'un demi-siècle sur ma tête
Achève aujourd'hui de passer.
Oh! combien nos jours sont rapides!
Oh! combien j'ai perdu d'instants!
Oh! combien je me sens de rides!
Hélas! hélas! j'ai cinquante ans.

A cet âge, tout nous échappe;
Le fruit meurt sur l'arbre jauni.
Mais à ma porte quelqu'un frappe;
N'ouvrons point: mon rôle est fini.
C'est, je gage, un docteur qui jette
Sa carte où s'est logé le temps.
Jadis, j'aurais dit: C'est Lisette.
Hélas! hélas! j'ai cinquante ans.

En maux cuisants vieillesse abonde:
C'est la goutte qui nous meurtrit;
La cécité, prison profonde;
La surdité, dont chacun rit.
Puis la raison, lampe qui baisse,
N'a plus que des feux tremblotants.
Enfants, honorez la vieillesse!
Hélas! hélas! j'ai cinquante ans.

Ciel! j'entends la Mort, qui, joyeuse,
Arrive en se frottant les mains.
A ma porte la fossoyeuse
Frappe; adieu, messieurs les humains!
En bas, guerre, famine et peste;
En haut, plus d'astres éclatants.
Ouvrons, tandis que Dieu me reste.
Hélas! hélas! j'ai cinquante ans.

Mais non! c'est vous! vous, jeune amie,
Sœur de charité des amours!
Vous tirez mon ame endormie
Du cauchemar des mauvais jours.

26

Semant les roses de votre âge,
Partout, comme fait le printemps,
Parfumez les rêves d'un sage.
Hélas! hélas! j'ai cinquante ans.

This is the last scene of the *grisette*, of whom we read in so many songs sparkling with youth and gaiety.

A certain intellectuality, however, pervades Béranger's love-songs. You seem to feel, to see, not merely the emotion, but the mind in the background viewing that emotion. You are conscious of a considerateness qualifying and contrasting with the effervescing champagne of the feelings described. Desire is rarefied; sense half becomes an idea. You may trace a similar metamorphosis in the poetry of passion itself. It we contrast such a poem as Shelley's 'Epipsychidion' with the natural language of common passion, we see how curiously the intellect can take its share in the dizziness of sense. In the same way, in the lightest poems of Béranger we feel that it may be infused, may interpenetrate the most buoyant effervescence.

Nothing is more odd than to contrast the luxurious and voluptuous nature of much of Béranger's poetry with the circumstances of his life. He never in all his productive time has more than 80*l.* a year; the smallest party of pleasure made him live, he tells us himself, most ascetically for a week; so far from leading the life of a Sybarite, his youth was one of anxiety and privation. A more worldly poet has probably never written, but no poet has shown in life so philosophic an estimate of this world's goods. His origin is very unaristocratic. He was born in August, 1780, at the house of his grandfather, a poor old tailor. Of his mother we hear nothing. His father was a speculative, sanguine, man, who never succeeded. His principal education was given him by an aunt, who taught him to read and to write, and perhaps generally incited his mind. His school-teaching tells of the philosophy of the revolutionary time. By way of primary school for the town of Péronne, a patriotic member of the National Assembly had founded an *institut d'enfants.* 'It offered,' we are told, 'at once the image of a club and that of a camp; the boys wore a military uniform; at every public event they named deputations, delivered orations, voted addresses: letters were written to the citizen Robespierre and the citizen Tallien.' Naturally, amid so great affairs there was no time for mere grammar; they did not teach *Latin.* Nor did Béranger ever acquire any knowledge of that language; and he may be said to be destitute of what is in the usual sense called culture. Accordingly, it has in these days been made a matter of wonder by critics, whom we may think pedantic, that one so destitute should be able to produce such works. But a far keener judge has pronounced the contrary. Goethe, who certainly did not undervalue the most elaborate and artful cultivation, at once pronounced Béranger to have 'a nature most happily endowed, firmly grounded in himself, purely developed from himself, and quite in harmony with himself.' In fact, as these words mean, Béranger, by happiness of nature or self-attention, has that *centrality* of mind which is the really valuable result of colleges and teaching. He puts things together; he refers things to a principle; rather, they group themselves in his intelligence insensibly round a principle. There is nothing *distrait* in his genius; the man has attained to be himself; a cool oneness, a poised personality pervades him. 'The unlearned,' it has been said, 'judge at random.' Béranger is not unlearned in this sense. There is no one who judges more simply, smoothly, and uniformly. His ideas refer to an exact measure. He has mastered what comes before him. And though doubtless unacquainted with foreign and incongruous literatures, he has mastered his own literature, which was shaped by kindred persons, and has been the expression of analogous natures; and this has helped him in expressing himself.

In the same way, his poor youth and boyhood have given a reality to his productions. He seems to have had this in mind in praising the 'practical education which I have received.' He was bred a printer; and the highest post he attained was a clerkship at the university, worth, as has been said, 80*l.* per annum. Accordingly, he has everywhere a sympathy with the common people, an unsought familiarity with them and their life. Sybarite poetry commonly wants this. The aristocratic nature is superficial; it relates to a life protected from simple wants, depending on luxurious artifices. 'Mamma,' said the simpleminded nobleman, 'when poor people have no bread, why do not they eat buns? they are much better.' An over-perfumed softness pervades the poetry of society. You see this in the songs of Moore, the best of the sort we have; all is beautiful, soft, half-sincere. There is a little falsetto in the tone, everything reminds you of the drawing-room and the *pianoforte*; and not only so—for all poetry of society must in a measure do this—but it seems fit for no other scene. Naturalness is the last word of praise that would be suitable. In the scented air we forget that there is a *pavé* and a multitude. Perhaps France is, of all countries

28

which have ever existed, the one in which we might seek an exception
for this luxurious limitation. A certain *égalité* may pervade its art as
its society. There is no such difference as with us between the shoe-
black and the gentleman. A certain refinement is very common; an
extreme refinement possibly rare. Béranger was able to write his
poems in poverty: they are popular with the poor.

A success even greater than what we have described as having been
achieved by Béranger in the first class of the poems of society—that
of amusement—has been attained by him in the second class, expressive
of epicurean speculation. Perhaps it is one of his characteristics that
the two are for ever running one into another. There is animation in
his thinking, there is meaning in his gaiety. It requires no elaborate explanation to make evident the connection between scepticism and
luxuriousness. Every one thinks of the Sadducee as in cool halls and
soft robes; no one supposes that the Sybarite believes. Pain not only
purifies the mind, but deepens the nature. A simply happy life is
animal; it is pleasant, and it perishes. All writers who have devoted
themselves to the explanation of this world's view of itself are necessarily in a certain measure Sadducees. The world is a Sadducee itself;
it cannot be anything else without recognising a higher creed, a more
binding law, a more solemn reality—without ceasing to be the world.
Equanimity is incredulous; impartiality does not care; an indifferent
politeness is sceptical. Though not a single speculative opinion is
expressed, we may feel this in *Roger Bontemps*:—

> *Roger Bontemps*
> Aux gens atrabilaires
> Pour exemple donné,
> En un temps de misères
> Roger Bontemps est né.
> Vivre obscur à sa guise,
> Narguer les mécontents;
> Eh gai! c'est la devise
> Du gros Roger Bontemps.
>
> Du chapeau de son père
> Coiffé dans les grands jours,
> De roses ou de lierre
> Le rajeunir toujours;
> Mettre un manteau de bure,

Vieil ami de vingt ans;
Eh gai! c'est la parure
Du gros Roger Bontemps.

Posséder dans sa hutte
Une table, un vieux lit,
Des cartes, une flûte,
Un broc que Dieu remplit,
Un portrait de maîtresse,
Un coffre et rien dedans;
Eh gai! c'est la richesse
Du gros Roger Bontemps.

Aux enfants de la ville
Montrer de petits jeux;
Etre un faiseur habile
De contes graveleux;
Ne parler que de danse
Et d'almanachs chantants;
Eh gai! c'est la science
Du gros Roger Bontemps.

Faute de vin d'élite,
Sabler ceux du canton;
Préférer Marguerite
Aux dames du grand ton;
De joie et de tendresse
Remplir tous ses instants;
Eh gai! c'est la sagesse
Du gros Roger Bontemps.

Dire au ciel: 'Je me fie,
Mon père, à ta bonté;
De ma philosophie
Pardonne la gaîté;
Que ma saison dernière
Soit encore un printemps;'
Eh gai! c'est la prière
Du gros Roger Bontemps.

Vous, pauvres pleins d'envie,
Vous, riches désireux,

Vous, dont le char dévie
Après un cours heureux;
Vous, qui perdrez peut-être
Des titres éclatants,
Eh gai! prenez pour maître
Le gros Roger Bontemps.

At the same time, in Béranger the scepticism is not extreme. The skeleton is not paraded. That the world is a passing show, a painted scene, is admitted; you seem to know that it is all acting and rouge and illusion: still the pleasantness of the acting is dwelt on, the rouge is never rubbed off, the dream runs lightly and easily. No nightmare haunts you, you have no uneasy sense that you are about to awaken. Persons who require a sense of reality may complain; pain is perhaps necessary to sharpen their nerves, a tough effort to harden their consciousness: but if you pass by this objection of the threshold, if you admit the possibility of a superficial and fleeting world, you will not find a better one than Béranger's world. Suppose all the world were a *restaurant*, his is a good *restaurant*; admit that life is an effervescing champagne, his is the best for the moment.

In several respects Béranger contrasts with Horace, the poet whom in general he most resembles. The song of *Roger Bontemps* suggests one of the most obvious differences. It is essentially democratic. As we have said before, Béranger is the poet of the people; he himself says, *Le peuple c'est ma muse.* Throughout Horace's writings, however much he may speak, and speak justly, of the simplicity of his tastes, you are always conscious that his position is exceptional. Everybody cannot be the friend of Mæcenas; every cheerful man of the world cannot see the springs of the great world. The intellect of most self-indulgent men must satisfy itself with small indulgences. Without a hard ascent you can rarely see a great view. Horace had the almost unequalled felicity of watching the characters and thoughts and tendencies of the governors of the world, the nicest manipulation of the most ingenious statesmen, the inner tastes and predilections which are the origin of the most important transactions; and yet had the ease and pleasantness of a[5] common and effortless life. So rare a fortune cannot be a general model; the gospel of Epicureanism must not ask a close imitation of one who had such very special advantages. Béranger gives the accepters of that creed a commoner type. Out of nothing but the most ordinary

[5] I have inserted 'a'.—Ed.

31

advantages—the garret, the almost empty purse, the not over-attired *grisette*—he has given them a model of the sparkling and quick existence for which their fancy is longing. You cannot imagine commoner materials. In another respect Horace and Béranger are remarkably contrasted. Béranger, sceptical and indifferent as he is, has a faith in, and zeal for, liberty. It seems odd that he should care for that sort of thing; but he does care for it. Horace probably had a little personal shame attaching to such ideas. No regimental officer of our own time can have 'joined' in a state of more crass ignorance than did the stout little student from Athens in all probability, the army of Brutus; the legionaries must have taken the measure of him, as the sergeants of our living friends. Anyhow he was not partial to such reflections; zeal for political institutions is quite as foreign to him as any other zeal. A certain hope in the future is characteristic of Béranger—

> Qui découvrit un nouveau monde?
> Un fou qu'on raillait en tout lieu.

Modern faith colours even bystanding scepticism. Though probably with no very accurate ideas of the nature of liberty, Béranger believes that it is a great good, and that France will have it.

The point in which Béranger most resembles Horace is that which is the most essential in the characters of them both—their geniality. This is the very essence of the poems of society; it springs in the verses of amusement, it harmonises with acquiescing sympathy the poems of indifference. And yet few qualities in writing are so rare. A certain malevolence enters into literary ink; the point of the pen pricks. Pope is the very best example of this. With every desire to imitate Horace, he cannot touch any of his subjects, or any kindred subjects, without infusing a bitter ingredient. It is not given to the children of men to be philosophers without envy. Lookers-on can hardly bear the spectacle of the great world. If you watch the carriages rolling down to the House of Lords, you will try to depreciate the House of Lords. Idleness is cynical. Both Béranger and Horace are exceptions to this. Both enjoy the roll of the wheels; both love the glitter of the carriages; neither is angry at the sun. Each knows that he is as happy as he can be—that he is all that he can be in his contemplative philosophy. In his means of expression for the purpose in hand, the Frenchman has the advantage. The Latin language is clumsy. Light pleasure was an exotic in the Roman world; the terms in which you strive to describe it suit rather the shrill camp and the droning law-court. In English, as we hinted just now, we have this too. Business is in our words; a too heavy sense clogs our literature: even in a writer so apt as Pope at the *finesse* of words, you feel the solid Gothic roots impede him. It is difficult not to be cumbrous. The horse may be fleet and light, but the wheels are ponderous and the road goes heavily. Béranger certainly has not this difficulty; nobody ever denied that a Frenchman could be light, that the French language was adapted for levity.

When we ascribed an absence of bitterness and malevolence to Béranger, we were far from meaning that he is not a satirist. Every light writer in a measure must be so. Mirth is the imagery of society; and mirth must make fun of somebody. The nineteenth century has not had many shrewder critics than its easy-natured poet. Its intense dullness particularly strikes him. He dreads the dreariness of the Academy; pomposity bores him; formalism tires him; he thinks, and may well think, it dreary to have

> Pour grands hommes des journalistes,
> Pour amusement l'Opéra.

But skilful as is the mirth, its spirit is genial and good-natured. 'You have been laughing at me constantly, Sidney, for the last seven years,' said a friend to the late Canon of St. Paul's, 'and yet in all that time you never said a single thing to me that I wished unsaid.' So far as its essential features are concerned, the nineteenth century may say the same of its musical satirist. Perhaps, however, the Bourbons might a little object. Clever people have always a *little* malice against the stupid.

There is no more striking example of the degree in which the gospel of good works has penetrated our modern society, than that Béranger has talked of 'utilising his talent.' The epicurean poet considers that he has been a political missionary. Well may others be condemned to the penal servitude of industry, if the lightest and idlest of skilful men boasts of being subjected to it. If Béranger thinks it necessary to think he has been useful, others may well think so too; let us accept the heavy doctrine of hard labour; there is no other way to heave the rubbish of this world. The mode in which Béranger is anxious to prove that he made his genius of use, is in diffusing a taste for liberty, and expressing an enthusiasm for it; and also, as we suppose, in quizzing those rulers of France who have not shared either the taste or the enthusiasm. Although, however, such may be the idea of the poet himself, posterity will scarcely confirm it. Political satire is the most ephemeral kind of literature. The circumstances to which it applies are local and temporary; the persons to whom it applies die. A very few months will make unintelligible what was at first strikingly plain. Béranger has illustrated this by an admission. There was a delay in publishing the last volume of his poems, many of which relate to the years or months immediately preceding the Revolution of 1830; the delay was not long, as the volume appeared in the first month of 1833, yet he says that many of the songs relate to the passing occurrences of a period 'déjà loin de nous.' On so shifting a scene as that of French political life, the jests of each act are forgotten with the act itself; the eager interest of each moment withdraws the mind from thinking of or dwelling on anything past. And in all countries administration is ephemeral; what relates to it is transitory. Satires on its detail are like the jests of a public office; the clerks change, oblivion covers their peculiarities; the point of the joke is forgotten. There are some considerable exceptions to the saying that foreign literary opinion is a 'contemporary posterity;' but in relation to satires on transitory transactions it is exactly expressive. No Englishman will now care for many of Béranger's songs which were once in the mouths of all his countrymen, which coloured the manners of revolutions, perhaps influenced their course. The fame of a poet may have a reference to politics; but it will be only to the wider species, to those social questions which never die, the elements of that active human nature which is the same age after age. Béranger can hardly hope for this. Even the songs which relate to liberty can hardly hope for this immortality. They have the vagueness which has made French aspirations for freedom futile. So far as they express distinct feeling, their tendency is rather anti-aristocratic than in favour of simple real liberty. And an objection to mere rank, though a potent, is neither a very agreeable nor a very poetical sentiment. Moreover, when the love of liberty is to be imaginatively expressed, it requires to an Englishman's ear a sound bigger and more trumpet-tongued than the voice of Béranger.

On a deeper view, however, an attentive student will discover a great deal that is most instructive in the political career of the not very business-like poet. His life has been contemporaneous with the course of a great change; and throughout it the view which he has taken of the current events is that which sensible men took at the time, and which a sensible posterity (and these events will from their size attract

34

attention enough to insure their being viewed sensibly) is likely to take. Béranger was present at the taking of the Bastille, but he was then only nine years old; the accuracy of opinion which we are claiming for him did not commence so early. His mature judgment begins with the career of Napoleon; and no one of the thousands who have written on that subject has viewed it perhaps more justly. He had no love for the despotism of the Empire, was alive to the harshness of its administration, did not care too much for its glory, must have felt more than once the social exhaustion. At the same time, no man was penetrated more profoundly, no literary man half so profoundly, with the popular admiration for the genius of the Empire. His own verse has given the truest and most lasting expression of it:

Les Souvenirs du Peuple
On parlera de sa gloire
Sous le chaume bien long-temps.
L'humble toit, dans cinquante ans,
Ne connaîtra plus d'autre histoire.
Là viendront les villageois,
Dire alors à quelque vieille:
'Par des récits d'autrefois,
Mère, abrégez notre veille.
Bien, dit-on, qu'il nous ait nui,
Le peuple encor le révère,
    Oui, le révère.
Parlez-nous de lui, grand'mère;
    Parlez-nous de lui.' (*bis.*)

'Mes enfants, dans ce village,
Suivi de rois, il passa.
Voilà bien longtemps de ça:
Je venais d'entrer en ménage.
A pied grimpant le coteau
Où pour voir je m'étais mise,
Il avait petit chapeau
Avec redingote grise.
Près de lui je me troublai;
Il me dit: "Bonjour, ma chère,
    Bonjour, ma chère." '
    'Il vous a parlé, grand'mère!
    Il vous a parlé!'

'L'an d'après, moi, pauvre femme,
A Paris étant un jour,
Je le vis avec sa cour:
Il se rendait à Notre-Dame.
Tous les cœurs étaient contents;
On admirait son cortège.
Chacun disait: "Quel beau temps!
Le ciel toujours le protége."
Son sourire était bien doux;
D'un fils Dieu le rendait père,
 Le rendait père.'
  'Quel beau jour pour vous, grand'mère!
  Quel beau jour pour vous!'

'Mais, quand la pauvre Champagne
Fut en proie aux étrangers,
Lui, bravant tous les dangers,
Semblait seul tenir la campagne.
Un soir, toute comme aujourd'hui,
J'entends frapper à la porte.
J'ouvre. Bon Dieu! c'était lui,
Suivi d'une faible escorte.
Il s'asseoit où me voilà,
S'écriant: "Oh! quelle guerre!
 Oh! quelle guerre!"'
  —'Il s'est assis là, grand'mère!
  Il s'est assis là!'

' "J'ai faim," dit-il; et bien vite
Je sers piquette et pain bis;
Puis il sèche ses habits,
Même à dormir le feu l'invite.
Au réveil, voyant mes pleurs,
Il me dit: "Bonne espérance!
Je cours, de tous ses malheurs,
Sous Paris, venger la France."
Il part; et comme un trésor
J'ai depuis gardé son verre,
 Gardé son verre.'
  —'Vous l'avez encor, grand'mère!
  Vous l'avez encor!'

'Le voici. Mais à sa perte
Le héros fut entraîné.
Lui, qu'un pape a couronné,
Est mort dans une île déserte.
Longtemps aucun ne l'a cru;
On disait: "Il va paraître;
Par mer il est accouru;
L'étranger va voir son maître."
Quand d'erreur on nous tira,
Ma douleur fut bien amère!
Fut bien amère!'
—'Dieu vous bénira, grand'mère;
Dieu vous bénira.'[6]

This is a great exception to the transitoriness of political poetry. Such a character as that of Napoleon displayed on so large a stage, so great a genius amid such scenery of action, insures an immortality. 'The page of universal history' which he was always coveting, he has attained; and it is a page which, from its singularity and its errors, its shame and its glory, will distract the attention from other pages. No one who has ever had in his mind the idea of Napoleon's character can forget it. Nothing too can be more natural than that the French should remember it. It has the primary imagination, the elementary conceiving power, in which they are deficient. So far from being restricted to the poetry of society, he would not have even appreciated it. A certain bareness marks his mind; his style is curt; the imaginative product is left rude; there is the distinct abstraction of the military diagram. The tact of light and passing talk, the detective imagination which is akin to that tact, and discovers the quick essence of social things,—he never had. In speaking of his power over popular fancies, Béranger has called him 'the greatest poet of modern times.' No genius can be more unlike his own, and therefore perhaps it is that he admires it so much. During the Hundred Days, Béranger says he was never under the illusion, then not rare, that the Emperor could become a constitutional monarch. The lion, he felt, would not change his skin. After the return of the Bourbons, he says, doubtless with truth, that his '*instinct du peuple*' told him they could never ally themselves with liberal principles, or unite with that new order of society which,

[6] I have punctuated this poem with speech marks, etc. to make it more intelligible. There are none in the 1851 edition.—Ed.

though dating from the Revolution, had acquired in five-and-twenty years a half-prescriptive right. They and their followers came in to *take* possession, and it was impossible they could unite with what *was* in possession. During the whole reign of the hereditary Bourbon dynasty, Béranger was in opposition. Representing the natural sentiments of the new Frenchman, he could not bear the natural tendency of the ruling power to the half-forgotten practices of old France. The legitimate Bourbons were by their position the chieftains of the party advocating their right by birth; they could not be the kings of a people; and the poet of the people was against them. After the genius of Napoleon, all other governing minds would seem tame and contracted; and Charles X. was not a man to diminish the inevitable feeling. Béranger despised him. As the poet warred with the weapons of poetry, the Government retorted with the penalties of state. He was turned out of his petty clerkship, he was twice imprisoned; but these things only increased his popularity; and a firm and genial mind, so far from being moved, sang songs at La Force itself. The Revolution of 1830 was willing to make his fortune.

'Je l'ai traitée,' he says, 'comme une puissance qui peut avoir des caprices auxquels il faut être en mesure de résister. Tous ou presque tous mes amis ont passé au ministère : j'en ai même encore un ou deux qui restent suspendus à ce mât de cocagne. Je me plais à croire qu'ils y sont accrochés par la basque, malgré les efforts qu'ils font pour descendre. J'aurais donc pu avoir part à la distribution des emplois. Malheureusement je n'ai pas l'amour des sinécures, et tout travail obligé m'est devenu insupportable, hors peut-être encore celui d'expéditionnaire. Des médisants ont prétendu que je faisais de la vertu. Fi donc! je faisais de la paresse. Ce défaut m'a tenu lieu de bien des qualités; aussi je le recommande à beaucoup de nos honnêtes gens. Il expose pourtant à de singuliers reproches. C'est à cette paresse si douce, que des censeurs rigides ont attribué l'éloignement où je me suis tenu de ceux de mes honorables amis qui ont eu le malheur d'arriver au pouvoir. Faisant trop d'honneur à ce qu'ils veulent bien appeler ma bonne tête, et oubliant trop combien il y a loin du simple bon sens à la science des grandes affaires, ces censeurs prétendent que mes conseils eussent éclairé plus d'un ministre. A les en croire, tapi derrière le fauteuil de velours de nos hommes d'état, j'aurais conjuré les vents, dissipé les orages, et fait nager la France dans un océan de délices. Nous aurions tous de la liberté à revendre ou plutôt à donner, car nous n'en savons pas bien encore le prix. Eh! messieurs mes deux ou trois amis, qui prenez un chansonnier pour un magicien, on ne vous a donc pas dit que le pouvoir est une cloche qui empêche ceux qui la mettent en branle d'entendre aucun autre son? Sans doute des ministres consultent quelquefois ceux qu'ils ont sous la main: consulter est un moyen de parler de soi qu'on néglige rarement. Mais il ne suffirait pas de consulter de bonne foi des gens qui conseilleraient de même. Il faudrait encore exécuter: ceci est la part du caractère. Les intentions les plus pures, le patriotisme le plus éclairé, ne le donnent pas toujours. Qui n'a vu de hauts personnages quitter un donneur d'avis avec une pensée courageuse, et, l'instant d'après, revenir vers lui, de je ne sais quel lieu de fascination, avec l'embarras d'un démenti donné aux résolutions les plus sages? "Oh!" disent-ils, "nous n'y serons plus repris! quelle galère!" Le plus honteux ajoute: "Je voudrais bien vous voir à ma place!" Quand un ministre dit cela, soyez sûr qu'il n'a plus la tête à lui. Cependant il en est un, mais un seul, qui, sans avoir perdu la tête, a répété souvent ce mot de la meilleure foi du monde; aussi ne l'adressait-il jamais à un ami.'

The statesman alluded to in the last paragraph is Manuel, his intimate friend, from whom he declares he could never have been separated, but whose death prevented his obtaining political honours. Nobody can read the above passage without feeling its tone of political sense. An enthusiasm for, yet half distrust of, the Revolution of July seems as sound a sentiment as could be looked for even in the most sensible contemporary. What he has thought of the present dynasty we do not know. He probably has as little concurred in the silly encomiums of its mere partisans as in the wild execrations of its disappointed enemies. His opinion could not have been either that of the English who *fêted* Louis Napoleon in 1855, or of those who despised him in 1851. The political fortunes of France during the last ten years must have been a painful scene of observation to one who remembered the taking of the Bastille. If there be such a thing as failure in the world, this looks like it.

Although we are very far from thinking that Béranger's claims on posterity are founded on his having utilised his talent in favour of liberty, it is very natural that he should think or half-think himself that it is so. His power over the multitude must have given him great pleasure; it is something to be able to write mottoes for a revolution; to write words for people to use, and hear people use those words. The same sort of pleasure which Horace derived from his nearness to the centre of great action, Béranger has derived from the power which his thorough sympathy with his countrymen has given him over them. A political satire may be ephemeral from the rapid oblivion of its circumstances; but it is not unnatural that the author, inevitably proud of its effect, may consider it of higher worth than mere verses of society.

This shrewd sense gives a solidity to the verses of Béranger which the social and amusing sort of poetry commonly wants; but nothing can redeem it from the reproach of wanting *back* thought. This is inevitable in such literature; as it professes to delineate for us the light essence of a fugitive world, it cannot be expected to dwell on those deep and eternal principles on which that world is based. It ignores them as light talk ignores them. The most opposite thing to the poetry of society is the poetry of inspiration. There exists, of course, a kind of imagination which detects the secrets of the universe; which fills us sometimes with dread, sometimes with hope; which awakens the soul, which makes pure the feelings, which explains nature, reveals what is above nature, chastens 'the deep heart of man.' Our senses teach us what the world is; our intuitions where it is. We see the blue and gold of the world, its lively amusements, its gorgeous if superficial splendour, its currents of men; we feel its light spirits, we enjoy its happiness; we enjoy it, and we are puzzled. What is the object of all this? Why do we do all this? What is the universe *for*? Such a book as Béranger's suggests this difficulty in its strongest form. It embodies the essence of all that pleasure-loving, pleasure-giving, unaccountable world in which men spend their lives,—which they are compelled to live in, but which the moment you get out of it seems so odd that you can hardly believe it is real. On this account, as we were saying before, there is no book the impression of which varies so much in different moods of mind. Sometimes no reading is so pleasant; at others you half-despise and half-hate the idea of it; it seems to sum up and make clear the littleness of your own nature. Few can bear the theory of their amusements; it is essential to the pride of man to believe that he is industrious. We are irritated at literary laughter, and wroth at printed mirth. We turn angrily away to that higher poetry which gives the outline within which all these light colours are painted. From the capital of levity and its self-amusing crowds, from the elastic *vaudeville* and the grinning actors, from *chansons* and *cafés*, we turn away to the solemn nature, to the blue over-arching sky: the one remains, the many pass; no number of seasons impairs the bloom of those hues, they are as soft to-morrow as to-day. The immeasurable depth folds us in. 'Eternity,' as the original thinker said, 'is everlasting.' We breathe a deep breath. And perhaps we have higher moments. We comprehend the 'unintelligible world;' we see into 'the life of things;' we fancy we know whence we come and whither we go; words we have repeated for years have a meaning for the first time; texts of old Scripture seem to apply to *us*. . . . And—and—Mr. Thackeray would say, You come back into the town, and order dinner at a *restaurant*, and read Béranger once more.

And though this is true—though the author of *Le Dieu des Bonnes Gens* has certainly no claim to be called a profound divine—though we do not find in him any proper expression, scarcely any momentary recognition, of those intuitions which explain in a measure the scheme and idea of things, and form the back-thought and inner structure of such minds as ours,—his sense and sympathy with the people enable him, perhaps compel him, to delineate those essential conditions which constitute the structure of exterior life, and determine with inevitable certainty the common life of common persons. He has no call to deal with heaven or the universe, but he knows the earth; he is restricted to the boundaries of time, but he understands time. He has extended his delineations beyond what in this country could be considered correct; *Les Cinq Étages* can scarcely be quoted here; but a perhaps higher example of the same kind of art may be so:

Le Vieux Vagabond
Dans ce fossé cessons de vivre;
Je finis vieux, infirme et las.
Les passants vont dire: 'Il est ivre.'
Tant mieux! ils ne me plaindront pas.
J'en vois qui détournent la tête;
D'autres me jettent quelques sous.
Courez vite, allez à la fête.
Vieux vagabond, je puis mourir sans vous.

Oui, je meurs ici de vieillesse,
Parce qu'on ne meurt pas de faim.
J'espérais voir de ma détresse
L'hôpital adoucir la fin.
Mais tout est plein dans chaque hospice,

Tant le peuple est infortuné.
La rue, hélas! fut ma nourrice.
Vieux vagabond, mourons où je suis né.

Aux artisans, dans mon jeune âge,
J'ai dit: 'Qu'on m'enseigne un métier.'
'Va, nous n'avons pas trop d'ouvrage,'
Répondaient-ils, 'va mendier.'
Riches, qui me disiez: 'Travaille,'
J'eus bien des os de vos repas;
J'ai bien dormi sur votre paille.
Vieux vagabond, je ne vous maudis pas.

J'aurais pu voler, moi, pauvre homme;
Mais non: mieux vaut tendre la main.
Au plus, j'ai dérobé la pomme
Qui mûrit au bord du chemin.
Vingt fois pourtant on me verrouille
Dans les cachots, de par le roi.
De mon seul bien on me dépouille.
Vieux vagabond, le soleil est à moi.

Le pauvre a-t-il une patrie?
Que me font vos vins et vos blés,
Votre gloire et votre industrie,
Et vos orateurs assemblés?
Dans vos murs ouverts à ses armes,
Lorsque l'étranger s'engraissait,
Comme un sot j'ai versé des larmes.
Vieux vagabond, sa main me nourrissait.

Comme un insecte fait pour nuire,
Hommes, que ne m'écrasiez-vous?
Ah! plutôt vous deviez m'instruire
A travailler au bien de tous.
Mis à l'abri du vent contraire,
Le ver fût devenu fourmi;
Je vous aurais chéris en frère.
Vieux vagabond, je meurs votre ennemi.[7]

[7] The punctuation, especially speech marks, has been altered somewhat from the 1851 edition for the sake of intelligibility.—Ed.

Pathos in such a song as this enters into poetry. We sympathise with the essential lot of man. Poems of this kind are doubtless rare in Béranger. His commoner style is lighter and more cheerful; but no poet who has painted so well the light effervescence of light society can, when he likes, paint so well the solid stubborn forms with which it is encompassed. The genial, firm sense of a large mind sees and comprehends all of human life which lies within the sphere of sense. He is an epicurean, as all merely sensible men by inevitable consequence are; and as an epicurean, he prefers to deal with the superficial and gay forms of life; but he can deal with others when he chooses to be serious. Indeed, there is no melancholy like the melancholy of the epicurean. He is alive to the fixed conditions of earth, but not to that which is above earth. He muses on the temporary, as such; he admits the skeleton, but not the soul. It is wonderful that Béranger is so cheerful as he is.

We may conclude as we began. In all his works,—in lyrics of levity, of politics, of worldly reflection,—Béranger, if he had not a single object, has attained a uniform result. He has given us an idea of the essential French character, such as we fancy it must be, but can never for ourselves hope to see that it is. We understand the nice tact, the quick intelligence, the gay precision; the essence of the drama we know, the spirit of what we have seen. We know his feeling:

> J'aime qu'un Russe soit Russe,
> Et qu'un Anglais soit Anglais;
> Si l'on est Prussien en Prusse,
> En France soyons Français.

He has acted accordingly: he has delineated to us the essential Frenchman.

Walter Scott

Introductory note

Walter Scott (1771–1832) was the son of an Edinburgh writer to the signet, and after being apprenticed to his father and then studying law, he was called to the bar in 1792. He had early become interested in the ballads and tales of the border country, and between 1802–3 published three volumes of *Border Minstrelsy*. His romantic poem *The Lay of the Last Minstrel*, 1805, was immensely popular and determined his literary career. He became a partner in a printing business, and during the next eight years published much poetry and also contributed to the *Edinburgh Review*. In spite of the great popularity of Scott's verse, Byron began to eclipse him in public interest, and Scott turned his attention to the novel. *Waverley* appeared in 1814, followed by very many others. The secret of their authorship was kept until 1826, partly to protect Scott's reputation as a poet, partly to indulge his love of the mysterious. In this year he was involved in the ruin of his partner, James Ballantyne, and of his publisher, Constable, and became liable for a debt of £130,000. He now wrote in order to pay off the debt, which was eventually settled by the sale of his copyrights after his death. He died at Abbotsford in 1832.

The Waverley Novels[1]

IT is not commonly on the generation which was contemporary with the production of great works of art that they exercise their most magical influence. Nor is it on the distant people whom we call posterity. Contemporaries bring to new books formed minds and stiffened creeds; posterity, if it regard them at all, looks at them as old subjects, worn-out topics, and hears a disputation on their merits with languid impartiality, like aged judges in a court of appeal. Even standard authors exercise but slender influence on the susceptible minds of a rising generation; they are become 'papa's books;' the walls of the library are adorned with their regular volumes; but no hand touches them. Their fame is itself half an obstacle to their popularity; a delicate fancy shrinks from employing so great a celebrity as the companion of an idle hour. The generation which is really most influenced by a work of genius is commonly that which is still young when the first controversy respecting its merits arises; with the eagerness of youth they read and re-read; their vanity is not unwilling to adjudicate: in the process their imagination is formed; the creations of the author range themselves in the memory; they become part of the substance of the very mind. The works of Sir Walter Scott can hardly be said to have gone through this exact process. Their immediate popularity was unbounded. No one—a few most captious critics apart—ever questioned their peculiar power. Still, they are subject to a transition which is in principle the same. At the time of their publication mature contemporaries read them with delight. Superficial the reading of grown men in some sort must ever be; it is only once in a lifetime

---

[1] *Library Edition.* Illustrated by upwards of Two Hundred Engravings on Steel, after Drawings by Turner, Landseer, Wilkie, Stanfield, Roberts, &c., including Portraits of the Historical Personages described in the Novels. 25 vols. demy 8vo. *Abbotsford Edition.* With One Hundred and Twenty Engravings on Steel, and nearly Two Thousand on Wood. 12 vols. super-royal 8vo. *Author's favourite Edition.* 48 vols. post 8vo. *Cabinet Edition.* 25 vols. foolscap 8vo. *Railway Edition.* Now publishing, and to be completed in 25 portable volumes, large type. *People's Edition.* 5 large volumes royal 8vo. This essay was first published in the *National Review* for April 1858, Volume VI, pp. 444-71.

that we can know the passionate reading of youth; men soon lose its eager learning power. But from peculiarities in their structure, which we shall try to indicate, the novels of Scott suffered less than almost any book of equal excellence from this inevitable superficiality of perusal. Their plain, and, so to say, cheerful merits suit the occupied man of genial middle life. Their appreciation was to an unusual degree coincident with their popularity. The next generation, hearing the praises of their fathers in their earliest reading time, seized with avidity on the volumes; and there is much in very many of them which is admirably fitted for the delight of boyhood. A third generation has now risen into at least the commencement of literary life, which is quite removed from the unbounded enthusiasm with which the Scotch novels were originally received, and does not always share the still more eager partiality of those who, in the opening of their minds, first received the tradition of their excellence. New books have arisen to compete with these; new interests distract us from them. The time, therefore, is not perhaps unfavourable for a slight criticism of these celebrated fictions; and their continual republication, without any criticism for many years, seems almost to demand it.

There are two kinds of fiction which, though in common literature they may run very much into one another, are yet in reality distinguishable and separate. One of these, which we may call the *ubiquitous*, aims at describing the whole of human life in all its spheres, in all its aspects, with all its varied interests, aims, and objects. It searches through the whole life of man; his practical pursuits, his speculative attempts, his romantic youth, and his domestic age. It gives an entire picture[2] of all these; or if there be any lineaments which it forbears to depict, they are only such as the inevitable repression of a regulated society excludes from the admitted province of literary art. Of this kind are the novels of Cervantes and Le Sage, and, to a certain extent, of Smollett or Fielding. In our own time, Mr. Dickens is an author whom nature intended to write to a certain extent with this aim. He should have given us *not* disjointed novels, with a vague attempt at a romantic plot, but sketches of diversified scenes, and the obvious life of varied mankind. The literary fates, however, if such beings there are, allotted otherwise. By a very terrible example of the way in which in this world great interests are postponed to little ones, the genius of authors is habitually sacrificed to the tastes of readers. In this

[2] The *National Review* has 'feature' for 'picture'.—p. 445.

age, the great readers of fiction are young people. The 'addiction' of these is to romance; and accordingly a kind of novel has become so familiar to us as almost to engross the name, which deals solely with the passion of love; and if it uses other parts of human life for the occasions of its art, it does so only cursorily and occasionally, and with a view of throwing into a stronger or more delicate light those sentimental parts of earthly affairs which are the special objects of delineation. All prolonged delineation of other parts of human life is considered 'dry,' stupid, and distracts the mind of the youthful generation from the 'fantasies' which peculiarly charm it. Mr. Olmsted has a story of some deputation of the Indians, at which the American orator harangued the barbarian audience about the 'great spirit,' and 'the land of their fathers,' in the style of Mr. Cooper's novels; during a moment's pause in the great stream, an old Indian asked the deputation, 'Why does your chief speak thus to us? we did not wish great instruction or fine words; we desire brandy and tobacco.' No critic in a time of competition will speak uncourteously of any reader of either sex; but it is indisputable that the old kind of novel, full of 'great instruction' and varied pictures, does not afford to some young gentlemen and some young ladies either the peculiar stimulus or the peculiar solace which they desire.

The Waverley Novels were published at a time when the causes that thus limit the sphere of fiction were coming into operation, but when they had not yet become so omnipotent as they are now. Accordingly, these novels everywhere bear marks of a state of transition. They are not devoted with anything like the present exclusiveness to the sentimental part of human life. They describe great events, singular characters, strange accidents, strange states of society; they dwell with a peculiar interest, and as if for their own sake, on antiquarian details relating to a past society. Singular customs, social practices, even political institutions which existed once in Scotland, and even elsewhere, during the Middle Ages, are explained with a careful minuteness. At the same time the sentimental element assumes a great deal of prominence. The book is in fact, as well as in theory, a narrative of the feelings and fortunes of the hero and heroine. An attempt, more or less successful, has been made to insert an interesting love-story in each novel. Sir Walter was quite aware that the best delineation of the oddest characters, or the most quaint societies, or the strangest incidents, would not in general satisfy his readers. He has invariably attempted an account of youthful, sometimes of decidedly juvenile, feelings and actions. The difference between Sir Walter's novels and the specially romantic fictions of the present day is, that in the former the love-story is always, or nearly always, connected with some great event, or the fortunes of some great historical character, or the peculiar movements and incidents of some strange state of society; and that the author did not suppose or expect that his readers would be so absorbed in the sentimental aspect of human life as to be unable or unwilling to be interested in, or to attend to, any other. There is always a *locus in quo*, if the expression may be pardoned, in the Waverley Novels. The hero and heroine walk among the trees of the forest according to rule, but we are expected to take an interest in the forest as well as in them.

No novel, therefore, of Sir Walter Scott's can be considered to come exactly within the class which we have called the ubiquitous. None of them in any material degree attempts to deal with human affairs in all their spheres—to delineate as a whole the life of man. The canvas has a large background, in some cases too large either for artistic effect or the common reader's interest; but there are always real boundaries—Sir Walter had no *thesis* to maintain. Scarcely any writer will set himself to delineate the whole of human life, unless he has a doctrine concerning human life to put forth and inculcate. The effort is *doctrinaire*. Scott's imagination was strictly conservative. He could understand (with a few exceptions) any considerable movement of human life and action, and could always describe with easy freshness everything which he did understand; but he was not obliged by stress of fanaticism to maintain a dogma concerning them, or to show their peculiar relation to the general sphere of life. He described vigorously and boldly the peculiar scene and society which in every novel he had selected as the theatre of romantic action. Partly from their fidelity to nature, and partly from a consistency in the artist's mode of representation, these pictures group themselves from the several novels in the imagination, and an habitual reader comes to think of and understand what is meant by 'Scott's world;' but the writer had no such distinct object before him. No one novel was designed to be a delineation of the world as Scott viewed it. We have vivid and fragmentary histories; it is for the slow critic of after-times to piece together their teaching.

From this intermediate position of the Waverley Novels, or at any rate in exact accordance with its requirements, is the special characteristic for which they are most remarkable. We may call this in a brief phrase their *romantic sense*; and perhaps we cannot better illustrate it than by a quotation from the novel to which the series owes its most usual name. It occurs in the description of the court-ball which Charles Edward is described as giving at Holyrood House the night before his march southward on his strange adventure. The striking interest of the scene before him, and the peculiar position of his own sentimental career, are described as influencing the mind of the hero.

'Under the influence of these mixed sensations, and cheered at times by a smile of intelligence and approbation from the Prince as he passed the group, Waverley exerted his powers of fancy, animation and eloquence, and attracted the general admiration of the company. The conversation gradually assumed the tone best qualified for the display of his talents and acquisitions. The gaiety of the evening was exalted in character, rather than checked, by the approaching dangers of the morrow. All nerves were strung for the future, and prepared to enjoy the present. This mood of mind is highly favourable for the exercise of the powers of imagination, for poetry, and for that eloquence which is allied to poetry.'

Neither 'eloquence' nor 'poetry' are the exact words with which it would be appropriate to describe the fresh style of the Waverley Novels; but the imagination of their author was stimulated by a fancied mixture of sentiment and fact, very much as he describes Waverley's to have been by a real experience of the two at once. The second volume of *Waverley* is one of the most striking illustrations of this peculiarity. The character of Charles Edward, his adventurous undertaking, his ancestral rights, the mixed selfishness and enthusiasm of the Highland chiefs, the fidelity of their hereditary followers, their striking and strange array, the contrast with the Baron of Bradwardine and the Lowland gentry; the collision of the motley and half-appointed host with the formed and finished English society, its passage by the Cumberland mountains and the blue lake of Ullswater,—are unceasingly and without effort present to the mind of the writer, and incite with their historical interest the susceptibility of his imagination. But at the same time the mental struggle, or rather transition, in the mind of Waverley,—for his mind was of the faint order which scarcely struggles,—is never for an instant lost sight of. In the very midst of the inroad and the conflict, the acquiescent placidity with which the hero exchanges the service of the imperious for the appreciation of the 'nice' heroine is kept before us, and the imagination of Scott wandered without effort from the great scene of martial affairs to the natural but rather unheroic sentiments of a young gentleman not very difficult to please. There is no trace of effort in the transition, as is so common in the inferior works of later copyists. Many historical novelists, especially those who with care and pains have 'read up' their detail, are often evidently in a strait how to pass from their history to their sentiment. The fancy of Sir Walter could not help connecting the two. If he had given us the English side of the race to Derby, he would have described the Bank of England paying in sixpences, and also the loves of the cashier.

It is not unremarkable in connection with this, the special characteristic of the 'Scotch novels,' that their author began his literary life by collecting the old ballads of his native country. Ballad poetry is, in comparison at least with many other kinds of poetry, a sensible thing. It describes not only romantic events, but historical ones, incidents in which there is a form and body and consistence,—events which have a result. Such a poem as 'Chevy Chace', we need not explain, has its prosaic side. The latest historian of Greece has nowhere been more successful than in his attempt to derive from Homer, the greatest of ballad poets, a thorough and consistent account of the political working of the Homeric state of society. The early natural imagination of men seizes firmly on all which interests the minds and hearts of natural men. We find in its delineations the council as well as the marriage, the harsh conflict as well as the deep love-affair. Scott's own poetry is essentially a modernised edition of the traditional poems which his early youth was occupied in collecting. The *Lady of the Lake* is a sort of *boudoir* ballad, yet it contains its element of common sense and broad delineation. The exact position of Lowlander and Highlander would not be more aptly described in a set treatise than in the well-known lines:

> Saxon, from yonder mountain high,
> I mark'd thee send delighted eye,
> Far to the south and east, where lay,
> Extended in succession gay,
> Deep waving fields and pastures green,
> With gentle slopes and groves between:
> These fertile plains, that soften'd vale,

Were once the birthright of the Gael;
The stranger came with iron hand,
And from our fathers rent the land.
Where dwell we now? See, rudely swell
Crag over crag, and fell o'er fell.
Ask we this savage hill we tread
For fattened steer or household bread;
Ask we for flocks those shingles dry,
And well the mountain might reply—
'To you, as to your sires of yore,
Belong the target and claymore!
I give you shelter in my breast,
Your own good blades must win the rest.'
Pent in this fortress of the North,
Think'st thou we will not sally forth,
To spoil the spoiler as we may,
And from the robber rend the prey?
Ay, by my soul! While on yon plain
The Saxon rears one shock of grain,
While of ten thousand herds there strays
But one along yon river's maze,
The Gael, of plain and river heir,
Shall with strong hand redeem his share.

We need not search the same poem for specimens of the romantic element, for the whole poem is full of them. The incident in which Ellen discovers who Fitz-James really is, is perhaps excessively romantic. At any rate the lines,—

To him each lady's look was lent;
On him each courtier's eye was bent;
Midst furs and silks and jewels sheen,
He stood in simple Lincoln green,
The centre of the glittering ring:
And Snowdoun's knight is Scotland's king,—

may be cited as very sufficient example of the sort of sentimental incident which is separable from extreme feeling. When Scott, according to his own half-jesting but half-serious expression, was 'beaten out of poetry' by Byron, he began to express in more pliable prose the same combination which his verse had been used to convey. As might have been expected, the sense became in the novels more free, vigorous, and flowing, because it is less cramped by the vehicle in which it is conveyed. The range of character which can be adequately delineated in narrative verse is much narrower than that which can be described in the combination of narrative with dramatic prose; and perhaps even the sentiment of the novels is manlier and freer; a delicate unreality hovers over the *Lady of the Lake.*

The sensible element, if we may so express it, of the Waverley Novels appears in various forms. One of the most striking is in the delineation of great political events and influential political institutions. We are not by any means about to contend that Scott is to be taken as an infallible or an impartial authority for the parts of history which he delineates. On the contrary, we believe all the world now agrees that there are many deductions to be made from, many exceptions to be taken to, the accuracy of his delineations. Still, whatever period or incident we take, we shall always find in the error a great, in one or two cases perhaps an extreme, mixture of the mental element which we term common sense. The strongest *un*sensible feeling in Scott was perhaps his Jacobitism, which crept out even in small incidents and recurring prejudice throughout the whole of his active career, and was, so to say, the emotional aspect of his habitual Toryism. Yet no one can have given a more sensible delineation, we might say a more statesmanlike analysis, of the various causes which led to the momentary success, and to the speedy ruin, of the enterprise of Charles Edward. Mr. Lockhart says that, notwithstanding Scott's imaginative readiness to exalt Scotland at the expense of England, no man would have been more willing to join in emphatic opposition to an anti-English party, if any such had presented itself with a practical object. Similarly his Jacobitism, though not without moments of real influence, passed away when his mind was directed to broad masses of fact and general conclusions of political reasoning. A similar observation may be made as to Scott's Toryism; although it is certain that there was an enthusiastic and, in the malicious sense, poetical element in Scott's Toryism, yet it quite as indisputably partook largely of two other elements, which are in common repute prosaic. He shared abundantly in the love of administration and organisation, common to all men of great active powers. He liked to contemplate method at work and order in action. Everybody hates to hear that the Duke of Wellington asked 'how the king's government was to be carried on.' No amount of warning wisdom will bear so fearful a repetition. Still, he *did* say it, and Scott had a sympathising foresight of the oracle before it was spoken. One element of his conservatism is his sympathy with the administrative arrangement, which is confused by the objections of a Whiggish opposition, and is liable to be altogether destroyed by uprisings of the populace. His biographer, while pointing out the strong contrast between Scott and the argumentative and parliamentary statesmen of his age, avows his opinion that in other times, and with sufficient opportunities, Scott's ability in managing men would have enabled him to 'play the part of Cecil or of Gondomar.' We may see how much an insensible enthusiasm for such abilities breaks out, not only in the description of hereditary monarchs, where the sentiment might be ascribed to a different origin, but also in the delineation of upstart rulers who could have no hereditary sanctity in the eyes of any Tory. Roland Græme, in the *Abbot*, is well described as losing in the presence of the Regent Murray the natural impertinence of his disposition. 'He might have braved with indifference the presence of an earl merely distinguished by his belt and coronet; but he felt overawed in that of the eminent soldier and statesman, the wielder of a nation's power, and the leader of her armies.' It is easy to perceive that the author shares the feeling of his hero by the evident pleasure with which he dwells on the Regent's demeanour: 'He then turned slowly round toward Roland Græme, and the marks of gaiety, real or assumed, disappeared from his countenance as completely as the passing bubbles leave the dark mirror of a still profound lake into which a traveller has cast a stone; in the course of a minute his noble features had assumed their natural expression of a deep and even melancholy gravity,' &c. In real life, Scott used to say that he never remembered feeling abashed in any one's presence except the Duke of Wellington's. Like that of the hero of his novel, his imagination was very susceptible to the influence of great achievement and prolonged success in wide-spreading affairs.

The view which Scott seems to have taken of democracy indicates exactly the same sort of application of a plain sense to the visible parts of the subject. His imagination was singularly penetrated with the strange varieties and motley composition of human life. The extraordinary multitude and striking contrast of the characters in his novels show this at once. And even more strikingly is the same habit of mind indicated by a tendency never to omit an opportunity of describing those varied crowds and assemblages which concentrate for a moment into a unity the scattered and unlike varieties of mankind.

Thus, but a page or two before the passage which we alluded to in *The Abbot,* we find the following:

It was indeed no common sight to Roland, the vestibule of a palace, traversed by its various groups,—some radiant with gaiety—some pensive, and apparently weighed down by affairs concerning the state, or concerning themselves. Here the hoary statesman, with his cautious yet commanding look, his furred cloak and sable pantoufles; there the soldier in buff and steel, his long sword jarring against the pavement, and his whiskered upper lip and frowning brow looking an habitual defiance of danger which perhaps was not always made good; there again passed my lord's serving-man, high of heart and bloody of hand, humble to his master and his master's equals, insolent to all others. To these might be added the poor suitor, with his anxious look and depressed mien—the officer, full of his brief authority, elbowing his betters, and possibly his benefactors, out of the road—the proud priest, who sought a better benefice—the proud baron, who sought a grant of church lands—the robber chief, who came to solicit a pardon for the injuries he had inflicted on his neighbours—the plundered franklin, who came to seek vengeance for that which he had himself received. Besides, there was the mustering and disposition of guards and soldiers—the despatching of messengers, and the receiving them—the trampling and neighing of horses without the gate—the flashing of arms, and rustling of plumes, and jingling of spurs within it. In short, it was that gay and splendid confusion, in which the eye of youth sees all that is brave and brilliant, and that of experience much that is doubtful, deceitful, false, and hollow—hopes that will never be gratified—promises which will never be fulfilled—pride in the disguise of humility—and insolence in that of frank and generous bounty.

As in the imagination of Shakespeare, so in that of Scott, the principal form and object were the structure—that is a hard word—the undulation and diversified composition of human society; the picture of this stood in the centre, and everything else was accessory and secondary to it. The old 'rows of books,' in which Scott so peculiarly delighted, were made to contribute their element to this varied imagination of humanity. From old family histories, odd memoirs, old law-trials, his fancy elicited new traits to add to the motley assemblage. His objection to democracy—an objection of which we can only appreciate the emphatic force when we remember that his youth was contemporary with the first French Revolution and the controversy as to the uniform and stereotyped rights of man—was, that it would sweep away this entire picture, level prince and peasant in a common *égalité,* substitute a scientific rigidity for the irregular and picturesque growth of centuries, replace an abounding and genial life by a symmetrical but lifeless mechanism. All the descriptions of society in the novels,—whether of feudal society, of modern Scotch society, or of English society,—are largely coloured by this feeling. It peeps out everywhere, and liberal critics have endeavoured to show that it was a narrow Toryism; but in reality it is a subtle compound of the natural instinct of the artist with the plain sagacity of the man of the world.

It would be tedious to show how clearly the same sagacity appears in his delineation of the various great events and movements in society which are described in the Scotch novels. There is scarcely one of them which does not bear it on its surface. Objections may, as we shall show, be urged to the delineation which Scott has given of the Puritan resistance and rebellions, yet scarcely any one will say there is not a worldly sense in it. On the contrary, the very objection is, that it is too worldly, and far too exclusively sensible.

The same thoroughly well-grounded sagacity and comprehensive appreciation of human life is shown in the treatment of what we may call *anomalous* characters. In general, monstrosity is no topic for art. Every one has known in real life characters which if, apart from much experience, he had found described in books, he would have thought unnatural and impossible. Scott, however, abounds in such characters. Meg Merrilies, Edie Ochiltree, Ratcliffe, are more or less of that description. That of Meg Merrilies especially is as distorted and eccentric as anything can be. Her appearance is described as making Mannering 'start;' and well it might:

She was full six feet high, wore a man's greatcoat over the rest of her dress, had in her hand a goodly sloethorn cudgel, and in all points of equipment except the petticoats seemed rather masculine than feminine. Her dark elf-locks shot out like the snakes of the Gorgon between an old-fashioned bonnet called a bongrace, heightening the singular effect of her strong and weather-beaten features, which they partly shadowed, while her eye had a wild roll that indicated something like real or affected insanity.

Her career in the tale corresponds with the strangeness of her exterior. 'Harlot, thief, witch, and gipsy,' as she describes herself, the hero is preserved by her virtues; half-crazed as she is described to be, he owes his safety on more than one occasion to her skill in stratagem and ability in managing those with whom she is connected, and who are

55

most likely to be familiar with her weakness and to detect her craft. Yet on hardly any occasion is the natural reader conscious of this strangeness. Something is of course attributable to the skill of the artist; for no other power of mind could produce the effect, unless it were aided by the unconscious tact of detailed expression. But the fundamental explanation of this remarkable success is the distinctness with which Scott saw how such a character as Meg Merrilies arose and was produced out of the peculiar circumstances of gipsy life in the localities in which he has placed his scene. He has exhibited this to his readers not by lengthy or elaborate description, but by chosen incidents, short comments, and touches of which he scarcely foresaw the effect. This is the only way in which the fundamental objection to making eccentricity the subject of artistic treatment can be obviated. Monstrosity ceases to be such when we discern the laws of nature which evolve it: when a real science explains its phenomena, we find that it is in strict accordance with what we call the natural type, but that some rare adjunct or uncommon casualty has interfered and distorted a nature, which is really the same, into a phenomenon which is altogether different. Just so with eccentricity in human character; it becomes a topic of literary art only when its identity with the ordinary principles of human nature is exhibited in the midst of, and as it were, by means of, the superficial unlikeness. Such a skill, however, requires an easy careless familiarity with usual human life and common human conduct. A writer must have a sympathy with health before he can show us how, and where, and to what extent, that which is unhealthy deviates from it; and it is this consistent acquaintance with regular life which makes the irregular characters of Scott so happy a contrast to the uneasy distortions of less sagacious novelists.

A good deal of the same criticism may be applied to the delineation which Scott has given us of the *poor*. In truth, poverty is an anomaly to rich people. It is very difficult to make out why people who want dinner do not ring the bell. One half of the world, according to the saying, do not know how the other half lives. Accordingly, nothing is so rare in fiction as a good delineation of the poor. Though perpetually with us in reality, we rarely meet them in our reading. The requirements of the case present an unusual difficulty to artistic delineation. A good deal of the character of the poor is an unfit topic for continuous art, and yet we wish to have in our books a lifelike exhibition of the whole of that character. Mean manners and mean vices are unfit for prolonged delineation; the every-day pressure of narrow necessities is too petty a pain and too anxious a reality to be dwelt upon. We can bear the mere description of the *Parish Register*—

> But this poor farce has neither truth nor art,
> To please the fancy or to touch the heart;
> Dark but not awful, dismal but yet mean,
> With anxious bustle moves the cumbrous scene;
> Presents no objects tender or profound,
> But spreads its cold unmeaning gloom around;—

but who could bear to have a long narrative of fortunes 'dismal but yet mean,' with characters 'dark but not awful,' and no objects 'tender or profound'? Mr. Dickens has in various parts of his writings been led by a sort of pre-Raphaelite *cultus* of reality into an error of this species. His poor people have taken to their poverty very thoroughly; they are poor talkers and poor livers, and in all ways poor people to read about. A whole array of writers have fallen into an opposite mistake. Wishing to preserve their delineations clear from the defects of meanness and vulgarity, they have attributed to the poor a fancied happiness and Arcadian simplicity. The conventional shepherd of ancient times was scarcely displeasing: that which is by everything except express avowal removed from the sphere of reality does not annoy us by its deviations from reality; but the fictitious poor of sentimental novelists are brought almost into contact with real life, half claim to be copies of what actually exists at our very doors, are introduced in close proximity to characters moving in a higher rank, over whom no such ideal charm is diffused, and who are painted with as much truth as the writer's ability enables him to give. Accordingly, the contrast is evident and displeasing: the harsh outlines of poverty will not bear the artificial rose-tint; they are seen through it, like high cheek-bones through the delicate colours of artificial youth; we turn away with some disgust from the false elegance and undeceiving art; we prefer the rough poor of nature to the petted poor of the refining describer. Scott has most felicitously avoided both these errors. His poor people are never coarse and never vulgar; their lineaments have the rude traits which a life of conflict will inevitably leave on the minds and manners of those who are to lead it; their notions have the narrowness which is inseparable from a contracted experience; their knowledge is not more extended than their restricted means of attaining it would render possible. Almost alone among novelists, Scott has given a thorough, minute, life-like description of poor persons, which is at the same time genial and pleasing. The reason seems to be, that the firm sagacity of his genius comprehended the industrial aspect of poor people's life thoroughly and comprehensively, his experience brought it before him easily and naturally, and his artist's mind and genial disposition enabled him to dwell on those features which would be most pleasing to the world in general. In fact, his own mind of itself and by its own nature, dwelt on those very peculiarities. He could not remove his firm and instructed genius into the domain of Arcadian unreality, but he was equally unable to dwell principally, peculiarly, or consecutively, on those petty, vulgar, mean details in which such a writer as Crabbe lives and breathes. Hazlitt said that Crabbe described a poor man's cottage like a man who came to distrain for rent; he catalogued every trivial piece of furniture, defects and cracks and all. Scott describes it as a cheerful but most sensible landlord would describe a cottage on his property: he has a pleasure in it. No detail, or few details, in the life of the inmates escape his experienced and interested eye; but he dwells on those which do not displease him. He sympathises with their rough industry and plain joys and sorrows. He does not fatigue himself or excite their wondering smile by theoretical plans of impossible relief. He makes the best of the life which is given, and by a sanguine sympathy makes it still better. A hard life many characters in Scott seem to lead; but he appreciates, and makes his reader appreciate, the full value of natural feelings, plain thoughts, and applied sagacity.

His ideas of political economy are equally characteristic of his strong sense and genial mind. He was always sneering at Adam Smith, and telling many legends of that philosopher's absence of mind and inaptitude for the ordinary conduct of life. A contact with the Edinburgh logicians had, doubtless, not augmented his faith in the formal deductions of abstract economy; nevertheless, with the facts before him, he could give a very plain and satisfactory exposition of the genial consequences of old abuses, the distinct necessity for stern reform, and the delicate humanity requisite for introducing that reform temperately and with feeling:

Even so the Laird of Ellangowan ruthlessly commenced his magisterial reform, at the expense of various established and superannuated pickers and stealers, who had been his neighbours for half a century. He wrought his miracles like a second Duke Humphrey; and by the influence of the beadle's rod, caused the lame to walk, the blind to see, and the palsied to labour. He detected poachers, black-fishers, orchard-breakers, and pigeon-shooters; had the applause of the bench for his reward, and the public credit of an active magistrate.

All this good had its ratable proportion of evil. Even an admitted nuisance, of ancient standing, should not be abated without some caution. The zeal of our worthy friend now involved in great distress sundry personages whose idle and mendicant habits his own *lachesse* had contributed to foster until these habits had become irreclaimable, or whose real incapacity for exertion rendered them fit objects, in their own phrase, for the charity of all well-disposed Christians. 'The long-remembered beggar,' who for twenty years had made his regular rounds within the neighbourhood, received rather as an humble friend than as an object of charity, was sent to the neighbouring workhouse. The decrepit dame, who travelled round the parish upon a hand-barrow, circulating from house to house like a bad shilling, which every one is in haste to pass to his neighbour—she, who used to call for her bearers as loud, or louder, than a traveller demands post-horses, even she shared the same disastrous fate. The 'daft Jock', who, half knave, half idiot, had been the sport of each succeeding race of village children for a good part of a century, was remitted to the county bridewell, where, secluded from free air and sunshine, the only advantages he was capable of enjoying, he pined and died in the course of six months. The old sailor, who had so long rejoiced the smoky rafters of every kitchen in the country by singing *Captain Ward* and *Bold Admiral Benbow*, was banished from the country for no better reason than that he was supposed to speak with a strong Irish accent. Even the annual rounds of the pedlar were abolished by the Justice, in his hasty zeal for the administration of rural police.

These things did not pass without notice and censure. We are not made of wood or stone, and the things which connect themselves with our hearts and habits cannot, like bark or lichen, be rent away without our missing them. The farmer's dame lacked her usual share of intelligence, perhaps also the self-applause which she had felt while distributing the *awmous* (alms), in shape of a *gowpen* (handful) of oatmeal to the medicant who brought the news. The cottage felt inconvenience from interruption of the petty trade carried on by the itinerant dealers. The children lacked their supply of sugar-plums and toys; the young women wanted pins, ribbons, combs, and ballads; and the old could no longer barter their eggs for salt, snuff, and tobacco. All these circumstances brought the busy Laird of Ellangowan into discredit, which was the more general on account of his former popularity. Even his lineage was brought up in judgment against him. They thought 'naething of what the like of Greenside, or Burnville, or Viewforth might do, that were strangers in the country; but Ellangowan! that had been a name amang them since the mirk Monanday, and lang before—*him* to be grinding the puir at that rate!—They ca'd his grandfather the Wicked Laird; but though he was whiles fractious aneuch, when he got into roving company and had ta'en the drap drink, he would have scorned to gang on at this gate. Na, na, the muckle chumlay in the Auld Place reeked like a killogie in his time, and there were as mony puir folk riving at the banes in the court and about the door, as there were gentles in the ha'. And the leddy, on ilka Christmas night as it came round, gae twelve siller pennies to ilka puir body about, in honour of the twelve apostles like. They were fond to ca' it papistrie; but I think our great folk might take a lesson frae the papists whiles. They gie another sort o' help to puir folk than just dinging down a saxpence in the brod on the Sabbath, and kilting, and scourging, and drumming them a' the sax days o' the week besides.'

Many other indications of the same healthy and natural sense, which gives so much of their characteristic charm to the Scotch novels, might be pointed out, if it were necessary to weary our readers by dwelling longer on a point we have already laboured so much. One more, however, demands notice because of its importance, and perhaps also because, from its somewhat less obvious character, it might otherwise escape without notice. There has been frequent controversy as to the penal code, if we may so call it, of fiction; that is, as to the apportionment of reward and punishment respectively to the good and evil personages therein delineated; and the practice of authors has been as various as the legislation of critics. One school abandons all thought on the matter, and declares that in the real life we see around us, good people often fail, and wicked people continually prosper; and would deduce the precept, that it is unwise in an art which should hold the 'mirror up to nature,' not to copy the uncertain and irregular distribution of its sanctions. Another school, with an exactness which savours at times of pedantry, apportions the success and the failure, the pain and the pleasure, of fictitious life to the moral qualities of those who are living in it—does not think at all, or but little, of every other quality in those characters, and does not at all care whether the penalty and reward are evolved in natural sequence from the circumstances and characters of the tale, or are owing to some monstrous accident far removed from all relation of cause or consequence to those facts and people. Both these classes of writers produce works which jar on the natural sense of common readers, and are at issue with the analytic criticism of the best critics. One school leaves an impression of an uncared-for world, in which there is no right and no wrong; the other, of a sort of Governesses' Institution of a world, where all praise and all blame, all good and all pain, are made to turn on special graces and petty offences, pesteringly spoken of and teasingly watched for. The manner of Scott is thoroughly different; you can scarcely lay down any novel of his without a strong feeling that the world in which the fiction has been laid, and in which your imagination has been moving, is one subject to *laws* of retribution which, though not apparent on a superficial glance, are yet in steady and consistent operation, and will be quite sure to work their due effect, if time is only given to them. Sagacious men know that this is in its best aspect the condition of life. Certain of the ungodly may, notwithstanding the Psalmist, flourish even through life like a green bay-tree; for providence, in external appearance (far differently from the real truth of things, as we may one day see it), works by a scheme of averages. Most people who ought to succeed, do succeed; most people who do fail, ought to fail. But there is no exact adjustment of 'mark' to merit; the competitive examination system appears to have an origin more recent than the creation of the world;—'on the whole,' 'speaking generally,' 'looking at life as a whole,' are the words in which we must describe the providential adjustment of visible good and evil to visible goodness and badness. And when we look more closely, we see that these general results are the consequences of certain principles which work half unseen, and which are effectual in the main, though thwarted here and there. It is this comprehensive though inexact distribution of good and evil which is suited to the novelist, and it is exactly this which Scott instinctively adopted. Taking a firm and genial view of the common facts of life,—seeing it as an experienced observer and tried man of action,— he could not help giving the representation of it which is insensibly borne in on the minds of such persons. He delineates it as a world moving according to laws which are always producing their effect, never *have* produced it; sometimes fall short a little; are always nearly successful. Good sense produces its effect as well as good intention; ability is valuable as well as virtue. It is this peculiarity which gives to his works, more than anything else, the life-likeness which distinguishes them; the average of the copy is struck on the same scale as that of reality; an unexplained uncommented-on adjustment works in the one, just as a hidden imperceptible principle of apportionment operates in the other.

The romantic susceptibility of Scott's imagination is as obvious in his novels as his matter-of-fact sagacity. We can find much of it in the place in which we should naturally look first for it,—his treatment of his heroines. We are no indiscriminate admirers of these young ladies, and shall shortly try to show how much they are inferior as imaginative creations to similar creations of the very highest artists. But the mode in which the writer speaks of them everywhere indicates an imagination continually under the illusion which we term romance. A gentle tone of manly admiration pervades the whole delineation of their words and actions. If we look carefully at the narratives of some remarkable female novelists—it would be invidious to give the instances by name—we shall be struck at once with the absence of this; they do not half like their heroines. It would be satirical to say that they were jealous of them; but it is certain that they analyse the mode in which their charms produce their effects, and the *minutiæ* of their operation, much in the same way in which a slightly jealous lady examines the claims of the heroines of society. The same writers have invented the atrocious species of *plain* heroines. Possibly none of the frauds which are now so much the topic of common remark are so irritating as that to which the purchaser of a novel is a victim on finding that he has only to peruse a narrative of the conduct and sentiments of an ugly lady. 'Two-and-sixpence to know the heart which has high cheek-bones!' Was there ever such an imposition? Scott would have recoiled from such conception. Even Jeanie Deans, though no heroine like Flora MacIvor, is described as 'comely,' and capable of looking almost pretty when required, and she has a compensating set-off in her sister, who is beautiful as well as unwise. Speaking generally, as is the necessity of criticism, Scott makes his heroines, at least by profession, attractive, and dwells on their attractiveness, though not with the wild ecstasy of insane youth, yet with the tempered and mellow admiration common to genial men of this world. Perhaps at times we are rather displeased at his explicitness, and disposed to hang back and carp at the admirable qualities displayed to us. But this is only a stronger evidence of the peculiarity which we speak of,—of the unconscious sentiments inseparable from Scott's imagination.

The same romantic tinge undeniably shows itself in Scott's pictures of the past. Many exceptions have been taken to the detail of mediæval life as it is described to us in *Ivanhoe*; but one merit will always remain to it, and will be enough to secure to it immense popularity. It describes the middle ages as we should have wished them to have been. We do not mean that the delineation satisfies those accomplished admirers of the old Church system who fancy that they have found among the prelates and barons of the fourteenth century a close approximation to the theocracy which they would recommend for our adoption. On the contrary, the theological merits of the middle ages are not prominent in Scott's delineation. 'Dogma' was not in his way: a cheerful man of the world is not anxious for a precise definition of peculiar doctrines. The charm of *Ivanhoe* is addressed to a simpler sort of imagination,—to that kind of boyish fancy which idolises mediæval society as the 'fighting time.' Every boy has heard of tournaments, and has a firm persuasion that in an age of tournaments life was thoroughly well understood. A martial society, where men fought hand to hand on good horses with large lances, in peace for pleasure, and in war for business, seems the very ideal of perfection to a bold and simply fanciful boy. *Ivanhoe* spreads before him the full landscape of such a realm, with Richard Cœur-de-Lion, a black horse, and the passage of arms at Ashby. Of course he admires it, and thinks there was never such a writer, and will nevermore be such a world. And a mature critic will share his admiration, at least to the extent of admitting that nowhere else have the elements of a martial romance been so gorgeously accumulated without becoming oppressive; their fanciful charm been so powerfully delineated, and yet so constantly relieved by touches of vigorous sagacity. One single fact shows how great the romantic illusion is. The pressure of painful necessity is scarcely so great in this novel as in novels of the same writer in which the scene is laid in modern times. Much may be said in favour of the mediæval system as contradistinguished from existing society; much has been said. But no one can maintain that general comfort was as much diffused as it is now. A certain case pervades the structure of later society. Our houses may not last so long, are not so picturesque, will leave no such ruins behind them; but they are warmed with hot water, have no draughts, and contain sofas instead of rushes. A slight daily unconscious luxury is hardly ever wanting to the dwellings in civilisation; like the gentle air of a genial climate, it is a perpetual minute enjoyment. The absence of this marks a rude barbaric time. We may avail ourselves of rough pleasures, stirring amusement, exciting actions, strange rumours; but life is hard and harsh. The cold air of the keen North may brace and invigorate, but it cannot soothe us. All sensible people know that the middle ages must have been very uncomfortable; there was a difficulty about 'good food;' almost insuperable obstacles to the cultivation of nice detail and small enjoyment. No one knew the abstract facts on which this conclusion rests better than Scott; but his delineation gives no general idea of the result. A thoughtless reader rises with the impression that the middle ages had the same elements of happiness which we have at present, and that they had fighting besides. We do not assert that this tenet is explicitly taught; on the contrary, many facts are explained, and many customs elucidated, from which a discriminating and deducing reader would infer the meanness of poverty and the harshness of barbarism. But these less imposing traits escape the rapid, and still more the boyish reader. His general impression is one of romance; and though, when roused, Scott was quite able to take a distinct view of the opposing facts, he liked his own mind to rest for the most part in the same pleasing illusion.

The same sort of historical romance is shown likewise in Scott's picture of remarkable historical characters. His Richard I is the traditional Richard, with traits heightened and ennobled in perfect conformity to the spirit of tradition. Some illustration of the same quality might be drawn from his delineations of the Puritan rebellions and the Cavalier enthusiasm. We might show that he ever dwells on the traits and incidents most attractive to a genial and spirited imagination. But the most remarkable instance of the power which romantic illusion exercised over him is his delineation of Mary Queen of Scots. He refused at one time of his life to write a biography of that princess 'because his opinion was contrary to his feeling.' He evidently considered her guilt to be clearly established, and thought, with a distinguished lawyer, that he should 'direct a jury to find her guilty;' but his fancy, like that of most of his countrymen, took a peculiar and special interest in the beautiful lady who, at any rate, had suffered so much and so fatally at the hands of a queen of England. He could not bring himself to dwell with nice accuracy on the evidence which substantiates her criminality, or on the still clearer indications of that unsound and over-crafty judgment, which was the fatal inheritance of the Stuart family, and which, in spite of advantages that scarcely any other family in the world has enjoyed, has made their name an historical byword for misfortune. The picture in the *Abbot*, one of the best historical pictures which Scott has given us, is principally the picture of the queen as the fond tradition of his countrymen exhibited her. Her entire innocence, it is true, is never alleged: but the enthusiasm of her followers is dwelt on with approving sympathy; their confidence is set forth at large; her influence over them is skilfully delineated; the fascination of charms chastened by misfortune is delicately indicated. We see a complete picture of the beautiful queen, of the suffering and sorrowful but yet not insensible woman. Scott could not, however, as a close study will show us, quite conceal the unfavourable nature of his fundamental opinion. In one remarkable passage the struggle of the judgment is even conspicuous, and in others the sagacity of the practised lawyer,—the thread of the attorney, as he used to call it, in his nature,—qualifies and modifies the sentiment hereditary in his countrymen and congenial to himself.

This romantic imagination is a habit or power (as we may choose to call it) of mind which is almost essential to the highest success in the historical novel. The aim, at any rate the effect, of this class of works seems to be to deepen and confirm the received view of historical personages. A great and acute writer may, from an accurate study of original documents, discover that those impressions are erroneous, and by a process of elaborate argument substitute others which he deems more accurate. But this can only be effected by writing a regular history. The essence of the achievement is the proof. If Mr. Froude had put forward his view of Henry the Eighth's character in a professed novel, he would have been laughed at. It is only by a rigid adherence to attested facts and authentic documents, that a view so original could obtain even a hearing. We start back with a little anger from a representation which is avowedly imaginative, and which contradicts our impressions. We do not like to have our opinions disturbed by reasoning; but it is impertinent to attempt to disturb them by fancies. A writer of the historical novel is bound by the popular conception of his subject; and commonly it will be found that this popular impression is to some extent a romantic one. An element of exaggeration clings to the popular judgment: great vices are made greater, great virtues greater also; interesting incidents are made more interesting, soft[3] legends more soft. The novelist who disregards this tendency will do so at the peril of his popularity. His business is to make attraction

[3] The *National Review* has 'softer' for 'soft'.—p. 463.

more attractive, and not to impair the pleasant pictures of ready-made romance by an attempt at grim reality.

We may therefore sum up the indications of this characteristic excellence of Scott's novels by saying, that more than any novelist he has given us fresh pictures of practical human society, with its cares and troubles, its excitements and its pleasures; that he has delineated more distinctly than any one else the framework in which this society inheres, and by the boundaries of which it is shaped and limited; that he has made more clear the way in which strange and eccentric characters grow out of that ordinary and usual system of life; that he has extended his view over several periods of society, and given an animated description of the external appearance of each, and a firm representation of its social institutions; that he has shown very graphically what we may call the worldly laws of moral government; and that over all these he has spread the glow of sentiment natural to a manly mind, and an atmosphere of generosity congenial to a cheerful one. It is from the collective effect of these causes, and from the union of sense and sentiment which is the principle of them all, that Scott derives the peculiar healthiness which distinguishes him. There are no such books as his for the sick-room, or for freshening the painful intervals of a morbid mind. Mere sense is dull, mere sentiment unsubstantial; a sensation of genial healthiness is only given by what combines the solidity of the one and the brightening charm of the other.

Some guide to Scott's defects, or to the limitations of his genius, if we would employ a less ungenial and perhaps more correct expression, is to be discovered, as usual, from the consideration of his characteristic excellence. As it is his merit to give bold and animated pictures of this world, it is his defect to give but insufficient representations of qualities which this world does not exceedingly prize, of such as do not thrust themselves very forward in it, of such as are in some sense above it. We may illustrate this in several ways.

One of the parts of human nature which are systematically omitted in Scott is the searching and abstract intellect. This did not lie in his way. No man had a stronger sagacity, better adapted for the guidance of common men and the conduct of common transactions. Few could hope to form a more correct opinion on things and subjects which were brought before him in actual life; no man had a more useful intellect. But on the other hand, as will be generally observed to be the case, no one was less inclined to that probing and seeking and anxious inquiry into things in general which is the necessity of some minds, and a sort of intellectual famine in their nature. He had no call to investigate the theory of the universe, and he would not have been able to comprehend those who did. Such a mind as Shelley's would have been entirely removed from his comprehension. He had no call to mix 'awful talk and asking looks' with his love of the visible scene. He could not have addressed the universe:

> I have watched
> Thy shadow, and the darkness of thy steps,
> And my heart ever gazes on the depth
> Of thy deep mysteries. I have made my bed
> In charnels and on coffins, where black death
> Keeps records of the trophies won from thee,
> Hoping to still these obstinate questionings
> Of thee and thine, by forcing some lone ghost,
> Thy messenger, to render up the tale
> Of what we are.

Such thoughts would have been to him 'thinking without an object,' 'abstracted speculations,' 'cobwebs of the unintelligible brain.' Above all minds his had the Baconian propensity to work upon 'stuff.' At first sight, it would not seem that this was a defect likely to be very hurtful to the works of a novelist. The labours of the searching and introspective intellect, however needful, absorbing, and in some degree delicious, to the seeker himself, are not in general very delightful to those who are not seeking. Genial men in middle life are commonly intolerant of that philosophising which their prototype in old times classed side by side with the lisping of youth. The theological novel, which was a few years ago so popular, and which is likely to have a recurring influence in times when men's belief is unsettled, and persons who cannot or will not read large treatises have thoughts in their minds and inquiries in their hearts, suggests to those who are accustomed to it the absence elsewhere of what is necessarily one of its most distinctive and prominent subjects. The desire to attain a belief, which has become one of the most familiar sentiments of heroes and heroines, would have seemed utterly incongruous to the plain sagacity of Scott, and also to his old-fashioned art. Creeds are *data* in his novels: people have different creeds, but each keeps his own. Some persons will think that this is not altogether amiss; nor do we particularly wish to take up the defence of the dogmatic novel. Nevertheless, it will strike those who are accustomed to the youthful generation of a cultivated time, that the passion of intellectual inquiry is one of the strongest impulses in many of them, and one of those which give the predominant colouring to the conversation and exterior mind of many more. And a novelist will not exercise the most potent influence over those subject to that passion, if he entirely omit the delineation of it. Scott's works have only one merit in this relation: they are an excellent rest to those who have felt this passion, and have had something too much of it.

The same indisposition to the abstract exercises of the intellect shows itself in the reflective portions of Scott's novels, and perhaps contributes to their popularity with that immense majority of the world who strongly share in that same indisposition: it prevents, however, their having the most powerful intellectual influence on those who have at any time of their lives voluntarily submitted themselves to this acute and refining discipline. The reflections of a practised thinker have a peculiar charm, like the last touches of the accomplished artist. The cunning exactitude of the professional hand leaves a trace in the very language. A nice discrimination of thought makes men solicitous of the most apt expressions to diffuse their thoughts. Both words and meaning gain a metallic brilliancy, like the glittering precision of the pure Attic air. Scott's is a healthy and genial world of reflection, but it wants the charm of delicate exactitude.

The same limitation of Scott's genius shows itself in a very different portion of art—in his delineation of his heroines. The same blunt sagacity of imagination which fitted him to excel in the rough description of obvious life, rather unfitted him for delineating the less substantial essence of the female character. The nice *minutiæ* of society, by means of which female novelists have been so successful in delineating their own sex, were rather too small for his robust and powerful mind. Perhaps, too, a certain unworldliness of *imagination* is necessary to enable men to comprehend or delineate that essence: unworldliness of *life* is no doubt not requisite; rather, perhaps, worldliness is necessary to the acquisition of a sufficient experience. But an absorption in the practical world does not seem favourable to a comprehension of anything which does not precisely belong to it. Its interests are too engrossing; its excitements too keen; it modifies the fancy, and in the change unfits it for everything else. Something too, in Scott's character and history made it more difficult for him to give a representation of women than of men. Goethe used to say that his idea of woman was not drawn from his experience, but that it came to him before experience, and that he explained his experience by a reference to it. And though this is a German, and not very happy, form of expression, yet it appears to indicate a very important distinction. Some efforts of the imagination are made so early in life, just as it were at the dawn of the conscious faculties, that we are never able to fancy ourselves as destitute of them. They are part of the mental constitution with which, so to speak, we awoke to existence. These are always far more firm, vivid, and definite than any other images of our fancy, and we apply them, half unconsciously, to any facts and sentiments and actions which may occur to us later in life, whether arising from within or thrust upon us from the outward world. Goethe doubtless meant that the idea of the female character was to him one of these first elements of imagination; not a thing puzzled out, or which he remembered having conceived, but a part of the primitive conceptions which, being coeval with his memory, seemed inseparable from his consciousness. The descriptions of women likely to be given by this sort of imagination will probably be the best descriptions. A mind which would arrive at this idea of the female character by this process, and so early, would be one obviously of more than usual susceptibility. The early imagination does not commonly take this direction; it thinks most of horses and lances, tournaments and knights; only a mind with an unusual and instinctive tendency to this kind of thought, would be borne thither so early or so effectually. And even independently of this probable peculiarity of the individual, the primitive imagination in general is likely to be the most accurate which men can form; not, of course, of the external manifestations and detailed manners, but of the inner sentiment and characteristic feeling of women. The early imagination conceives what it does conceive very justly; fresh from the facts, stirred by the new aspect of things, undimmed by the daily passage of constantly forgotten images, not misled by the irregular analogies of a dislocated life,—the early mind sees what it does see with a spirit and an intentness never given to it again. A mind like Goethe's, of very strong imagination, aroused at the earliest age,— not of course by passions, but by an unusual strength in that undefined longing which is the prelude to our passions,—will form the best idea of the inmost female nature which masculine nature can form. The difference[4] is evident in the characters of women formed by Goethe's imagination or Shakespeare's, and those formed by such an imagination as that of Scott. The latter seems so external. We have traits, features, manners; we know the heroine as she appeared in the street; in some degree we know how she talked, but we never know how she felt—least of all what she was: we always feel there is a world behind, unanalysed, unrepresented, which we cannot attain to. Such a character as Margaret in *Faust* is known to us to the very soul; so is Imogen; so is Ophelia. Edith Bellenden, Flora MacIvor, Miss Wardour, are young ladies who, we are told, were good-looking, and well-dressed (according to the old fashion), and sensible; but we feel we know but very little of them, and they do not haunt our imaginations. The failure of Scott in this line of art is more conspicuous, because he had not in any remarkable degree the later experience of female detail, with which some minds have endeavoured to supply the want of the early essential imagination, and which Goethe possessed in addition to it. It was rather late, according to his biographer, before Scott set up for 'a squire of dames;' he was a 'lame young man, very enthusiastic about ballad poetry;' he was deeply in love with a young lady, supposed to be imaginatively represented by Flora MacIvor, but he was unsuccessful. It would be over-ingenious to argue, from his failing in a single love-affair, that he had no peculiar interest in young ladies in general; but the whole description of his youth shows that young ladies exercised over him a rather more divided influence than is usual. Other pursuits intervened, much more than is common with persons of the imaginative temperament, and he never led the life of flirtation from which Goethe believed that he derived so much instruction. Scott's heroines, therefore, are, not unnaturally, faulty, since from a want of the very peculiar instinctive imagination he could not give us the essence of women, and from the habits of his life he could not delineate to us their detailed life with the appreciative accuracy of habitual experience. Jeanie Deans is probably the best of his heroines, and she is so because she is the least of a heroine. The plain matter-of-fact element in the peasant-girl's life and circumstances suited a robust imagination. There is little in the part of her character that is very finely described which is characteristically feminine. She is not a masculine, but she is an epicene heroine. Her love-affair with Butler, a single remarkable scene excepted, is rather commonplace than otherwise.

4 The *National Review* has 'trace' for 'difference'.—p. 466.

A similar criticism might be applied to Scott's heroes. Everyone feels how commonplace they are—Waverley excepted, whose very vacillation gives him a sort of character. They have little personality. They are all of the same type;—excellent young men—rather strong— able to ride and climb and jump. They are always said to be sensible, and bear out the character by being not unwilling sometimes to talk platitudes. But we know nothing of their inner life. They are said to be in love; but we have no special account of their individual sentiments. People show their character in their love more than in anything else. These young gentlemen all love in the same way—in the vague commonplace way of this world. We have no sketch or dramatic expression of the life within. Their souls are quite unknown to us. If there is an exception, it is Edgar Ravenswood. But if we look closely, we may observe that the notion which we obtain of his character, unusually broad as it is, is not a notion of him in his capacity of hero, but in his capacity of distressed peer. His proud poverty gives a distinctness which otherwise his lineaments would not have. We think little of his love; we think much of his narrow circumstances and compressed haughtiness.

The same exterior delineation of character shows itself in its treatment of men's religious nature. A novelist is scarcely, in the notion of ordinary readers, bound to deal with this at all; if he does, it will be one of his great difficulties to indicate it graphically, yet without dwelling on it. Men who purchase a novel do not wish a stone or a sermon. All lengthened reflections must be omitted,—the whole armory of pulpit eloquence. But no delineation of human nature can be considered complete which omits to deal with man in relation to the questions which occupy him as man, with his convictions as to the theory of the universe and his own destiny; the human heart throbs on few subjects with a passion so intense, so peculiar, and so typical. From an artistic view, it is a blunder to omit an element which is so characteristic of human life, which contributes so much to its animation, and which is so picturesque. A reader of a more simple mind, little apt to indulge in such criticism, feels 'a want of depth', as he would speak, in delineations from which so large an element of his own most passionate and deepest nature is omitted. It can hardly be said that there is an omission of the religious nature in Scott. But at the same time there is no adequate delineation of it. If we refer to the facts of his life, and the view of his character which we collect from thence, we shall find that his religion

71

was of a qualified and double sort. He was a genial man of the world, and had the easy faith in the kindly *Dieu des bons gens* which is natural to such a person; and he had also a half-poetic principle of superstition in his nature, inclining him to believe in ghosts, legends, fairies, and elfs, which did not affect his daily life or possibly his superficial belief, but was nevertheless very constantly present to his fancy, and which affected, as is the constitution of human nature, through that frequency, the undefined, half-expressed, inexpressible feelings which are at the root of that belief.[5] Superstition was a kind of Jacobitism in his religion; as a sort of absurd reliance on the hereditary principle modified insensibly his leanings in the practical world, so a belief in the existence of unevidenced, and often absurd, supernatural beings, qualified his commonest speculations on the higher world. Both these elements may be thought to enter into the highest religion; there is a principle of cheerfulness which will justify in its measure a genial enjoyment, and also a principle of fear which those who think only of that enjoyment will deem superstition, and which will really become superstition in the over-anxious and credulous acceptor of it. But in a true religion these two elements will be combined. The character of God images itself very imperfectly in any human soul, but in the highest it images itself as a whole; it leaves an abiding impression which will justify anxiety and allow of happiness. The highest aim of the religious novelist would be to show how this operates in human character; to exhibit in their curious modification our religious love, and also our religious fear. In the novels of Scott the two elements appear in a state of separation, as they did in his own mind. We have the superstition of the peasantry in the *Antiquary*, in *Guy Mannering*, everywhere almost; we have likewise a pervading tone of genial easy reflection characteristic of the man of the world who produced, and agreeable to the people of the world who read, these works. But we have no picture of the two in combination. We are scarcely led to think on the subject at all, so much do other subjects distract our interest; but if we do think, we are puzzled at the contrast. We do not know which is true, the uneasy belief of superstition, or the easy satisfaction of the world; we waver between the two, and have no suggestion even hinted to us of the possibility of a reconciliation. The character of the Puritans certainly

[5] The *National Review* sentence runs 'and affected, as is the constitution of human nature, by that frequency, the indefined, half-expressed, inexpressible feelings which are at the root of that belief'.—p. 468. As this does not make very good sense the text has been amended accordingly.

did not in general embody such a reconciliation, but it might have been made by a sympathising artist the vehicle for a delineation of a struggle after it. The two elements of love and fear ranked side by side in their minds with an intensity which is rare even in minds that feel only one of them. The delineation of Scott is amusing, but superficial. He caught the ludicrous traits which tempt the mirthful imagination, but no other side of the character pleased him. The man of the world was displeased with their obstinate interfering zeal; their intensity of faith was an opposition force in the old Scotch polity, of which he liked to fancy the harmonious working. They were superstitious enough; but nobody likes other people's superstitions. Scott's were of a wholly different kind. He made no difficulty as to the observance of Christmas Day, and would have eaten potatoes without the faintest scruple, although their name does not occur in Scripture. Doubtless also his residence in the land of Puritanism did not incline him to give anything except a satirical representation of that belief. You must not expect from a dissenter a faithful appreciation of the creed from which he dissents. You cannot be impartial on the religion of the place in which you live; you may believe it, or you may dislike it; it crosses your path in too many forms for you to be able to look at it with equanimity. Scott had rather a rigid form of Puritanism forced upon him in his infancy; it is asking too much to expect him to be partial to it. The aspect of religion which Scott delineates best is that which appears in griefs, especially in the grief of strong characters. His strong *natural* nature felt the power of death. He has given us many pictures of rude and simple men subdued, if only for a moment, into devotion by its presence.

On the whole, and speaking roughly, these defects in the delineation which Scott has given us of human life are but two. He omits to give us a delineation of the soul. We have mind, manners, animation, but it is the stir of this world. We miss the consecrating power; and we miss it not only in its own peculiar sphere, which, from the difficulty of introducing the deepest elements into a novel, would have been scarcely matter for a harsh criticism, but in the place in which a novelist might most be expected to delineate it. There are perhaps such things as the love-affairs of immortal beings, but no one would learn it from Scott. His heroes and heroines are well dressed for this world, but not for another; there is nothing even in their love which is suitable for immortality. As has been noticed, Scott also omits any delineation of the abstract unworldly intellect. This too might not have been so

73

severe a reproach, considering its undramatic, unanimated nature, if it had stood alone; but taken in connection with the omission which we have just spoken of, it is most important. As the union of sense and romance makes the world of Scott so characteristically agreeable,—a fascinating picture of this world in the light in which we like best to dwell on[6] it; so the deficiency in the attenuated, striving intellect, as well as in the supernatural soul, gives to the 'world' of Scott the cumbrousness and temporality, in short, the materialism, which is characteristic of the world.

We have dwelt so much on what we think are the characteristic features of Scott's imaginative representations that we have left ourselves no room to criticise the two most natural points of criticism in a novelist—plot and style. This is not, however, so important in Scott's case as it would commonly be. He used to say, 'It was of no use having a plot; you could not keep to it.' He modified and changed his thread of story from day to day,—sometimes even from bookselling reasons, and on the suggestion of others. An elaborate work of narrative art could not be produced in this way, everyone will concede; the highest imagination, able to look far over the work, is necessary for that task. But the plots produced, so to say, by the pen of the writer as he passes over the events are likely to have a freshness and a suitableness to those events which is not possessed by the inferior writers who make up a mechanical plot before they commence. The procedure of the highest genius doubtless is scarcely a procedure: the view of the whole story comes at once upon its imagination like the delicate end and the distinct beginning of some long vista. But all minds do not possess the highest mode of conception; and among lower modes, it is doubtless better to possess the vigorous fancy which creates each separate scene in succession as it goes, than the pedantic intellect which designs everything long before it is wanted. There is a play in unconscious creation which no voluntary elaboration and preconceived fitting of distinct ideas can ever hope to produce. If the whole cannot be created by one bounding effort, it is better that each part should be created separately and in detail.

The style of Scott would deserve the highest praise if M. Thiers could establish his theory of narrative language. He maintains that a historian's language approaches perfection in proportion as it aptly communicates what is meant to be narrated without drawing any

[6] The *National Review* has 'in' for 'on'.—p. 470.

attention to itself. Scott's style fulfils this condition. Nobody rises from his works without a most vivid idea of what is related, and no one is able to quote a single phrase in which it has been narrated. We are inclined, however, to differ from the great French historian, and to oppose to him a theory derived from a very different writer. Coleridge used to maintain that all good poetry was untranslatable into words of the same language without injury to the sense: the meaning was, in his view, to be so inseparably intertwined even with the shades of the language, that the change of a single expression would make a difference in the accompanying feeling, if not in the bare signification: consequently, all good poetry must be remembered exactly,—to change a word is to modify the essence. Rigidly this theory can only be applied to a few kinds of poetry, or special passages in which the imagination is exerting itself to the utmost, and collecting from the whole range of associated language the very expressions which it requires. The highest excitation of feeling is necessary to this peculiar felicity of choice. In calmer moments the mind has either a less choice, or less acuteness of selective power. Accordingly, in prose it would be absurd to expect any such nicety. Still, on great occasions in imaginative fiction, there should be passages in which the words seem to cleave to the matter. The excitement is as great as in poetry. The words should become part of the sense. They should attract our attention, as this is necessary to impress them on the memory; but they should not in so doing distract attention from the meaning conveyed. On the contrary, it is their inseparability from their meaning which gives them their charm and their power. In truth, Scott's language, like his sense, was such as became a bold sagacious man of the world. He used the first sufficient words which came uppermost, and seems hardly to have been sensible, even in the works of others, of that exquisite accuracy and inexplicable appropriateness of which we have been speaking.

To analyse in detail the faults and merits of even a few of the greatest of the Waverley Novels would be impossible in the space at our command on the present occasion. We have only attempted a general account of a few main characteristics. Every critic must, however, regret to have to leave topics so tempting to remark as many of Scott's stories, and a yet greater number of his characters.

Charles Dickens
Introductory note

Charles Dickens (1812–1870) was the son of a clerk in the navy pay-office; in childhood he underwent considerable hardship and received little formal education as a result of the poverty of his family. He became a solicitor's clerk, and meanwhile taught himself shorthand and read widely. In 1835 he became a reporter of the Commons debates for the *Morning Chronicle*; his contributions to other periodicals were republished in 1836 as *Sketches by Boz*. The monthly publication in twenty numbers of *The Posthumous Papers of the Pickwick Club* began in April, 1836, and this was the beginning of Dickens's success and fame. A steady stream of novels appeared, and in 1850 Dickens founded a weekly periodical, *Household Words*. At the time of Bagehot's essay the main body of Dickens's novels had been written, and he was at the height of his fame and popularity: in this year he began to give public readings of his work. The only major novels to appear after Bagehot's essay were *A Tale of Two Cities*, 1859, and *Great Expectations*, 1860–61.

Charles Dickens[1]

IT must give Mr. Dickens much pleasure to look at the collected series of his writings. He has told us of the beginnings of *Pickwick*.

'I was,' he relates in what is now the preface to that work, 'a young man of three and twenty, when the present publishers, attracted by some pieces I was at that time writing in the *Morning Chronicle* newspaper (of which one series had lately been collected and published in two volumes, illustrated by my esteemed friend Mr. George Cruikshank), waited upon me to propose a something that should be published in shilling numbers—then only known to me, or I believe to anybody else, by a dim recollection of certain interminable novels in that form, which used, some five-and-twenty years ago, to be carried about the country by pedlars, and over some of which I remember to have shed innumerable tears, before I served my apprenticeship to Life. When I opened my door in Furnival's Inn to the managing partner who represented the firm, I recognised in him the person from whose hands I had bought, two or three years previously, and whom I had never seen before or since, my first copy of the magazine in which my first effusion—dropped stealthily one evening at twilight, with fear and trembling, into a dark letter-box, in a dark office, up a dark court in Fleet Street—appeared in all the glory of print; on which occasion, by the by,—how well I recollect it!—I walked down to Westminster Hall, and turned into it for half-an-hour, because my eyes were so dimmed with joy and pride that they could not bear the street, and were not fit to be seen there. I told my visitor of the coincidence, which we both hailed as a good omen; and so fell to business.'

After such a beginning, there must be great enjoyment in looking at the long series of closely printed green volumes, in remembering their marvellous popularity, in knowing that they are a familiar literature wherever the English language is spoken,—that they are read with

---

[1] *Cheap Edition of the Works of Mr. Charles Dickens. The Pickwick Papers, Nicholas Nickleby, &c.* London, 1857–8. Chapman and Hall. This essay was first published in the *National Review* for October 1858, Volume VII, pp. 458–86.

admiring appreciation by persons of the highest culture at the centre of civilisation,—that they amuse, and are fit to amuse, the roughest settler in Vancouver's Island.

The penetrating power of this remarkable genius among all classes at home is not inferior to its diffusive energy abroad. The phrase 'household book' has, when applied to the works of Mr. Dickens, a peculiar propriety. There is no contemporary English writer whose works are read so generally through the whole house, who can give pleasure to the servants as well as to the mistress, to the children as well as to the master. Mr. Thackeray without doubt exercises a more potent and plastic fascination within his sphere, but that sphere is limited. It is restricted to that part of the middle class which gazes inquisitively at the 'Vanity Fair' world. The delicate touches of our great satirist have, for such readers, not only the charm of wit, but likewise the interest of valuable information; he tells them of the topics which they want to know. But below this class there is another and far larger, which is incapable of comprehending the idling world or of appreciating the accuracy of delineations drawn from it, which would not know the difference between a picture of Grosvenor Square by Mr. Thackeray and the picture of it in a Minerva-Press novel, which only cares for or knows of its own multifarious, industrial, fig-selling world,—and over these also Mr. Dickens has power.

It cannot be amiss to take this opportunity of investigating, even slightly, the causes of so great a popularity. And if, in the course of our article, we may seem to be ready with over-refining criticism, or to be unduly captious with theoretical objection, we hope not to forget that so great and so diffused an influence is a *datum* for literary investigation,—that books which have been thus *tried* upon mankind and have thus succeeded, must be books of immense genius,—and that it is our duty as critics to explain, as far as we can, the nature and the limits of that genius, but never for one moment to deny or question its existence.

Men of genius may be divided into regular and irregular. Certain minds, the moment we think of them, suggest to us the ideas of symmetry and proportion. Plato's name, for example, calls up at once the impression of something ordered, measured, and settled: it is the exact contrary of everything eccentric, immature, or undeveloped. The opinions of such a mind are often erroneous, and some of them may, from change of time, of intellectual *data*, or from chance, seem not to be quite worthy of it; but the mode in which those opinions are expressed, and (as far as we can make it out) the mode in which they are framed, affect us, as we have said, with a sensation of symmetricalness. It is not very easy to define exactly to what peculiar internal characteristic this external effect is due: the feeling is distinct, but the cause is obscure; it lies hid in the peculiar constitution of great minds, and we should not wonder that it is not very easy either to conceive or to describe. On the whole, however, the effect seems to be produced by a peculiar proportionateness, in each instance, of the mind to the tasks which it undertakes, amid which we see it, and by which we measure it. Thus we feel that the powers and tendencies of Plato's mind and nature were more fit than those of any other philosopher for the due consideration and exposition of the highest problems of philosophy, of the doubts and difficulties which concern man as man. His genius was measured to its element; any change would mar the delicacy of the thought or the polished accuracy of the expression. The weapon was fitted to its aim. Every instance of proportionateness does not, however, lead us to attribute this peculiar symmetry to the whole mind we are observing. The powers must not only be suited to the task undertaken, but the task itself must also be suited to a human being, and employ all the marvellous faculties with which he is endowed. The neat perfection of such a mind as Talleyrand's is the antithesis to the symmetry of genius; the niceties neither of diplomacy nor of conversation give scope to the entire powers of a great nature. We may lay down as the condition of a regular or symmetrical genius, that it should have the exact combination of powers suited to graceful and easy success in an exercise of mind great enough to task the whole intellectual nature.

On the other hand, men of irregular or unsymmetrical genius are eminent either for some one or some few peculiarities of mind, have possibly special defects on other sides of their intellectual nature, at any rate want what the scientific men of the present day would call the *definite proportion* of faculties and qualities suited to the exact work they have in hand. The foundation of many criticisms of Shakespeare is that he is deficient in this peculiar proportion. His overteeming imagination gives at times, and not unfrequently, a great feeling of irregularity; there seems to be confusion. We have the tall trees of the forest, the majestic creations of the highest genius; but we have, besides, a bushy second growth, an obtrusion of secondary images and fancies, which prevent our taking an exact measure of such grandeur. We have not the sensation of intense simplicity which must probably accompany the highest conceivable greatness. Such is also the basis of Mr. Hallam's criticism on Shakespeare's language, which Mr. Arnold has lately revived. 'His expression is often faulty,' because his illustrative imagination, somewhat predominating over his other faculties, diffuses about the main expression a supplement of minor metaphors which sometimes distract the comprehension, and almost always deprive his style of the charm that arises from undeviating directness. Doubtless this is an instance of the very highest kind of irregular genius, in which all the powers exist in the mind in a very high, and almost all of them in the very highest measure, but in which from a slight excess in a single one, the charm of proportion is lessened. The most ordinary cases of irregular genius are those in which single faculties are abnormally developed, and call off the attention from all the rest of the mind by their prominence and activity. Literature, as the 'fragment of fragments' is so full of the fragments of such minds that it is needless to specify instances.

Possibly it may be laid down that one of two elements is essential to a symmetrical mind. It is evident that such a mind must either apply itself to that which is theoretical or that which is practical, to the world of abstraction or to the world of objects and realities. In the former case the deductive understanding, which masters first principles and makes deductions from them,—the thin ether of the intellect, the 'mind itself by itself,'—must evidently assume a great prominence. To attempt to comprehend principles without it, is to try to swim without arms, or to fly without wings. Accordingly, in the mind of Plato, and in others like him, the abstract and deducing understanding fills a great place; the imagination seems a kind of eye to descry its data; the artistic instinct an arranging impulse which sets in order its inferences and conclusions. On the other hand, if a symmetrical mind busy itself with the active side of human life, with the world of concrete men and real things, its principal quality will be a practical sagacity, which forms with ease a distinct view and just appreciation of all the mingled objects that the world presents,—which allots to each its own place and its intrinsic and appropriate rank. Possibly no mind gives such an idea of this sort of symmetry as Chaucer's. Everything in it seems in its place. A healthy sagacious man of the world has gone through the world; he loves it, and knows it; he dwells on it with a fond appreciation; every object of the old life of 'merry England' seems to fall into its precise niche in his ordered and symmetrical comprehension. The *Prologue to the Canterbury Tales* is in itself a series of memorial tablets to mediæval society; each class has its tomb, and each its apt inscription. A man without such an apprehensive and broad sagacity must fail in every extensive delineation of various life; he might attempt to describe what he did not penetrate, or if by a rare discretion he avoided that mistake, his works would want the *binding element*; he would be deficient in that distinct sense of relation and combination which is necessary for the depiction of the whole of life, which gives to it unity at first, and imparts to it a mass in the memory ever afterwards. And eminence in one or other of these marking faculties,—either in the deductive abstract intellect, or the practical seeing sagacity,—seems essential to the mental constitution of a symmetrical genius, at least in man. There are, after all, but two principal all-important spheres in human life—thought and action; and we can hardly conceive of a masculine mind symmetrically developed, which did not evince its symmetry by an evident perfection in one or other of those pursuits, which did not leave the trace of its distinct reflection upon the one, or of its large insight upon the other of them. Possibly it may be thought that in the sphere of pure art there may be room for a symmetrical development different from these; but it will perhaps be found, on examination of such cases, either that under peculiar and appropriate disguises one of these great qualities is present, or that the apparent symmetry is the narrow perfection of a limited nature, which may be most excellent in itself, as in the stricter form of sacred art, but which, as we explained, is quite opposed to that broad perfection of the thinking being to which we have applied the name of the symmetry of genius.

If this classification of men of genius be admitted, there can be no hesitation in assigning to Mr. Dickens his place in it. His genius is essentially irregular and unsymmetrical. Hardly any English writer perhaps is much more so. His style is an example of it. It is descriptive, racy, and flowing; it is instinct with new imagery and singular illustration; but it does not indicate that due proportion of the faculties to one another which is a beauty in itself, and which cannot help diffusing beauty over every happy word and moulded clause. We may choose an illustration at random. The following graphic description will do:

If Lord George Gordon had appeared in the eyes of Mr. Willet, overnight, a nobleman of somewhat quaint and odd exterior, the impression was confirmed this morning, and increased a hundred fold. Sitting bolt upright upon his bony steed, with his long, straight hair dangling about his face and fluttering in the wind; his limbs all angular and rigid, his elbows stuck out on either side ungracefully, and his whole frame jogged and shaken at every motion of his horse's feet,—a more grotesque or more ungainly figure can hardly be conceived. In lieu of whip, he carried in his hand a great gold-headed cane, as large as any footman carries in these days; and his various modes of holding this unwieldy weapon—now upright before his face like the sabre of a horse-soldier, now over his shoulder like a musket, now between his finger and thumb, but always in some uncouth and awkward fashion—contributed in no small degree to the absurdity of his appearance. Stiff, lank, and solemn, dressed in an unusual manner, and ostentatiously exhibiting—whether by design or accident—all his peculiarities of carriage, gesture, and conduct, all the qualities, natural and artificial, in which he differed from other men;—he might have moved the sternest looker-on to laughter, and fully provoked the smiles and whispered jests which greeted his departure from the Maypole inn.

Quite unconscious, however, of the effect he produced, he trotted on beside his secretary, talking to himself nearly all the way, until they came within a mile or two of London, when now and then some passenger went by who knew him by sight, and pointed him out to some one else, and perhaps stood looking after him, or cried, in jest or earnest, as it might be, 'Hurrah, Geordie! No Popery!' At which he would gravely pull off his hat, and bow. When they reached the town and rode along the streets, these notices became more frequent; some laughed, some hissed, some turned their heads and smiled, some wondered who he was, some ran along the pavement by his side and cheered. When this happened in a crush of carts and chairs and coaches, he would make a dead stop, and pulling off his hat, cry, 'Gentlemen, No Popery!' to which the gentlemen would respond with lusty voices, and with three times three; and then, on he would go again with a score or so of the raggedest following at his horse's heels, and shouting till their throats were parched.

The old ladies too—there were a great many old ladies in the streets, and these all knew him. Some of them—not those of the highest rank, but such as sold fruit from baskets and carried burdens—clapped their shrivelled hands, and raised a weazen, piping, shrill 'Hurrah, my lord.' Others waved their hands or handkerchiefs, or shook their fans or parasols, or threw up windows, and called in haste to those within to come and see. All these marks of popular esteem he received with profound gravity and respect; bowing very low, and so frequently that his hat was more off his head than on; and looking up at the houses as he passed along, with the air of one who was making a public entry, and yet was not puffed-up or proud.

No one would think of citing such a passage as this, as exemplifying the proportioned beauty of finished writing; it is not the writing of an evenly developed or of a highly cultured mind; it abounds in jolts and odd turns; it is full of singular twists and needless complexities: but, on the other hand, no one can deny its great and peculiar merit. It is an odd style, and it is very odd how much you read it. It is the overflow of a copious mind, though not the chastened expression of an harmonious one.

The same quality characterises the matter of his works. His range is very varied. He has attempted to describe every kind of scene in English life, from quite the lowest to almost the highest. He has not endeavoured to secure success by confining himself to a single path, nor wearied the public with repetitions of the subjects by the delineation of which he originally obtained fame. In his earlier works he never writes long without saying something well, something which no other man would have said; but even in them it is the characteristic of his power that it is apt to fail him at once; from masterly strength we pass without interval to almost infantine weakness,—something like disgust succeeds in a moment to an extreme admiration. Such is the natural fate of an unequal mind employing itself on a vast and various subject. On a recent occasion we ventured to make a division of novels into the ubiquitous,—it would have been perhaps better to say the miscellaneous,—and the sentimental: the first, as its name implies, busying itself with the whole of human life, the second restricting itself within a peculiar and limited theme. Mr. Dickens's novels are all of the former class. They aim to delineate nearly all that part of our national life which can be delineated,—at least, within the limits which social morality prescribes to social art; but you cannot read his delineation of any part without being struck with its singular incompleteness. An artist once said of the best work of another artist, 'Yes, it is a pretty patch.' If we might venture on the phrase, we should say that Mr. Dickens's pictures were graphic scraps; his best books are compilations of them.

The truth is that Mr. Dickens wholly wants the two elements which we have spoken of as one or other requisite for a symmetrical genius. He is utterly deficient in the faculty of reasoning. 'Mamma, what shall I think about?' said the small girl. 'My dear, don't think,' was the old-fashioned reply. We do not allege that in the strict theory of education this was a correct reply; modern writers think otherwise; but we wish someone would say it to Mr. Dickens. He is often troubled with the idea that he must reflect, and his reflections are perhaps the worst reading in the world. There is a sentimental confusion about them; we never find the consecutive precision of mature theory, or the cold distinctness of clear thought. Vivid facts stand out in his imagination, and a fresh illustrative style brings them home to the imagination of his readers; but his continuous philosophy utterly fails in the attempt to harmonise them,—to educe a theory or elaborate a precept from them. Of his social thinking we shall have a few words to say in detail; his didactic humour is very unfortunate: no writer is less fitted for an excursion to the imperative mood. At present we only say what is so obvious as scarcely to need saying, that his abstract understanding is so far inferior to his picturesque imagination as to give even to his best works the sense of jar and incompleteness, and to deprive them altogether of the crystalline finish which is characteristic of the clear and cultured understanding.

Nor has Mr. Dickens the easy and various sagacity which, as has been said, gives a unity to all which it touches. He has, indeed, a quality which is near allied to it in appearance. His shrewdness in some things, especially in traits and small things, is wonderful. His works are full of acute remarks on petty doings, and well exemplify the telling power of minute circumstantiality. But the minor species of perceptive sharpness is so different from diffused sagacity, that the two scarcely ever are to be found in the same mind. There is nothing less like the great lawyer, acquainted with broad principles and applying them with distinct deduction, than the attorney's clerk who catches at small points like a dog biting at flies. 'Over-sharpness' in the student is the most unpromising symptom of the logical jurist. You must not ask a horse in blinkers for a large view of a landscape. In the same way, a detective ingenuity in microscopic detail is of all mental qualities most unlike the broad sagacity by which the great painters of human affairs have unintentionally stamped the mark of unity on their productions. They show by their treatment of each case that they understand the whole of life; the special delineator of fragments and points shows that he understands them only. In one respect the defect is more striking in Mr. Dickens than in any other novelist of the present day. The most remarkable deficiency in modern fiction is its omission of the business of life, of all those countless occupations, pursuits, and callings in which most men live and move, and by which they have

84

their being. In most novels money *grows*. You have no idea of the toil, the patience, and the wearing anxiety by which men of action provide for the day, and lay up for the future, and support those that are given into their care. Mr. Dickens is not chargeable with this omission. He perpetually deals with the pecuniary part of life. Almost all his characters have determined occupations, of which he is apt to talk even at too much length. When he rises from the toiling to the luxurious classes, his genius in most cases deserts him. The delicate refinement and discriminating taste of the idling orders are not in his way; he knows the dry arches of London Bridge better than Belgravia. He excels in inventories of poor furniture, and is learned in pawnbrokers' tickets. But, although his creative power lives and works among the middle class and industrial section of English society, he has never painted the highest part of their daily intellectual life. He made, indeed, an attempt to paint specimens of the apt and able man of business in *Nicholas Nickleby*; but the Messrs. Cheeryble are among the stupidest of his characters. He forgot that breadth of platitude is rather different from breadth of sagacity. His delineations of middle-class life have in consequence a harshness and meanness which do not belong to that life in reality. He omits the relieving element. He describes the figs which are sold, but not the talent which sells figs well. And it is the same want of the diffused sagacity in his own nature which has made his pictures of life so odd and disjointed, and which has deprived them of symmetry and unity.

The *biʒarrerie* of Mr. Dickens's genius is rendered more remarkable by the inordinate measure of his special excellences. The first of these is his power of observation in detail. We have heard,—we do not know whether correctly or incorrectly,—that he can go down a crowded street and tell you all that is in it, what each shop was, what the grocer's name was, how many scraps of orange-peel there were on the pavement. His works give you exactly the same idea. The amount of detail which there is in them is something amazing,—to an ordinary writer something incredible. There are pages containing telling *minutiæ* which other people would have thought enough for a volume. Nor is his sensibility to external objects, though omnivorous, insensible to the artistic effect of each. There are scarcely anywhere such pictures of London as he draws. No writer has equally comprehended the artistic material which is given by its extent, its congregation of different elements, its mouldiness, its brilliancy.

Nor does his genius—though from some idiosyncrasy of mind or accident of external situation, it is more especially directed to city life—at all stop at the city-wall. He is especially at home in the picturesque and obvious parts of country life, particularly in the comfortable and (so to say) mouldering portion of it. The following is an instance; if not the best that could be cited, still one of the best:

They arranged to proceed upon their journey next evening, as a stage-wagon, which travelled for some distance on the same road as they must take, would stop at the inn to change horses, and the driver for a small gratuity would give Nell a place inside. A bargain was soon struck when the wagon came, and in due time it rolled away; with the child comfortably bestowed among the softer packages, her grandfather and the schoolmaster walking on beside the driver, and the landlady and all the good folks of the inn screaming out their good wishes and farewells.

What a soothing, luxurious, drowsy way of travelling, to lie inside that slowly-moving mountain, listening to the tinkling of the horses' bells, the occasional smacking of the carter's whip, the smooth rolling of the great broad wheels, the rattle of the harness, the cheery goodnights of passing travellers jogging past on little short-stepped horses—all made pleasantly indistinct by the thick awning, which seemed made for lazy listening under, till one fell asleep! The very going to sleep, still with an indistinct idea, as the head jogged to and fro upon the pillow, of moving onward with no trouble or fatigue, and hearing all these sounds like dreamy music, lulling to the senses—and the slow waking up, and finding one's self staring out through the breezy curtain half-opened in the front, far up into the cold bright sky with its countless stars, and downward at the driver's lantern dancing on like its namesake Jack of the swamps and marshes, and sideways at the dark grim trees, and forward at the long bare road rising up, up, up, until it stopped abruptly at a sharp high ridge as if there were no more road, and all beyond was sky; and the stopping at the inn to bait, and being helped out, and going into a room with fire and candles, and winking very much, and being agreeably reminded that the night was cold, and anxious for very comfort's sake to think it colder than it was! What a delicious journey was that journey in the wagon!

Then the going on again—so fresh at first, and shortly afterwards so sleepy. The waking from a sound nap as the mail came dashing past like a highway comet, with gleaming lamps and rattling hoofs, and visions of a guard behind, standing up to keep his feet warm, and of a gentleman in a fur cap opening his eyes and looking wild and stupefied; the stopping at the turnpike, where the man was gone to bed, and knocking at the door until he answered with a smothered shout from under the bed-clothes in the little room above, where the faint light was burning, and presently came down, night-capped and shivering, to throw the gate wide open, and wish all wagons off the road except by day. The cold sharp interval between night and morning; the distant streak of light widening and spreading, and turning from gray to white, and from white to yellow, and from yellow to burning red; the presence of day, with all its cheerfulness and life; men and horses at the plough; birds in the trees and hedges, and boys in solitary fields frightening them away with rattles. The coming to the town:—people busy in the market; light carts and chaises round the tavern yard; tradesmen standing at their doors; men running horses up and down the streets for sale; pigs plunging and grunting in the dirty distance, getting off with long strings at their legs, running into clean chemists' shops and being dislodged with brooms by 'prentices; the night-coach changing horses—the passengers cheerless, cold, ugly, and discontented, with three months' growth of hair in one night, the coachman fresh as from a bandbox and exquisitely beautiful by contrast:—so much bustle, so many things in motion, such a variety of incidents—when was there a journey with so many delights as that journey in the wagon!

Or, as a relief from a very painful series of accompanying characters, it is pleasant to read and remember the description of the fine morning on which Mr. Jonas Chuzzlewit does not reflect. Mr. Dickens has, however, no feeling analogous to the nature-worship of some other recent writers. There is nothing Wordsworthian in his bent; the interpreting inspiration (as that school speak) is not his. Nor has he the erudition in difficult names which has filled some pages in late novelists with mineralogy and botany. His descriptions of nature are fresh and superficial; they are not sermonic or scientific.

Nevertheless, it may be said that Mr. Dickens's genius is especially suited to the delineation of city life. London is like a newspaper. Everything is there, and everything is disconnected. There is every kind of person in some houses; but there is no more connection between the houses than between the neighbours in the lists of 'births, marriages, and deaths.' As we change from the broad leader to the squalid police-report, we pass a corner and we are in a changed world. This is advantageous to Mr. Dickens's genius. His memory is full of instances of old buildings and curious people, and he does not care to piece them together. On the contrary, each scene, to his mind, is a separate scene,—each street a separate street. He has, too, the peculiar alertness of observation that is observable in those who live by it. He describes London like a special correspondent for posterity.

A second most wonderful special faculty which Mr. Dickens possesses is what we may call his *vivification* of character, or rather of characteristics. His marvellous power of observation has been exercised upon men and women even more than upon town or country; and the store of human detail, so to speak, in his books is endless and enormous. The boots at the inn, the pickpockets in the street, the undertaker, the Mrs. Gamp, are all of them at his disposal; he knows each trait and incident, and he invests them with a kind of perfection in detail which in reality they do not possess. He has a very peculiar power of taking hold of some particular traits, and making a character out of them. He is especially apt to incarnate particular professions in this way. Many of his people never speak without some allusion to their occupation. You cannot separate them from it. Nor does the writer ever separate them. What would Mr. Mould be if not an undertaker? or Mrs. Gamp if not a nurse? or Charley Bates if not a pickpocket? Not only is human nature in them subdued to what it works in, but there seems to be no nature to subdue; the whole character is the idealisation of a trade, and is not in fancy or thought distinguishable from it. Accordingly, of necessity, such delineations become caricatures. We do not in general contrast them with reality; but as soon as we do, we are struck with the monstrous exaggerations which they present. You could no more fancy Sam Weller, or Mark Tapley, or the Artful Dodger really existing, walking about among common ordinary men and women, than you can fancy a talking duck or a writing bear. They are utterly beyond the pale of ordinary social intercourse. We suspect, indeed, that Mr. Dickens does not conceive his characters to himself as mixing in the society he mixes in. He sees people in the street, doing certain things, talking in a certain way, and his fancy petrifies them in the act. He goes on fancying hundreds of reduplications of that act and that speech; he frames an existence in which there is nothing else but that aspect which attracted his attention. Sam Weller is an example. He is a man-servant who makes a peculiar kind of jokes, and is wonderfully felicitous in certain similes. You see him at his first introduction:

'My friend,' said the thin gentleman.

'You're one o' the adwice gratis order,' thought Sam, 'or you wouldn't be so werry fond o' me all at once.' But he only said, 'Well, sir?'

'My friend,' said the thin gentleman, with a conciliatory 'hem,' 'Have you got many people stopping here now? Pretty busy? Eh?'

Sam stole a look at the inquirer. He was a little high-dried man, with a dark squeezed-up face, and small restless black eyes, that kept winking and twinkling on each side of his little inquisitive nose, as if they were playing a perpetual game of peep-bo with that feature. He was dressed all in black, with boots as shiny as his eyes, a low white neckcloth, and a clean shirt with a frill to it. A gold watch-chain, and seals, depended from his fob. He carried his black kid gloves *in* his hands, not *on* them; and as he spoke, thrust his wrists beneath his coat-tails, with the air of a man who was in the habit of propounding some regular posers.

'Pretty busy, eh?' said the little man.

'Oh, werry well, sir,' replied Sam: 'we shan't be bankrupts, and we shan't make our fort'ns. We eats our biled mutton without capers, and don't care for horse-radish wen ve can get beef.'

'Ah,' said the little man, 'you're a wag, ain't you?'

'My eldest brother was troubled with that complaint,' said Sam, 'it may be catching—I used to sleep with him.'

'This is a curious old house of yours,' said the little man, looking round him.

'If you'd sent word you was a coming, we'd ha' had it repaired,' replied the imperturbable Sam.

The little man seemed rather baffled by these several repulses, and a short consultation took place between him and the two plump gentlemen. At its conclusion, the little man took a pinch of snuff from an oblong silver box, and was apparently on the point of renewing the conversation, when one of the plump gentlemen, who, in addition to a benevolent countenance, possessed a pair of spectacles and a pair of black gaiters, interfered—

'The fact of the matter is,' said the benevolent gentleman, 'that my friend here '(pointing to the other plump gentleman) 'will give you half a guinea if you'll answer one or two—'

'Now, my dear sir—my dear sir,' said the little man, 'pray allow me— my dear sir, the very first principle to be observed in these cases is this: if you place a matter in the hands of a professional man, you must in no way interfere in the progress of the business; you must repose implicit confidence in him. Really, Mr.' (he turned to the other plump gentleman, and said)— 'I forget your friend's name.'

'Pickwick,' said Mr. Wardle, for it was no other than that jolly personage.

'Ah, Pickwick: really, Mr. Pickwick, my dear sir, excuse me—I shall be happy to receive any private suggestions of yours, as *amicus curiæ*, but you must see the impropriety of your interfering with my conduct in this case, with such an *ad captandum* argument as the offer of half a guinea. Really, my dear sir, really'—and the little man took an argumentative pinch of snuff and looked very profound.

'My only wish, sir,' said Mr. Pickwick, 'was to bring this very unpleasant matter to as speedy a close as possible.'

'Quite right—quite right,' said the little man.

'With which view,' continued Mr. Pickwick, 'I made use of the argument which my experience of men has taught me is the most likely to succeed in any case.'

'Ay, ay,' said the little man, 'very good, very good indeed; but you should have suggested it to *me*. My dear sir, I'm quite certain you cannot be ignorant of the extent of confidence which must be placed in professional men. If any authority can be necessary on such a point, my dear sir, let me refer you to the well-known case in Barnwell and—'

'Never mind George Barnwell,' interrupted Sam, who had remained a wondering listener during this short colloquy: 'everybody knows what sort of a case his was, tho' it's always been my opinion, mind you, that the young 'ooman deserved scragging a precious sight more than he did. Hows'ever, that's neither here nor there. You want me to except of half a guinea. Werry well, I'm agreeable: I can't say no fairer than that, can I, sir? (Mr. Pickwick smiled.) Then the next question is, what the devil do you want with me? as the man said wen he see the ghost.'

'We want to know—' said Mr. Wardle.

'Now my dear sir—my dear sir,' interposed the busy little man.

Mr. Wardle shrugged his shoulders, and was silent.

'We want to know,' said the little man, solemnly;—'and we ask the question of you, in order that we may not awaken apprehensions inside— we want to know who you've got in this house, at present.'

'Who there is in the house!' said Sam, in whose mind the inmates were always represented by that particular article of their costume which came under his immediate superintendence. 'There's a wooden leg in number six; there's a pair of Hessians in thirteen; there's two pair of halves in the commercial; there's these here painted tops in the snuggery inside the bar; and five more tops in the coffee-room.'

'Nothing more?' said the little man.

'Stop a bit,' replied Sam, suddenly recollecting himself. 'Yes; there's a pair of Wellingtons a good deal worn, and a pair o' lady's shoes, in number five.'

'What sort of shoes?' hastily inquired Wardle, who, together with Mr. Pickwick, had been lost in bewilderment at the singular catalogue of visitors.

'Country make,' replied Sam.

'Any maker's name?'

'Brown.'

'Where of?'

'Muggleton.'

'It *is* them,' exclaimed Wardle. 'By Heavens, we've found them.'
'Hush!' said Sam. 'The Wellingtons has gone to Doctors' Commons.'
'No,' said the little man.
'Yes, for a licence.'
'We're in time,' exclaimed Wardle. 'Show us the room; not a moment is to be lost.'
'Pray, my dear sir—pray,' said the little man; 'caution, caution.' He drew from his pocket a red silk purse, and looked very hard at Sam as he drew out a sovereign.
Sam grinned expressively.
'Show us into the room at once, without announcing us,' said the little man, 'and it's yours.'

One can fancy Mr. Dickens hearing a dialogue of this sort,—not nearly so good, but something like it,—and immediately setting to work to make it better and put it in a book; then changing a little the situation, putting the boots one step up in the scale of service, engaging him as footman to a stout gentleman (but without for a moment losing sight of the peculiar kind of professional conversation and humour which his first dialogue presents), and astonishing all his readers by the marvellous fertility and magical humour with which he maintains that style. Sam Weller's father is even a stronger and simpler instance. He is simply nothing but an old coachman of the stout and extinct sort: you cannot separate him from the idea of that occupation. But how amusing he is! We dare not quote a single word of his talk; because we should go on quoting so long, and everyone knows it so well. Some persons may think that this is not a very high species of delineative art. The idea of personifying traits and trades may seem to them poor and meagre. Anybody, they may fancy, can do that. But how would they do it? Whose fancy would not break down in a page,—in five lines? Who could carry on the vivification with zest and energy and humour for volume after volume? Endless fertility in laughter-causing detail is Mr. Dickens's most astonishing peculiarity. It requires a continuous and careful reading of his works to be aware of his enormous wealth. Writers have attained the greatest reputation for wit and humour, whose whole works do not contain so much of either as are to be found in a very few pages of his.

Mr. Dickens's humour is indeed very much a result of the two peculiarities of which we have been speaking. His power of detailed observation and his power of idealising individual traits of character—

sometimes of one or other of them, sometimes of both of them together. His similes on matters of external observation are so admirable that everybody appreciates them, and it would be absurd to quote specimens of them; nor is it the sort of excellence which best bears to be paraded for the purposes of critical example. Its off-hand air and natural connection with the adjacent circumstances are inherent parts of its peculiar merit. Every reader of Mr. Dickens's works knows well what we mean. And who is not a reader of them?

But his peculiar humour is even more indebted to his habit of vivifying external traits, than to his power of external observation. He, as we have explained, expands traits into people; and it is a source of true humour to place these, when so expanded, in circumstances in which only people—that is, complete human beings—can appropriately act. The humour of Mr. Pickwick's character is entirely of this kind. He is a kind of incarnation of simple-mindedness and what we may call obvious-mindedness. The conclusion which each occurrence or position in life most immediately presents to the unsophisticated mind is that which Mr. Pickwick is sure to accept. The proper accompaniments are given to him. He is a stout gentleman in easy circumstances, who is irritated into originality by no impulse from within, and by no stimulus from without. He is stated to have 'retired from business.' But no one can fancy what he was in business. Such guileless simplicity of heart and easy impressibility of disposition would soon have induced a painful failure amid the harsh struggles and the tempting speculations of pecuniary life. As he is represented in the narrative, however, nobody dreams of such antecedents. Mr. Pickwick moves easily over all the surface of English life from Goswell Street to Dingley Dell, from Dingley Dell to the Ipswich elections, from drinking milk-punch in a wheelbarrow to sleeping in the approximate pound, and no one ever thinks of applying to him the ordinary maxims which we should apply to any common person in life, or to any common personage in a fiction. Nobody thinks it is wrong in Mr. Pickwick to drink too much milk-punch in a wheelbarrow, to introduce worthless people of whom he knows nothing to the families of people for whom he really cares; nobody holds him responsible for the consequences; nobody thinks there is anything wrong in his taking Mr. Bob Sawyer and Mr. Benjamin Allen to visit Mr. Winkle senior, and thereby almost irretrievably offending him with his son's marriage.

We do not reject moral remarks such as these, but they never occur to us. Indeed, the indistinct consciousness that such observations are possible, and that they are hovering about our minds, enhances the humour of the narrative. We are in a conventional world, where the mere maxims of common life do not apply, and yet which has all the amusing detail, and picturesque elements, and singular eccentricities of common life. Mr. Pickwick is a personified ideal; a kind of amateur in life, whose course we watch through all the circumstances of ordinary existence, and at whose follies we are amused just as really skilled people are at the mistakes of an amateur in their art. His being in the pound is not wrong; his being the victim of Messrs. Dodson is not foolish. 'Always shout with the mob,' said Mr. Pickwick. 'But suppose there are two mobs,' said Mr. Snodgrass. 'Then shout with the loudest,' said Mr. Pickwick. This is not in him weakness or time-serving or want of principle, as in most even of fictitious people it would be. It is his way. Mr. Pickwick was expected to say something, so he said 'Ah!' in a grave voice. This is not pompous as we might fancy, or clever as it might be if intentionally devised; it is simply his way. Mr. Pickwick gets late at night over the wall behind the back-door of a young-ladies' school, is found in that sequestered place by the school-mistress and the boarders and the cook, and there is a dialogue between them. There is nothing out of possibility in this; it is his way. The humour essentially consists in treating as a moral agent a being who really is not a moral agent. We treat a vivified accident as a man, and we are surprised at the absurd results. We are reading about an acting thing, and we wonder at its scrapes, and laugh at them as if they were those of the man. There is something of this humour in every sort of farce. Everybody knows these are not real beings acting in real life, though they talk as if they were, and want us to believe that they are. Here, as in Mr. Dickens's books, we have exaggerations pretending to comport themselves as ordinary beings, caricatures acting as if they were characters.

At the same time it is essential to remember, that however great may be and is the charm of such exaggerated personifications, the best specimens of them are immensely less excellent, belong to an altogether lower range of intellectual achievements, than the real depiction of actual living men. It is amusing to read of beings *out of* the laws of morality, but it is more profoundly interesting, as well as more instructive, to read of those whose life in its moral conditions resembles

93

our own. We see this most distinctly when both[2] the representations are given by the genius of the same writer. Falstaff is a sort of sack-holding paunch, an exaggerated over-development which no one thinks of holding down to the commonplace rules of the ten commandments and the statute-law. We do not think of them in connection with him. They belong to a world apart. Accordingly, we are vexed when the king discards him and reproves him. Such a fate was a necessary adherence on Shakespeare's part to the historical tradition; he never probably thought of departing from it, nor would his audience have perhaps endured his doing so. But to those who look at the historical plays as pure works of imaginative art, it seems certainly an artistic misconception to have developed so marvellous an *un*moral impersonation, and then to have subjected it to an ethical and punitive judgment. Still, notwithstanding this error, which was very likely inevitable, Falstaff is probably the most remarkable specimen of caricature-representation to be found in literature. And its very excellence of execution only shows how inferior is the kind of art which creates only such representations. Who could compare the genius, marvellous as must be its fertility, which was needful to create a Falstaff, with that shown in the higher productions of the same mind in Hamlet, Ophelia, and Lear? We feel instantaneously the difference between the aggregating accident which rakes up from the externalities of life other accidents analogous to itself, and the central ideal of a real character which cannot show itself wholly in any accidents, but which exemplifies itself partially in many, which unfolds itself gradually in wide spheres of action, and yet, as with those we know best in life, leaves something hardly to be understood, and after years of familiarity is a problem and a difficulty to the last. In the same way, the embodied characteristics and grotesque exaggerations of Mr. Dickens, notwithstanding all their humour and all their marvellous abundance, can never be for a moment compared with the great works of the real painters of essential human nature.

There is one class of Mr. Dickens's pictures which may seem to form an exception to this criticism. It is the delineation of the outlaw, we might say the anti-law, world in *Oliver Twist*. In one or two instances Mr. Dickens has been so fortunate as to hit on characteristics which, by his system of idealisation and continual repetition, might really be brought to look like a character. A man's trade or profession

[2] I have inserted 'both'.—Ed.

in regular life can only exhaust a very small portion of his nature; no approach is made to the essence of humanity by the exaggeration of the traits which typify a beadle or an undertaker. With the outlaw world it is somewhat different. The bare fact of a man belonging to that world is so important to his nature, that if it is artistically developed with coherent accessories, some approximation to a distinctly natural character will be almost inevitably made. In the characters of Bill Sykes and Nancy this is so. The former is the skulking ruffian who may be seen any day at the police-courts, and whom any one may fancy he sees by walking through St. Giles's. You cannot attempt to figure to your imagination the existence of such a person without being thrown into the region of the passions, the will, and the conscience; the mere fact of his maintaining, as a condition of life and by settled profession, a struggle with regular society, necessarily brings these deep parts of his nature into prominence; great crime usually proceeds from abnormal impulses or strange effort. Accordingly, Mr. Sykes is the character most approaching to a coherent man who is to be found in Mr. Dickens's works. We do not say that even here there is not some undue heightening admixture of caricature; but this defect is scarcely thought of amid the general coherence of the picture, the painful subject, and the wonderful command of strange accessories. Miss Nancy is a still more delicate artistic effort. She is an idealisation of the girl who may also be seen at the police-courts and St. Giles's; as bad, according to occupation and common character, as a woman can be, yet retaining a tinge of womanhood, and a certain compassion for interesting suffering, which under favouring circumstances might be the germ of a regenerating influence. We need not stay to prove how much the imaginative development of such a personage must concern itself with our deeper humanity; how strongly, if excellent, it must be contrasted with everything conventional or casual or superficial. Mr. Dickens's delineation is in the highest degree excellent. It possesses not only the more obvious merits belonging to the subject, but also that of a singular delicacy of expression and idea. Nobody fancies for a moment that they are reading about anything beyond the pale of ordinary propriety. We read the account of the life which Miss Nancy leads with Bill Sykes without such an idea occurring to us: yet when we reflect upon it, few things in literary painting are more wonderful than the depiction of a professional life of sin and sorrow, so as not even to startle those to whom the deeper forms of either are but names and shadows. Other writers would have given as vivid a picture: Defoe would have poured out even a more copious measure of telling circumstantiality, but he would have narrated his story with an inhuman distinctness which, if not impure is *un*pure; French writers, whom we need not name, would have enhanced the interest of their narrative by trading on the excitement of stimulating scenes. It would be injustice to Mr. Dickens to say that he has surmounted these temptations; the unconscious evidence of innumerable details proves that, from a certain delicacy of imagination and purity of spirit, he has not even experienced them. Criticism is the more bound to dwell at length on the merits of these delineations, because no artistic merit can make *Oliver Twist* a pleasing work. The squalid detail of crime and misery oppresses us too much. If it is to be read at all, it should be read in the first hardness of the youthful imagination, which no touch can move too deeply, and which is never stirred with tremulous suffering at the 'still sad music of humanity.' The coldest critic in later life may never hope to have again the apathy of his boyhood.

It perhaps follows from what has been said of the characteristics of Mr. Dickens's genius, that he would be little skilled in planning plots for his novels. He certainly is not so skilled. He says in his preface to the *Pickwick Papers*, 'that they were designed for the introduction of diverting characters and incidents; that no ingenuity of plot was attempted, or even at that time considered very feasible by the author in connection with the desultory plan of publication adopted;' and he adds an expression of regret that 'these chapters had not been strung together on a stronger thread of more general interest.' It is extremely fortunate that no such attempt was made. In the cases in which Mr. Dickens has attempted to make a long connected story, or to develop into scenes or incidents a plan in any degree elaborate, the result has been a complete failure. A certain consistency of genius seems necessary for the construction of a consecutive plot. An irregular mind naturally shows itself in incoherency of incident and aberration of character. The method in which Mr. Dickens's mind works, if we are correct in our criticism upon it, tends naturally to these blemishes. Caricatures are necessarily isolated; they are produced by the exaggeration of certain conspicuous traits and features; each being is enlarged on its greatest side; and we laugh at the grotesque grouping and the startling contrast. But the connection between human beings on which a plot depends is rather severed than elucidated by the en-

CHARLES DICKENS

hancement of their diversities. Interesting stories are founded on the
intimate relations of men and women. These intimate relations are
based not on their superficial traits, or common occupations, or most
visible externalities, but on the inner life of heart and feeling. You
simply divert attention from that secret life by enhancing the perceptible diversities of common human nature, and the strange anoma-
lies into which it may be distorted. The original germ of *Pickwick*
was a 'Club of Oddities.' The idea was professedly abandoned; but
traces of it are to be found in all Mr. Dickens's books. It illustrates the
professed grotesqueness of the characters as well as their slender
connection.

The defect of plot is heightened by Mr. Dickens's great, we might
say complete, inability to make a love-story. A pair of lovers is by
custom a necessity of narrative fiction, and writers who possess a great
general range of mundane knowledge, and but little knowledge of the
special sentimental subject, are often in amusing difficulties. The watchful reader observes the transition from the hearty description of well-
known scenes, of prosaic streets, or journeys by wood and river, to the
pale colours of ill-attempted poetry, to such sights as the novelist
wishes he need not try to see. But few writers exhibit the difficulty
in so aggravated a form as Mr. Dickens. Most men by taking thought
can make a lay figure to look not so very unlike a young gentleman,
and can compose a telling schedule of ladylike charms. Mr. Dickens
has no power of doing either. The heroic character—we do not mean
the form of character so-called in life and action, but that which is
hereditary in the heroes of novels—is not suited to his style of art.
Hazlitt wrote an essay to inquire 'Why the heroes of romances are
insipid;' and without going that length, it may safely be said that the
character of the agreeable young gentleman who loves and is loved
should not be of the most marked sort. Flirtation ought not to be an
exaggerated pursuit. Young ladies and their admirers should not
express themselves in the heightened and imaginative phraseology
suited to Charley Bates and the Dodger. Humour is of no use, for
no one makes love in jokes: a tinge of insidious satire may perhaps be
permitted as a rare and occasional relief, but it will not be thought
'a pretty book' if so malicious an element be at all habitually perceptible.
The broad farce in which Mr. Dickens indulges is thoroughly out of
place. If you caricature a pair of lovers ever so little, by the necessity
of their calling you make them ridiculous. One of Sheridan's best

comedies is remarkable for having no scene in which the hero and heroine are on the stage together; and Mr. Moore suggests that the shrewd wit distrusted his skill in the light dropping love-talk which would have been necessary. Mr. Dickens would have done well to imitate so astute a policy; but he has none of the managing shrewdness which those who look at Sheridan's career attentively will probably think not the least remarkable feature in his singular character. Mr. Dickens, on the contrary, pours out painful sentiments as if he wished the abundance should make up for the inferior quality. The excruciating writing which is expended on Miss Ruth Pinch passes belief. Mr. Dickens is not only unable to make lovers talk, but to describe heroines in mere narrative. As has been said, most men can make a jumble of blue eyes and fair hair and pearly teeth, that does very well for a young lady, at least for a good while; but Mr. Dickens will not, probably cannot, attain even to this humble measure of descriptive art. He vitiates the repose by broad humour, or disenchants the delicacy by an unctuous admiration.

This deficiency is probably nearly connected with one of Mr. Dickens's most remarkable excellencies. No one can read Mr. Thackeray's writings without feeling that he is perpetually treading as close as he dare to the border-line that separates the world which may be described in books from the world which it is prohibited so to describe. No one knows better than this accomplished artist where that line is, and how curious are its windings and turns. The charge against him is that he knows it but too well; that with an anxious care and a wistful eye he is ever approximating to its edge, and hinting with subtle art how thoroughly he is familiar with, and how interesting he could make the interdicted region on the other side. He never violates a single conventional rule; but at the same time the shadow of the immorality that is not seen is scarcely ever wanting to his delineation of the society that is seen. Everyone may perceive what is passing in his fancy. Mr. Dickens is chargeable with no such defect: he does not seem to feel the temptation. By what we may fairly call an instinctive purity of genius, he not only observes the conventional rules, but makes excursions into topics which no other novelist could safely handle, and, by a felicitous instinct, deprives them of all impropriety. No other writer could have managed the humour of Mrs. Gamp without becoming unendurable. At the same time it is difficult not to believe that this singular insensibility to the temptations to which many of the greatest novelists have succumbed is in some measure connected with his utter inaptitude for delineating the portion of life to which their art is specially inclined. He delineates neither the love-affairs which ought to be, nor those which ought not to be.

Mr. Dickens's indisposition to 'make capital' out of the most commonly tempting part of human sentiment is the more remarkable because he certainly does not show the same indisposition in other cases. He has naturally great powers of pathos; his imagination is familiar with the common sorts of human suffering; and his marvellous conversancy with the detail of existence enables him to describe sick-beds and death-beds with an excellence very rarely seen in literature. A nature far more sympathetic than that of most authors has familiarised him with such subjects. In general, a certain apathy is characteristic of book-writers, and dulls the efficacy of their pathos. Mr. Dickens is quite exempt from this defect; but, on the other hand, is exceedingly prone to a very ostentatious exhibition of the opposite excellence. He dwells on dismal scenes with a kind of fawning fondness; and he seems unwilling to leave them, long after his readers have had more than enough of them. He describes Mr. Dennis the hangman as having a professional fondness for his occupation: he has the same sort of fondness apparently for the profession of death-painter. The painful details he accumulates are a very serious drawback from the agreeableness of his writings. Dismal 'light literature' is the dismallest of reading. The reality of the police-reports is sufficiently bad, but a fictitious police-report would be the most disagreeable of conceivable compositions. Some portions of Mr. Dickens's books are liable to a good many of the same objections. They are squalid from noisome trivialities, and horrid with terrifying crime. In his earlier books this is commonly relieved at frequent intervals by a graphic and original mirth. As—we will not say age, but maturity, has passed over his powers, this counteractive element has been lessened; the humour is not so happy as it was, but the wonderful fertility in painful *minutiæ* still remains.

Mr. Dickens's political opinions have subjected him to a good deal of criticism, and to some ridicule. He has shown, on many occasions, the desire,—which we see so frequent among able and influential men,—to start as a political reformer. Mr. Spurgeon said, with an application to himself, 'If you've got the ear of the public, *of course* you must begin to tell it its faults.' Mr. Dickens has been quite disposed to make this use of his popular influence. Even in *Pickwick* there are many traces of this tendency; and the way in which it shows itself in that book and in others is very characteristic of the time at which they appeared. The most instructive political characteristic of the years from 1825 to 1845 is the growth and influence of the scheme of opinion which we call radicalism. There are several species of creeds which are comprehended under this generic name, but they all evince a marked reaction against the worship of the English constitution and the affection for the English *status quo*, which were then the established creed and sentiment. All radicals are anti-Eldonites. This is equally true of the Benthamite or philosophical radicalism of the early period, and the Manchester or 'definite-grievance' radicalism, among the last vestiges of which we are now living. Mr. Dickens represents a species different from either. His is what we may call the 'sentimental radicalism;' and if we recur to the history of the time, we shall find that there would not originally have been any opprobrium attaching to such a name. The whole course of the legislation, and still more of the administration, of the first twenty years of the nineteenth century were marked by a harsh unfeelingness which is of all faults the most contrary to any with which we are chargeable now. The world of the 'Six Acts,' of the frequent executions,[3] of the Draconic criminal law, is so far removed from us that we cannot comprehend its having ever existed. It is more easy to understand the recoil which has followed. All the social speculation, and much of the social action of the few years succeeding the Reform Bill bear the most marked traces of the reaction. The spirit which animates Mr. Dickens's political reasonings and observations expresses it exactly. The vice of the then existing social authorities and of the then existing public had been the forgetfulness of the pain which their own acts evidently produced,—an unrealising habit which adhered to official rules and established maxims, and which would not be shocked by the evident consequences, by proximate human suffering. The sure result of this habit was the excitement of the habit precisely opposed to it. Mr. Carlyle, in his *Chartism*, we think, observes of the poor-law reform: 'It was then, above all things, necessary that outdoor relief should cease. But how? What means did great Nature take for accomplishing that most desirable end? She created a race of men who believed the cessation of outdoor relief to be the one thing needful.' In the same way, and by the same

[3] The *National Review* has 'frequent executions for death', p. 480 and I have omitted 'for death'.

propensity to exaggerated opposition which is inherent in human nature, the unfeeling obtuseness of the early part of this century was to be corrected by an extreme, perhaps an excessive, sensibility to human suffering in the years which have followed. There was most adequate reason for the sentiment in its origin, and it had a great task to perform in ameliorating harsh customs and repealing dreadful penalties; but it has continued to repine at such evils long after they ceased to exist, and when the only facts that at all resemble them are the necessary painfulness of due punishment and the necessary rigidity of established law.

Mr. Dickens is an example both of the proper use and of the abuse of the sentiment. His earlier works have many excellent descriptions of the abuses which had descended to the present generation from others whose sympathy with pain was less tender. Nothing can be better than the description of the poor debtors' gaol in *Pickwick*, or of the old parochial authorities in *Oliver Twist*. No doubt these descriptions are caricatures, all his delineations are so; but the beneficial use of such art can hardly be better exemplified. Human nature endures the aggravation of vices and foibles in written description better than that of excellencies. We cannot bear to hear even the hero of a book for ever called 'just;' we detest the recurring praise even of beauty, much more of virtue. The moment you begin to exaggerate a character of true excellence, you spoil it; the traits are too delicate not to be injured by heightening or marred by over-emphasis. But a beadle is made for caricature. The slight measure of pomposity that humanises his unfeelingness introduces the requisite comic element; even the turnkeys of a debtors' prison may by skilful hands be similarly used. The contrast between the destitute condition of Job Trotter and Mr. Jingle and their former swindling triumph, is made comic by a rarer touch of unconscious art. Mr. Pickwick's warm heart takes so eager an interest in the misery of his old enemies, that our colder nature is tempted to smile. We endure the over-intensity, at any rate the unnecessary aggravation, of the surrounding misery; and we endure it willingly, because it brings out better than anything else could have done the half-comic intensity of a sympathetic nature.

It is painful to pass from these happy instances of well-used power to the glaring abuses of the same faculty in Mr. Dickens's later books. He began by describing really removable evils in a style which would induce all persons, however insensible, to remove them if they could;

he has ended by describing the natural evils and inevitable pains of the present state of being in such a manner as must tend to excite discontent and repining. The result is aggravated, because Mr. Dickens never ceases to hint that these evils are removable, though he does not say by what means. Nothing is easier than to show the evils of anything. Mr. Dickens has not unfrequently spoken, and what is worse, he has taught a great number of parrot-like imitators to speak, in what really is, if they knew it, a tone of objection to the necessary constitution of human society. If you will only write a description of it, any form of government will seem ridiculous. What is more absurd than a despotism, even at its best? A king of ability or an able minister sits in an orderly room filled with memorials, and returns, and documents, and memoranda. These are his world; among these he of necessity lives and moves. Yet how little of the real life of the nation he governs can be represented in an official form! How much of real suffering is there that statistics can never tell! how much of obvious good is there that no memorandum to a minister will ever mention! how much deception is there in what such documents contain! how monstrous must be the ignorance of the closet statesman, after all his life of labour, of much that a ploughman could tell him of! A free government is almost worse, as it must read in a written delineation. Instead of the real attention of a laborious and anxious statesman, we have now the shifting caprices of a popular assembly—elected for one object, deciding on another; changing with the turn of debate; shifting in its very composition; one set of men coming down to vote to-day, to-morrow another and often unlike set, most of them eager for the dinner-hour, actuated by unseen influences,—by a respect for their constituents, by the dread of an attorney in a far-off borough. What people are these to control a nation's destinies, and wield the power of an empire, and regulate the happiness of millions! Either way we are at fault. Free government seems an absurdity, and despotism is so too. Again, every form of law has a distinct expression, a rigid procedure, customary rules and forms. It is administered by human beings liable to mistake, confusion, and forgetfulness, and in the long run, and on the average, is sure to be tainted with vice and fraud. Nothing can be easier than to make a case, as we may say, against any particular system, by pointing out with emphatic caricature its inevitable miscarriages, and by pointing out nothing else. Those who so address us may assume a tone of philanthropy, and for ever exult that they are not so unfeeling as other men are; but the real tendency of their exhortations is to make men dissatisfied with their inevitable condition, and what is worse, to make them fancy that its irremediable evils can be remedied, and indulge in a succession of vague strivings and restless changes. Such, however,—though in a style of expression somewhat different,—is very much the tone with which Mr. Dickens and his followers have in later years made us familiar. To the second-hand repeaters of a cry so feeble, we can have nothing to say; if silly people cry because they think the world is silly, let them cry; but the founder of the school cannot, we are persuaded, peruse without mirth the lachrymose eloquence which his disciples have perpetrated. The soft moisture of irrelevant sentiment cannot have entirely entered into his soul. A truthful genius must have forbidden it. Let us hope that this pernicious example may incite someone of equal genius to preach with equal efficiency a sterner and a wiser gospel; but there is no need just now for us to preach it without genius.

There has been much controversy about Mr. Dickens's taste. A great many cultivated people will scarcely concede that he has any taste at all; a still larger number of fervent admirers point, on the other hand, to a hundred felicitous descriptions and delineations which abound in apt expressions and skilful turns and happy images,—in which it would be impossible to alter a single word without altering for the worse; and naturally inquire whether such excellences in what is written do not indicate good taste in the writer. The truth is that Mr. Dickens has what we may call creative taste; that is to say, the habit or faculty, whichever we may choose to call it, which at the critical instant of artistic production offers to the mind the right word, and the right word only. If he is engaged on a good subject for caricature, there will be no defect of taste to preclude the caricature from being excellent. But it is only in moments of imaginative production that he has any taste at all. His works nowhere indicate that he possesses in any degree the passive taste which decides what is good in the writings of other people and what is not, and which performs the same critical duty upon a writer's own efforts when the confusing mists of productive imagination have passed away. Nor has Mr. Dickens the gentlemanly instinct which in many minds supplies the place of purely critical discernment, and which, by constant association with those who know what is best, acquires a second-hand perception of that which is best. He has no tendency to conventionalism for good or for

103

evil; his merits are far removed from the ordinary path of writers, and it was not probably so much effort to him as to other men to step so far out of that path: he scarcely knew how far it was. For the same reason he cannot tell how faulty his writing will often be thought, for he cannot tell what people will think.

A few pedantic critics have regretted that Mr. Dickens had not received what they call a regular education. And if we understand their meaning, we believe they mean to regret that he had not received a course of discipline which would probably have impaired his powers. A regular education should mean that ordinary system of regulation and instruction which experience has shown to fit men best for the ordinary pursuits of life. It applies the requisite discipline to each faculty in the exact proportion in which that faculty is wanted in the pursuits of life; it develops understanding, and memory, and imagination, each in accordance with the scale prescribed. To men of ordinary faculties this is nearly essential; it is the only mode in which they can be fitted for the inevitable competition of existence. To men of regular and symmetrical genius also, such a training will often be beneficial. The world knows pretty well what are the great tasks of the human mind, and has learnt in the course of ages with some accuracy what is the kind of culture likely to promote their exact performance. A man of abilities, extraordinary in degree but harmonious in proportion, will be the better for having submitted to the kind of discipline which has been ascertained to fit a man for the work to which powers in that proportion are best fitted; he will do what he has to do better and more gracefully; culture will add a touch to the finish of nature. But the case is very different with men of irregular and anomalous genius, whose excellences consist in the *aggravation* of some special faculty, or at the most of one or two. The discipline which will fit him for the production of great literary works is that which will most develop the peculiar powers in which he excels; the rest of the mind will be far less important; it will not be likely that the culture which is adapted to promote this special development will also be that which is most fitted for expanding the powers of common men in common directions. The precise problem is to develop the powers of a strange man in a strange direction. In the case of Mr. Dickens, it would have been absurd to have shut up his observant youth within the walls of a college. They would have taught him nothing about Mrs. Gamp there; Sam Weller took no degree. The kind of early life fitted to develop the power of

CHARLES DICKENS

apprehensive observation is a brooding life in stirring scenes; the idler in the streets of life knows the streets; the bystander knows the picturesque effect of life better than the player; and the meditative idler amid the hum of existence is much more likely to know its sound and to take in and comprehend its depths and meanings than the scholastic student intent on books, which if they represent any world, represent one which has long passed away, which commonly try rather to develop the reasoning understanding than the seeing observation, which are written in languages that have long been dead. You will not train by such discipline a caricaturist of obvious manners.

Perhaps, too, a regular instruction and daily experience of the searching ridicule of critical associates would have detracted from the *pluck* which Mr. Dickens shows in all his writings. It requires a great deal of courage to be a humorous writer; you are always afraid that people will laugh at you instead of with you: undoubtedly there is a certain eccentricity about it. You take up the esteemed writers, Thucydides and the *Saturday Review*; after all, they do not make you laugh. It is not the function of really artistic productions to contribute to the mirth of human beings. All sensible men are afraid of it, and it is only with an extreme effort that a printed joke attains to the perusal of the public: the chances are many to one that the anxious producer loses heart in the correction of the press, and that the world never laughs at all. Mr. Dickens is quite exempt from this weakness. He has what a Frenchman might call the courage of his faculty. The real daring which is shown in the *Pickwick Papers*, in the whole character of Mr. Weller senior, as well as in that of his son, is immense, far surpassing any which has been shown by any other contemporary writer. The brooding irregular mind is in its first stage prone to this sort of courage. It perhaps knows that its ideas are 'out of the way;' but with the infantine simplicity of youth it supposes that originality is an advantage. Persons more familiar with the ridicule of their equals in station (and this is to most men the great instructress of the college time) well know that of all qualities this one most requires to be clipped and pared and measured. Posterity, we doubt not, will be entirely perfect in every conceivable element of judgment; but the existing generation like what they have heard before—it is much easier. It required great courage in Mr. Dickens to write what his genius has compelled them to appreciate.

We have throughout spoken of Mr. Dickens as he was, rather than as he is; or, to use a less discourteous phrase, and we hope a truer, of his early works rather than of those which are more recent. We could not do otherwise consistently with the true code of criticism. A man of great genius, who has written great and enduring works, must be judged mainly by them; and not by the inferior productions which, from the necessities of personal position, a fatal facility of composition, or other cause, he may pour forth at moments less favourable to his powers. Those who are called on to review these inferior productions themselves, must speak of them in the terms they may deserve; but those who have the more pleasant task of estimating as a whole the genius of the writer, may confine their attention almost wholly to those happier efforts which illustrate that genius. We should not like to have to speak in detail of Mr. Dickens's later works, and we have not done so. There are, indeed, peculiar reasons why a genius constituted as his is (at least if we are correct in the view which we have taken of it) would not endure without injury during a long life the applause of the many, the temptations of composition, and the general excitement of existence. Even in his earlier works it was impossible not to fancy that there was a weakness of fibre unfavourable to the longevity of excellence. This was the effect of his deficiency in those masculine faculties of which we have said so much,—the reasoning understanding and firm far-seeing sagacity. It is these two component elements which stiffen the mind, and give a consistency to the creed and a coherence to its effects,—which enable it to protect itself from the rush of circumstances. If to a deficiency in these we add an extreme sensibility to circumstances,—a mobility, as Lord Byron used to call it, of emotion, which is easily impressed, and still more easily carried away by impression,—we have the idea of a character peculiarly unfitted to bear the flux of time and chance. A man of very great determination could hardly bear up against them with such slight aids from within and with such peculiar sensibility to temptation. A man of merely ordinary determination would succumb to it; and Mr. Dickens has succumbed. His position was certainly unfavourable. He has told us that the works of his later years, inferior as all good critics have deemed them, have yet been more read than those of his earlier and healthier years. The most characteristic part of his audience, the lower middle-class, were ready to receive with delight the least favourable productions of his genius. Human nature cannot endure this; it is too much to have to endure a coincident temptation both from within and from without.

Mr. Dickens was too much inclined by natural disposition to lachrymose eloquence and exaggerated caricature. Such was the kind of writing which he wrote most easily. He found likewise that such was the kind of writing that was read most readily; and of course he wrote that kind. Who would have done otherwise? No critic is entitled to speak very harshly of such degeneracy, if he is not sure that he could have coped with difficulties so peculiar. If that rule is to be observed, who is there that will not be silent? No other Englishman has attained such a hold on the vast populace; it is little, therefore, to say that no other has surmounted its attendant temptations.

John Milton
Introductory note

John Milton (1608–74) was the son of a scrivener and notary. He was educated at St. Paul's School and at Cambridge. He afterwards lived for five years with his father in Buckinghamshire, and his shorter poems *L'Allegro, Il Penseroso, Arcades* and *Comus* belong to this period. The next two years were spent in France and Italy, where he wrote *Lycidas*, 1637. The approaching Civil War brought him home, and he now devoted himself to writing state papers and letters in Latin, and many pamphlets, among them *Doctrine and Discipline of Divorce*, 1643, and *Areopagitica*, 1644, on the liberty of the press. In 1649 he was appointed Secretary to the newly formed Council of State. After the Restoration he was heavily fined but not otherwise punished. He had become blind in 1652. In the years which elapsed between *Lycidas* and *Paradise Lost*, which was published in 1667, Milton wrote no poetry save for the sonnets and some Latin and Italian pieces. His last poems, *Paradise Regained* and *Samson Agonistes* were published together in 1672.

John Milton[1]

THE *Life of Milton*, by Professor Masson, is a difficulty for the critics. It is very laborious, very learned, and in the main, we believe, very accurate. It is exceedingly long,—there are 780 pages in this volume, and there are to be two volumes more: it touches on very many subjects, and each of these has been investigated to the very best of the author's ability. No one can wish to speak with censure of a book on which so much genuine labour has been expended and yet we are bound, as true critics, to say that we think it has been composed upon a principle that is utterly erroneous. In justice to ourselves we must explain our meaning.

There are two methods on which biography may consistently be written. The first of these is what we may call the exhaustive method. Every fact which is known about the hero may be told us; everything which he did, everything which he would not do, everything which other people did to him, everything which other people would not do to him,—may be narrated at full length. We may have a complete picture of all the events of his life; of all which he underwent, and all which he achieved. We may, as Mr. Carlyle expresses it, have a complete account 'of his effect upon the universe, and of the effect of the universe upon him.' We admit that biographies of this species would be very long and generally very tedious, we know that the world could not contain very many of them; but nevertheless the principle on which they may be written is intelligible.

The second method on which the life of a man may be written is the selective. Instead of telling everything, we may choose what we will tell. We may select out of the numberless events, from among the

[1] *The Life of John Milton, narrated in connection with the Political, Ecclesiastical, and Literary History of his Time.* By David Masson, M.A., Professor of English Literature in University College, London. Cambridge: Macmillan. *An Account of the Life, Opinions, and Writings of John Milton.* By Thomas Keightley; with an Introduction to *Paradise Lost.* London: Chapaman and Hall. *The Poems of Milton*, with Notes by Thomas Keightley. London: Chapman and Hall.
This essay was first published in the *National Review* for July 1859, Volume IX, pp. 150–86.

innumerable actions of his life, those events and those actions which exemplify his true character, which prove to us what were the true limits of his talents, what was the degree of his deficiencies, which were his defects, which his vices,—in a word, we may select the traits and the particulars which seem to give us the best idea of the man as he lived and as he was. On this side the flood, as Sydney Smith would have said, we should have fancied that this was the only practicable principle on which biographies can be written about persons of whom many details are recorded. For ancient heroes the exhaustive method is possible. All that can be known of them is contained in a few short passages of Greek and Latin, and it is quite possible to say whatever can be said about every one of these: the result would not be unreasonably bulky, though it might be dull. But in the case of men who have lived in the thick of the crowded modern world, no such course is admissible; overmuch *may* be said, and we must choose what we will say. Biographers, however, are rarely bold enough to adopt the selective method consistently. They have, we suspect, the fear of the critics before their eyes. They do not like that it should be said that 'the work of the learned gentleman contains serious omissions: the events of 1562 are not mentioned; those of October 1579 are narrated but very cursorily:' and we fear that in any case such remarks will be made. Very learned people are pleased to show that they know what is *not* in the book; sometimes they may hint that perhaps the author did not know it, or surely he would have mentioned it. But a biographer who wishes to write what most people of cultivation will be pleased to read, must be courageous enough to face the pain of such censures. He must choose, as we have explained, the characteristic parts of his subject; and all that he has to take care of besides, is so to narrate them that their characteristic elements shall be shown: to give such an account of the general career as may make it clear what these chosen events really were; to show their respective bearings to one another; to delineate what is expressive in such a manner as to make it expressive.

This plan of biography is, however, by no means that of Mr. Masson. He has no dread of overgrown bulk and overwhelming copiousness. He finds, indeed, what we have called the exhaustive method insufficient. He not only wishes to narrate in full the life of Milton, but to add those of his contemporaries likewise: he seems to wish to tell us not only what Milton did, but also what every one else did in Great Britain during his lifetime. He intends his book to be not merely a biography of Milton, but also in some sort a continuous history of his time. ... The suggestions of Milton's life have indeed determined the tracks of these historical researches and expositions, sometimes through the literature of the period, sometimes through its civil and ecclesiastical politics; but the extent to which I have pursued them, and the space which I have assigned to them, have been determined by my desire to present, by their combination, something like a connected historical view of British thought and British society in general prior to the Revolution.

We need not do more than observe that this union of heterogeneous aims must always end, as it has in this case, in the production of a work at once overgrown and incomplete. A great deal which has only a slight bearing on the character of Milton is inserted; much that is necessary to a true history of 'British thought and British society' is of necessity left out. The period of Milton's life which is included in the published volume makes the absurdity especially apparent. In middle life Milton was a great controversialist on contemporary topics; and though it would not be proper for a biographer to load his pages with a full account of all such controversies, yet some notice of the most characteristic of them would be expected from him. In this part of Milton's life some reference to public events would be necessary; and we should not severely censure a biographer, if the great interest of those events induced him to stray a little from his topic. But the first thirty years of Milton's life require a very different treatment. He passed those years in the ordinary musings of a studious and meditative youth; it was the period of *Lycidas* and of *Comus*; he then dreamed

> Such sights as youthful poets dream
> On summer eves by haunted stream.

We do not wish to have this part of his life disturbed, to a greater extent than may be necessary, with the harshness of public affairs. Nor is it necessary that it should be so disturbed. A life of poetic retirement requires but little reference to anything except itself. In a biography of Mr. Tennyson we should not expect to hear of the Reform Bill, or the Corn Laws. Mr. Masson is, however, of a different opinion. He thinks it necessary to tell us, not only all which Milton did, but everything also that he might have heard of.

The biography of Mr. Keightley is on a very different scale. He tells the story of Milton's career in about half a small volume. Probably this is a little too concise, and the narrative is somewhat dry and bare. It is often, however, acute, and is always clear; and even were its defects greater than they are, we should think it unseemly to criticise the last work of one who has performed so many useful services to literature with extreme severity. And we must observe,[2] that in one respect Mr. Keightley contrasts very favourably with Mr. Masson: he only tells his readers what he knows did happen; Mr. Masson is fond of telling us what he thinks may have happened. We have some such passages as the following:

Look back, reader, and see him as I do! Now, under the elms on his father's lawn, he listens to the rural hum, and marks the branches as they wave, and the birds as they fly; now, in the garden, he notes the annual series of the plants and the daily blooming of the roses. In his walks in the neighbourhood, also, he observes not only the wayside vegetation, but the whole wide face of the landscape, rich in wood and meadow, to the royal towers of Windsor and the bounding line of the low Surrey hills. Over this landscape, changing its livery from day to day, fall the varying seasons. Light green spring comes with its showers and its days of keener blue, when nature is warm at the root, and all things gain in liveliness; spring changes into summer, when all is one wealth of leafage, and the gorgeous bloom of the orchards passes into the forming fruit; summer deepens into autumn, gathering the tanned haycocks and tumbling the golden grain; and, at last, when the brown and yellow leaves have fallen, and the winds have blown them and the rains rotted them, comes winter with his biting breath, and the fields are either all white, so that the most familiar eye hardly knows them, or they lie in mire, and, in the dull brumous air, the stripped stems and netted twig-work of the trees are like a painting in China ink. And these seasons have each their occupations. Now the plough is afield; now the sower casts the seed; now the sheep are shorn; now the mower whets his scythe. There is, moreover, the quicker continual alternation of night and day, dipping the landscape in darkness or in lunar tints, and bringing it back again, as Aurora rises, in all the colours of the morn. In summer the twilight steals slowly over the lawn, and, seated at the open window, the poet, who has heard the lark's carol abroad by day, will listen in the stillness for the first song of the nightingale; and when the night is farther advanced, may there not be a walk on the lawn, to observe the trembling tops of the poplars, and to drink, ere the soul is done with that day more, the solemnising glory of the tranquil stars? Look on, thou glorious youth, at stars and trees, at the beauties of

[2] From 'And we must observe . . .' to 'Mr. Carlyle is almost our only master of delineative conjecture' has been omitted in editions of Bagehot before the present one. It is found in the *National Review* at pp. 153–4.

day and the beauties of night, at the changing aspects of the seasons, and at all that the seasons bring!

Perhaps this is what Mr. Punch would call 'moonshine,' and Mr. Masson 'lunar tints.' Such fanciful eloquence is teasing to the reader. If we are to have fancies, we like to have our own. At least, if our own are disturbed, we wish them to be replaced by others which are better. Mr. Masson has neither the humour of imagination, nor the delicacy of style, which in other hands have made these hypotheses pleasing. Mr. Carlyle is almost our only master of delineative conjecture.

The bare outline of Milton's life is very well known. We have all heard that he was born in the later years of King James, just when Puritanism was collecting its strength for the approaching struggle; that his father and mother were quiet good people, inclined, but not immoderately, to that persuasion; that he went up to Cambridge early, and had some kind of dissension with the authorities there; that the course of his youth was in a singular degree pure and staid; that in boyhood he was a devourer of books, and that he early became, and always remained, a severely studious man; that he married, and had difficulties of a peculiar character with his first wife; that he wrote on divorce; that after the death of his first wife, he married a second time a lady who died very soon, and a third time a person who survived him more than fifty years; that he wrote early poems of singular beauty, which we still read; that he travelled in Italy, and exhibited his learning in the academies there; that he plunged deep in the theological and political controversies of his time; that he kept a school, or rather, in our more modern phrase, took pupils; that he was a republican of a peculiar kind, and of 'no church,' which Dr. Johnson thought dangerous; that he was Secretary for Foreign Languages under the Long Parliament, and retained that office after the *coup-d'état* of Cromwell; that he defended the death of Charles the First, and became blind from writing a book in haste upon that subject; that after the Restoration he was naturally in a position of some danger and much difficulty; that in the midst of that difficulty he wrote *Paradise Lost*; that he did not fail in heart or hope, but lived for fourteen years after the destruction of all for which he had laboured, in serene retirement, 'though fallen on evil days, though fallen on evil times;'—all this we have heard from our boyhood. How much is wanting to complete the picture, how many traits, both noble and painful, might be recovered from the past, we shall never know, till some biographer skilled in interpreting the details of human nature shall select this subject for his art.

All that we can hope to do in an essay like this is to throw together some miscellaneous remarks on the character of the Puritan poet, and on the peculiarities of his works; and if in any part of them we may seem to make unusual criticisms, and to be over-ready with depreciation or objection, our excuse must be that we wish to paint a likeness, and that the harsher features of the subject should have a prominence, even in an outline.

There are two kinds of goodness conspicuous in the world, and often made the subject of contrast there; for which, however, we seem to want exact words, and which we are obliged to describe rather vaguely and incompletely. These characters may in one aspect be called the sensuous and the ascetic. The character of the first is that which is almost personified in the poet-king of Israel, whose actions and whose history have been 'improved' so often by various writers, that it now seems trite even to allude to them. Nevertheless, the particular virtues and the particular career of David seem to embody the idea of what may be called sensuous goodness far more completely than a living being in general comes near to an abstract idea. There may have been shades in the actual man which would have modified the resemblance; but in the portrait which has been handed down to us the traits are perfect and the approximation exact. The principle of this character is its sensibility to outward stimulus; it is moved by all which occurs, stirred by all which happens, open to the influences of whatever it sees, hears, or meets with. The certain consequence of this mental constitution is a peculiar liability to temptation. Men are, according to the divine, 'put upon their trial through the senses.' It is through the constant suggestions of the outer world that our minds are stimulated, that our will has the chance of a choice, that moral life becomes possible. The sensibility to this external stimulus brings with it, when men have it to excess, an unusual access of moral difficulty. Everything acts on them, and everything has a chance of turning them aside; the most tempting things act upon them very deeply, and their influence, in consequence, is extreme. Naturally, therefore, the errors of such men are great. We need not point the moral.

> Dizzied faith, and guilt, and woe,
> Loftiest aims by earth defiled,

114

Gleams of wisdom sin-beguiled,
Sated power's tyrannic mood,
Counsels shared with men of blood,
Sad success,parental tears,
And a dreary gift of years.

But, on the other hand, the excellence of such men has a charm, a kind
of sensuous sweetness, that is its own. Being conscious of frailty, they
are tender to the imperfect; being sensitive to this world, they sympathise with the world; being familiar with all the moral incidents of
life, their goodness has a richness and a complication: they fascinate
their own age, and in their deaths they are 'not divided' from the love
of others. Their peculiar sensibility gives a depth to their religion; it is
at once deeper and more human than that of other men. As their sympathetic knowledge of those whom they have seen is great, so it is with
their knowledge of Him whom they have not seen; and as is their
knowledge, so is their love: it is deep, from their nature; rich and
intimate, from the variety of their experience; chastened by the ever-
present sense of their weakness and of its consequences.

In extreme opposition to this is the ascetic species of goodness. This
is not, as is sometimes believed, a self-produced ideal—a simply
voluntary result of discipline and restraint. Some men have by nature
what others have to elaborate by effort. Some men have a repulsion
from the world. All of us have, in some degree, a protective instinct;
an impulse, that is to say, to start back from what may trouble us, to
shun what may fascinate us, to avoid what may tempt us. On the moral
side of human nature this preventive check is occasionally imperious;
it holds the whole man under its control,—makes him recoil from the
world, be offended at its amusements, be repelled by its occupations,
be scared by its sins. The consequences of this tendency, when it is
thus in excess, upon the character are very great and very singular. It
secludes a man in a sort of natural monastery; he lives in a kind of moral
solitude; and the effects of his isolation for good and for evil on his
disposition are very many. The best result is a singular capacity for
meditative religion. Being aloof from what is earthly, such persons are
shut up with what is spiritual; being unstirred by the incidents of time,
they are alone with the eternal; rejecting this life, they are alone with
what is beyond. According to the measure of their minds, men of this
removed and secluded excellence become eminent for a settled and
brooding piety, for a strong and predominant religion. In human life

too, in a thousand ways, their isolated excellence is apparent. They walk through the whole of it with an abstinence from sense, a zeal of morality, a purity of ideal, which other men have not. Their religion has an imaginative grandeur, and their life something of an unusual impeccability. And these are obviously singular excellencies. But the deficiencies to which the same character tends are equally singular. In the first place, their isolation gives them a certain pride in themselves, and an inevitable ignorance of others. They are secluded by their constitutional δαίμων from life; they are repelled from the pursuits which others care for; they are alarmed at the amusements which others enjoy. In consequence, they trust in their own thoughts; they come to magnify both them and themselves—for being able to think and to retain them. The greater the nature of the man, the greater is this temptation. His thoughts are greater, and, in consequence, the greater is his tendency to prize them, the more extreme is his tendency to overrate them. This pride, too, goes side by side with a want of sympathy. Being aloof from others, such a mind is unlike others; and it feels, and sometimes it feels bitterly, its own unlikeness. Generally, however, it is too wrapt up in its own exalted thoughts to be sensible of the pain of moral isolation; it stands apart from others, unknowing and unknown. It is deprived of moral experience in two ways,—it is not tempted itself, and it does not comprehend the temptations of others. And this defect of moral experience is almost certain to produce two effects, one practical, and the other speculative. When such a man is wrong, he will be apt to believe that he is right. If his own judgment err, he will not have the habit of checking it by the judgment of others; he will be accustomed to think most men wrong; differing from them would be no proof of error, agreeing with them would rather be a basis for suspicion. He may, too, be very wrong, for the conscience of no man is perfect on all sides. The strangeness of secluded excellence will be sometimes deeply shaded by very strange errors. To be commonly above others, still more to think yourself above others, is to be below them every now and then, and sometimes much below. Again, on the speculative side, this defect of moral experience penetrates into the distinguishing excellence of the character,—its brooding and meditative religion. Those who see life under only one aspect, can see religion under only one likewise. This world is needful to interpret what is beyond; the seen must explain the unseen. It is from a tried and a varied and a troubled moral life that the deepest and truest ideas of

God arise. The ascetic character wants these; therefore in its religion there will be a harshness of outline, a bareness, so to say, as well as a grandeur. In life we may look for a singular purity; but also, and with equal probability, for singular self-confidence, a certain unsympathising straitness, and perhaps a few singular errors.

The character of the ascetic, or austere species of goodness, is almost exactly embodied in Milton. Men, indeed, are formed on no ideal type. Human nature has tendencies too various, and circumstances too complex. All men's characters have sides and aspects not to be comprehended in a single definition; but in this case, the extent to which the character of the man, as we find it delineated, approaches to the moral abstraction which we sketch from theory, is remarkable. The whole being of Milton may, in some sort, be summed up in the great commandment of the austere character, 'Reverence thyself.' We find it expressed in almost every one of his singular descriptions of himself,— of those striking passages which are scattered through all his works, and which add to whatever interest may intrinsically belong to them one of the rarest of artistic charms, that of magnanimous autobiography. They have been quoted a thousand times, but one of them may perhaps be quoted again.

I had my time, readers, as others have, who have good learning bestowed upon them, to be sent to those places where, the opinion was, it might be soonest attained; and as the manner is, was not unstudied in those authors which are most commended; whereof some were grave orators and historians, whose matter methought I loved indeed, but as my age then was, so I understood them; others were the smooth elegiac poets, whereof the schools are not scarce, whom both for the pleasing sound of their numerous writing, which in imitation I found most easy, and most agreeable to nature's part in me, and for their matter, which what it is, there be few who know not, I was so allured to read, that no recreation came to me better welcome: for that it was then those years with me which are excused, though they be least severe, I may be saved the labour to remember ye. Whence having observed them to account it the chief glory of their wit, in that they were ablest to judge, to praise, and by that could esteem themselves worthiest to love those high perfections which under one or other name they took to celebrate, I thought with myself by every instinct and presage of nature, which is not wont to be false, that what emboldened them to this task might with such diligence as they used embolden me; and that what judgment, wit, or elegance was my share, would herein best appear, and best value itself, by how much more wisely, and with more love of virtue I should choose (let rude ears be absent) the object of not unlike praises: for albeit these thoughts to some will seem virtuous and commendable, to others only pardonable, to a third sort perhaps idle; yet the mentioning of them now will end in serious. Nor blame it, readers, in those years to propose to themselves such a reward, as the noblest dispositions above other things in this life have sometimes preferred: whereof not to be sensible when good and fair in one person meet, argues both a gross and shallow judgment, and withal an ungentle and swainish breast: for by the firm settling of these persuasions, I became, to my best memory, so much a proficient, that if I found those authors any where speaking unworthy things of themselves, or unchaste of those names which before they had extolled; this effect it wrought with me, from that time forward their art I still applauded, but the men I deplored; and above them all preferred the two famous renowners of Beatrice and Laura, who never write but honour of them to whom they devote their verse, displaying sublime and pure thoughts without transgression. And long it was not after, when I was confirmed in this opinion, that he who would not be frustrate of his hope to write well hereafter in laudable things, ought himself to be a true poem; that is, a composition and pattern of the best and honourablest things; not presuming to sing high praises of heroic men, or famous cities, unless he have in himself the experience and the practice of all that which is praiseworthy.

It may be fanciful to add, and we may be laughed at, but we believe that the self-reverencing propensity was a little aided by his singular personal beauty. All the describers of his youth concur in telling us that this was very remarkable. Mr. Masson has the following account of it:

When Milton left Cambridge in July 1632, he was twenty-three years and eight months old. In stature, therefore, at least, he was already whatever he was to be. 'In stature,' he says himself at a later period, when driven to speak on the subject, 'I confess I am not tall, but still of what is nearer to middle height than to little: and what if I were of little; of which stature have often been very great men both in peace and war—though why should that be called little which is great enough for virtue?' (*'Staturâ, fateor, non sum procerâ, sed quæ mediocri tamen quàm parvæ propior sit; sed quid si parvâ, quâ et summi sæpe tum pace tum bello viri fuere—quanquam parva cur dicitur, quæ ad virtutem satis magna est?'*) This is precise enough; but we have Aubrey's words to the same effect. 'He was scarce so tall as I am,' says Aubrey; to which, to make it more intelligible, he appends this marginal note:— '*Qu. Quot* feet I am high? *Resp.* Of middle stature;'—*i.e.* Milton was a little under middle height. 'He had light brown hair,' continues Aubrey,—putting the word 'abrown' ('auburn') in the margin by way of synonym for 'light brown;'—'his complexion exceeding fair; oval face; his eye a dark gray.'

118

We are far from accusing Milton of personal vanity. His character was too enormous, if we may be allowed so to say, for a fault so petty. But a little tinge of excessive self-respect will cling to those who can admire themselves. Ugly men are and ought to be ashamed of their existence. Milton was not so.

The peculiarities of the austere type of character stand out in Milton more remarkably than in other men who partake of it, because of the extreme strength of his nature. In reading him this is the first thing that strikes us. We seem to have left the little world of ordinary writers. The words of some authors are said to have 'hands and feet;' they seem, that is, to have a vigour and animation which only belongs to things which live and move. Milton's words have not this animal life. There is no rude energy about them. But, on the other hand, they have, or seem to have, a soul, a spirit which other words have not. He was early aware that what he wrote, 'by certain vital signs it had,' was such as the world would not 'willingly let die.' After two centuries we feel the same. There is a solemn and firm music in the lines; a brooding sublimity haunts them; the spirit of the great writer moves over the face of the page. In life there seems to have been the same peculiar strength that his works suggest to us. His moral tenacity is amazing. He took his own course, and he kept his own course; and we may trace in his defects the same characteristics. 'Energy and ill-temper,' some say, 'are the same thing;' and though this is a strong exaggeration, yet there is a basis of truth in it. People who labour much will be cross if they do not obtain that for which they labour; those who desire vehemently will be vexed if they do not obtain that which they desire. As is the strength of the impelling tendency, so, other things being equal, is the pain which it will experience if it be baffled. Those, too, who are set on what is high, will be proportionately offended by the intrusion of what is low. Accordingly, Milton is described by those who knew him as a 'harsh and choleric man.' 'He had,' we are told, 'a gravity in his temper, not melancholy, or not till the latter part of his life,—not sour, not morose, or ill-natured; but a certain severity of mind; a mind not condescending to little things;'—and this, although his daughter remembered that he was delightful company, the life of conversation, and that he was so 'on account of a flow of subjects and an unaffected cheerfulness and civility.' Doubtless this may have been so when he was at ease, and at home. But there are unmistakable traces of the harsher tendency in almost all his works.

Some of the peculiarities of the ascetic character were likewise augmented by his studious disposition. This began very early in life, and continued till the end. 'My father,' he says, 'destined me to the study of polite literature, which I embraced with such avidity, that from the twelfth year of my age I hardly ever retired to rest from my studies till midnight; which was the first source of injury to my eyes, to the natural weakness of which were added frequent headaches: all of which not retarding my eagerness after knowledge, he took care to have me instructed,' &c. Every page of his works shows the result of this education. In spite of the occupations of manhood, and the blindness and melancholy of old age, he still continued to have his principal pleasure in that 'studious and select reading' which, though often curiously transmuted, is perpetually involved in the very texture of his works. We need not stay to observe how a habit in itself so austere conduces to the development of an austere character. Deep study, especially deep study which haunts and rules the imagination, necessarily removes men from life, absorbs them in themselves; purifies their conduct, with some risk of isolating their sympathies; developes that loftiness of mood which is gifted with deep inspirations and indulged with great ideas, but which tends in its excess to engender a contempt for others, and a self-appreciation which is even more displeasing to them.

These same tendencies were aggravated also by two defects which are exceedingly rare in great English authors, and which perhaps Milton alone amongst those of the highest class is in a remarkable degree chargeable with. We mean a deficiency in humour, and a deficiency in a knowledge of plain human nature. Probably when, after the lapse of ages, English literature is looked at in its larger features only, and in comparison with other literatures which have preceded or which may follow it, the critics will lay down that its most striking characteristic as a whole is its involution, so to say, in life; the degree to which its book-life resembles real life; the extent to which the motives, dispositions, and actions of common busy persons are represented in a medium which would seem likely to give us peculiarly the ideas of secluded, and the tendencies of meditative men. It is but an aspect of this fact, that English literature abounds,—some critics will say abounds excessively,—with humour. This is in some sense the imaginative element of ordinary life,—the relieving charm, partaking at once of contrast and similitude, which gives a human and an intellectual interest to the world of clowns and cottages, of fields and farmers. The degree to which Milton is deficient in this element is conspicuous in every page of his writings where its occurrence could be looked for; and if we do not always look for it, this is because the subjects of his most remarkable works are on a removed elevation, where ordinary life, the world of 'cakes and ale,' is never thought of and never expected. It is in his dramas, as we should expect, that Milton shows this deficiency the most. 'Citizens' never talk in his pages, as they do in Shakespeare. We feel instinctively that Milton's eye had never rested with the same easy pleasure on the easy, ordinary, shop-keeping world. Perhaps, such is the complication of art, that it is on the most tragic occasions that we feel this want the most. It may seem an odd theory, and yet we believe it to be a true principle, that catastrophes require a comic element. We appear to feel the same principle in life. We may read solemn descriptions of great events in history,—say of Lord Strafford's trial, and of his marvellous speech, and his appeal to his 'saint in heaven'; but we comprehend the whole transaction much better when we learn from Mr. Baillie, the eye-witness, that people ate nuts and apples, and talked, and laughed, and betted on the great question of acquittal and condemnation. Nor is it difficult to understand why this should be so. It seems to be a law of the imagination, at least in most men, that it will not bear concentration. It is essentially a glancing faculty. It goes and comes, and comes and goes, and we hardly know whence or why. But we most of us know that when we try to fix it, in a moment it passes away. Accordingly, the proper procedure of art is to let it go in such a manner as to ensure its coming back again. The force of artistic contrasts effects exactly this result. Skilfully disposed opposites suggest the notion of each other. We realise more perfectly and easily the great idea, the tragic conception, when we are familiarised with its effects on the minds of little people, with the petty consequences which it causes, as well as with the enormous forces from which it comes. The catastrophe of *Samson Agonistes* discloses Milton's imperfect mastery of this element of effect. If ever there was an occasion which admitted its perfect employment, it was this. The kind of catastrophe is exactly that which is sure to strike, and strike forcibly, the minds of common persons. If their observations on the occasion were really given to us, we could scarcely avoid something rather comic. The eccentricity, so to speak, of ordinary persons, shows itself peculiarly at such times, and they say the queerest things. Shakespeare has exemplified this principle most skilfully on various occasions: it is the sort of art which is just in his way. His imagination always seems to be floating between the contrasts of things; and if his mind had a resting-place that it liked, it was this ordinary view of extraordinary events. Milton was under the greater obligation to use this relieving principle of art in the catastrophe of Samson, because he has made every effort to heighten the strictly tragic element, which requires that relief. His art, always serious, was never more serious. His Samson is not the incarnation of physical strength which the popular fancy embodies in the character; nor is it the simple and romantic character of the Old Testament. On the contrary, Samson has become a Puritan: the observations he makes would have done much credit to a religious pikeman in Cromwell's army. In consequence, his death requires some lightening touches to make it a properly artistic event. The pomp of seriousness becomes too oppressive.

> At length, for intermission sake, they led him
> Between the pillars; he his guide requested
> (For so from such as nearer stood we heard),
> As over-tired, to let him lean a while
> With both his arms on those two massy pillars,
> That to the archèd roof gave main support.
> He unsuspicious led him; which when Samson
> Felt in his arms, with head a while inclined,
> And eyes fast fixed, he stood, as one who pray'd,
> Or some great matter in his mind revolved:
> At last, with head erect, thus cry'd aloud:—
> 'Hitherto, Lords, what your commands imposed
> I have perform'd, as reason was, obeying,
> Not without wonder or delight beheld;
> Now, of my own accord, such other trial
> I mean to show you of my strength yet greater
> As with amaze shall strike all who behold.'
> This uttered, straining all his nerves, he bowed;
> As with the force of winds and waters pent
> When mountains tremble, those two massy pillars
> With horrible convulsion to and fro
> He tugged, he shook, till down they came, and drew
> The whole roof after them with burst of thunder
> Upon the heads of all who sat beneath,
> Lords, ladies, captains, counsellors, or priests,

Their choice nobility and flower, not only
Of this, but each Philistian city round,
Met from all parts to solemnise this feast.
Samson with these immixed, inevitably
Pulled down the same destruction on himself;
The vulgar only 'scaped who stood without.
 Chor. O dearly bought revenge, yet glorious!
Living or dying thou has fulfilled
The work for which thou wast foretold
To Israel, and now liest victorious
Among thy slain self-killed;
Not willingly, but tangled in the fold
Of dire Necessity, whose law in death conjoined
Thee with thy slaughtered foes, in number more
Than all thy life hath slain before.

This is grave and fine; but Shakespeare would have done it differently and better.

We need not pause to observe how certainly this deficiency in humour and in the delineation of ordinary human feeling is connected with a recluse, a solitary, and to some extent an unsympathising life. If we combine a certain natural aloofness from common men with literary habits and an incessantly studious musing, we shall at once see how powerful a force is brought to bear on an instinctively austere character, and how sure it will be to develop the peculiar tendencies of it, both good and evil. It was to no purpose that Milton seems to have practised a sort of professional study of life. No man could rank more highly the importance to a poet of an intellectual insight into all-important pursuits and 'seemly arts.' But it is not by the mere intellect that we can take in the daily occupations of mankind; we must sympathise with them, and see them in their human relations. A chimney-sweeper, *quâ* chimney-sweeper, is not very sentimental; it is in himself that he is so interesting.

Milton's austere character is in some sort the more evident, because he possessed in large measure a certain relieving element, in which those who are eminent in that character are very deficient. Generally such persons have but obtuse senses. We are prone to attribute the purity of their conduct to the dullness of their sensations. Milton had no such obtuseness. He had every opportunity for knowing the world of eye and ear. You cannot open his works without seeing how much he did know of it. The austerity of his nature was not caused by the deficiency of his senses, but by an excess of the warning instinct. Even when he professed to delineate the world of sensuous delight, this instinct shows itself. Dr. Johnson thought he could discern melancholy in *L'Allegro*. If he had said solitariness, it would have been correct.

The peculiar nature of Milton's character is very conspicuous in the events of his domestic life, and in the views which he took of the great public revolutions of his age. We can spare only a very brief space for the examination of either of these; but we will endeavour to say a few words upon each of them.

The circumstances of Milton's first marriage are as singular as any in the strange series of the loves of the poets. The scene opens with an affair of business. Milton's father, as is well known, was a scrivener— a kind of professional money-lender, then well known in London; and having been early connected with the vicinity of Oxford, continued afterwards to have pecuniary transactions of a certain nature with country gentlemen of that neighbourhood. In the course of these he advanced 500*l.* to a certain Mr. Richard Powell, a squire of fair landed estate, residing at Forest Hill, which is about four miles from the town of Oxford. The money was lent on the 11th of June 1627; and a few months afterwards Mr. Milton the elder gave 312*l.* of it to his son the poet, who was then a youth at college, and made a formal memorandum of the same in the form then usual, which still exists. The debt was never wholly discharged; for in 1651 we find Milton declaring on oath that he had never received more than 180*l.*, 'in part satisfaction of his said just and principal debt, with damages for the same, and his costs of suit.' Mr. Keightley supposes him to have 'taken many a ride over to Forest Hill' after he left Cambridge and was living at Horton, which is not very far distant; but of course this is only conjecture. We only know that about 1643 'he took,' as his nephew relates, 'a journey into the country, nobody about him certainly knowing the reason, or that it was any more than a journey of recreation. After a month's stay, home; he returns a married man, that went out a bachelor; his wife being Mary, the eldest daughter of Mr. Richard Powell, then a justice of the peace' for the county of Oxford. The suddenness of the event is rather striking; but Philips was at the time one of Milton's pupils, and it is possible that some pains may have been taken to conceal the love-affair from the 'young gentlemen.' Still, as Philips was Milton's nephew, he was likely to hear such intelligence tolerably early; and as he does not seem to have done so, the *dénouement* was probably rather prompt. At any rate, he was certainly married at that time, and took his bride home to his house in Aldersgate Street; and there was feasting and gaiety according to the usual custom of such events. A few weeks after, the lady went home to her friends, in which there was of course nothing remarkable; but it is singular that when the natural limit of her visit at home was come, she absolutely refused to return to her husband. The grounds of so strange a resolution are very difficult to ascertain. Political feeling ran very high: old Mr. Powell adhered to the side of the king, and Milton to that of the parliament; and this might be fancied to have caused an estrangement. But on the other hand, these circumstances must have been well known three months before. Nothing had happened in that quarter of a year to change very materially the position of the two parties in the state. Some other cause for Mrs. Milton's conduct must be looked for. She herself is said to have stated that she did not like her husband's 'spare diet and hard study.' No doubt, too, she found it dull in London; she had probably always lived in the country, and must have been quite unaccustomed to the not very pleasant scene in which she found herself. Still, many young ladies have married schoolmasters, and many young ladies have gone from Oxfordshire to London; and nevertheless no such dissolution of matrimonial harmony is known to have occurred.

The fact we believe to be, that the bride took a dislike to her husband. We cannot but have a suspicion that she did not like him before marriage, and that pecuniary reasons had their influence. If, however, Mr. Powell exerted his paternal influence, it may be admitted that he had unusual considerations to advance in favour of the alliance he proposed. It is not every father whose creditors are handsome young gentlemen with a fair income. Perhaps it seemed no extreme tyranny to press the young lady a little to do that which some others might have done without pressing. Still, all this is but hypothesis; the evidence of the love-affairs of the time of King Charles I. is but meagre. But whatever the feelings of Miss Powell may have been, those of Mrs. Milton are exceedingly certain. She would not return to her husband; she did not answer his letters; and a messenger whom he sent to bring her back was handled rather roughly. Unquestionably, she was deeply to blame, by far the most to blame of the two. Whatever may be alleged against him, is as nothing compared with her offence in leaving him.

To defend so startling a course, we must adopt views of divorce even more extreme than those which Milton was himself driven to inculcate; and whatever Mrs. Milton's practice may have been, it may be fairly conjectured that her principles were strictly orthodox. Yet, if she could be examined by a commission to the ghosts, she would probably have some palliating circumstances to allege in mitigation of judgment. There were, perhaps, peculiarities in Milton's character which a young lady might not improperly dislike. The austere and ascetic character is of course far less agreeable to women than the sensuous and susceptible. The self-occupation, the pride, the abstraction of the former are to the female mind disagreeable; studious habits and unusual self-denial seem to it purposeless; lofty enthusiasm, public spirit, the solitary pursuit of an elevated ideal, are quite out of its way,—they rest too little on the visible world to be intelligible, they are too little suggested by the daily occurrences of life to seem possible. The poet in search of an imaginary phantom has never been successful with women,—there are innumerable proofs of that; the ascetic moralist is even less interesting. A character combined out of the two—and this to some extent was Milton's—is singularly likely to meet with painful failure; with a failure the more painful, that it could never anticipate or explain it. Possibly he was absorbed in an austere self-conscious excellence; it may never have occurred to him that a lady might prefer the trivial detail of daily happiness.

Milton's own view of the matter he has explained to us in his book on divorce; and it is a very odd one. His complaint was that his wife would not talk. What he wished in marriage was an 'intimate and speaking help;' he encountered a 'mute and spiritless mate.' One of his principal incitements to the 'pious necessity of divorcing,' was an unusual deficiency in household conversation. A certain loquacity in their wives has been the complaint of various eminent men; but his domestic affliction was a different one. The 'ready and reviving associate,' whom he had hoped to have found, appeared to be a 'co-inhabiting mischief,' who was sullen, and perhaps seemed bored and tired. And at times he is disposed to cast the blame of his misfortune on the uninstructive nature of youthful virtue. The 'soberest and best-governed men,' he says, are least practised in such affairs, are not very well aware that 'the bashful muteness' of a young lady 'may oft-times hide the unliveliness and natural sloth which is really unfit for conversation;' and are rather in too great haste to light the nuptial torch:

whereas those 'who have lived most loosely, by reason of their bold accustoming, prove most successful in their matches; because their wild affections, unsettling at will, have been as so many divorces to teach them experience.' And he rather wishes to infer that the virtuous man should, in case of mischance, have his resource of divorce likewise.

In truth, Milton's book on divorce—though only containing principles which he continued to believe long after he had any personal reasons for wishing to do so—were clearly suggested at first by the unusual phenomena of his first marriage. His wife began by not speaking to him, and finished by running away from him. Accordingly, like most books which spring out of personal circumstances, his treatises on this subject have a frankness, and a mastery of detail, which others on the same topic sometimes want. He is remarkably free from one peculiarity of modern writers on such matters. Several considerate gentlemen are extremely anxious for the 'rights of woman.' They think that women will benefit by removing the bulwarks which the misguided experience of ages has erected for their protection. A migratory system of domestic existence might suit Madame Dudevant, and a few cases of singular exception; but we cannot fancy that it would be, after all, so much to the taste of most ladies as the present more permanent system. We have some reminiscence of the stories of the wolf and the lamb, when we hear amiable men addressing a female auditory (in books of course) on the advantages of a freer 'development.' We are perhaps wrong, but we cherish an indistinct suspicion that an indefinite extension of the power of selection would rather tend to the advantage of the sex which more usually chooses. But we have no occasion to avow such opinions now. Milton had no such modern views. He is frankly and honestly anxious for the rights of the man. Of the doctrine that divorce is only permitted for the help of wives, he exclaims, 'Palpably uxorious! who can be ignorant that woman was created for man, and not man for woman? What an injury is it after wedlock to be slighted! what to be contended with in point of house-rule who shall be the head; not for any parity of wisdom, for that were something reasonable, but out of a female pride! "I suffer not," saith St. Paul, "the woman to usurp authority over the man." If the Apostle could not suffer it,' he naturally remarks, 'into what mould is he mortified that can?' He had a sincere desire to preserve men from the society of unsocial and unsympathising women; and that was his principal idea.

His theory, to a certain extent, partakes of the same notion. The following passage contains a perspicuous exposition of it:

Moses, Deut. xxiv. 1, established a grave and prudent law, full of moral equity, full of due consideration towards nature, that cannot be resisted, a law consenting with the wisest men and civilest nations; that when a man hath married a wife, if it come to pass that he cannot love her by reason of some displeasing natural quality or unfitness in her, let him write her a bill of divorce. The intent of which law undoubtedly was this: that if any good and peaceable man should discover some helpless disagreement or dislike, either of mind or body, whereby he could not cheerfully perform the duty of a husband without the perpetual dissembling of offence and disturbance to his spirit; rather than to live uncomfortably and unhappily both to himself and to his wife, rather than to continue undertaking a duty which he could not possibly discharge, he might dismiss her whom he could not tolerably, and so not conscionably, retain. And this law the Spirit of God by the mouth of Solomon, Prov. xxx. 21, 23, testifies to be a good and a necessary law, by granting it that 'a hated woman' (for so the Hebrew word signifies, rather than 'odious,' though it come all to one), that 'a hated woman, when she is married, is a thing that the earth cannot bear.'

And he complains that the civil law of modern states interferes with the 'domestical prerogative of the husband.'

His notion would seem to have been that a husband was bound not to dismiss his wife, except for a reason really sufficient; such as a thoroughly incompatible temper, an incorrigible 'muteness,' and a desertion like that of Mrs. Milton. But he scarcely liked to admit that, in the use of this power, he should be subject to the correction of human tribunals. He thought that the circumstances of each case depended upon 'utterless facts;' and that it was practically impossible for a civil court to decide on a subject so delicate in its essence, and so imperceptible in its data. But though amiable men doubtless suffer much from the deficiencies of their wives, we should hardly like to intrust them, in their own cases, with a jurisdiction so prompt and summary.

We are far from being concerned, however, just now with the doctrine of divorce on its intrinsic merits: we were only intending to give such an account of Milton's opinions upon it as might serve to illustrate his character. We think we have shown that it is possible there may have been, in his domestic relations, a little overweening pride; a tendency to overrate the true extent of masculine rights, and to dwell on his wife's duty to be social towards him rather than on his duty to be social towards her,—to be rather sullen whenever she was not quite cheerful. Still, we are not defending a lady for leaving her husband for defects of such inferior magnitude. Few households would be kept together, if the right of transition were exercised on such trifling occasions. We are but suggesting that she may share the excuse which our great satirist has suggested for another unreliable lady: 'My mother was an angel; but angels are not always *commodes à vivre*.'

This is not a pleasant part of our subject, and we must leave it, It is more agreeable to relate that on no occasion of his life was the substantial excellence of Milton's character more conclusively shown than in his conduct at the last stage of this curious transaction. After a very considerable interval, and after the publication of his book on divorce, Mrs. Milton showed a disposition to return to her husband; and in spite of his theories, he received her with open arms. With great Christian patience, he received her relations too. The Parliamentary party was then victorious; and old Mr. Powell, who had suffered very much in the cause of the king, lived until his death untroubled, and 'wholly to his devotion,' as we are informed, in the house of his son-in-law.

Of the other occurrences of Milton's domestic life we have left ourselves no room to speak; we must turn to our second source of illustration for his character,—his opinions on the great public events of his time. It may seem odd, but we believe that a man of austere character naturally tends *both* to an excessive party spirit and to an extreme isolation. Of course the circumstances which develop the one must be different from those which are necessary to call out the other: party-spirit requires companionship; isolation, if we may be pardoned so original a remark, excludes it. But though, as we have shown, this species of character is prone to mental solitude, tends to[3] an intellectual isolation where it is possible and as soon as it can, yet when invincible circumstances throw it into mental companionship, when it is driven into earnest association with earnest men on interesting topics, its zeal becomes excessive. Such a man's mind is at home only with its own enthusiasm; it is cooped up within the narrow limits of its own ideas, and it can make no allowance for those who differ from or oppose them. We may see something of this excessive party-zeal in Burke. No one's reasons are more philosophical; yet no one who acted

[3] The *National Review* has 'lends' for 'tends to'.—p. 169.

with a party went further in aid of it or was more violent in support of it. He forgot what could be said for the tenets of the enemy; his imagination made that enemy an abstract incarnation of his tenets. A man, too, who knows that he formed his opinions originally by a genuine and intellectual process, is but little aware of the undue energy those ideas may obtain from the concurrence of those around. Persons who first acquired their ideas at second-hand, are more open to a knowledge of their own weakness, and better acquainted with the strange force which there is in the sympathy of others. The isolated mind, when it acts with the popular feeling, is apt to exaggerate that feeling for the most part by an almost inevitable consequence of the feelings which render it isolated. Milton is an example of this remark. In the commencement of the struggle between Charles I. and the Parliament, he sympathised strongly with the popular movement, and carried to what seems now a strange extreme his partisanship. No one could imagine that the first literary Englishman of his time could write the following passage on Charles I.:

Who can with patience hear this filthy, rascally Fool speak so irreverently of Persons eminent both in Greatness and Piety? Dare you compare King *David* with King *Charles*; a most Religious King and Prophet with a Superstitious Prince, and who was but a Novice in the Christian Religion; a most prudent, wise Prince with a weak one; a valiant Prince with a cowardly one; finally, a most just Prince with a most unjust one? Have you the impudence to commend his Chastity and Sobriety, who is known to have committed all manner of Leudness in company with his Confident the Duke of *Buckingham*? It were to no purpose to enquire into the private Actions of his life, who publickly at Plays would embrace and kiss the Ladies.

Whatever may be the faults of that ill-fated monarch,—and they assuredly were not small,—no one would now think this absurd invective to be even an excusable exaggeration. It misses the true mark altogether, and is the expression of a strongly imaginative mind which has seen something that it did not like, and is unable in consequence to see anything that has any relation to it distinctly or correctly. But with the supremacy of the Long Parliament Milton's attachment to their cause ceased. No one has drawn a more unfavourable picture of the rule which they established. Years after their supremacy had passed away, and the restoration of the monarchy had covered with a new and strange scene the old actors and the old world, he thrust into a most unlikely part of his *History of England* the following attack on them:

But when once the superficiall zeal and popular fumes that acted their New Magistracy were cool'd and spent in them, strait every one betook himself (setting the Commonwealth behind, his privat ends before) to doe as his own profit or ambition ledd him. Then was justice delay'd, and soon after deni'd spight and favour determin'd all: hence faction, thence treachery, both at home and in the field: ev'ry where wrong, and oppression: foull and horrid deeds committed daily, or maintain'd, in secret, or in open. Som who had bin call'd from shops and warehouses, without other merit, to sit in Supreme Councills and Committees (as thir breeding was) fell to huckster the Commonwealth. Others did therafter as men could soothe and humour them best; so hee who would give most, or, under covert of hypocriticall zeale, insinuat basest, enjoy'd unworthily the rewards of lerning and fidelity; or escap'd the punishment of his crimes and misdeeds. Thir Votes and Ordinances, which men looked should have contain'd the repealing of bad laws, and the immediat constitution of better, resounded with nothing els, but new Impositions, Taxes, Excises; yeerly, monthly, weekly. Not to reckon the Offices, Gifts and Preferments bestow'd and shar'd among themselvs.

His dislike of this system of committees, and of the generally dull and unemphatic administration of the Commonwealth, attached him to the Puritan army and to Cromwell; but in the continuation of the passage we have referred to, he expresses, with something, let it be said, of a schoolmaster feeling, an unfavourable judgment on their career.

For *Britan*, to speak a truth not oft'n spok'n, as it is a Land fruitful enough of men stout and courageous in warr, soe it is naturally not over-fertill of men able to govern justly and prudently in peace, trusting onely in thir Motherwit; who consider not justly, that civility, prudence, love of the Publick good, more then of money or vaine honour, are to this soile in a manner outlandish; grow not here, but in mindes well implanted with solid and elaborat breeding, too impolitic els and rude, if not headstrong and intractable to the industry and vertue either of executing or understanding true Civill Government. Valiant indeed, and prosperous to win a field; but to know the end and reason of winning, unjudicious, and unwise: in good or bad success, alike unteachable. For the Sun, which wee want, ripens wits as well as fruits; and as Wine and Oil are imported to us from abroad, soe must ripe understanding, and many Civill Vertues, be imported into our mindes from Foren Writings, and examples of best Ages; we shall els miscarry still, and com short in the attempts of any great enterprize. Hence did thir Victories prove as fruitles, as thir Losses dang'rous; and left them still conq'ring under the same greevances, that Men suffer conquer'd: which was indeed

131

unlikely to goe otherwise, unles Men more then vulgar bred up, as few of them were, in the knowledg of antient and illustrious deeds, invincible against many and vaine Titles, impartial to Freindships and Relations, had conducted thir Affairs: but then from the Chapman to the Retailer, many whose ignorance was more audacious then the rest, were admitted with all thir sordid Rudiments to bear no meane sway among them, both in Church and State.

We need not speak of Milton's disapprobation of the restoration. Between him and the world of Charles II. the opposition was inevitable and infinite. Therefore the general fact remains, that except in the early struggles, when he exaggerated the popular feeling, he remained solitary in opinion, and had very little sympathy with any of the prevailing parties of his time.

Milton's own theory of government is to be learned from his works. He advocated a free commonwealth, without rule of a single person or House of Lords: but the form of his projected commonwealth was peculiar. He thought that a certain perpetual council, which should be elected by the nation once for all, and the number of which should be filled up as vacancies might occur, was the best possible machine of government. He did not confine his admiration to abstract theory, but proposed the immediate establishment of such a council in this country. We need not go into an elaborate discussion to show the errors of this conclusion. Hardly any one, then or since, has probably adopted it. The interest of the theoretical parts of Milton's political works is entirely historical. The tenets advocated are not of great value, and the arguments by which he supports them are perhaps of less; but their relation to the times in which they were written gives them a very singular interest. The time of the Commonwealth was the only period in English history in which the fundamental questions of government have been thrown open for popular discussion in this country. We read in French literature discussions on the advisability of establishing a monarchy, on the advisability of establishing a republic, on the advisability of establishing an empire; and before we proceed to examine the arguments, we cannot help being struck at the strange contrast which this multiplicity of open questions presents to our own uninquiring acquiescence in the hereditary polity which has descended to us. 'King, Lords, and Commons' are, we think, ordinances of nature. Yet Milton's political writings embody the reflections of a period when, for a few years, the government of England was nearly as much a subject of fundamental discussion as that of France was in 1851. An 'invitation to thinkers,' to borrow the phrase of Neckar, was given by the circumstances of the time; and, with the habitual facility of philosophical speculation, it was accepted, and used to the utmost. Such are not the kind of speculations in which we expect assistance from Milton. It is not in its transactions with others, in its dealings with the manifold world, that the isolated and austere mind shows itself to the most advantage. Its strength lies in itself. It has 'a calm and pleasing solitariness.' It hears thoughts which others cannot hear. It enjoys the quiet and still air of delightful studies; and is ever conscious of such musing and poetry 'as is not to be obtained by the invocation of Dame Memory and her twin daughters, but by devout prayer to that Eternal Spirit, who can enrich with all utterance and knowledge, and sends out his Seraphim with the hallowed fire of his altar.'

> Descend from Heaven, Urania, by that name
> If rightly thou art called, whose voice divine
> Following, above the Olympian hill I soar,
> Above the flight of Pegaséan wing!
> The meaning, not the name, I call; for thou
> Nor of the Muses nine, nor on the top
> Of old Olympus dwell'st; but heav'nly born,
> Before the hills appeared, or fountain flowed,
> Thou with eternal Wisdom didst converse,
> Wisdom thy sister, and with her didst play
> In presence of the Almighty Father, pleased
> With thy celestial song. Up led by thee,
> Into the Heaven of Heavens I have presumed,
> An earthly guest, and drawn empyreal air,
> Thy tempering. With like safety guided down,
> Return me to my native element;
> Lest, from this flying steed unreined (as once
> Bellerophon, though from a lower clime)
> Dismounted, on the Aleian field I fall,
> Erroneous there to wander and forlorn.
> Half yet remains unsung, but narrower bound
> Within the visible Diurnal Sphere.
> Standing on Earth, not rapt above the pole,
> More safe I sing with mortal voice, unchanged
> To hoarse or mute, though fallen on evil days,
> On evil days though fallen, and evil tongues,

In darkness, and with dangers compassed round,
And solitude; yet not alone, while thou
Visit'st my slumbers nightly, or when Morn
Purples the East. Still govern thou my song,
Urania, and fit audience find, though few.
But drive far off the barbarous dissonance
Of Bacchus and his revellers, the race
Of that wild rout that tore the Thracian bard
In Rhodope, where woods and rocks had ears
To rapture, till the savage clamour drown'd
Both harp and voice; nor could the Muse defend
Her son. So fail not thou who thee implores;
For thou art heavenly, she an empty dream.

'An ancient clergyman of Dorsetshire, Dr. Wright, found John Milton in a small chamber hung with rusty green, sitting in an elbow-chair, and dressed neatly in black: pale, but not cadaverous.' He used also to sit in a gray coarse cloth coat at the door of his house near Bunhill Fields, in warm sunny weather;' and the common people said he was inspired.

If from the man we turn to his works, we are struck at once with two singular contrasts. The first of them is this. The distinction between ancient and modern art is sometimes said, and perhaps truly, to consist in the simple bareness of the imaginative conceptions which we find in ancient art, and the comparatively complex clothing in which all modern creations are embodied. If we adopt this distinction, Milton seems in some sort ancient, and in some sort modern. Nothing is so simple as the subject-matter of his works. The two greatest of his creations—the character of Satan and the character of Eve—are two of the simplest—the latter probably the very simplest—in the whole field of literature. On this side Milton's art is classical. On the other hand, in no writer is the imagery more profuse, the illustrations more various, the dress altogether more splendid. And in this respect the style of his art seems romantic and modern. In real truth, however, it is only ancient art in a modern disguise. The dress is a mere dress, and can be stripped off when we will. We all of us do perhaps in memory strip it off for ourselves. Notwithstanding the lavish adornments with which her image is presented, the character of Eve is still the simplest sort of feminine essence,—the pure embodiment of that inner nature which we believe and hope that women have. The character of Satan, though it is not so easily described, has nearly as few elements in it. The most purely modern conceptions will not bear to be unclothed in this manner. Their romantic garment clings inseparably to them. Hamlet or Lear are not to be thought of except as complex characters, with very involved and complicated embodiments. They are as difficult to draw out in words as the common characters of life are; that of Hamlet, perhaps, is more so. If we make it, as perhaps we should, the characteristic of modern and romantic art that it presents us with creations which we cannot think of or delineate except as very varied, and, so to say, circumstantial, we must not rank Milton among the masters of romantic art. And without involving the subject in the troubled sea of an old controversy, we may say that the most striking of the poetical peculiarities of Milton is the bare simplicity of his ideas, and the rich abundance of his illustrations.

Another of his peculiarities is equally striking. There seems to be such a thing as second-hand poetry. Some poets, musing on the poetry of other men, have unconsciously shaped it into something of their own: the new conception is like the original, it would never probably have existed had not the original existed previously; still it is sufficiently different from the original to be a new thing, not a copy or a plagiarism; it is a creation, though, so to say, a suggested creation. Gray is as good an example as can be found of a poet whose works abound in this species of semi-original conceptions. Industrious critics track his best lines back, and find others like them which doubtless lingered near his fancy while he was writing them. The same critics have been equally busy with the works of Milton, and equally successful. They find traces of his reading in half his works; not, which any reader could do, in overt similes and distinct illustrations, but also in the very texture of the thought and the expression. In many cases, doubtless, they discover more than he himself knew. A mind like his, which has an immense store of imaginative recollections, can never know which of his own imaginations is exactly suggested by which recollection. Men awake with their best ideas; it is seldom worth while to investigate very curiously whence they came. Our proper business is to adapt, and mould, and act upon them. Of poets perhaps this is true even more remarkably than of other men; their ideas are suggested in modes, and according to laws, even more impossible to specify than the ideas of the rest of the world. Second-hand poetry, so to say, often seems quite original to the poet himself; he frequently does not know that he derived it from an old memory; years afterwards it may strike him as it does others. Still, in general, such inferior species of creation is not so likely to be found in minds of singular originality as in those of less. A brooding, placid, cultivated mind, like that of Gray, is the place where we should expect to meet with it. Great originality disturbs the adaptive process, removes the mind of the poet from the thoughts of other men, and occupies it with its own heated and flashing thoughts. Poetry of the second degree is like the secondary rocks of modern geology,—a still, gentle, alluvial formation; the igneous glow of primary genius brings forth ideas like the primeval granite, simple, astounding, and alone. Milton's case is an exception to this rule. His mind has marked originality, probably as much of it as any in literature; but it has as much of moulded recollection as any mind too. His poetry in consequence is like an artificial park, green, and soft, and beautiful, yet with outlines bold, distinct, and firm, and the eternal rock ever jutting out; or, better still, it is like our own lake scenery, where nature has herself the same combination—where we have Rydal Water side by side with the everlasting upheaved mountain. Milton has the same union of softened beauty with unimpaired grandeur; and it is his peculiarity.

These are the two contrasts which puzzle us at first in Milton, and which distinguish him from other poets in our remembrance afterwards. We have a superficial complexity in illustration, and imagery, and metaphor; and in contrast with it we observe a latent simplicity of idea, an almost rude strength of conception. The underlying thoughts are few, though the flowers on the surface are so many. We have likewise the perpetual contrast of the soft poetry of the memory, and the firm, as it were fused, and glowing poetry of the imagination. His words, we may half fancifully say, are like his character. There is the same austerity in the real essence, the same exquisiteness of sense, the same delicacy of form which we know that he had, the same music which we imagine there was in his voice. In both his character and his poetry there was an ascetic nature in a sheath of beauty.

No book, perhaps, which has ever been written is more difficult to criticise than *Paradise Lost*. The only way to criticise a work of the imagination, is to describe its effect upon the mind of the reader,— at any rate, of the critic; and this can only be adequately delineated by strong illustrations, apt similes, and perhaps a little exaggeration.

The task is in its very nature not an easy one; the poet paints a picture on the fancy of the critic, and the critic has in some sort to copy it on the paper. He must say what it is before he can make remarks upon it. But in the case of *Paradise Lost* we hardly like to use illustrations. The subject is one which the imagination rather shrinks from. At any rate, it requires courage, and an effort to compel the mind to view such a subject as distinctly and vividly as it views other subjects. Another peculiarity of *Paradise Lost* makes the difficulty even greater. It does not profess to be a mere work of art; or rather, it claims to be by no means that, and that only. It starts with a dogmatic aim; it avowedly intends to

> assert eternal Providence,
> And justify the ways of God to men.

In this point of view we have always had a sympathy with the Cambridge mathematician who has been so much abused. He said, 'After all, *Paradise Lost proves* nothing;' and various persons of poetical tastes and temperament have been very severe on the prosaic observation. Yet, 'after all,' he was right. Milton professed to prove something. He was too profound a critic,—rather, he had too profound an instinct of those eternal principles of art which criticism tries to state,— not to know that on such a subject he must prove something. He professed to deal with the great problem of human destiny; to show why man was created, in what kind of universe he lives, whence he came, and whither he goes. He dealt of necessity with the greatest of subjects. He had to sketch the greatest of objects. He was concerned with infinity and eternity even more than with time and sense; he undertook to delineate the ways, and consequently the character, of Providence, as well as the conduct and the tendencies of man. The essence of success in such an attempt is to satisfy the religious sense of man; to bring home to our hearts what we know to be true; to teach us what we have not seen; to awaken us to what we have forgotten; to remove the 'covering' from all people, and 'the veil' that is spread over all nations; to give us, in a word, such a conception of things, divine and human, as we can accept, believe, and trust. The true doctrine of criticism demands what Milton invites—an examination of the degree in which the great epic attains this aim. And if, in examining it, we find it necessary to use unusual illustrations, and plainer words than are customary, it must be our excuse that we do not think the subject can be made clear without them.

The defect of *Paradise Lost* is that, after all, it is founded on a *political* transaction. The scene is in heaven very early in the history of the universe, before the creation of man or the fall of Satan. We have a description of a court. The angels,

> By imperial summons called,

appear

> Under their hierarchs in orders bright.
> Ten thousand thousand ensigns high advanced,
> Standards and gonfalons, 'twixt van and rear,
> Stream in the air, and for distinction serve
> Of hierarchies, of orders, and degrees.

To this assemblage 'th' Omnipotent' speaks:

> Hear, all ye Angels, progeny of light,
> Thrones, Dominations, Princedoms, Virtues, Powers,
> Hear my decree, which unrevoked shall stand!
> This day I have begot whom I declare
> My only Son, and on this holy hill
> Him have anointed, whom ye now behold
> At my right hand. Your head I him appoint;
> And by myself have sworn to him shall bow
> All knees in Heaven, and shall confess him Lord.
> Under his great vicegerent reign abide,
> United as one individual soul,
> For ever happy. Him who disobeys
> Me disobeys, breaks union, and, that day,
> Cast out from God and blessed vision, falls
> Into utter darkness deep engulfed, his place
> Ordained without redemption, without end.

This act of patronage was not popular at court; and why should it have been? The religious sense is against it. The worship which sinful men owe to God is not transferable to lieutenants and vicegerents. The whole scene of the court jars upon a true feeling. We seem to be reading about some emperor of history, who admits his son to a share in the empire, who confers on him a considerable jurisdiction, and requires officials, with 'standards and gonfalons,' to bow before him.

JOHN MILTON

The orthodoxy of Milton is quite as questionable as his accuracy. The old Athanasian creed was not made by persons who would allow such a picture as that of Milton to stand before their imaginations. The generation of the Son was to them a fact 'before all time,' an eternal fact. There was no question in their minds of patronage or promotion. The Son was the Son before all time, just as the Father was the Father before all time. Milton had in such matters a bold but not very sensitive imagination. He accepted the inevitable materialism of biblical, and, to some extent, of all religious language as distinct revelation. He certainly believed, in contradiction to the old creed, that God had both 'parts and passions.' He imagined that earth

> Is but the shadow of Heaven, and, things therein
> Each to other like, more than on Earth is thought!

From some passages it would seem that he actually thought of God as having 'the members and form' of a man. Naturally, therefore, he would have no toleration for the mysterious notions of time and eternity which are involved in the traditional doctrine. We are not, however, now concerned with Milton's belief, but with his representation of his creed—his picture, so to say, of it in *Paradise Lost*; still, as we cannot but think, that picture is almost irreligious, and certainly different from that which has been generally accepted in Christendom. Such phrases as 'before all time,' 'eternal generation,' are doubtless very vaguely interpreted by the mass of men; nevertheless, no sensitively orthodox man *could* have drawn the picture of a generation, not to say an exaltation, *in* time.

We shall see this more clearly by reading what follows in the poem:

> All seemed well pleased; all seemed, but were not all.

One of the archangels, whose name can be guessed, decidedly disapproved, and calls a meeting, at which he explains that

> orders and degrees
> Jar not with liberty, but well consist;

but still, that the promotion of a new person, on grounds of relationship merely, above, even infinitely above, the old angels with imperial titles, was 'a new law,' and rather tyrannical. Abdiel,

> than whom none with more zeal adored
> The Deity, and divine commands obeyed,

139

attempts a defence:

> Grant it thee unjust
> That equal over equals monarch reign—
> Thyself, though great and glorious, dost thou count,
> Or all angelic nature join'd in one,
> Equal to him, begotten Son, by whom?
> As by his Word, the mighty Father made
> All things, even thee, and all the Spirits of Heaven
> By him created in their bright degrees,
> Crowned them with glory, and to their glory named
> Thrones, Dominations, Princedoms, Virtues, Powers?—
> Essential Powers; nor by his reign obscured,
> But more illustrious made; since he, the head,
> One of our number thus reduced becomes;
> His laws our laws; all honour to him done
> Returns our own. Cease then this impious rage,
> And tempt not these; but hasten to appease
> The incensed Father and the incensed Son,
> While pardon may be found, in time besought.

Yet though Abdiel's intentions were undeniably good, his argument is rather specious. Acting as an instrument in the process of creation would scarcely give a valid claim to the obedience of the created being. Power may be shown in the act, no doubt; but mere power gives no true claim to the obedience of moral beings. It is a kind of principle of all manner of idolatries and false religions to believe that it does so. Satan, besides, takes issue on the fact:

> That we were formed then, say'st thou? and the work
> Of secondary hands, by task transferred
> From Father to his Son? Strange point and new!
> Doctrine which we would know whence learned!

And we must say that the speech in which the new ruler is introduced to the 'thrones, dominations, princedoms, virtues, powers,' is hard to reconcile with Abdiel's exposition. '*This day*' he seems to have come into existence, and could hardly have assisted at the creation of the angels, who are not young, and who converse with one another like old acquaintances.

We have gone into this part of the subject at length, because it is the source of the great error which pervades *Paradise Lost*. Satan is made *interesting*. This has been the charge of a thousand orthodox and even heterodox writers against Milton. Shelley, on the other hand, has gloried in it; and fancied, if we remember rightly, that Milton intentionally ranged himself on the Satanic side of the universe, just as Shelley himself would have done, and that he wished to show the falsity of the ordinary theology. But Milton was born an age too early for such aims, and was far too sincere to have advocated any doctrine in a form so indirect. He believed every word he said. He was not conscious of the effect his teaching would produce in an age like this, when scepticism is in the air, and when it is not possible to help looking coolly on his delineations. Probably in our boyhood we can recollect a period when any solemn description of celestial events would have commanded our respect; we should not have dared to read it intelligently, to canvass its details and see what it meant: it was a religious book; it sounded reverential, and that would have sufficed. Something like this was the state of mind of the seventeenth century. Even Milton probably shared in a vague reverence for religious language. He hardly felt the moral effect of the pictures he was drawing. His artistic instinct, too, often hurries him away. His Satan was to him, as to us, the hero of his poem. Having commenced by making him resist on an occasion which in an earthly kingdom would have been excusable and proper, he probably a little sympathised with him, just as his readers do.

The interest of Satan's character is at its height in the first two books. Coleridge justly compared it to that of Napoleon. There is the same pride, the same satanic ability, the same will, the same egotism. His character seems to grow with his position. He is far finer after his fall, in misery and suffering, with scarcely any resource except in himself, than he was originally in heaven; at least if Raphael's description of him can be trusted. No portrait which imagination or history has drawn of a revolutionary anarch is nearly so perfect; there is all the grandeur of the greatest human mind, and a certain infinitude in his circumstances which humanity must ever want. Few Englishmen feel a profound reverence for Napoleon I. There was no French alliance in *his* time; we have most of us some tradition of antipathy to him. Yet hardly any Englishman can read the account of the campaign of 1814 without feeling his interest for the Emperor to be strong, and without perhaps being conscious of a latent wish that he may succeed. Our opinion is against him, our serious wish is of course for England; but the imagination has a sympathy of its own, and will not give place. We read about the great general—never greater than in that last emergency—showing resources of genius that seem almost infinite, and that assuredly have never been surpassed, yet vanquished, yielding to the power of circumstances, to the combined force of adversaries, each of whom singly he outmatches in strength, and all of whom together he surpasses in majesty and in mind. Something of the same sort of interest belongs to the Satan of the first two books of *Paradise Lost*. We know that he will be vanquished; his name is not a recommendation. Still we do not imagine distinctly the minds by which he is to be vanquished; we do not take the same interest in them that we do in him; our sympathies, our fancy, are on his side.

Perhaps much of this was inevitable; yet what a defect it is! Especially what a defect in Milton's own view, and looked at with the stern realism with which he regarded it! Suppose that the author of evil in the universe were the most attractive being in it; suppose that the source of all sin were the origin of all interest to us! We need not dwell upon this.

As we have said, much of this was difficult to avoid, if indeed it could be avoided, in dealing with such a theme. Even Milton shrank, in some measure, from delineating the divine character. His imagination evidently halts when it is required to perform that task. The more delicate imagination of our modern world would shrink still more. Any person who will consider what such an attempt must end in will find his nerves quiver. But by a curiously fatal error, Milton has selected for delineation exactly that part of the divine nature which is most beyond the reach of the human faculties, and which is also, when we try to describe our fancy of it, the least effective to our minds. He has made God *argue*. Now, the procedure of the divine mind from truth to truth must ever be incomprehensible to us; the notion, indeed, of his proceeding at all, is a contradiction: to some extent, at least, it is inevitable that we should use such language, but we know it is in reality inapplicable. A long train of reasoning in such a connection is so out of place as to be painful; and yet Milton has many. He relates a series of family prayers in heaven, with sermons afterwards, which are very tedious. Even Pope was shocked at the notion of Providence talking like 'a school-divine.' And there is the still worse error, that if you once attribute reasoning to Him, subsequent logicians may discover that He does not reason very well.

Another way in which Milton has contrived to strengthen our

interest in Satan is the number and insipidity of his good angels. There are old rules as to the necessity of a supernatural machinery for an epic poem, worth some fraction of the paper on which they are written, and derived from the practice of Homer, who believed his gods and goddesses to be real beings, and would have been rather harsh with a critic who called them machinery. These rules had probably an influence with Milton, and induced him to manipulate these serious angels more than he would have done otherwise. They appear to be excellent administrators with very little to do; a kind of grand chamberlains with wings, who fly down to earth and communicate information to Adam and Eve. They have no character; they are essentially messengers, merely conductors, so to say, of the providential will: no one fancies that they have an independent power of action; they seem scarcely to have minds of their own. No effect can be more unfortunate. If the struggle of Satan had been with Deity directly, the natural instincts of religion would have been awakened; but when an angel with mind is only contrasted to angels with wings, we sympathise with the former.

In the first two books, therefore, our sympathy with Milton's Satan is great; we had almost said unqualified. The speeches he delivers are of well-known excellence. Lord Brougham, no contemptible judge of emphatic oratory, has laid down that if a person had not an opportunity of access to the great Attic masterpieces, he had better choose these for a model. What is to be regretted about the orator is that he scarcely acts up to his sentiments. 'Better to reign in hell than serve in heaven' is, at any rate, an audacious declaration. But he has no room for exhibiting similar audacity in action. His offensive career is limited. In the nature of the subject there was scarcely the possibility for the fallen archangel to display in the detail of his operations the surpassing intellect with which Milton has endowed him. He goes across chaos, gets into a few physical difficulties; but these are not much. His grand aim is the conquest of our first parents; and we are at once struck with the enormous inequality of the conflict. Two beings just created, without experience, without guile, without knowledge of good and evil, are expected to contend with a being on the delineation of whose powers every resource of art and imagination, every subtle suggestion, every emphatic simile, has been lavished. The idea in every reader's mind is, and must be, not surprise that our first parents should yield, but wonder that Satan should not think it beneath him to attack them. It is as if an army should invest a cottage.

We have spoken more of theology than we intended; and we need not say how much the monstrous inequalities attributed to the combatants affect our estimate of the results of the conflict. The state of man is what it is, because the defenceless Adam and Eve of Milton's imagination yielded to the nearly all-powerful Satan whom he has delineated. Milton has in some sense invented this difficulty; for in the book of Genesis there is no such inequality. The serpent may be subtler than any beast of the field; but he is not necessarily subtler or cleverer than man. So far from Milton having justified the ways of God to man, he has loaded the common theology with a new encumbrance.

We may need refreshment after this discussion; and we cannot find it better than in reading a few remarks of Eve.

> That day I oft remember, when from sleep,
> I first awaked, and found myself reposed,
> Under a shade, on flow'rs, much wond'ring where
> And what I was, whence thither brought, and how.
> Not distant far from thence a murm'ring sound
> Of waters issued from a cave, and spread
> Into a liquid plain; then stood unmoved,
> Pure as the expanse of Heav'n. I thither went
> With unexperienced thought, and laid me down
> On the green bank, to look into the clear
> Smooth lake, that to me seem'd another sky.
> As I bent down to look, just opposite
> A shape within the watery gleam appear'd,
> Bending to look on me. I started back;
> It started back: but pleased I soon returned;
> Pleased it returned as soon with answering looks
> Of sympathy and love. There I had fix'd
> Mine eyes till now, and pined with vain desire,
> Had not a voice thus warned me: 'What thou seest,
> What there thou seest, fair creature, is thyself;
> With thee it came and goes: but follow me,
> And I will bring thee where no shadow stays
> Thy coming, and thy soft embraces—he
> Whose image thou art; him thou shalt enjoy
> Inseparably thine; to him shalt bear
> Multitudes like thyself, and thence be call'd

Mother of Human Race.' What could I do
But follow straight, invisibly thus led?
Till I espied thee, fair, indeed, and tall,
Under a platan; yet methought less fair,
Less winning soft, less amiably mild,
Than that smooth watery image. Back I turn'd:
Thou, following, cry'dst aloud, 'Return, fair Eve;
Whom fly'st thou?'

Eve's character, indeed, is one of the most wonderful efforts of the human imagination. She is a kind of abstract woman; essentially a typical being; an official 'mother of all living.' Yet she is a real interesting woman, not only full of delicacy and sweetness, but with all the undefinable fascination, the charm of personality, which such typical characters hardly ever have. By what consummate miracle of wit this charm of individuality is preserved, without impairing the general idea which is ever present to us, we cannot explain, for we do not know.

Adam is far less successful. He has good hair,—'hyacinthine locks' that 'from his parted forelock manly hung;' a 'fair large front' and 'eye sublime;' but he has little else that we care for. There is, in truth, no opportunity of displaying manly virtues, even if he possessed them. He has only to yield to his wife's solicitations, which he does. Nor are we sure that he does it well. He is very tedious; he indulges in sermons which are good; but most men cannot but fear that so delightful a being as Eve must have found him tiresome. She steps away, however, and goes to sleep at some of the worst points.

Dr. Johnson remarked, that, after all, *Paradise Lost* was one of the books which no one wished longer: we fear, in this irreverent generation, some wish it shorter. Hardly any reader would be sorry if some portions of the later books had been spared him. Coleridge, indeed, discovered profound mysteries in the last; but in what could not Coleridge find a mystery if he wished? Dryden more wisely remarked, that Milton became tedious when he entered upon a 'tract of Scripture.' Nor is it surprising that such is the case. The style of many parts of Scripture is such that it will not bear addition or subtraction. A word less, or an idea more, and the effect upon the mind is the same no longer. Nothing can be more tiresome than a sermonic amplification of such passages. It is almost too much when, as from the pulpit, a paraphrastic commentary is prepared for our spiritual improvement.

In deference to the intention we bear it, but we bear it unwillingly; and we cannot endure it at all when, as in poems, the object is to awaken our fancy rather than to improve our conduct. The account of the creation in the book of Genesis is one of the compositions from which no sensitive imagination would subtract an iota, to which it could not bear to add a word. Milton's paraphrase is alike copious and ineffective. The universe is, in railway phrase, 'opened,' but not created; no green earth springs in a moment from the indefinite void. Instead, too, of the simple loneliness of the Old Testament, several angelic officials are in attendance, who help in nothing, but indicate that heaven must be plentifully supplied with tame creatures.

There is no difficulty in writing such criticisms, and, indeed, other unfavourable criticisms, on *Paradise Lost*. There is scarcely any book in the world which is open to a greater number, or which a reader who allows plain words to produce a due effect will be less satisfied with. Yet what book is really greater? In the best parts the words have a magic in them; even in the inferior passages you are hardly sensible of their inferiority till you translate them into your own language. Perhaps no style ever written by man expressed so adequately the conceptions of a mind so strong and so peculiar; a manly strength, a haunting atmosphere of enhancing suggestions, a firm continuous music, are only some of its excellencies. To comprehend the whole of the others, you must take the volume down and read it,—the best defence of Milton, as has been said most truly, against all objections.

Probably no book shows the transition which our theology has made, since the middle of the seventeenth century, at once so plainly and so fully. We do not now compose long narratives to 'justify the ways of God to men.' The more orthodox we are, the more we shrink from it; the more we hesitate at such a task, the more we allege that we have no powers for it. Our most celebrated defences of established tenets are in the style of Butler, not in that of Milton. They do not profess to show a satisfactory explanation of human destiny; on the contrary, they hint that probably we could not understand such an explanation if it were given us; at any rate, they allow that it is not given us. Their course is palliative. They suggest an 'analogy of difficulties.' If our minds were greater, so they reason, we should comprehend these doctrines: now we cannot explain analogous facts which we see and know. No style can be more opposite to the bold argument, the boastful exposition of Milton. The teaching of the eighteenth century is in the very atmosphere we breathe. We read it in the teachings of Oxford; we hear it from the missionaries of the Vatican. The air of the theology is clarified. We know our difficulties, at least; we are rather prone to exaggerate the weight of some than to deny the reality of any.

We cannot continue a line of thought which would draw us on too far for the patience of our readers. We must, however, make one more remark, and we shall have finished our criticism on *Paradise Lost*. It is analogous to that which we have just made. The scheme of the poem is based on an offence against positive morality. The offence of Adam was not against nature or conscience, not against anything of which we can see the reason, or conceive the obligation, but against an unexplained injunction of the Supreme Will. The rebellion in heaven, as Milton describes it, was a rebellion, not against known ethics, or immutable spiritual laws, but against an arbitrary selection and an unexplained edict. We do not say that there is no such thing as positive morality; we do not think so; even if we did, we should not insert a proposition so startling at the conclusion of a literary criticism. But we are sure that wherever a positive moral edict is promulgated, it is no subject, except perhaps under a very peculiar treatment, for literary art. By the very nature of it, it cannot satisfy the heart and conscience. It is a difficulty; we need not attempt to explain it away. There are mysteries enough which will never be explained away. But it is contrary to every principle of criticism to state the difficulty as if it were not one; to bring forward the puzzle, yet leave it to yourself; to publish so strange a problem, and give only an untrue solution of it: and yet such, in its bare statement, is all which Milton has done.

Of Milton's other writings we have left ourselves no room to speak; and though every one of them, or almost every one of them, would well repay a careful criticism, yet few of them seem to throw much additional light on his character, or add much to our essential notion of his genius, though they may exemplify and enhance it. *Comus* is the poem which does so the most. Literature has become so much lighter than it used to be, that we can scarcely realise the position it occupied in the light literature of our forefathers. We have now in our own language many poems that are pleasanter in their subject, more graceful in their execution, more flowing in their outline, more easy to read. Dr. Johnson, though perhaps no very excellent authority on the more intangible graces of literature, was disposed to deny to

Milton the capacity of creating the lighter literature: 'Milton, madam, was a genius that could cut a colossus from a rock, but could not carve heads upon cherry-stones.' And it would not be surprising if this generation, which has access to the almost indefinite quantity of lighter compositions which have been produced since Johnson's time, were to echo his sentence. In some degree, perhaps, the popular taste does so. *Comus* has no longer the peculiar exceptional popularity which it used to have. We can talk without general odium of its defects. Its characters are nothing, its sentiments are tedious, its story is not interesting. But it is only when we have realised the magnitude of its deficiencies that we comprehend the peculiarity of its greatness. Its power is in its style. A grave and firm music pervades it: it is soft, without a thought of weakness; harmonious and yet strong; impressive, as few such poems are, yet covered with a bloom of beauty and a complexity of charm that few poems have either. We have, perhaps, light literature in itself better, that we read oftener and more easily, that lingers more in our memories; but we have not any, we question if there ever will be any, which gives so true a conception of the capacity and the dignity of the mind by which it was produced. The breath of solemnity which hovers round the music attaches us to the writer. Every line, here as elsewhere in Milton, excites the idea of indefinite power.

And so we must draw to a close. The subject is an infinite one, and if we pursued it, we should lose ourselves in miscellaneous commentary, and run on far beyond the patience of our readers. What we have said has at least a defined intention. We have wished to state the impression which the character of Milton and the greatest of Milton's works are likely to produce on readers of the present generation,— a generation, almost more than any other, different from his own.

Georgiana Marion Craik
(Mrs. A. W. May)

Introductory note

Georgiana Craik (1831–95) was the author of many novels, and of numerous stories for children. *Lost and Won* and *Patience Holt* were the best known of her works.

Lost and Won[1]

WE have frequently had occasion to regret that the language of criticism is defective in terms to express the minor degrees of excellence in novel writing. The number of novels is so great, and the shades of merit are so many, that we need a finely pointed nomenclature. The language of trade is far more effective. It has very accurate, though often very odd words to distinguish the hundred sorts and qualities of the various articles of commerce; and it is especially copious in marking the minute shades between 'middling' and 'good' which it is so difficult to distinguish sharply. There is one well-known commodity which, even in the printed circulars, has the six gradations of 'ordinary,' 'middling,' 'fair,' 'good fair,' 'good,' and 'fine;' besides others which we are told the oral language of the market would accurately define. No one believes that literary excellence has fewer shades of distinction than cotton, and yet how few are the words of the critic in comparison with those of the broker.

If we might for once use trade language, we should venture to describe *Lost and Won* as a 'fine middling,' or 'readable second quality' novel. The language is good, the narrative spirited, the characters are fairly selected and fairly delineated, the dialogue has considerable dramatic force, and yet the work, as a whole, is by no means of the first excellence. A really good novel will bear to be read again and again, to be thought over in various connexions, to be meditated upon in various moods, to be discussed and commented on. *Lost and Won* would not bear so extreme a test; its merits are almost certain to strike us at a first reading, and quite sure to escape us at a second. We liked the spirited narrative yesterday—to-day it seems poor, for we know what we are going to be told. The characters seemed not amiss at first, for we were always expecting a new insight into them; but on a second reading we can scarcely endure them, because

[1] *Lost and Won*. By Georgiana M. Craik, Author of 'Riverston.' London: Smith and Elder. 1859. This article was first published in the *Saturday Review* for April 16 1859, Volume VII, pp. 474–5. Mrs. Russell Barrington mentions this review as being by Bagehot in her biography (p. 272) but she does not include it in her edition of the works.

we know that this insight into their essence is never to be given us, and that the delineations will be sketchy and external to the last page. 'If you are pleased with a common acquaintance,' we have been warned, 'be rather careful not to see him again.' If you have read a common novel with pleasure, the warning of criticism is never to open it again.

We can scarcely compliment the authoress of *Lost and Won* upon her plot. The narrative purports to be written by the heroine—or the quietest of the heroines—of the book. The scene opens with a description of her domestication with an aunt and two male cousins, in a very quiet situation, and an account of one of the latter—a very large young man—getting extremely wet. The repose of their life is broken by the occurrence—it is difficult to use any other word—of a young lady called 'Hildred Kane,' who has been in Italy, and has been in Brussels, has splendid hair, is the daughter of an actress, and is altogether an exciting and astonishing sort of personage. The large young man whom we have mentioned immediately falls in love with this young lady, and being in the same house has considerable opportunities of rendering himself acceptable. He does not, however, succeed completely. She is intellectual, cultivated, and accustomed—though we are not very distinctly told where—to intellectual conversation. He is manly and bulky—according to the traditional type in novels of the common young Englishman—but is not remarkable for many ideas, and has only a cumbrous way of expressing those he possesses. She accepts him, however, at last, and they are to be married, when a certain Lord Carstairs appears on the scene. This nobleman did not bear, we are informed, the best of reputations in that neighbourhood, as there had been an unpleasant affair with a governess in those parts—still he was received in society. His first introduction is thus described:—'Hildred sat before the piano, and the room was filled round about her; but there were two especially who stood nearest to her. One of these was Frankland; the other, Alice whispered to me, was Lord Carstairs. *He* was standing at the side of her chair, so turned that I could not see his face, except once when, at the sound of some slight movement behind him, he stirred, and looked round. I saw it then for one moment, and forgot it no more. It was a proud, keen, beautiful face—and yet a face that was not young, that was all scathed and lined and worn—that might have passed through fire, it was so strangely seared.' As every reader will expect, Hildred is fascinated with this singular face. Lord Carstairs, as well as herself, has been in Italy, and they have a good deal doubtless respecting that country to say to one another. Several exciting incidents occur. There is a fire, and he saves her life—he goes out in a life-boat towards a ship in difficulties, and she strains her eyes after it, regardless of her bulky *fiancé*, who has again got wet. Considerable skill and taste are shown in the description of her struggles: she has no money, and is only prevented from going upon the stage by a promise that she would not do so, made to her father on his death-bed. She exerts herself very much to fasten her mind down to ordinary English life, and the simple attractions of her commonplace admirer, but in vain. The moral of the book evidently is, that a certain excitement is necessary for persons whose excitability is naturally great; and that it is very dangerous by artificial moralities, or conventional distinctions, to exclude them from the pursuits which naturally afford that excitement. If Hildred had been allowed to go on the stage, the authoress almost tells us, she would have had a career—an opening for her strongest tendencies, a sphere for using her higher powers of mind. Common English society affords an Englishwoman no such opportunity. She must bend her mind—ordinarily it does not require much bending—to a rather pleasant but still not very exciting routine. Needlework is appointed her—she is quite forbidden to be theatrical. Hildred revolts at this necessity, and listens to Lord Carstairs. He seduces her, and they live together for awhile in Italy, where he leaves her, and she ends, after all, by going on the stage.

This is one half of the plot of the book. The other half relates to the narratress. We have said that she begins by describing herself as domesticated with two young cousins—both young gentlemen—one of whom falls in love with their anomalous visitor Hildred. Of course the other falls in love with the supposed authoress, and is successful. He is a good young clergyman, who, we are informed, is clever and accomplished, but who never does anything or says anything which evinces those qualities. The narratress is a quiet and tolerably clever girl, who delineates herself incidentally, and by short allusions, in a very skilful way, and who accepts first the intellectual guidance, and then the hand of her clerical cousin with gentle gratitude, and constant, if rather tame affection. The sole interruption to their tranquil course is a somewhat anomalous relation of the gentleman with a consumptive young lady who is much in love with him, but at the point of death.

She ultimately dies, to the evident relief of her especial friend the narratress, and no other difficulties intervene. The quiet course of this love affair is evidently intended as a relief from the exciting story of Hildred Kane, and answers that purpose extremely well.

It will be seen from this sketch of the plot that there is little in this novel which will require or bear very special criticism. As we have said, it is rather good, but not very good; and the language of criticism would ineffectually exhaust itself in endeavouring to give a more accurate or expressive description of it. It has, however, one peculiarity, in relation to which it may be instructive to consider it somewhat further. We have said that the narrative professes to have been composed by the quiet heroine, and there are evident advantages which not unfrequently just now induce writers of novels to tell their story from that point of view. It is the greatest of these that the necessary limitations of the life which it is proper to describe in the novel, exactly coincide with the necessary limitations of the knowledge of the person who, on this supposition, professedly writes it. Nothing is, by the received rules, permitted in novels, which does not suit the perusal of young ladies as well as of young gentlemen. Such a writer as Mr. Thackeray is constantly irritated at this restraint. He has evidently to reject illustrations which would be telling, and remarks which would be very appropriate, because they belong to the unladylike and inter-dicted world. Every man, in proportion to the variety of his acquaint-ance with life, will feel the same constraint. The obvious remedy is, that the writer should throw himself once for all into the position of a young lady in the story—hear only what she hears, see only what she sees, know only what she knows. His dramatic instincts will then preserve him even from wishing to overstep the prescribed boundary. Whatever he may wish to say himself, he will not wish that a quiet heroine of his delineation should say anything which it would not be quite proper that she should say. If the novel be written, as we know is now not very uncommon, by a young lady, she will find an additional advantage in selecting as the point of delineation the exact point of view with which she is inevitably most familiar, and which is more or less her own. She will be sure of describing only what she can describe, as well as be protected from all risk, if by possibility there should be any, of trespassing on what she ought not to describe.

But there are drawbacks on these advantages. Not only does the extreme limitation of the field of delineation after a time weary all those whose range of knowledge is more varied, but a less evident result follows, of which *Lost and Won* is a striking instance. The narrative becomes very melodramatic. A little reflection will, indeed, enable us to perceive why this must be so. By a melodramatic incident, we mean a startling incident of which no rational or intelligible account is given us. By a melodramatic character, we mean one which has the startling features and exaggerated qualities which tell upon the stage, but of which no real *rationale* is offered. In the case of the event, we have either no idea of its cause, or we perceive that cause to be improbable. In the case of the man, we do not know the inner nature out of which his startling peculiarities arise. These peculiarities are described to us, and we are told that they belong to a certain man, but what that man is we do not know. Some such delineation as this is the inevitable result of that limited knowledge which it is proper to attribute to the favourite narratress of modern fiction—the quiet heroine. A young lady of that kind can only in a modified way understand that which passes around her. Not to speak of other limitations, the entire sphere of masculine action is wholly shut out from her perception. Half the incidents in life have their origin in events belonging to the active world, which she has no means of knowing. All around her people move and act from impulses and causes which she only very vaguely, if at all, apprehends, and which never enter her real world of secret thought. In consequence, she acquires a habit of accepting the obvious incidents of life as what they are, without concerning herself with the reasons for them, or much thinking if there are any reasons. As soon as this state of mind is made the point of view from which a narrative is imagined to be told us, we have inevitably one of the principal elements of a melodrama. We have recounted to us events—probably rather striking events, for no one likes telling a story 'about nothing'—of which no rational account is given to us, or, from knowledge appropriate to the imagined narratress, can be given to us. The same result, to an extent even greater, is true of characters. For example, nothing can be more melodramatic than the delineation of Lord Carstairs in *Lost and Won*. He is a very bad but very picturesque young nobleman. He treats Hildred in what may possibly be an attractive sort of way, but it is not a sort of way which enables us to understand his character. He is intended to be a person of much ability, much cultivation, and much daring, but utterly unscrupulous in his relations with women, and much disposed, if they will permit it, to amuse himself at their expense. No one can deny that such a character is possible, or that, in the hands of a master of literary delineation, it might be made a telling subject for the exercise of his art. But it is equally certain that such a character is beyond the mental experience of a common lady. She can have no idea of the early life by which such a man is formed into what he is, or of the more mature life which he leads when he has been so formed. Both conceptions are beyond her sphere. We do not say that a woman of genius may not emancipate herself from these limits; the task is difficult, but we quite believe that it may be possible for an intuitive imagination to divine all that is essential in such a character. But no similar divination must be attributed to an ordinary young heroine. She is not intended to be a woman of genius. Her mind is timid, and its range is narrow. No acquaintance with the real existence of a bad young nobleman can be acquired by such a person except under very peculiar circumstances, or at her own cost. To attribute such knowledge to a gentle young lady who has never had any experience would be monstrous. The authoress of *Lost and Won* has escaped this error. She has not made Lord Carstairs a real character. We have only a sketch of certain obvious traits and picturesque features of his, which a young lady could not help noticing. But, in consequence, the novel as a delineation of life is inevitably very imperfect. We are shown, as moving among the real people of the book, a kind of wicked lay figure that destroys their happiness and ruins their fortunes. The same defect must attend every attempt to describe the striking characters and startling incidents of real life from a point of view at which the real nature of the former, and the producing causes of the latter, are altogether invisible.

The Dean[1]

NOVELS perhaps reflect better than any other species of light literature that change of sentiment in regard to standing subjects of interest which appears to be constantly taking place in the minds of the curious and sensitive. It is a flux and reflux which is highly interesting; for though not in itself a very important matter, it is determined by causes which are at once very deep-seated and most momentous.

For readers who look upon novels from this point of view the *Dean* may have a certain interest—an interest which may in some cases prove sufficiently strong to induce them to read it through. We have also no doubt that the composition of it gave the author considerable pleasure, and enabled her (for Berkeley Aikin is obviously the pseudonym of a woman) to give to feelings creditable in themselves a degree of clearness which it was no doubt satisfactory to arrive at. There is a large class of people who think that they have a sort of inarticulate solution of the various problems of life lying hid in their minds, and to whom nothing is so delightful as the task of giving it outward and visible, if not very coherent or systematic shape. A book written under this impression is rarely altogether dull, inasmuch as it is usually pervaded by a certain *bonâ fide* belief that the author is preaching something which his, or very frequently her, readers really ought to know for their own sakes. The gospels according to novels never had much charm for us; but the books which contain them do undeniably stand on a different and rather a higher level than the mere three volumes made to order, which are perhaps among the most melancholy products of a high state of civilisation.

The *Dean* is a story about one of those awful ogres who are systematically hypocritical, and take the trouble of telling themselves so every time they do a hypocritical action. A naughty Irish boy, Mick Moore, is seized with a burning thirst for knowledge and an unlimited

[1] *The Dean; or, the Popular Preacher.* By Berkeley Aikin. London: Saunders and Otley. 1859. This article was first published in the *Saturday Review* for May 7 1859, Volume VII, pp. 566–7. Mrs. Russell Barrington attributes it to Bagehot in her biography (p. 272) but omits it from her collected edition of the works.

ambition. A legacy of 400*l*., paid in sovereigns, falls to his father, and is hidden in the thatch of his cabin. Mick sets fire to the cabin, steals the money, goes to Dublin as a student at Trinity, becomes a famous popular preacher, marries for love (slighting a rich widow), and on his first wife's death marries a still richer widow than the first—a Countess, with 12,000*l*. a-year—within three months after her husband's death. He becomes one of the most popular preachers in London, and gets a deanery. His eldest son, by his first wife, turns out a sort of genius, milder of mood than his father, but such a beautiful preacher, and such an angelic creature in all other ways as never was heard of out of a novel. The second son gets into all manner of sinful courses. There are various sisters, a heartless aristocratic heroine, and a virtuous popular one, who act after their respective kinds. The Dean, who is a bully, a liar, a hypocrite of the first water, and everything else that is bad—and who is also a man of profound genius, and that sort of adamantine character which novelists favour so much at present —dies in a lurid glow. His good son marries the good heroine, his bad son is drawn into forgery by the woman whom his father slighted, and the other characters all get their appropriate bits of poetical justice according to the form of the statutes. Besides these main characters, there is a female novelist, who assumes the name of Sydney Acton (her real name being Graham), a dissenting minister of extraordinary genius, called Pulseford Pember, and a variety of minor personages, whose manœuvres give the authoress an opportunity of indulging all her special crotchets in the most effective manner.

The story has nothing in it at all, but the gossip and the morality of the book have a sort of interest, for the reasons which we have already stated. They show us what sort of impression the present state of society makes upon a pious, amiable, susceptible lady, who is sincerely anxious to be useful in her generation, and who thinks that she confers upon it the greatest benefit in her power by giving as emphatic a shape as she possibly can to her likes and dislikes. The great object which attracts her attention is of course the clergy. Clergymen of all denominations crowd her canvas. Whether the moral is to be pointed and the tale adorned by virtue or vice, strength or weakness, a clerical face of some shade or other looks out of the picture—the black coat having exactly the same attraction which in old-fashioned novels the red-coat used to be said to have for the female mind. The absorbing contemplation of the clerical genus does not, however, prevent a predilection—both characteristic and interesting—for some particular specimens of the race. High Churchmen, Low Churchmen, and Dissenters are all passed in review, with more or less appreciation of their weaknesses; but there is one school which secures a heartfelt admiration as amusing as it is simple. That 'man of God C——K——,' and that noble work *Alton Locke*, which, with the Bible and the *Pilgrim's Progress* forms the library of the earnest parish clerk, supply the authoress with her real standard; yet it is fair to say that she indicates her preference very briefly, though, to our minds, quite conclusively. The *naïveté* with which she delights in Mr. Kingsley's views of life is exceedingly amusing. To find that, after all, a religious person may not only write novels, but even read them—that a fondness for Smollett and Fielding is permissible to a Christian woman, and that she may even go the length, in a protesting sort of way, of owning a mild preference for such books over others usually looked upon as far more respectable—all these things seem to have come upon her as revelations which have won her heart. We would not quarrel, for the world, with what is no doubt a most innocent delight in a liberty which, if not newly discovered, is at any rate newly recognised—though there are certainly not a few chapters in the novels of the eighteenth century which we should have thought could do good neither to man, woman, nor child. Profane swearing is a very wicked habit; but great allowance is to be made for the mild expletives of a lad very strictly brought up, whose elder brother has just told him that 'Hang it,' and 'Confound it' are not forbidden by the third commandment.

Having thus anchored herself to a warm-hearted, and, as it is called, a genial view of this world and the next—though it is certainly rather a vague one—the authoress of the *Dean* has an excellent standing-ground from which she may throw her various dislikes into as bold relief as she pleases; and she certainly takes occasion to do so in a manner which must, we should think, give the parties attacked the benevolent pleasure which arises from being the objects of assaults which gratify the assailant and do not hurt the patient. The little arrows shot at various Church parties are so very little, and so exceedingly free from venom, that it is interesting to see how pertinaciously they are launched; nor can anything be more curious than to find how much more importance a volunteer controversialist attaches to controversy than those who are actually engaged in it. Berkeley

Aikin—for we suppose that we must not attach to that curious alias either Mr. or Mrs.—introduces us to a clerical dinner-party which a peacemaking and somewhat romantic young clergyman gives to a large number of his brethren, with a view of bringing them into kindly relations; but such an awful scene takes place between the High-church Rector of Beyedoers and the Low-church Vicar of Allfaithnoworks (the attempt at characteristic names is curiously impotent), that the Evangelical party leave the house in indignation, and are shortly after followed by their High-Church enemies. There is something pre-eminently feminine in such a notion. That half-a-dozen clergymen, whose theological views might differ, should not be able to treat each other, in the dining-room of a common friend, with the most ordinary decency, is just the sort of conception of the *odium theologicum* which a person would form who was debarred by her sex from any other connexion with the subject than an irritable and absorbing sympathy with such disputes, founded upon a very imperfect conception and a very one-sided experience of their relations to practical charity.

The last qualification is one which it is only fair to the authoress to point out. A strong vein of benevolence of a very genuine kind pervades the whole book. The sentiment that the rich have got more, and the poor less, than their share of the comforts of life, and that the parable of Dives and Lazarus contains the only comment that can be made on a great part of our social system, is constantly present to her mind, and gives occasionally an air of something which borders on pathos, and even on dignity, to much of what would otherwise be unmitigated twaddle. As soon, however, as the sentiment is thrown into an intellectual shape, the incapacity of the writer for any real intellectual effort becomes painfully apparent. General denunciations of wrath to come die away into gossip, and small-talk, and paltry little mares'-nests which would have been simply tiresome if they had stood alone. Thus, for example, one of the sins of the nation which engages the special attention of a person who has such very awful warnings to give to us all, is the evil treatment of governesses. She once wrote a book, it seems, about the sorrows of that ill-treated class, and, with a true womanly pertinacity, she cannot be induced to give up her point. All the wicked people in the *Dean* have governesses at 15*l.* a-year; and one particularly unkind and absurd remark which was made by a lady of rank to a member of the class in question, and by her repeated to Mrs. Aikin, 'in the summer of 1856,' and taken down on the spot (such was that lady's determination to give a sort of legal authenticity to the evidence which she had to produce), is triumphantly brought forward as a proof of the thesis that the rich have a great deal to answer for.

Good novels by women are amongst the best books of their kind. The *Dean* is very far indeed from belonging to that class; but it is not altogether bad nor altogether unamusing. It is a dishevelled unprotected sort of composition; but it is well meant and kindly and shows here and there traces of power which might by cultivation be much improved. There is a chapter about the herculean dissenting minister's adventures in London, whither he walked up from the country to get his living, which is an obvious and not a very bad imitation of Goldsmith. If Mrs. Aikin could satisfy herself, once for all, that the world will never be any better or any wiser in any respect whatever, she would greatly improve her own chance of writing good novels.

Samuel Rogers
Introductory note

Samuel Rogers (1763–1855) was the son of Thomas Rogers, a banker. He entered the bank in which his father was a partner. In 1792 he published *The Pleasures of Memory*, which was very popular and established his reputation. Thomas Rogers died in 1793, leaving Samuel Rogers in control of the bank and possessed of considerable income. He moved in 1803 to the house in St. James's Place where for the next fifty years he entertained the great literary and political figures of his time, at the famous 'Breakfasts at Rogers's.' He was benevolent as well as hospitable: Moore, Jeffrey, Wordsworth, Sheridan and many others were indebted to his influence or personal generosity. Although he enjoyed a considerable poetic reputation during his lifetime, it is as host and conversationalist that he is chiefly remembered. He published *Epistle to a Friend*, 1798; *Jacqueline*, 1814, and *Human Life*, 1819. He declined the Laureateship in 1850 on Wordsworth's death. Alexander Dyce recorded many of the anecdotes about celebrated people with which Rogers's conversation abounded, and from a great mass of this material Dyce made a selection which he published as *Recollections of The Table-Talk of Samuel Rogers*, 1856. Rogers himself kept records of his conversations with such men as the Duke of Wellington, Fox, Burke, Scott and Horne Tooke, and these were published by Rogers's nephew William Sharpe, in 1859.

Rogers's Recollections[1]

MR. ROGERS is one of the authors who have taken too much pains with their writings. The *Pleasures of Memory* employed him seven years, *Columbus* fourteen, *Human Life* six, *Italy* fourteen; and even after the publication of these poems he did not cease to correct them. In these days of hasty composition it is impossible not to respect so much patience and so much concentrated labour, and well-known maxims would lead us to anticipate that very great excellence would be their result. We believe, however, that in most cases these maxims are erroneous. We incline to think that such extremely slow production is very rarely favourable to the perfection of works of genius. Writers forget what they mean to say. Who can answer for the exact line of thought which he intended to express nine years ago? The author knows as little about it as any one else. If the subject is a favourite one, he is very apt to confuse it with other thoughts which have come and gone in the intermediate period. In consequence, when he is correcting, as he calls it, the work of former years, he is apt to substitute a thought materially different from the original one, and less suitable to the connexion in which it occurs. The first thought, at any rate, arose out of the thought which preceded it in the course of composition. The interpolated idea was suggested by the circumstances of succeeding years. Again, even if the writer exactly remembers what he meant to say, the effect is often worse. Probably the idea is a fixed idea to him— a notion which he carries through the earth, and which never leaves him. In that case the thought is apt to be so familiar to him that he hardly knows whether any particular words convey it or not. All words on the same subject convey it to his mind, and he is apt to expect that they will convey it to others. Especially when he has altered his own words—as in the course of nine or ten years a man well may, in a short poem, many times—he cannot say whether the thought is ade-

[1] *Recollections*. By Samuel Rogers. London: Longmans. 1859. This article was first published in the *Saturday Review* for August 6 1859, Volume VIII, pp. 166–7. Mrs. Russell Barrington attributes it to Bagehot in her biography (p. 272) but does not include it in her collected edition.

quately expressed or not. The very place in the poem calls up the idea to him; and any words at all near the mark which satisfy his ear are very apt to satisfy his mind. Accordingly, a student of the most celebrated poems of Mr. Rogers will discover many expressions out of which a patient elaboration has extracted the whole meaning, and many paragraphs of which the first flow has been destroyed by inter-polated thoughts and gradually modified ideas.

But however applicable the practice of very elaborate composition might be thought to be to the production of very exquisite poems, hardly any one, we should have imagined, would have fancied that it was applicable to memoirs and anecdotes. We might as well apply it to letter-writing. Who would like to receive compositions which had been days under cultivation, and which worthily conveyed the elabor-ate dullness of patient attention? We may like the schoolboy scrawl, but we are certain to dislike the meritorious theme. Accordingly, the great pains and labour which we are told that Mr. Rogers spent on these Memoirs have been very perniciously spent. He had exceedingly valuable materials. He was in the habit of more or less constant inter-course with the best society in London for about fifty years, and he entered in careful journals what he heard there. If he had confined his attention to setting down with distinctness and accuracy the substance of what occurred on the occasions which interested him the most, we could not have failed to have a work full of valuable in-formation, and exhibiting the sensitive taste, cool sense and refined cultivation which he indisputably possessed. We could have borne with some triviality, for much of it would probably have been charac-teristic of the times, and even more of it of the writer. Mr. Rogers has unfortunately adopted a very different course. Instead of telling us that he went to dine with Horne Tooke at such and such a time, that he had such and such a coat on, that he was amusing or not amusing, he has given us selected scraps of his conversation on very many different occasions. We have sets of such sayings as the follow-ing:—'Plays and Epic poems mislead us. A leader is often led. He has a thousand opinions to struggle with.—Pieces of money are so many tickets for sheep, oxen, &c.—When a pension is given or a salary, a draft is issued on the tiller of the soil.' Even if the sayings were in themselves happy, they would lose much of their interest from our not being told to whom they were said, before whom, and in what con-nexion; and when they have, as is the case with the dicta we have quoted, no intrinsic value at all, it is easy to imagine the folly of the labour which has separated them from all extrinsic sources of interest. We can conceive nothing duller than this book to a person who had never heard of Charles Fox, or Horne Tooke, or Lord Erskine. A reader who is familiar with their characters and their circumstances will occasionally, however, find something which is agreeable to him, because his imagination will enable him to supply the attendant circumstances and living details which Mr. Rogers spent some years in omitting.

Mr. Fox is one of the best known persons of whom Mr. Rogers recollected much, and many persons will therefore feel a slight interest in looking over the disconnected memoranda which he has left us. Sometimes the buoyancy and life of Mr. Fox's character almost prevail over the jejuneness of the reminiscent. We like to read the following of the great statesman:—'Very candid—Retracts instantly —Continually putting wood on the fire—His Trajan, his Venus, his Mosaics from Tivoli—His attachment to particular books—his common-place book—they keep a journal at home and abroad.' . . . 'When Francis said that Wilberforce, if it was left to him to decide whether Pitt should go out of office for ten months and the Slave-trade be abolished for ever, or Pitt remain in, with the Slave-trade, would decide for Pitt—"Yes," said Fox, "I'm afraid he would be for Barabbas." '

'After all, Burke was a damned wrong-headed fellow through life, always jealous and contradictory.' There is something of the simple emphasis of real conversation in these phrases—we feel that they were said. Mr. Rogers observes that his memorials of Mr. Fox show 'his playfulness, his love of letters, and his good nature in unbending himself to a young man.' There is no doubt that they do so; and if Mr. Rogers had told us the actual details of what happened, they would have shown these estimable qualities still more. Few statesmen have felt so ardent a love of letters as Fox—fewer still have recurred to them with the same fresh gaiety in the midst of a very unsuccessful political career. He thought poetry the 'great thing, after all,' and agreed with Burke that there was 'no truth'—no adequate representation, that is, of great subjects—elsewhere. His insensibility to the kindred art is in contrast curious:—'Mrs. Fox said the only fault she could find with him was his aversion to music. The utmost she could say for him was that he *could* read Homer, while she played and sung

165

to herself.' But we cannot say that the undress conversations of this volume will tend to raise the fame of Mr. Fox as a statesman. His situation in later life was singularly unfortunate for a person who had spent his earlier life as he did. He had passed a youth of fashionable excess qualified by fractious debating. From neither of these pursuits had he acquired—for in neither of them had he an opportunity of acquiring—a great store of political reflection. On these subjects, as he declared in the House of Commons, he sat at the feet of Mr. Burke. If he had been thrown, as Mr. Pitt was, among the details of office, there is considerable evidence that he would have mastered them with real vigour—thought upon them with fresh originality. But he had no such opportunity. The twenty years of his life in which his mind would have been most fit for such a task were passed in Opposition. His views, in consequence, were almost always defective—often singularly so for a man of his ability in his position. We do not dwell on his dislike of political economy, which is curiously shown in these *Recollections*. 'We knew nothing on that subject,' said Lord Lauderdale, 'before Adam Smith wrote.' 'Pooh,' says Fox, 'your Adam Smiths are nothing.' We have no right to complain of a statesman of even the end of the eighteenth century for not having given a real attention to the true theory of trade. Those who then did so deserve great praise, but those who were deficient in it scarcely merit great blame. Lord Derby said he was born in the 'prescientific period,' and Mr. Fox certainly was so. But the volume before us shows distinct traces of a very uncultivated mind on parts of politics which do not need so elaborate a treatment. Mr. Rogers heard him say—'I always say, and always think, that of all the countries in Europe, England will be the last to be free. Russia will be free before England. The Russians know no better, and knowledge might and would operate on them to good; but the English have the knowledge and the slavery too.' Of course such reflections are but childish absurdities.

The reminiscences of Horne Tooke, in Mr. Rogers's *Memorandum-book*, are likewise occasionally curious. His literal kind of wit—set off, as tradition recounts, by a courteous manner and by imperturbable coolness—is not ill shown in the following:—' "Power," said Lord ——— to Tooke, "should follow property." "Very well," he replied, "then we will take the property from you, and the power shall follow it." ' ... ' "Now, young man, as you are settled in town," said my uncle, "I would advise you to take a wife." "With all my heart, sir;

whose wife shall I take?" ' It is a trait of manners that the 'Rev. Mr. Horne' must have been a young clergyman at the time of this conversation; he did not, as is well known, take the name of Tooke till a later period. We have a trace, too, of his philological acuteness in Mr. Rogers's pages:—'An illiterate people is most tenacious of their language. In traffic the seller learns that of the buyer before the buyer learns his. A bull in the field, when brought to town and cut up in the market, becomes bœuf, beef; a calf, veal; a sheep, mouton; a pig, pork;—because there the Norman purchased, and the seller soon learnt *his* terms; while the peasantry retained their own.' It is not surprising that a sharp logical wit should be an acute interpreter of language.

If, as is generally thought, the general reader be a person of no information, we do not recommend him to read the disconnected scraps to which the punctilious care of Mr. Rogers has reduced his reminiscences; but any one who knows a little of the principal people who have appeared in England during the last sixty or seventy years will find something to interest him, though much less than he would have found if the same materials had been used more freely and more naturally.

Emily Eden
Introductory note

Emily Eden (1797–1869) was the seventh daughter of William Eden, first Baron Auckland, and was born at Westminster in 1797. She accompanied her brother George Eden to India, and remained with him there during his term as governor-general from 1835–42. She wrote about this period on her return. She then published *The Semi-Detached House*, 1859 and later *The Semi-Attached Couple*. Emily Eden's name did not appear on the title-page of the first novel, which was advertised as being edited by Lady Teresa Lewis, a life-long friend of Emily Eden. Both novels had a considerable sale. Emily Eden died at Richmond, Surrey, in 1869.

The Semi-Detached House[1]

ALTHOUGH this is not exactly a novel with a dogma, it is a novel with a notion. The notion is that we ought not to dislike to live in a semi-detached house. 'Oh, Aunt Sarah,' exclaims one of the ladies in the first page, 'you don't mean that you expect me to live in a semi-detached house.'—'Why not, my dear, if it suits you in other respects?' —'Why, because I should hate my semi-detachment, or whatever the occupants of the other half may call themselves.'—'They call themselves Hopkinson,' continued Aunt Sarah, coolly.—'I knew it,' said Blanche triumphantly, 'I felt certain their names would be either Tomkinson or Hopkinson. . . . Did you see any of the Hopkinsons when you went to look at the house?'—'Yes, they went in at their door just as I went in at yours. The mother, as I suppose, and two daughters, and a little boy.'—'Oh dear me! a little boy, who will always be throwing stones at the palings, and making me jump; daughters who will be always playing "Partant pour la Syrie;" and the mother'—'Well, what will she do to offend your Highness?'—'She will be immensely fat, wear mittens, thick, heavy mittens, and contrive to know what I have for dinner every day.'

The lady who objects to the 'semi-detachment' is a certain Lady Chester, and the book is to teach us that she ought not to object. Mrs. Hopkinson does turn out to be fat, but also turns out to be very sensible, good-humoured, and obliging, to have two nice daughters, and to be capable of giving wise counsel on the management of the kitchen chimney. The purpose of the book, in so far as it has a purpose, is to teach us that we should take life easily and frankly—associate with the people whom chance throws in our way, if they seem sensible and pleasant—that we should not be too much pleased at speaking to persons of superior rank, nor too anxious to avoid those who may be below us. Our readers will say that, after all, this is not very new,

[1] *The Semi-Detached House*. Edited by Lady Teresa Lewis. London: Bentley. 1859. This article was first published in the *Saturday Review* for August 27 1859, Volume VIII, pp. 261–2. Mrs. Russell Barrington attributes it to Bagehot in her biography but does not include it in her collected edition.

and it certainly is not. But it is a great achievement to teach an old lesson in an enlivening way, and this is a lesson which it is rather difficult to teach with perfect good taste. Mr. Thackeray, for example, has been teaching it with consummate ability for many years; but perhaps he makes too much of it. We fancy he considers it both more difficult and more important than it really is. He a little overrates the intensity of the snobbish propensities—he dwells on them almost sympathizingly. A certain dean of a departed generation cautioned his hearers against 'That besetting liquor, old port wine, by which even some of our clergy have been led astray.' In a somewhat similar spirit our great satirist warns us that no literary ability, no fame, no mental power is an effectual protection against the desire to speak to Dukes. Wherever he looks through the world, this is the desire he perceives. The insidious temptation creeps into all hearts, and injures wherever it enters. We own that we think this an exceedingly exaggerated kind of teaching. The snobbish desires undoubtedly exist, and are diffused most widely; but it is only in rare cases that they are extremely powerful. They would take most people a little way, but very few people a great way. Mr. Thackeray, too, we think, fancies his lesson too important. Like all missionaries, he intensifies the evil against which he is preaching. Many people who do care too much about the great, and who are too much afraid of talking to those below them, are nevertheless very good people. They have their fault, as others have theirs; but for all that their nature may in the main be sound, and their capacity for substantial excellence may in most of its parts not be much impaired. Snobbishness is an insidious endemic, but it is rarely a mortal malady. We can scarcely perhaps give the *Semi-Detached House* a higher sort of praise than that it teaches Mr. Thackeray's peculiar doctrine in a healthier and better way than he does. The two varieties of snobbishness—that of running from our inferiors and that of making up to our superiors—both occur pretty often in this book, and both are laughed at. They are allowed to be venial sins, but it is shown that they are ludicrous—that they interfere with the tranquillity of life and with the chances of enjoyment that turn up in it—that sensible persons, whatever their rank may be, laugh at them. Of course there is nothing new in the lesson; but there is a good-natured contempt in the way it is given that is telling. We can fancy it curing, or half-curing, the vice. Mr. Thackeray, we fear, only teaches people to hide the indications of it.

A novel of this sort necessarily has its scene in the middle rank of social life—with some people who are lords and ladies and some who are neither; and it has the sort of merits which such a novel may be expected to have. The dialogue is very good, very witty and buoyant— jolly, though yet ladylike. The events are the ordinary ones of social life. Two families live in the two halves of one house, and are naturally thrown together; and as one is of rank, and the other by no means of rank, the scenes can be made amusing. The lady of no rank fancies, moreover, that the lady of rank is not all which she should be, and this is made amusing too. The authoress has one peculiarity which is invaluable to a painter of common social life—she has a genius for middle-aged women. For obvious reasons young people are made more prominent in novels than they are in reality. Perhaps the discovery of this is one of the sorest disappointments of early life. Young people come out with romantic notions of various sorts, and it is disappointing to find middle-aged people with the influence which they in fact have. As to men, it does not seem to matter so much; they have occupations, and briefs, and offices, which seem to explain it. But that the social half of life should be subject to the administrative vivacity of ladies with historical complexions is for a time a trial. A novel like the *Semi-Detached House*, which brings out this fact, and shows how far the middle-aged *régime* may be made tolerable, is instructive.

There are two middle-aged women in this book—one good and the other bad, but both fat and both energetic. We may give a specimen of the conversation of the former:—

'Ah, there they are,' said Mrs. Hopkinson, jumping up in a fright. 'Oh, John, what shall we do? I knew they would come to us in our turn.'

'Who would come, Jane?' said Captain Hopkinson, who was half asleep.

'Why, the burglars, of course! What will become of us! Where's my purse? I always keep a purse ready to give them, it makes them so good-humoured. Oh, dear, what a noise they make, and they will be quite savage if they are kept waiting,' she said, as another violent ringing was heard. 'John, John, you must not go down to them; they will knock you down. Let me go.'

'I don't see,' said John, laughing, 'why I am to let you go and be knocked down instead of me. But, my dear, there is no danger; burglars do not come and ring the bell and ask to be let in like a morning visitor. It must be the policeman.'

'Ah, poor man! I dare say with his head knocked to pieces with a life-preserver, and all over kicks and bites. But, perhaps, he is only come to tell us the house is on fire,' said Mrs. Hopkinson, with a sudden accession of cheerfulness. 'I should not mind that, anything is better than robbers. Oh, John, now don't put your head out so far, those ticket-of-leave men fire in all directions. And do keep calling out Thomas and John, and I will answer in a gruff voice,' said poor Mrs. Hopkinson, who was so terrified her whisper could scarcely be heard.

'My dear,' said John, withdrawing his head, 'there is nothing to be alarmed at. It is Lord Chester; Lady Chester is taken ill, and he wants you to go to her.'

'And so that is all,' said Mrs. Hopkinson, instantly beginning to dress. 'Ah, poor soul, of course I will. Well, now, this is neighbourly of them, and I take it very kindly their sending for me. Why, they are two babies themselves, and they can't know what to do with a third.'

The snobbish fat lady is a certain Baroness Sampson, the wife of a certain Jewish *millionaire* in the City, who is discovered at the end of the book not to be a *millionaire*, and decamps. This lady is not, indeed, asked to the Queen's balls, but intends to bring her Majesty 'to her senses next year,' and lives upon that pretension in the mean time. That she pretends to know persons whom she has never seen, and is very anxious to know people who will upon no account know her, it is not necessary for us to relate.

One defect of the lesson not to object to a 'semi-detached house' is that it will not make a plot of itself. The authoress of the book, wishing to have a plot, like other novelists, has been obliged to annex one from other sources. She has not, however, thought it worth while to look out for a complicated one. The hero is a certain man named Willis, who has lost his wife, and trades on his disconsolateness ever after. He really makes a great deal of it in general society. Much attention is paid him by way of relief, and the minor comforts of life are constantly offered to him by way of compensation. These, however, he resists, and perseveres in his unconquerable depression, naturally feeling that while it obtained him so many pleasant things it would be foolish to relinquish it. There is one pursuit in life in which a conspicuous grief for a deceased wife is likely to be rather an incumbrance than a help—and that is, the wooing of a second. In Mr. Willis's case the difficulty is increased by his having selected a matter-of-fact young lady who works out her ideas with unusual distinctness. 'Either,' she says to Mr. Willis, 'you do not still care for your late wife, for whom you are in the deepest mourning, or you do not care for me. If you like me, leave off your mourning; if you must keep your mourning, leave me alone. Either your love is false or your grief is false; please make your selection.' Mr. Willis is logician enough to feel the force of this reasoning, and ceases to be disconsolate.

We do not know whether such a plot was intended to be anything; but it is nothing. No art could spin much out of so slight a material. Besides, the moment Mr. Willis ceases to be mournful, he ceases to be anything. He has, in other respects, no more character than the mute in a funeral. He displays all through the book one trait, and one only. The moment he loses that, he vanishes in our fancy entirely. As this is the case, we need not say that the merit of the book does not lie in the story, but in its sparkling dialogue, its good subsidiary characters, and its cheerful and habitual good sense.

Tennyson's Idylls
Introductory note

This essay, which appeared in the *National Review* for October 1859 has never before been included in any edition of Bagehot's works. My attention was first drawn to the essay by Dr. Robert Tener who attributed it to Bagehot in a letter to the *Times Literary Supplement* of August 21 1959. In my opinion the evidence for Bagehot's authorship is overwhelming and I have no doubt that the essay came from his pen. Bagehot was, of course, an editor of the *National Review* from 1855 to 1864, and often wrote for it, so that it would be a natural place for an essay to be published by him.

A major piece of evidence in favour of Bagehot's authorship is the following passage: 'In our last Number we had occasion, in writing on another subject, to draw out at some length the delineation of the two kinds of *goodness* which have long been contrasted, and always seem likely to be contrasted, in the world,—the ascetic and the sensuous' (p. 383).[1] This is an allusion to Bagehot's essay on Milton which appeared in the *National Review* for July 1859 (IX: 150–86). At pages 155–7 this essay discusses the two forms of goodness, a discussion which includes these words: 'There are two kinds of goodness conspicuous in the world, and often made the subject of contrast there; for which, however, we seem to want exact words, and which we are obliged to describe rather vaguely and incompletely. These characters may in one aspect be called the sensuous and the ascetic . . . .' In both essays the author develops the theme in a very similar manner.

This is strong evidence of Bagehot's authorship but it does not stand alone. The comparisons of Tennyson with Shelley and Keats and to a lesser extent with Wordsworth and Milton are typical of Bagehot. So is the remark that Caxton's defence of King Arthur's historical authenticity 'would hardly satisfy Sir G. C. Lewis or Mr. Grote.' (p. 373.) Sir George Cornewall Lewis was a close friend of Bagehot's and Bagehot admired him greatly.

[1] Page references are to the *National Review* in the case of *Tennyson's Idylls*, others are to this edition.

Bagehot's idiosyncratic sense of humour is also found in the essay. Commenting on the idealising of medieval life in chivalric literature the author writes: 'If King Arthur existed, there were peasants in his time and these peasants had wives, and these wives had children, and these children had measles; but no one wishes to hear of the peasants, the wives, or the babies, but of Queen Guinevere and Lancelot, of the king himself, and all the "Table Round".' (p. 375.) Again, when the author is discussing love at first sight as being more 'rational' in the age of chivalry, there is a typically Bagehotian flavour: 'It came under the precept, "use your opportunities". Unless you became enamoured at a first view, you might never be so,—you might never get a second.' (p. 377.) When comparing Shelley and Keats for their sustained faculty of lyrical expression the author again shows a gleam of Bagehotian fun: 'They seem hurried into song; and, what is more, kept there when they have been hurried there. Shelley's *Skylark* is the most familiar example of this. A rather young musician was once asked, what was Jenny Lynd's charm in singing. "Oh," he replied, "she went up so high, and staid up high so long." ' (p. 388.)

Another trace of Bagehot's style is found in a passage where he makes the point that poetry principally influences young men and that this is especially true of Tennyson's poetry: 'His audience formerly consisted entirely of young men of cultivated tastes and susceptible imaginations; and it was so because his poetry contained most of the elements which are suitable to such persons in a country like England, and an age such as this is.' (p. 371.) This may be compared with the closing paragraph of *The English Constitution*: 'I do not count as an anomaly the existence of our double government, with all its infinite accidents, though half the superficial peculiarities that are often complained of arise out of it. The co-existence of a Queen's seeming prerogative and Downing Street's real government is just suited to such a country as this, in such an age as our's.'

The author of *Tennyson's Idylls* includes the following passage in the essay: 'The English mind, which like its great philosophers, likes to work upon 'stuff', is more pleased with general chivalric pictures than with chiselled phantoms and intense lyrics.' (p. 389.) This may be compared with the passage in Bagehot's essay on Scott where he writes: 'Above all minds his had the Baconian propensity to work upon stuff.' Volume II, p. 67.

When the author is discussing the dangers of *Maud*'s appealing to youth, a period when feeling is semi-diseased, he quotes from Keats' preface to *Endymion*. 'Keats, who knew much about such matters, remarked this. "The imagination," he said, "of a man is healthy, and the imagination of a boy is healthy; but between" there is an uncertain time, when the fancy is restless, the principles are unfixed, the sentiments waver, and the highest feelings have not acquired consistency.' (p. 372.) Bagehot quotes the same passage in his essay on Hartley Coleridge (1852), Volume I, p. 151. Again the misquotation of Milton's *L'Allegro* (p. 371) is the same in this essay as in Bagehot's *Milton* (1859), Volume II, p. 111. I have corrected both.

Finally it is worth noting that the author of the essay states: 'Everybody admires Tennyson now; but to admire him fifteen years or so ago was to be a "Tennysonian"' (pp. 369–70). As Saintsbury has pointed out, Bagehot was one of the first to recognise Browning and Tennyson as 'among the leaders of mid-nineteenth century poetry.'[2]

Since assembling the internal evidence for Bagehot's authorship new and conclusive external evidence has come to light to show that this essay is indeed by Bagehot. I have in my possession the diary of Eliza Bagehot for 1859, kindly given to me by the late Colonel Noël Halsey, a descendant of the Wilson family through his mother who was one of Eliza Bagehot's (*née* Wilson) five sisters. On September 2 1859 there is the following entry: 'Walter stayed at home all day and began his article on Tennyson's *Idylls of the King* for next *National*.' On September 8 and September 10 there are further references to Walter's working on the article. On September 18 we find 'Walter wrote to nearly end of *Idylls*' and on September 19 'Walter took holiday being the last day he could be at Claverton and finished his article.' The evidence for Bagehot's authorship is thus overwhelming.

Alfred Lord Tennyson

Alfred Tennyson (1809–1892) was the son of the Rev. George Tennyson, vicar of Somersby in Lincolnshire. He was educated principally by his father, and at Trinity College, Cambridge, where he first met

[2] See *A History of English Criticism*. Edinburgh, 1911, p. 496.

Arthur Hallam. He published *Poems, Chiefly Lyrical*, 1830, and a further volume, *Poems*, 1833. These were scathingly reviewed, and he published no more until his poems began to appear in magazines some years later. A two-volume collection appeared in 1842, containing *Morte d'Arthur, Locksley Hall*, and *Ulysses*; his fame, though not yet his popularity began to be established. He published *The Princess*, 1847, and in 1850 *In Memoriam*, which he had begun in 1833 on the death of his friend Hallam. He became Poet Laureate in 1850, in succession to Wordsworth. He published *Maud*, 1855, and in 1859 four *Idylls of The King*, which established his fame and popularity. Tennyson was made a peer in 1884.

Tennyson's Idylls[1]

IT is a hardship on quarterly reviewers that good books should be published at the beginning of a quarter. Before the next number of the Review appears, they are scarcely new books at all. Everything which need be, or ought to be, perhaps everything which can be said, has been said. Doubtless the best remarks are forestalled. Yet what is to be done? A critical journal, which hopes to influence the taste of its time, must not omit to notice any remarkable books. When they are so attractive as the *Idylls of the King*, what critic can neglect a chance of reviewing them? Although, therefore, the last poem of Mr. Tennyson has already been some time before the public, and much has already been written about it, we must devote a few words to the delineation of its peculiarities.

The *Idylls of the King* is, we think, more popular with the general public than with Mr. Tennyson's straiter disciples. It is the characteristic—in some cases it is the calamity—of every great and peculiar poet, to create for himself a school of readers. Wordsworth did so during the first twenty years of the century. For the whole of that time, and perhaps for some years longer, his works could scarcely be said to belong to general English literature: the multitude did not read them. Some of the acutest of those who gave away reputation in those days laughed at them. But a secret worship was all the while forming itself; a sect accumulated. If you read the reviews of that time, you will find that the Wordsworthians were considered a kind of Quakers in literature, that rejected finery, disliked ornate art, and preferred a 'thee and thou' simplicity in poetry. Some of the defects of Wordsworth's poems may be in part traced to the narrowing influence of this species of readers. Even the greatest artist thinks sometimes of his peculiar public. The more solitary his life is, the more he broods on it. The more rejected he is by the multitude, the more he thinks of his few disciples. It is scarcely conceivable that such a habit

[1] *Idylls of the King*. By Alfred Tennyson. London, Moxon and Co. 1859. This essay was first published in the *National Review* for October 1859, Volume IX, pp. 368–94.

should not narrow the mind and straiten the sympathies. The class of persons who are the first to take up a very peculiar writer, are themselves commonly somewhat peculiar. 'I am not sure of missionaries,' said some one; 'but I detest converts.' The first believers in anything are rarely good critics of it. The first enthusiasts for a great poet are heedless in their faith; a fault in their idol is like a fault in themselves: they have to defend him in discussion, and in consequence they come to admire the most those parts of his poems which are attacked most frequently: they have a logical theory in defence of them, and are attached to the instances that show its ingenuity and that exemplify its nature: in short, they admire, not what is best in the great writer, but what is most characteristic of him; they incite him to display his eccentricities and to develop his peculiarities. 'Beware of thy friends,' says the oriental proverb; 'for affection is but the flattery of the soul.' Many of Wordsworth's best poems would have been better if he had been more on his guard against the misleading influence of a sectarian sympathy. A few years ago Mr. Tennyson was in a rather similar position. We should not like to specify the date of his ratified acceptance by the public at large; but it is indisputable that at one time he was not so accepted. Everybody admires Tennyson now; but to admire him fifteen years or so ago, was to be a 'Tennysonian.' We know what the *Quarterly* said of his first volume, and the feeling there indicated lingered a long time in many quarters. He has now vanquished it; but an observant eye may still detect in literary, and still more in semi-literary society, several differences in taste and in feeling between the few disciples of the early school and the numerous race of new admirers.

Perhaps the first Tennysonians were not among the wisest of men,— at least they were not taken from the class which is apt to be the wisest. The early poetry of Mr. Tennyson—and the same may be said of nearly all the poetry of Shelley and Keats—labours under the defect that it is written, almost professedly, for young people—especially young men—of rather heated imaginations. All poetry, or almost all poetry, finds its way more easily to the brains of young men, who are at once intellectual and excitable, than to those of men of any other kind. Persons engaged in life have rarely leisure for imaginative enjoyment: the briefs, the sums, the politics intervene. Slowly, even in the case of young men, does the influence of a new poet enter into the mind; you hear the snatch of a stanza here; you see an extract in a periodical; you get the book and read it; you are pleased with it, but you do not know whether the feeling will last. It is the habitual pleasure that such works give which alone is the exact criterion of their excellence. But what number of occupied men read new poetry habitually? What number of them really surrender their minds to the long task of gradually conceiving new forms of imagery, to the even more delicate task of detecting the healthiness or unhealthiness of unfamiliar states of feeling? Almost all poetry, in consequence, is addressed more to young men than to others. But the early poetry of Tennyson, and of the other poets we have named, is addressed to that class even more peculiarly. In the greatest poets, in Shakespeare and in Homer, there is a great deal besides poetry. There are broad descriptions of character, dramatic scenes, eloquence, argument, a deep knowledge of manly and busy life. These interest readers who are no longer young; they refer to the world in which almost all of us have to act; they reflect with the strong light of genius the scenes of life in which the mass of men live and move. By the aid of these extraneous elements, the poetry of these great writers reaches and impresses those who would never be attracted by it in itself, or take the pains to understand it if it had been presented to them alone. Shelley and Keats, on the other hand, have presented their poetry to the world in its pure essence; they have not added—we scarcely know whether they would have been able to add—the more worldly and terrestrial elements; probably their range in the use of these would have been but limited; at any rate, they have not tried—parts of Shelley's *Cenci* perhaps excepted—to use them; they have been content to rely on imaginatively expressed sentiment, and sentiment-exciting imagery; in short, on that which in its more subtle sense we call poetry, exclusively and wholly. In consequence, their works have had a great influence on young men; they retain a hold on many mature men only because they are associated with their youth; they delineate

> Such sights as youthful poets dream
> On summer eves by haunted stream:

and young men, who were not poets, have eagerly read them, have fondly learned them, and have long remembered them.—A good deal of this description applies to the writings of Tennyson,—some years ago we should have said that almost the whole of it was applicable to him. His audience formerly consisted entirely of young men of cultivated tastes and susceptible imaginations; and it was so because his poetry contained most of the elements which are suitable to such persons in a country like England, and an age such as this is. But whatever be the cause,—whether or not our analysis of the ingredients in Mr. Tennyson's poetry which attracted young men of this kind be correct or otherwise,—the fact that it did so attract them, and that it attracted but few others with great force, is very certain. His public was limited and peculiar; it was almost as much so as Wordsworth's was at an earlier time.

When Mr. Tennyson published *Maud*, we feared that the influence of this class of admirers was deteriorating his powers. The subject was calculated to call out the unhealthier sort of youthful imaginations; and his treatment of it, so far from lessening the danger, seemed studiously selected to increase it. The hero of *Maud* is a young man who lives very much out of the world, who has no definite duties or intelligible occupations, who hates society because he is bound by no social ties and is conscious of no social courage. This young gentleman sees a young lady who is rich, and whose father has an unpleasant association with his own father, who was a bankrupt. He has all manner of feelings about the young lady, and she is partial to him; but there is a difficulty about their interviews. As he is poor and she is wealthy, they do not meet in common society; and a stolen visit in her garden ends, if we understand the matter, in his killing her brother. After this he leads a wandering life, and expresses his sentiments. Such a story is evidently very likely to bring into prominence the exaggerated feelings and distorted notions which we call unhealthy. The feelings of a young man who has nothing to do, and tries to do nothing; who is very poor, and regrets that he is not very rich; who is in love, and cannot speak to the lady he loves; who knows he cannot marry her, but notwithstanding wanders vaguely about her,—are sure to be unhealthy. Solitude, social mortification, wounded feeling, are the strongest sources of mental malaria; and all of these are here crowded together, and are conceived to act at once. Such a representation, therefore, if it was to be true, must be partially tinctured with unhealthiness. This was inevitable; and it was inevitable, too, that this taint should be rather agreeable than otherwise to many of the poet's warmest admirers. The Tennysonians, as we have said, were young men; and youth is the season of semi-diseased feeling. Keats, who knew much about such matters, remarked this. 'The imagination,' he said, 'of a man is healthy, and the imagination of a boy is healthy; but between' there is an uncertain time, when the fancy is restless, the principles are unfixed, the sentiments waver, and the highest feelings have not acquired consistency. Upon young men in such a frame of mind a delineation like that of the hero of *Maud*, adorned, as it was, with rare fragments of beautiful imagery, and abiding snatches of the sweetest music, could not but be attractive, and could not but be dangerous. It seemed to be the realised ideal of their hopes, of their hearts, of themselves; it half consecrated their characteristic defects, it confirmed their hope that their eccentricities were excellencies. Such a danger could not be avoided; but Mr. Tennyson, so far from trying to shun it, seemed intentionally to choose to aggravate it. He seemed to sympathise with the feverish railings, the moody nonsense, the very entangled philosophy, which he put into the mouth of his hero. There were some odd invectives against peace, against industry, against making your livelihood, which seemed by no means to be dramatic exhibitions of represented character, but, on the contrary, confidential expositions of the poet's own belief. He not only depicted the natural sentiments of an inactive, inexperienced, and neglected young man, but seemed to agree with them. He sympathised with moody longings; he was not severe on melancholy vanity; he rather encouraged a general disaffection to the universe. He appeared not only to have written, but to have accepted the 'Gospel according to the Unappreciated.' The most charitable reader could scarcely help fancying, that in describing an irritable confusion of fancy and a diseased moodiness of feeling, the poet for the time imbibed a certain taint of those defects.

The *Idylls of the King* suggest to us a peculiar doubt. Was not Mr. Tennyson, after all, laughing at his admirers? *Did* he believe in *Maud*, though he seemed to say he did? We do not know; but at all events we have now a poem not only of a different, but of the very opposite kind. Every line of it is defined with the delicate grace of a very composed genius; shows the trace of a very mature judgment; will bear the scrutiny of the most choice and detective taste. The feelings are natural, the thoughts such as people in life have or might have. The situations, though in a certain sense unnatural, have, we believe, a peculiar artistic propriety. There is a completeness in the whole.

> For when the Roman left us, and their law
> Relax'd its hold upon us, and the ways

Were fill'd with rapine, here and there a deed
Of prowess done redress'd a random wrong.
But I was first of all the kings who drew
The knighthood-errant of this realm and all
The realms together under me, their Head,
In that fair Order of my Table Round,
A glorious company, the flower of men,
To serve as model for the mighty world,
And be the fair beginning of a time.

The general public will like this, but scarcely the youthful admirers of broken art and incomplete beauties who accepted *Maud* with great delight. The world we know is opposed to earnest enthusiasts and fond disciples, and Mr. Tennyson has sided with the world.

We think that it is no chance which has made several of our poets dream of a poem on King Arthur. The story of that monarch became *par excellence the* legend of chivalry. Nothing, indeed, can be much stranger than that it should have done so. There is no evidence that such a king ever existed; and the fact has very long been questioned. Caxton, who first printed *La Mort d'Arthure* in English, relates a conversation which he either had, or feigned himself to have had, with a lover of chivalric literature, who advised the printing: 'To whom,' he says, 'I answered that dyvers men hold opinion that there was no such Arthur, and that all such books as been made of him, been but fayned and fables, because that some chronicles make of him no mention, nor remember him nothing nor of his knyhts.' And the argument in reply would hardly satisfy Sir G. C. Lewis or Mr. Grote. 'First, ye may see his sepulture in the monasterye of Glastynburye;' and next, his name, 'Patricius Arthurus, Britanniæ, Galliæ, Germaniæ, Daciæ imperator,' on Saint Edward's shrine in Westminster Abbey; also, 'Gauvayn's skull and Cradok's mantel,' at Dover; 'at Winchester, the round table; and in other places, Launcelotte's sword, and many other things.' It was a touching theory of ancient credulity, that relics prove the existence of the hero to whom it is said that they belonged. The scrupulous modern doctrine, as we know, is that they must first *prove themselves.* Even when we are certain that the hero existed, it must likewise be shown by connected links of evidence that the alleged relics—the sword or the skull—ever belonged to him. However, most people in former ages believed otherwise; 'the bricks' continued 'to testify' not only to the existence of the bricklayer, but also to his name and his lineage; the non-existent King Arthur was accepted as the hero of chivalry, the model of its excellence, and the incarnation of its virtues. Yet even admitting his existence, the conception of him was peculiarly fanciful. If Arthur ever existed, he was a British king, who resisted the northern invaders. Knighthood was the undesigned development of the feudal system—of that system which the northern conquerors of modern Europe invented, and imposed on its half-romanised inhabitants. Even in legendary history, which is naturally the most singular of histories, scarcely anything is more singular than that the hero of knighthood, the traditional model of chivalric virtues, should have been a romanised Briton, whose very name seems to have come from Britanny; whose whole character, if he had been a real person, must have been cast in a very different mould; whose exploits were alleged to have been performed over the northern hordes, but for whose victory chivalry would never have existed; who could never have comprehended the graces assigned to him, who would have lamented the barrenness of his victories, and grieved at the downfall of his race. Yet such was the case. It did not matter that the hero of the conquerors was of the race of the conquered. A literature was required to be the expression of the chivalric imagination; minstrels sang it; chroniclers wrote it. And when the conditions of knightly life were passing away with the decay of the feudal institutions, its ideal was prized more. The feeling that all trace of it was departing, that its possibility was ceasing, that a new world of tamer life and fainter features was coming in, gave to the literary embodiments of the chivalrous ideal a saddened charm, a melancholy refinement, which they had not in themselves. It is not easy to read *The History of King Arthur* now, yet it was once a treasured volume; and the French book from which it was translated was, as was natural in 'knightly France,' treasured still more.

Yet when we come to examine the chivalric romance, we shall find that, though dull and tedious in its actual form, it contains many elements of great artistic value; that, though it can never again be popular itself, something more than accident has attracted our poets to it. Leibnitz spoke of the medieval philosophy as the least agreeable of out-of-door heaps; but he added, 'there is gold in it.' We will not dare to imitate the grave coarseness of the philosophic style; but we will say, that it was the real gold of a genuine poetic interest which has attracted Milton and Dryden, and now another poet, to medieval romance.

The value of the subject lies, if we may be allowed the expression, in its supernaturalness. Poets are frequently advised to make choice of modern subjects: it is said that ancient ones are worn out; that all which can correctly be said of them has been said; that a new world, with ardent life, and tender grace, and bold energy, is around us; that in it we should seek the topics of our art, and especially the themes of our poetry. Yet the practice of our poets does not as yet conform itself much to the teaching of this criticism. They seem to have, or to believe they have, a restraining instinct which disinclines them to act on the exhortation; they undoubtedly have an impelling tendency which incites them to select their subjects from the older world. One of our poets has said, in answer to the critics, 'a great action' is a great action anywhere; surely it is as good if it happened in former ages as if it had happened yesterday. And unquestionably this is so; yet it only amounts, after all, to a claim of equality for the older poetic subjects, it does not justify the distinct preference which the practice of poets seems to give to them.

We believe the reason of that preference to be, that in describing the ancient life it is easy to select, and it is admissible to exaggerate. The chivalrous legend is in itself both a selection and an exaggeration. A few parts of life are chosen out of many, and those few are heightened in colour and augmented in size. *Ivanhoe* is an illustration of this which everyone can understand. Scott was fond of the old chivalric life, and he told stories of it as a sagacious man of this modern world would tell them. He describes it as, in the first place, a fighting period; and in the next place, a falling-in-love period. We rise from the romance with the idea that some centuries ago there were black horses, and large lances, knights in armour, and beautiful ladies: and that there was little else. These elements of life are already selected in the traditional imagination; in speaking of those times we gratify a preconceived idea in speaking of these elements and of these only. We need not apologise for our choice; on the contrary, we should jar upon latent anticipations if we extended our range, or if we chose differently. If King Arthur existed, there were peasants in his time, and these peasants had wives, and these wives had children, and these children had measles; but no one wishes to hear of the peasants, the wives, or the babies, but of Queen Guinevere and Lancelot, of the king himself, and all the 'Table Round.' In the modern world it is different, everything runs into everything else; every detail suggests an approximate

186

detail; every fact another fact. We see this in the appropriate description of modern life, the modern novel. No form of art has perhaps ever existed in which the detail of ordinary existence has been used with such copiousness,—in crude hands doubtless with absurd prolixity, but in the hands of the greater artists—in those, for instance, of Mr. Thackeray—with a sort of defined abundance, and the restrained tact of measured fertility. 'The novelist,' our satirist tells us, 'knows everything;' and he certainly knows all the little facts, the trivial details, the 'knives and forks' of ordinary life. But how few of these details are fit for poetry! how few of them are consistent with its sustained tone! how few would not jar upon its characteristic associations! how many would mar its effect! We are not, we own, of any formal school in poetry; we do not, as certain French critics, object to the 'mouse stirring' of the dramatist. We only mean to say, that all the facts of a life with which we are familiar have a hundred associations—that in sustained and high poetry any one of these might have an unintended influence and a disenchanting effect. In ancient life such details are few, and those few have been sifted by a sort of legendary tradition; by the testing imagination of ages of story-tellers and story-hearers.

We have said that the traditional conception of the age of medieval chivalry is that of a fighting period, and of a falling-in-love period. If we consider the peculiar nature of these pursuits, and the peculiar mode in which we are accustomed to believe that they then existed, we shall understand their artistic value. It will be conceded that these two pursuits present human nature in what to most people is its most interesting aspect. How many people read the account of a war when it is brought to them in the newspaper, who read nothing else there! how few in proportion care for a debate in parliament, the great labours of the Chancellor of the Exchequer, or the ordinary administration of peaceful existence! Still more of love-stories we need not speak; it does not need critical ink to prove that *they* are perused. All kinds of war and all kinds of love are for ever attractive. But if we consider the form in which these pursuits appear in the chivalric legend, it will be found to be in both cases that which is most striking to the unsophisticated imagination. Without having recourse needlessly to deep metaphysics, it may be said that the imagination is more strongly impressed by strong qualities and strong passions that are vividly displayed, than by less intense elements less vividly displayed. Now the love-making in the time of chivalry was not the matter of detail

187

that it is now—women lived in comparative seclusion; their intercourse with men was rare, was not very familiar, and was scarcely at all intellectual. Under these circumstances falling in love at first sight was rather rational than otherwise. It came under the precept, 'use your opportunities.' Unless you became enamoured at a first view, you might never be so,—you might never get a second. Intellectual calculation would therefore not forbid the practice, and there was much else to encourage it; wherever ladies are much secluded, it will always be common enough. Mr. Meadows has an anecdote in his book on China, which is, he says, authentic.

'A Chinese, who had experienced bitter disenchantments in marriage, and suffered grievously through women in many other ways,—and who, in consequence, considered them simply as unmitigated sources of trouble and mischief,—retired with his infant son to the peaks of a mountain range in Kwei chow, to a spot quite inaccessible for little-footed Chinese women; through whom he was resolved that his son should never experience similar miseries. He trained up the youth to worship the gods, and stand in awe and abhorrence of devils; but he never mentioned woman to him, and always descended the mountains alone to buy food. The infirmities of age, however, at length compelled him to take the young man with him, to carry the heavy bag of rice. But he very reasonably argued: "I shall always accompany my son, and take care that if he does see a woman by chance, he shall never speak to one; he is very obedient; he has never heard of women; he does not know what they are; and as he has lived in that way for twenty years already, he is, of course, now pretty safe."

'As they were, on the first occasion, leaving the market-town together, the son suddenly stopped short, and, pointing to three approaching objects, inquired: "Father, what are these things? Look! look! what are they?" The father hastily answered with the peremptory order: "Turn away your head: they are devils." The son, in some alarm, instantly turned away from things so bad, and which were gazing at his motions with surprise from under their fans. He walked to the mountain top in silence, ate no supper, and from that day lost his appetite and was afflicted with melancholy. For some time his anxious and puzzled parent could get no satisfactory answer to his inquiries; but at length the poor young man burst out, almost crying from an inexplicable pain, "Oh, father, that tallest devil! that tallest devil, father!"

'He had idealised the first objective reality he met with, and had "fallen deeply in love at first sight." '

We need not stay to prove that such a mode of becoming enamoured is more striking to the imagination than our quieter modern mode. The suddenness, the violence, the painfulness, of the olden mode are evidently impressive.—Something of the same qualities may be observed in the antique mode of fighting. The interest in modern military operations is curiously divided. The scene is this: We have an intellectual general, calculating, arranging, combining, taxing all the forces of a superior intellect, skilful in tactics, abounding in ingenuity; we have likewise a body of soldiery, excelling in daring, quick in attack, steady in defence, organised into a machine. Here are two sources of interest, the mind and the fighting: but the mind does not fight; and that which fights is hardly mind. The general is removed from the conflict, and the regiments which he sends do not come home to our fancies as human beings; they seem rather to be implements and organisations. We can scarcely realise the complex combat. Our interest in it, even in as far as we imagine it, is lost in the multitude of the combatants, and the scientific framework which the devising mind has planned out for them. We never see, we never hope to see, a mind, which is great both in itself and in its position, which is the leading mind of the scene,—in real danger, confronting evident perils, overcoming visible foes. In old times it was otherwise. The characters, the real prominent characters of a fiction, can be made to fight. We know how Richard I. fights in *Ivanhoe*. Dr. Johnson, in the *Life of Addison*, has scoffed at the old style of describing battles, in which Marlborough was made to win Blenheim by his personal prowess, and he and Eugene were supposed to contend with the French marshals hand to hand. His literal mind was shocked at the unreality of the delineation; he saw its untruth, and could not but laugh at its impossibility: but he has not marked, and probably did not see, that in early times, and as long as it was true, this delineation had the merit of concentrating the interest derived from intellect and the interest derived from courage in a single spot; and that no more faithful representation of a modern battle, except in most exceptional cases, does or can do so.

These illustrations are far from exhausting the subject; but they are enough for our purpose. They show, we think, that the events of the chivalric legend are better adapted to sustained and prolonged poetry than the events of recent times and of the present day; and that they are so because they abound much less in dangerous detail, are confined to selected events and chosen characters, show us human passions in a more vivid form, present human actions in a more easily intelligible shape, give us a sort of large-hand copy of life which it is comparatively easy to understand and imitate.

Mr. Tennyson has in the *Idylls* used these elements of the chivalric legend with instinctive felicity and dexterity. The tale of Prince Geraint, as the first Idyll might be called, is, in its main incidents, as pure a tale of chivalry as could be conceived. His love of Enid at first sight; his single combat with her cousin, who keeps her out of her inheritance; the general plentifulness of banditti, and his conquests over them,—are all features belonging essentially to that kind of story. It would be needless criticism to show that the poet has made a great deal of them, that the narrative is very clear and very flowing, that the choice of the events is very skilful; every reader must have perceived these excellencies.

It is more necessary to point out what the careful art of the poet disguises—that he has avoided the greatest danger of such a theme. The danger of a topic abounding in romantic and extraordinary events is, that its treatment may have a sort of glare. The first miracle we meet petrifies us, the next only astonishes, the third tires, and a fourth bores. The perpetual stimulus of such events as those which we have shown to be particularly characteristic of the chivalric legend would become wearisomely tedious, if a relieving element were not introduced in order to prevent it. Mr. Tennyson has found us such an element. He has managed to introduce to us, incidentally and without effort, many pictures of the quieter parts of human nature. He has fully availed himself of the license which his subject gives him. He never goes into any detail of life, which cannot be made attractive, which may have disenchanting associations, which may touch with a prosaic breath the accomplished exquisiteness of his art. But no mistaken hesitation, none of the over-caution which a less practised artist would have felt, has restrained him from using to the utmost the entire range of that part of life which he can make attractive. We have spoken of the first Idyll, as in its story one of the most purely chivalric of the four. Yet even in this there are several relieving elements. There is scarcely anything to be imagined of higher excellence in this kind than the character of Yniol and his wife. Yniol is an old lord who has

lost his property, whose followers have deserted him, and who lives
in poverty at an old castle upon sufference. He thus describes how his
nephew ejected him, and what are the feelings with which he con-
templates his life:

> 'And since the proud man often is the mean,
> He sow'd a slander in the common ear,
> Affirming that his father left him gold,
> And in my charge, which was not render'd to him;
> Bribed with large promises the men who served
> About my person, the more easily
> Because my means were somewhat broken into
> Thro' open doors and hospitality;
> Raised my own town against me in the night
> Before my Enid's birthday, sack'd my house;
> From mine own earldom foully ousted me;
> Built that new fort to overawe my friends,
> For truly there are those who love me yet;
> And keeps me in this ruinous castle here,
> Where doubtless he would put me soon to death,
> But that his pride too much despises me:
> And I myself sometimes despise myself;
> For I have let men be, and have their way;
> Am much too gentle, have not used my power:
> Nor know I whether I be very base
> Or very manful, whether very wise
> Or very foolish; only this I know,
> That whatsoever evil happen to me,
> I seem to suffer nothing heart or limb,
> But can endure it all most patiently.'

The quiet contemplative character, which suffers so many calamities
in rude times, and which is often so puzzled to find out why it has
experienced them, is a most suitable shading element to relieve the
mind from always admiring great knights who strike hard, who throw
immense lances, and who can kill anyone they wish. The feminine
reflections—if such they can be called—of Yniol's wife, on the changes
of her fortune, are equally appropriate, and quite as true to nature:

> 'For I myself unwillingly have worn
> My faded suit, as you, my child, have yours,
> And howsoever patient, Yniol his.
> Ah, dear, he took me from a goodly house,

With store of rich apparel, sumptuous fare,
And page, and maid, and squire, and seneschal,
And pastime both of hawk and hound, and all
That appertains to noble maintenance.
Yea, and he brought me to a goodly house;
But since our fortune swerved from sun to shade,
And all thro' that young traitor, cruel need
Constrain'd us, but a better time has come;
So clothe yourself in this, that better fits
Our mended fortunes and a Prince's bride:
For tho' ye won the prize of fairest fair,
And tho' I heard him call you fairest fair,
Let never maiden think, however fair,
She is not fairer in new clothes than old.'

The whole story of the dress, of which this is a part, is a very delicate instance of relieving and softening skill; but we have no room to make any more remarks upon it.

Mr. Tennyson has, however, introduced another element into the description of the chivalric state of society, which, though in some sense it relieves it, does not so well harmonise with it. As we have observed, he avails himself of the peculiar manner—the sudden manner—of falling in love, characteristic of that society. In the first Idyll, Geraint falls in love with Enid on the first evening of their acquaintance; he proposes for her at once, fights a tournament, and is accepted the next morning. In the third Idyll we have the reverse history: a young lady named Elaine falls in love at once with the great Sir Lancelot; but as he does not like her as well as the Queen, she is not accepted. These are love affairs very characteristic of a state of society when women were seen but rarely, and even when seen were but little spoken to; but side by side with them in the Idyll there are other scenes indicative of a great familiarity between them and men, full of intellectual friction between the two, showing on both sides the nice and critical knowledge of our civilised world. It seems hardly fair that a writer should insist on the good side of both species of life; upon being permitted to use the sudden love which arises from not knowing women, and the love-tinged intercourse of thought and fancy which is the result of knowing them, together and at once. The nature of the story seems to have led Mr. Tennyson into this complication. The reign of Arthur, as is well known, was believed to have been for many years clouded,

and at length terminated, by the unlawful affection of his Queen
Guinevere for Sir Lancelot, the greatest and most renowned of his
courtiers. This is evidently a very delicate topic for art to handle.
King Arthur and Sir Lancelot are both to be made interesting: the
Queen, of

> imperial-moulded form,
> And beauty such as never woman wore,

is to be made interesting likewise. A great deal of intellectual detail
is necessary for this end; many slight touches of delicate insight must
conduce to it; a hundred pencillings of nice art must be accumulated
to effect it. If the subject was to be treated for modern readers, some
additions to the bareness of old romance and legend were indispens-
able; and even a critic could hardly object to them. But Mr. Tennyson
has gone further. There being a Queen at court who was not immacul-
ate, he has thought it proper that there should be ladies about her
who are no better. 'Vivien,' the young lady who gives her name to the
second Idyll, is more fitted for the court of Louis Quinze than for that
of the saintly king of chivalry. The delineation speaks for itself:

> For once, when Arthur walking all alone,
> Vext at a rumour issued from herself,
> Of some corruption, crept among his knights,
> Had met her, Vivien, being greeted fair,
> Would fain have wrought upon his cloudy mood
> With reverent eyes mock-loyal, shaken voice,
> And flutter'd adoration, and at last
> With dark sweet hints of some who prized him more
> Than who should prize him most; at which the King
> Had gazed upon her blankly and gone by:
> But one had watch'd, and had not held his peace:
> It made the laughter of an afternoon
> That Vivien should attempt the blameless King.
> And after that, she set herself to gain
> Him, the most famous man of all those times,
> Merlin, who knew the range of all their arts,
> Had built the King his havens, ships, and halls,
> Was also Bard, and knew the starry heavens;
> The people call'd him Wizard; whom at first
> She play'd about with slight and sprightly talk,
> And vivid smiles, and faintly venom'd points

Of slander, glancing here and grazing there;
And yielding to his kindlier moods, the Seer
Would watch her at her petulance, and play,
Ev'n when they seem'd unloveable, and laugh
As those that watch a kitten; thus he grew
Tolerant of what he half disdain'd, and she,
Perceiving that she was but half disdain'd,
Began to break her sports with graver fits,
Turn red or pale, would often when they met
Sigh fully, or all-silent gaze upon him
With such a fixt devotion, that the old man
Tho' doubtful, felt the flattery, and at times
Would flatter his own wish in age for love,
And half believe her true: for thus at times
He waver'd; but that other clung to him,
Fixt in her will, and so the seasons went.

There is undoubtedly much that is not modern in Merlin's character, or rather in his occupation, for he is a faint kind of being; but
the enchanter who has a charm of 'woven paces and of waving hands,'
and who has read lines of lore which no other person can read, does
not belong to the drawing-room. His pursuits, at any rate, do not.

'*Thou* read the book, my pretty Vivien!
O ay, it is but twenty pages long,
But every page having an ample marge,
And every marge enclosing in the midst
A square of text that looks a little blot,
The text no larger than the limbs of fleas;
And every square of text an awful charm,
Writ in a language that has long gone by.
So long, that mountains have arisen since
With cities on their flanks—*thou* read the book!
And every margin scribbled, crost, and cramm'd
With comment, densest condensation, hard
To mind and eye; but the long sleepless nights
Of my long life have made it easy to me.
And none can read the text, not even I;
And none can read the comment but myself;
And in the comment did I find the charm.
O, the results are simple; a mere child
Might use it to the harm of any one,
And never could undo it: ask no more:

For tho' you should not prove it upon me,
But keep that oath ye sware, ye might, perchance,
Assay it on some one of the Table Round,
And all because ye dream they babble of you.'

But however removed from us Merlin's character may be, that of
Vivien in its essence rather belongs to an over-civilised and satirical,
than to an uncultivated and romantic time. It rather mars our enjoyment of the new book of chivalry, to have a character so discordant
with its idea placed in such prominence, and drawn out in such development.

A similar charge cannot, however, be justly brought against the
main story of the poem. The contrast of character between King Arthur
and Sir Lancelot is one of those which exists in some degree in all
ages, but which the exciting circumstances of an unsettled time necessarily tend to bring out and exaggerate. In our last Number we had
occasion, in writing on another subject, to draw out at some length
the delineation of the two kinds of *goodness* which have long been
contrasted, and always seem likely to be contrasted, in the world,—
the ascetic and the sensuous. The characteristic of the latter is to be
sensitive to everything in this world, tempted by every stimulus,
exposed to every passion; the characteristic of the former is to be
repelled from the ordinary pleasures of the world, to be above them,
to feel a warning instinct against them. In the course of life the fate
of the ascetic character is to be absorbed in a somewhat chill ideal;
that of the sensuous character is to purchase a fascinating richness of
earthly experience by a serious number of grave errors. We had some
difficulty formerly in illustrating the distinction between the two
characters at once clearly and expressively, but we should have had
no such difficulty if Mr. Tennyson had published his new poem a
little earlier. The character of Arthur, absorbed in the ideal conception
of a chivalrous monarchy, is the very type of the highest abstract or
ascetic character; that of Lancelot, the great knight of many exploits
and full-lipped enjoyment, whom Guinevere prefers, is the type of the
sensuous and sensitive. The Queen's painting of the contrast is true
both to nature and to the female idea of nature.

'For what is true repentance but in thought—
Not ev'n in inmost thought to think again
The sins that made the past so pleasant to us:

And I have sworn never to see him more,
To see him more.'
    And ev'n in saying this,
Her memory from old habit of the mind
Went slipping back upon the golden days
In which she saw him first, when Lancelot came,
Reputed the best knight and goodliest man,
Ambassador, to lead her to his lord
Arthur, and led her forth, and far ahead
Of his and her retinue moving, they,
Rapt in sweet talk or lively, all on love
And sport and tilts and pleasure, (for the time
Was maytime, and as yet no sin was dream'd,)
Rode under groves that look'd a paradise
Of blossom, over sheets of hyacinth
That seem'd the heavens upbreaking thro' the earth,
And on from hill to hill, and every day
Beheld at noon in some delicious dale
The silk pavilions of King Arthur raised
For brief repast or afternoon repose
By couriers gone before; and on again,
Till yet once more ere set of sun they saw
The Dragon of the great Pendragonship,
That crown'd the state pavilion of the King,
Blaze by the rushing brook or silent well.

    But when the Queen immersed in such a trance,
And moving thro' the past unconsciously,
Came to that point when first she saw the King
Ride toward her from the city, sigh'd to find
Her journey done, glanced at him, thought him cold,
High, self-contain'd, and passionless, not like him,
'Not like my Lancelot'—

We need not observe upon the moral tact of making the Queen see
Lancelot first; it was necessary as an artistic palliation for her. It would
have been scarcely pleasant to think of her without it.

    There can be no doubt that Mr. Tennyson has judged wisely in
telling the story of Arthur and Guinevere in a series of tales rather
than in a single connected epic. The peculiar and painful nature of that
story requires, in a singular degree, the continual use of relieving
elements; and yet it is of the first importance that no one of these

elements should assume an undue prominence, or be more interesting than the story itself. If other interesting characters had been introduced into the main plot of a continuous poem, the latter effect would have been nearly inevitable. The imagination cannot rest with satisfaction either on Guinevere's relation to Arthur or on her relation to Lancelot. In each there is a disagreeable and disenchanting something. If a competing interest had been introduced into the central plot, it could hardly fail to be intrinsically pleasanter, and might have distracted the attention intended from the chosen theme. The form which the poet has adopted—that of a set of stories, with continual allusion to a latent thread—prevents this result, and also gives the requisite shading to the painful subject. There is a continued succession of relieving interests; but there is none which can compete with the central one, or be compared with it.

We have said enough of the merits of this poem to entitle us to say what ought to be said against it. We have not, indeed, a long list of defects to set forth. On the contrary, we think we perceive only one of real importance; and it is very probable that many critics will think us quite wrong as to that one. It appears to us that the *Idylls* are defective in dramatic power. Madame de Staël said that Coleridge was admirable in monologue, but quite incapable of dialogue. Something analogous may perhaps be said of Mr. Tennyson. His imagination seems to fix itself on a particular person in a particular situation; and he pours out, with ease and abundance, with delicacy and exactness, all which is suitable to that person in that situation. This was so with *Ulysses* in former years; it is so in his *Grandmother's Apology*, published the other day. Unnumbered instances of it may be found in the *Idylls*. But the power of writing a soliloquy is very different from that of writing a conversation; so different, indeed, that the person who is most likely to wish to write one, is most likely not to wish to write the other. Dialogue requires a very changing imagination, ready to move with ease from the mental position of one mind to the mental position of another, quick with the various language suited to either. Soliloquy—prolonged soliloquy, at any rate—requires a very steady imagination, steadily accumulating, slowly realising the exact position of a single person. The glancing mind will tend to one sort of composition; the meditative, solitary, and heavy mind to the other. All Mr. Tennyson's poems show more of the latter tendency than of the first. His genius gives the notion of a slow depositing instinct; day by day, as the hours pass, the delicate sand falls into beautiful forms—in stillness, in peace, in brooding. You fancy Shakespeare writing quick, the hasty dialogue of the parties passing quickly through his brain: we have no such idea of our great contemporary poet. He keeps his verses in his head: a meditative and scrupulous Muse is prayed to

> Let him write his random lines
> Ere they be half forgotten,
> Nor add or alter many times
> Till all be ripe and rotten.

The lightly-flowing dialogue is not so written. The lightly-moving imagination which is necessary to its composition gallops quicker, has a more varied tread, alters its point of view more frequently. If we look into the various dialogues of these *Idylls*, we shall not only observe that the tendency to monologue is great, and is greatest at the most striking points and telling situations, but also be struck with what is nearly the same phenomenon in another form—the remarkable similarity of the conversational powers of all the various personages. It is not only that a peculiar kind of language, a sort of a dialect of sentimental chivalry, pervades the whole,—this is quite in keeping with the design, and is perhaps essential to the perfect effect of such a book; but the similarity seems to go deeper: each dramatic personage is fully endowed with the expressive capacities of Mr. Tennyson's imagination; each one has them all, and consequently they are all on a level; no one has a superiority. No fact can more exactly and instructively define the precise difference between a genuine dramatic expression and the superficially analogous, but really different, art of delineative soliloquy. In the latter, it is right that the state of feeling to be expressed should be expressed with all the poet's power: we are representing the man's notion of himself; we take the liberty to say for him what he could never say; we translate into similes and phrases the half thoughts and floating feelings which he never could for a moment have expressed in that way, or probably in any other way. But in the genuine drama we are delineating a scene with more than one actor, and we are to state an imaginary dialogue. The mode in which people express themselves is an essential fact of that dialogue. The degree in which people can express themselves is one of the most dramatic parts of their characters; it is therefore contrary to all the principles of art to give to each character the same command, especially if it be a singular command over very imaginative language. The state of the supposed speaker's mind is no doubt brought out by that mode more effectually than by any other; but the effect of the scene—of the speaking mind which can delineate itself, and of the dumb mind which cannot—is altogether impaired, for the striking contrast is destroyed.

The only other defect with which the *Idylls* are, we think, to be charged, is not so much a positive defect in the poetry itself, as rather a negative deficiency in it when compared with other poems of Mr. Tennyson's that we have known for many years. A certain subtlety seems to pervade some of the latter; and it is in part ascribable to the subtlety of thought, and is greatly heightened by a peculiar subtlety of expression. There are lines in some of the older poems for which perhaps every one has

A pleasurable feeling of blind love.

We know what they express: they *do* express it to us: they dwell in our memories; they haunt us with their echo. Yet, if we try to analyse them, their charm is gone. Is the meaning expressed? Did Mr. Tennyson really mean this?—is there not this ambiguity? Might he not have intended something else? We can conceive a foreign critic, thoroughly acquainted with our language for almost all other purposes, to be quite incapable of seeing the merit of some of the more characteristic of these poems, from a want of those early floating and mysterious associations with language, in the instinctive and delicate use of which that charm consists. We have known literal-minded English persons, who preferred the plainer phraseology—the 'commin print,' as Lisbeth would have called it—of every-day rhymers. And, in some sense, their preference was correct. All that they could perceive was more perfect in the entirely valueless rhyme than in the entirely invaluable. The logical structure is better; it would construe better into other words, or into a foreign language: and this the literal critics perceive. The hovering air of power and beauty which the words really have, they do not perceive. If you were to suggest the existence they would smile. We believe that of this subtle sort of beauty, there is less in the *Idylls* than in Mr. Tennyson's earlier poetry. Perhaps they have not been in our hands long enough for us to judge. These super-logical beauties, if we may so say, are those which require the longest time to perceive, and the most perfect familiarity to appreciate. Still we do think so. We think there are few passages, considering the length of the poems, which will have years hence that inexplicable and magical power over our minds which some of Mr. Tennyson's old lines have. Perhaps the subject may have something to do with it. The sentiments in these poems are simpler than his sentiments used to be; they are not 'clothed in white samite, mystic, wonderful.' The thoughts are broader and plainer. The old mystic grace of language may, therefore, not have been so much used, only because it was no longer so much needed.

Every poem of Mr. Tennyson's must suggest the inquiry, what is the place which he occupies in the series of our poets? This poem must do so most of all; because, as we have explained, it removes some of the doubts which his warmest admirers formerly felt as to the limits of the range of his genius. It shows that he has the skill to adapt, the instinctive taste and self-restraint to preserve a continued interest of considerable length. Architectonic power the long-worded critics used to say he had not; but we have now discovered that he has it. The puzzling question returns, Where is Mr. Tennyson to be placed in the rank of our poets? We know that he has genius; but is that genius great or small, when compared with others like it?

It is most natural to compare him with Keats and Shelley. The kind of readers he addresses is, as we observed, the same: a sort of intellectual sentiment pervades his works as well as theirs: the superficial resemblances of the works of all the three are many. But, on the other hand, Mr. Tennyson is deficient in the most marked peculiarity which Shelley and Keats have in common. Both of these poets are singularly gifted with a sustained faculty of lyrical expression. They seem hurried into song; and, what is more, kept there when they have been hurried there. Shelley's *Skylark* is the most familiar example of this. A rather young musician was once asked, what was Jenny Lind's charm in singing. 'Oh,' he replied, 'she went up so high, and staid up high so long.' There is something of this sustainment at a great height in all Shelley's lyrics. His strains are profuse. He is ever soaring; and whilst soaring, ever singing. Keats, it is true, did not ascend to so extreme an elevation. He did not belong to the upper air. He had no abstract labour, no haunting speculations, no attenuated thoughts. He was the poet of the obvious beauty of the world. His genius was of the earth—of the autumn earth—rich and mellow; and it was lavish.

He did not carry his art high or deep; he neither enlightens our eyes much, nor expands our ears much; but pleases our fancies with a prolonged strain of simple rich melody. He does not pause, or stay, or hesitate. His genius is continuous; the flow of it is as obvious at the best moments as the excellence, and at inferior moments is more so. Mr. Tennyson, on the other hand, has no tendencies of this kind. He broods, as we have said. There are undoubtedly several beautiful songs in his writings,—several in which the sentiment cleaves to the words, and cannot even in our memories be divorced from them. But their beauty is not continuous. A few lines fasten upon us with an imperious and evermastering charm; but the whole composition, as a whole, has not much value. The run of it, as far as it has a run, expresses nothing. The genius of Mr. Tennyson is delineative; it muses and meditates; it describes moods, feelings, and objects of imagination; but it does not rush on to pour out passion, or express overwhelming emotion.

In the special lyrical impulse, therefore, we think it indisputable that Mr. Tennyson is inferior both to Keats and to Shelley. To Shelley he is moreover evidently inferior in general intensity of mind. This intense power of conception is, indeed, the most striking of all Shelley's peculiarities. There is something nervously exciting about his way of writing, even on simple subjects. He takes them up so vividly into his brain that they seem to make it quiver, and that of a sensitive reader at times quivers in sympathy. The subjects are no doubt often abstract; too abstract, perhaps, occasionally for art. But that only makes the result more singular. That an excitable mind should be stimulated by the strong interest of the facts of the world, by the phenomena of life, by the expectation of death, is what we should expect. It is intelligible to our understanding, and in obvious accordance with our experience. But that this extreme excitement should be caused in the poet's mind very often, and in the reader's mind sometimes, by the abstractions of singular tenuity, is what few would expect. So, however, it is. The mind of Shelley seems always to work in a kind of pure rare ether, clearer, sharper, more eager than the ordinary air. The reader feels that he is on a kind of mountainous elevation, and perhaps he feels vivified by it: at times almost all persons do so, but at times also they are chilled at its cold, and half-frightened at the lifelessness and singularity. It is characteristic of Shelley that he was obliged to abandon one of his favourite speculations, 'dizzy from thrilling horror.' Of all this abstract intensity Mr. Tennyson has not a particle. He is never very eager about anything, and he is certainly not over-anxious about phantoms and abstractions. In some respects this deficiency may not have injured his writings: it has rather contributed to his popularity. The English mind, which, like its great philosophers, likes to work upon 'stuff,' is more pleased with genial chivalric pictures than with chiselled phantoms and intense lyrics. Still, a critic who appreciates Shelley at all, will probably feel that he has a degree of inner power, of telling mental efficiency, which Mr. Tennyson does not equal. Horrible as the *Cenci* must ever be, it shows an eager and firmer grasp of mind—a greater tension of the imagination—than the *Idylls*.

Over Keats, however, Mr. Tennyson may perhaps claim a general superiority. We are, indeed, making a comparison which is scarcely fair; Keats died when he was still very young. His genius was immature; and his education, except the superficial musing education he gave himself, was very imperfect. Mr. Tennyson has lived till his genius is fully ripe, and he has gathered in the fruits of his century. No one can read his poems without feeling this: some of his readers have probably felt it painfully. Twenty years ago, when there was an idea in the high places of criticism that he was a silly and affected writer, many ignorant persons thought they were showing their knowledge in laughing at a language which nevertheless was both most emphatic and most accurate. The amount of thought which is held in solution,—if we may be pardoned so scientific a metaphor,—in Mr. Tennyson's poetry, is very great. If you come to his poems a hundred times, it is very probable that you will even to the end find there some new allusion, some recondite trace of high-bred thought, which you had not seen before. His reflections are often not new; he would not advance for himself perhaps, his just admirers, we are sure, would not claim for him, the fame of an absolutely original thinker. But he indicates the possession of a kind of faculty which in an age of intellect and cultivation is just as important, possibly is even more important, than the power of first-hand discovery. He is a first-rate *realiser*; and realisation is a test of truth. Out of the infinite thoughts, discoveries, and speculations which are scattered, more or less perfectly, through society, certain minds have a knack of taking up and making their own that which is true, and healthy, and valuable; and they reject the rest. It is often not by a very strict analysis or explicit logical statement that such minds arrive at their conclusions. They are continually thinking the subjects in question over: they have the details of them in their minds: they have a floating picture of endless particulars about them in their imaginations. In consequence, by musing over a true doctrine, they see that it is true: it fits their picture, adapts itself to it, forms at once a framework for it. On the contrary, they find that a false tenet does not suit the facts which they have in their minds: they muse over it, find out its unsuitability, and think no more of it. The belief of these remarkably sane and remarkably meditative persons about the facts to which they devote their own understandings is one of the best criteria of truth in this world. It is the discriminating winnow of civilisation, which receives the real corn of the true discoverer, and leaves the vexing chaff of the more pompous science to be forgotten and pass away. This kind of meditative tact and slow selective judgment Mr. Tennyson possesses in a very great measure; and there is nothing of which Keats was so entirely destitute. It does not, perhaps, occur to you while reading him that he is deficient in it. It belongs to an order of merit completely out of his way. It is the reflective gift of a mature man: Keats's best gifts are those of an impulsive, original, and refined boy. But if we compare— as in some degree we cannot help doing—the indications of general mind which are scattered through the three writers, we shall think, perhaps, that in these Mr. Tennyson excels Keats, even remembering the latter's early death, and, in consequence, giving him all fair credit for the possibilities of subsequent development; just as we found before that the intellectual balance seemed, when similarly adjusted, to incline against Mr. Tennyson, and in favour of Shelley.

Some one has said that Tennyson was a drawing-room Wordsworth. There is no deep felicity or instruction in the phrase, but it has some superficial appropriateness. Wordsworth's works have no claim to be in the drawing-room: they have the hill-side and the library, and those places are enough for them. Wordsworth, as we know, dealt with two subjects, and with two subjects only,—the simple elemental passions, 'the pangs by which the generations are prepared,' and in which they live and breathe and move; and secondly, the spiritual conception of nature, which implies that the universe is, in its beauties and its changes, but the expression of an inherent and animating spirit. Neither of these subjects suits the drawing-room. The simple passions are there carefully covered over; nature is out-of-doors. Mr. Tennyson, however, has given some accounts of the more refined and secondary passions in Wordsworth's intense manner; and if he does not give the exact sketches of external nature, or preach any gospel concerning it, he gives us a mental reflex of it, and a Lotus-eater's view of what it ought to be, and what it is rather a shame on the whole that it is not, which are not inadmissible in a luxurious drawing-room. A little of the spirit of Wordsworth, thus modified, may be traced in Mr. Tennyson; and perhaps this is the only marked trace of a recent writer that can be found in his writings. If we were to be asked as before, whether Mr. Wordsworth or Mr. Tennyson were the superior in general imaginative power, we think we should say that the latter was the superior, but that Wordsworth had achieved a greater task than he has as yet achieved, with inferior powers. The mind of Wordsworth was singularly narrow; his range peculiarly limited; the object he proposed to himself unusually distinct. He has given to us a complete embodiment of the two classes of subjects which he has treated of: perhaps it would be impossible to imagine one of them —the peculiar aspect of outward nature which we mentioned—to be better delineated; certainly as yet, we apprehend, it is not delineated nearly so well any where else. Although we should be inclined to believe that Mr. Tennyson's works indicate greater powers, we do not think that they evince so much concentrated efficiency, that they leave any single result upon the mind which is at once so high and so definite.

If we were asked, as we shall be asked, why we think Mr. Tennyson to have greater powers than Wordsworth, we would venture to allege two reasons. In the first place, Mr. Tennyson has a power of making fun. No one can claim that, of all powers, for Wordsworth, it is certain: no human being more entirely destitute of humour is perhaps discoverable anywhere in literature, or possibly even in society. Not a tinge of it seems ever to have influenced him. He had, through life, the narrow sincerity of the special missionary; but he had not, what is all but incompatible with it, the restraining tact of the man of the world, which teaches that all things and all gospels are only now and then in season; that it is absurd always to be teaching a single doctrine; that it is not wise to fatigue oneself by trying to interest others in that which it is perfectly certain they will not be interested in. The world of 'cakes and ale,' indisputably, is not that of Words-worth. There are quite sufficient indications that Mr. Tennyson appreciates it. Secondly, it may be said that, far more completely than Wordsworth, and far more completely than any other recent poet, Mr. Tennyson has conceived in his mind, and has delineated in his works, a general picture of human life. He certainly does not give us the whole of it, there is a considerable portion which he scarcely touches; but an acute eye can observe that he sees more than he says; and even judging exclusively and rigidly from what is said, the amount of life which Mr. Tennyson has delineated, even in these *Idylls* only, far surpasses in extent and range that which Wordsworth has described. Wordsworth's range is so narrow, and the extent of life and thought which these *Idylls* go over, slight as is their seeming structure, is so great, that perhaps no one will question this conclusion. Some may, however, deny its sufficiency; they may suggest that it does not prove our conclusion. In Shelley's case, it may be said that we allowed a certain defined intensity to have a higher imaginative value than a more diffused fertility and a less concentrated art; why is not Wordsworth entitled to share the benefit of this doctrine also? The plea is very specious, but we are not inclined to think that it is sound. Shelley has shown in a single direction, or in a few directions, an immense general power of imagination and mind. We may not pause to prove this: it is in the nature of allusive criticism to be dogmatic; we must appeal to the memory of our readers. On the other hand, we think, by a certain doggedness of nature, by high resolution, and even, in a certain sense, by an extreme limitation of mind, Wordsworth, with far less of imagination, was able in special directions to execute most admirable works. But the power displayed is, in a great degree, that of character rather than of imagination. He put all his mind into a single task, and he did it. Wordsworth's best works are the saved-up excellencies of a rather barren nature; those of Shelley are the rapid productions of a very fertile one. When we are speaking of mere intellectual and imaginative power, we run, therefore, no risk of contradiction in ranking Mr. Tennyson at a higher place than Wordsworth, notwithstanding that we have adjudged him to be inferior in the same quality to Shelley.

Perhaps we can, after this discussion, fix, at least approximately and incompletely, Mr. Tennyson's position in the hierarchy of our poets. We think that the poets of this century of whom we have been speaking,—and Coleridge may be added to the number,—may be, in a certain sense, classed together as the intellectualised poets. We do not, of course, mean that there ever was a great poet who was destitute of great intellect, or who did not show that intellect distinctly in his poems. But the poets of whom we speak show that intellect in a further and special sense. We are all conscious of the difference between talking to an educated man and to an uneducated. The difference by no means is, that the educated man talks better; that he either says better things, or says them in a more vigorous way. Possibly uneducated persons, as a rule, talk more expressively, and send whatever meaning they have farther into the hearer's mind; perhaps their meaning on the subjects which they have in common with educated men, is not very much inferior. Still there is a subtle charm about the conversation of the educated which that of other persons has not. That charm consists in the constant presence and constant trace of a cultivated intellect. The words are used with a certain distinct precision; a distinguishing tact of intellect is indicated by that which is said; a discriminating felicity is shown in the mode in which it is said. The charm of cultivated expression is like the charm of a cultivated manner; it is easy and yet cautious, natural and yet improved, ready and yet restrained. The fascination of a cultivated intellect in literature is the same. It is more easy to describe its absence, perhaps, than its presence. The style of Shakespeare, for example, wants entirely this peculiar charm. He had the manifold experience, the cheerful practicality, the easy felicity of the uneducated man; but he had not the measured abundance, the self-restraining fertility, which the very highest writer may be conceived to have. There is no subtle discretion in his words: there is the nice tact of native instinct; there is not the less necessary, but yet attractive, precision of an earnest and anxious education. Perhaps it will be admitted that the writers we have mentioned—Shelley, Coleridge, Keats, Wordsworth, and Tennyson— may all be called, as far as our own literature is concerned, in a peculiar sense the intellectualised poets. Milton indeed would, in positive knowledge, be superior to any of them, and to many of them put together, but he is an exceptional poet in English literature, to be classed apart, and seldom to be spoken of in contrast or comparison with any other; and even he, from a want of natural subtlety of mind, does not perhaps show us, in the midst of his amazing knowledge, the most acute and discriminating intellectuality. But if we except Milton, these poets may almost certainly be classed apart: and if they are to be so, we have indicated the place which Mr. Tennyson holds in this class in relation to all of them save Coleridge. A real estimate of the latter is not to be expected of us at the end of an article, and as a parenthesis in the estimate of another poet. He will long be a problem to the critics, and a puzzle to the psychologists. But, so far as the general powers of mind shown in his poems are concerned,—and this is the only aspect of his genius which we are at present considering,—we need have no hesitation in saying that they are much inferior to those shown in the poems of our greatest contemporary poet. Their great excellence is, in truth, almost confined to their singular power in the expression of one single idea. Both *Christabel* and the *Ancient Mariner* are substantially developments of the same conception; they delineate almost exclusively the power which the supernatural has, when it is thrust among the detail of the natural. This idea is worked out with astonishing completeness; but it is left to stand alone. There are no characters, no picture of life at large, no extraordinary thoughts, to be found in these poems; their metre and their strangeness are their charm. After what has been said, we need not prove at large that such an exclusive concentration upon such an idea proves that these poems are inferior, or rather indicate inferior imaginative genius to that of Tennyson. The range of the art is infinitely less; and the peculiar idea, which is naturally impressive, and in comparison with others easy to develop, hardly affords scope for the clear exhibition of a very creative genius, even if there were not other circumstances which would lead us to doubt whether Coleridge, rich and various as were his mental gifts, was possessed of that one. On the whole, we may pause in the tedium of our comparative dissertation. We may conclude, that in the series of our intellectualised poets Mr. Tennyson is to be ranked as inferior in the general power of the poetic imagination to Shelley, and to Shelley only;—and if this be true, the establishment of it is a contribution to criticism quite sufficient for a single article.

Lady Mary Wortley Montagu
Introductory note

Lady Mary Wortley Montagu (1689–1762), was the daughter of Evelyn Pierrepont, afterwards fifth earl and first duke of Kingston. In 1712 she married Edward Wortley Montagu, M.P. for Huntingdon, and in 1716 accompanied him to Constantinople where he had been sent as ambassador. She was one of the first western women to live in the near east, and sent from there a series of spirited letters which were published after her death. They had been copied and edited, and it is uncertain how many are in their original form. Her early poems, imitations of Pope, were published without her authorisation. Pope, once her admirer, became her bitter enemy, as was Horace Walpole, and these two depicted her as being cruel and eccentric almost to the point of insanity. She went to Italy in 1739, and returned to England on her husband's death in 1761, having been separated from him for thirty years. She died in England in 1762.

Lady Mary Wortley Montagu[1]

NOTHING is so transitory as second-class fame. The name of Lady Mary Wortley Montagu is hardly now known to the great mass of ordinary English readers. A generation has arisen which has had time to forget her. Yet only a few years since, an allusion to the 'Lady Mary' would have been easily understood by every well-informed person; young ladies were enjoined to form their style upon hers; and no one could have anticipated that her letters would seem in 1862 as different from what a lady of rank would then write or publish as if they had been written in the times of paganism. The very change, however, of popular taste and popular morality gives these letters now a kind of interest. The farther and the more rapidly we have drifted from where we once lay, the more do we wish to learn what kind of port it was. We venture, therefore, to recommend the letters of Lady Mary Wortley Montagu as an instructive and profitable study, not indeed to the youngest of young ladies, but to those maturer persons of either sex 'who have taken all knowledge to be their province,' and who have commenced their readings in 'universality' by an assiduous perusal of Parisian fiction.

It is, we admit, true that these letters are not at the present day very agreeable reading. What our grandfathers and grandmothers thought of them it is not so easy to say. But it now seems clear that Lady Mary was that most miserable of human beings,[2] an ambitious and wasted woman; that she brought a very cultivated intellect into a very cultivated society; that she gave to that society what it was most anxious to receive, and received from it all which it had to bestow; —and yet that this all was to her as nothing. The high intellectual

[1] *The Letters and Works of Lady Mary Wortley Montagu.* Edited by her Great-grandson, Lord Wharncliffe. Third edition, with Additions and Corrections derived from the original Manuscripts, illustrative Notes, and a new Memoir. By W. Moy Thomas. In two volumes. London: Henry Bohn.

This essay was first published in the *National Review*, January 1862, Volume XIV, pp. 198–223.

[2] The *National Review* has 'miserable beings' but 'human beings' seems more likely and has been substituted.

world of England has never been so compact, so visible in a certain sense, so enjoyable, as it was in her time. She had a mind to understand it, beauty to adorn it, and wit to amuse it; but she chose to pass a great part of her life in exile, and returned at last to die at home among a new generation, whose name she hardly knew, and to whom she herself was but a spectacle and a wonder.

Lady Mary Pierrepont—for that was by birth her name—belonged to a family which had a traditional reputation for ability and cultivation. The *Memoirs of Lucy Hutchinson*—(almost the only legacy that remains to us from the first generation of refined Puritans, the only book, at any rate, which effectually brings home to us how different they were in taste and in temper from their more vulgar and feeble successors)—contains a curious panegyric on *wise William* Pierrepont, to whom the Parliamentary party resorted as an oracle of judgment, and whom Cromwell himself, if tradition may be trusted, at times condescended to consult and court. He did not, however, transmit much of his discretion to his grandson, Lady Mary's father. This nobleman, for he inherited from an elder branch of the family both the marquisate of Dorchester and the dukedom of Kingston, was a mere man 'about town,' as the homely phrase then went, who passed a long life of fashionable idleness interspersed with political intrigue, and who signalised his old age by marrying a young beauty of fewer years than his youngest daughter, who, as he very likely knew, cared nothing for him and much for another person. He had the 'grand air,' however, and he expected his children when he visited them, to kneel down immediately and ask his blessing, which, if his character was what is said, must have been *very* valuable. The only attention he ever (that we know of) bestowed upon Lady Mary was a sort of theatrical outrage, pleasant enough to her at the time, but scarcely in accordance with the educational theories in which we now believe. He was a member of the Kit-Cat, a great Whig club, the Brooks's of Queen Anne's time, which, like Brooks's, appears not to have been purely political, but to have found time for occasional relaxation and for somewhat unbusiness-like discussions. They held annually a formal meeting to arrange the female toasts for that year; and we are told that a whim seized her father to nominate Lady Mary, 'then not eight years old, a candidate; alleging that she was far prettier than any lady on their list. The other members demurred, because the rules of the club forbade them to elect a beauty whom they had never seen. "Then you shall see her," cried he; and in the gaiety of the moment sent orders home to have her finely dressed and brought to him at the tavern, where she was received with acclamations, her claim unanimously allowed, her health drunk by every one present, and her name engraved in due form upon a drinking-glass. The company consisting of some of the most eminent men in England, she went from the lap of one poet, or patriot, or statesman, to the arms of another, was feasted with sweetmeats, overwhelmed with caresses, and, what perhaps already pleased her better than either, heard her wit and beauty loudly extolled on every side. Pleasure, she said, was too poor a word to express her sensations; they amounted to ecstasy: never again, throughout her whole future life, did she pass so happy a day. Nor, indeed, could she; for the love of admiration, which this scene was calculated to excite or increase, could never again be so fully gratified; there is always some alloying ingredient in the cup, some drawback upon the triumphs, of grown people. Her father carried on the frolic, and, we may conclude, confirmed the taste, by having her picture painted for the clubroom, that she might be enrolled a regular toast.' Perhaps some young ladies of more than eight years old would not much object to have lived in those times. Fathers may be wiser now than they were then, but they rarely make themselves so thoroughly agreeable to their children.

This stimulating education would leave a weak and vain girl still more vain and weak; but it had not that effect on Lady Mary. Vain she probably was, and her father's boastfulness perhaps made her vainer; but her vanity took an intellectual turn. She read vaguely and widely; she managed to acquire some knowledge—how much is not clear—of Greek and Latin, and certainly learned with sufficient thoroughness French and Italian. She used to say that she had the worst education in the world, and that it was only by the 'help of an uncommon memory and indefatigable labour' that she had acquired her remarkable attainments. Her father certainly seems to have been capable of any degree of inattention and neglect; but we should not perhaps credit too entirely all the legends which an old lady recounted to her grandchildren of the intellectual difficulties of her youth.

She seems to have been encouraged by her grandmother, one of the celebrated Evelyn family, whose memory is thus enigmatically but still expressively enshrined in the diary of the author of *Sylva*. 'Under this date,' we are informed, 'of the 2d of July 1649, he records a day spent at Godstone, where Sir John' (this lady's father) 'was on a visit with his daughter;' and he adds, 'Mem. The prodigious memory of Sir John of Wilts's daughter, since married to Mr. W. Pierrepont.' The lady who was thus formidable in her youth deigned in her old age to write frequently, as we should now say,—to open a 'regular commerce' of letters, as was said in that age,—with Lady Mary when quite a girl, which she always believed to have been beneficial to her, and probably believed rightly; for she was intelligent enough to comprehend what was said to her, and the old lady had watched many changes in many things.

Her greatest intellectual guide, at least so in after-life she used to relate, was Mr. Wortley, whom she afterwards married. 'When I was young,' she said, 'I was a great admirer of Ovid's *Metamorphoses*, and that was one of the chief reasons that set me upon the thoughts of stealing the Latin language. Mr. Wortley was the only person to whom I communicated my design, and he encouraged me in it. I used to study five or six hours a day for two years in my father's library; and so got that language, whilst everybody else thought I was reading nothing but novels and romances.' She perused, however, some fiction also; for she possessed, till her death, the whole library of Mrs. Lennox's *Female Quixote*, a ponderous series of novels in folio, in one of which she had written, in her fairest youthful hand, the names and characteristic qualities of 'the beautiful Diana, the volatile Clemene, the melancholy Doris, Celadon the faithful, Adamas the wise, and so on, forming two columns.'[3]

Of Mr. Wortley it is not difficult, from the materials before us, to decipher his character; he was a slow man, with a taste for quick companions. Swift's diary to Stella mentions an evening spent over a bottle of old wine with Mr. Wortley and Mr. Addison. Mr. Wortley was a rigid Whig, and Swift's transition to Toryism soon broke short that friendship. But with Addison he maintained an intimacy which lasted during their joint lives, and survived the marriages of both. With Steele likewise he was upon the closest terms, is said to have written some papers in the *Tatler* and *Spectator*; and the second volume of the former is certainly dedicated to him in affectionate and respectful terms.

Notwithstanding, however, these conspicuous testimonials to high ability, Mr. Wortley was an orderly and dull person. Every letter

[3] Morgan has 'two long columns.'

received by him from his wife during five-and-twenty years of absence, was found, at his death, carefully indorsed with the date of its arrival and with a *synopsis* of its contents. 'He represented,' we are told, 'at various times, Huntingdon, Westminster, and Peterborough in Parliament, and appears to have been a member of that class who win respectful attention by sober and business-like qualities; and his name is constantly found in the drier and more formal part of the politics of the time.'[4] He answered to the description given more recently of a similar person: 'Is not,' it was asked, 'Sir John —— a very methodical person?' 'Certainly he is,' was the reply, 'he files his invitations to dinner.' The Wortley papers, according to the descriptions of those who have inspected them, seem to contain the accumulations of similar documents during many years. He hoarded money, however, to more purpose, for he died one of the richest commoners in England; and a considerable part of the now marvellous wealth of the Bute family seems at first to have been derived from him.

Whatever good qualities Addison and Steele discovered in Mr. Wortley, they were certainly not those of a good writer. We have from his pen and from that of Lady Mary a description of the state of English politics during the three first years of George III.,[5] and any one who wishes to understand how much readability depends upon good writing would do well to compare the two. Lady Mary's is a clear and bright description of all the superficial circumstances of the time; Mr. Wortley's is equally superficial, often unintelligible and always lumbering, and scarcely succeeds in telling us more than that the writer was wholly unsuccessful in all which he tried to do. As to Mr. Wortley's contributions to the periodicals of his time, we may suspect that the jottings preserved at London[6] are all which he ever wrote of them, and that the style and arrangement were supplied by more skilful writers. Even a county member might furnish headings for the *Saturday Review*. He might say: '*Trent* British vessel — Americans always intrusive—Support Government—Kill all that is necessary.'

What Lady Mary discovered in Mr. Wortley it is easier to say and shorter, for he was very handsome. If his portrait can be trusted, there

[4] Morgan closes the inverted commas after 'business-like qualities' but Hutton follows the *National Review* text which has been preferred here.

[5] Morgan has 'George I' for 'George III'.

[6] The *National Review* has 'Loudon'; Morgan has 'Sandon' and Hutton has 'London'. I have used London as being the most likely and requiring the least alteration.

was a placid and business-like repose about him, which might easily be attractive to a rather excitable and wild young lady, especially when combined with imposing features and a quiet sweet expression. He attended *to her* also. When she was a girl of fourteen, he met her at a party, and evinced his admiration. And a little while later, it is not difficult to fancy that a literary young lady might be much pleased with a good-looking gentleman not uncomfortably older than herself, yet having a place in the world, and well known to the literary men of the age. He was acquainted with the classics too, or was supposed to be so; and whether it was a consequence of or a preliminary to their affections, Lady Mary wished to know the classics also.

Bishop Burnet was so kind as to superintend the singular studies— for such they were clearly thought—of this aristocratic young lady; and the translation of the *Enchiridion* of Epictetus, which he revised, is printed in this edition of her works. But even so grave an undertaking could not wholly withdraw her from more congenial pursuits. She commenced a correspondence with Miss Wortley, Mr. Wortley's unmarried sister, which still remains, though Miss Wortley's letters are hardly to be called hers, for her brother composed, and she merely copied them. The correspondence is scarcely in the sort of English or in the tone which young ladies, we understand, now use.

'It is as impossible,' says Miss Wortley, 'for my dearest Lady Mary to utter a[7] thought that can seem dull as to put on a look that is not beautiful. Want of wit is a fault that those who envy you most would not be able to find in your kind compliments. To me they seem perfect, since repeated assurances of your kindness forbid me to question their sincerity. You have often found that the most angry, nay, the most neglectful air you can assume, has made as deep a wound as the kindest; and these lines of yours, that you tax with dulness (perhaps because they were writ when you was not in a right humour, or when your thoughts were elsewhere employed), are so far from deserving the imputation, that the very turn of your expression, had I forgot the rest of your charms, would be sufficient to make me lament the only fault you have—your inconstancy.'

To which the reply is:

I am infinitely obliged to you, my dear Mrs. Wortley, for the wit, beauty, and other fine qualities, you so generously bestow upon me. Next to receiving them from Heaven, you are the person from whom I would choose

[7] The *National Review* has no 'a', neither has Hutton, but Morgan has inserted one.

to receive gifts and graces: I am very well satisfied to owe them to your own delicacy of imagination, which represents to you the idea of a fine lady, and you have good nature enough to fancy I am she. All this is mighty well, but you do not stop there; imagination is boundless. After giving me imaginary wit and beauty, you give me imaginary passions, and you tell me I'm in love: if I am, 'tis a perfect sin of ignorance, for I don't so much as know the man's name: I have been studying these three hours, and cannot guess who you mean. I passed the days of Nottingham races [at] Thoresby without seeing, or even wishing to see, one of the sex. Now, if I am in love, I have very hard fortune to conceal it so industriously from my own knowledge, and yet discover it so much to other people. 'Tis against all form to have such a passion as that, without giving one sigh for the matter. Pray tell me the name of him I love, that I may (according to the laudable custom of lovers) sigh to the woods and groves hereabouts, and teach it to the echo.

After some time Miss Wortley unfortunately died, and there was an obvious difficulty in continuing the correspondence without the aid of an appropriate sisterly screen. Mr. Wortley seems to have been tranquil and condescending; perhaps he thought placid tactics would be most effective, for Lady Mary was not so calm. He sent her some *Tatlers*, and received, by way of thanks, the following tolerably encouraging letter:

To Mr. Wortley Montagu

I am surprised at one of the *Tatlers* you send me; is it possible to have any sort of esteem for a person one believes capable of having such trifling inclinations? Mr. Bickerstaff has very wrong notions of our sex. I can say there are some of us that despise charms of show, and all the pageantry of greatness, perhaps with more ease than any of the philosophers. In contemning the world, they seem to take pains to contemn it; we despise it, without taking the pains to read lessons of morality to make us do it. At least I know I have always looked upon it with contempt, without being at the expense of one serious reflection to oblige me to it. I carry the matter yet farther; was I to choose of two thousand pounds a year or twenty thousand, the first would be my choice. There is something of an unavoidable *embarras* in making what is called a great figure in the world; [it] takes off from the happiness of life; I hate the noise and hurry inseparable from great estates and titles, and look upon both as blessings that ought only to be given to fools, for 'tis only to them that they are blessings. The pretty fellows you speak of, I own entertain me sometimes; but is it impossible to be diverted with what one despises? I can laugh at a puppet-show; at the same time I know there is nothing in it worth my attention or regard. General notions are generally wrong. Ignorance and folly are thought the best foundations for virtue, as if not knowing what a good wife is was necessary to make one so. I confess that can never be my way of reasoning; as I always forgive an *injury* when I think it not done out of malice, I can never think myself *obliged* by what is done without design. Give me leave to say it (I know it sounds vain), I know how to make a man of sense happy; but then that man must resolve to contribute something towards it himself. I have so much esteem for you, I should be very sorry to hear you was unhappy; but for the world I would not be the instrument of making you so; which (of the humour you are) is hardly to be avoided if I am your wife. You distrust me—I can neither be easy, nor loved, where I am distrusted. Nor do I believe your passion for me is what you pretend it; at least I am sure was I in love I could not talk as you do. Few women would have spoke so plainly as I have done; but to dissemble is among the things I never do. I take more pains to approve my conduct to myself than to the world; and would not have to accuse myself of a minute's deceit. I wish I loved you enough to devote myself to be for ever miserable, for the pleasure of a day or two's happiness. I cannot resolve upon it. You must think otherwise of me, or not all.

I don't enjoin you to burn this letter. I know you will. 'Tis the first I ever writ to one of your sex, and shall be the last. You must never expect another. I resolve against all correspondence of the kind; my resolutions are seldom made, and never broken.

Mr. Wortley, however, still grumbled. He seems to have expected a young lady to do something even more decisive than ask him to marry her. He continued to hesitate and pause. The lady in the comedy says, 'What right has a man to intend unless he states his intentions?' and Lady Mary's biographers are entirely of that opinion. They think her exceedingly ill-used, and Mr. Wortley exceedingly to blame. And so it may have been; certainly a love-correspondence is rarely found where activity and intrepidity on the lady's side so much contrasts with quiescence and timidity on the gentleman's. If, however, we could summon him before us, probably Mr. Wortley would have something to answer on his own behalf. It is tolerably plain that he thought Lady Mary too excitable. 'Certainly,' he doubtless reasoned, 'she is a handsome young lady, and very witty; but beauty and wit are dangerous as well as attractive. Vivacity is delightful; but my esteemed friend Mr. Addison has observed that excessive quickness of parts is not unfrequently the cause of extreme rapidity in action. Lady Mary makes love to me before marriage, and I like it; but may she not make love also to some one else after marriage, and then I shall not like it.' Accordingly he writes to her timorously as to her love of pleasure, her love of romantic reading, her occasional toleration of younger gentlemen and quicker admirers. At last, however, he proposed; and as far as the lady was concerned, there was no objection.

We might have expected, from a superficial view of the facts, that there would have been no difficulty either on the side of her father. Mr. Wortley died one of the richest commoners in England; was of the first standing in society, of good family, and he had apparently, therefore, money to settle and station to offer to his bride. And he did offer both. He was ready to settle an ample sum on Lady Mary, both as his wife and as his widow, and was anxious that, if they married, they should live in a manner suitable to her rank and his prospects. But nevertheless there was a difficulty. The *Tatler* had recently favoured its readers with dissertations upon social ethics not altogether dissimilar to those with which the *Saturday Review* frequently instructs its readers. One of these dissertations contained an elaborate exposure of the folly of settling your estate upon your unborn children. The arguments were of a sort very easily imaginable. 'Why,' it was said, 'should you give away that which you have to a person whom you do not know; whom you may never see; whom you may not like when you do see; who may be undutiful, unpleasant, or idiotic? Why, too, should each generation surrender its due control over the next? When the family estate is settled, men of the world know that the father's control is gone, for disinterested filial affection is an unfrequent though doubtless possible virtue; but so long as *property* is in suspense, all expectants will be attentive to those who have it in their power to give or not to give it.' These arguments had converted Mr. Wortley, who is said even to have contributed notes for the article, and they seem to have converted Lady Mary also. She was to have her money, and the most plain-spoken young ladies do not commonly care to argue much about the future provision for their possible children; the subject is always delicate and a little frightful, and, on the whole, must be left to themselves. But Lord Dorchester, her father, felt it his duty to be firm. It is an old saying, that 'you never know where a man's conscience may turn up,' and the advent of ethical feeling was in this case even unusually beyond calculation. Lord Dorchester had never been an anxious father, and was not now going to be a liberal father. He had never cared much about Lady Mary, except in so far as he could himself gain *éclat* by exhibiting her youthful beauty, and he was not now at her marriage about to do at all more than was necessary and decent in his station. It was not therefore apparently probable tha the would be irritatingly obstinate respecting the income of his daughter's children. He was so, however. He deemed it a duty to see that '*his* grandchild never should be a beggar,' and, for what reason does not so clearly appear, wished that his eldest male grandchild should be immensely richer than all his other grandchildren. The old feudal aristocrat, often in modern Europe so curiously disguised in the indifferent exterior of a careless man of the world, was, as became him, dictatorial and unalterable upon the duty of founding a family. Though he did not care much for his daughter, he cared much for the position of his daughter's eldest son. He had probably stumbled on the fundamental truth that 'girls were girls, and boys were boys,' and was disinclined to disregard the rule of primogeniture by which he had obtained his marquisate, and from which he expected a dukedom.

Mr. Wortley, however, was through life a man, if eminent in nothing else, eminent at least in obstinacy. He would not give up the doctrine of the *Tatler* even to obtain Lady Mary. The match was accordingly abandoned, and Lord Dorchester looked out for and found another gentleman whom he proposed to make his son-in-law; for he believed, according to the old morality, 'that it was the duty of the parents to find a husband for a daughter, and that when he was found, it was the daughter's duty to marry him.' It was as wrong in her to attempt to choose as in him to neglect to seek. Lady Mary was, however, by no means disposed to accept this passive theory of female obligation. She *had* sought and chosen; and to her choice she intended to adhere. The conduct of Mr. Wortley would have offended some ladies, but it rather augmented her admiration. She had exactly that sort of irritable intellect which sets an undue value on new theories of society and morality, and is pleased when others do so too. She thought Mr. Wortley was quite right not to 'defraud himself for a possible infant,' and admired his constancy and firmness. She determined to risk a step, as she herself said, unjustifiable to her own relatives, but which she nevertheless believed that she could justify to herself. She decided on eloping with Mr. Wortley.

Before, however, taking this audacious leap, she looked a little. Though she did not object to the sacrifice of the customary inheritance of her contingent son, she by no means approved of sacrificing the settlement which Mr. Wortley had undertaken at a prior period of the negotiation to make upon herself. And, according to common sense, she was undoubtedly judicious. She was going from her father, and foregoing the money which he had promised her; and therefore it was not reasonable that, by going *to* her lover, she should forfeit also the money which *he* had promised her. And there is nothing offensive in her mode of expression.

'Tis something odd for a woman that brings nothing to expect anything; but after the way of my education, I dare not pretend to live but in some degree suitable to it. I had rather die than return to a dependency upon relations I have disobliged. Save me from that fear, if you love me. If you cannot, or think I ought not to expect it, be sincere and tell me so. 'Tis better I should not be yours at all, than, for a short happiness, involve myself in ages of misery. I hope there will never be occasion for this precaution; but, however, 'tis necessary to make it.

But true and rational as all this seems, perhaps it is still truer and still more rational to say, that if a woman has not sufficient confidence in her lover to elope with him without a previous promise of a good settlement, she had better not elope with him at all. After all, if he declines to make the stipulated settlement, the lady will have either to return to her friends or to marry without it, and she would have the full choice between these satisfactory alternatives, even if she asked no previous promise from her lover. At any rate, the intrusion of coarse money among the refined materials of romance is, in this case, even more curious and remarkable than usual.

After some unsuccessful attempts, Lady Mary and Mr. Wortley did elope and did marry, and, after a certain interval, of course, Lord Dorchester received them, notwithstanding their contempt of his authority, into some sort of favour and countenance. They had probably saved him money by their irregularity, and economical frailties are rarely judged severely by men of fashion who are benefited by them. Lady Mary, however, was long a little mistrusted by her own relations, and never seems to have acquired much family influence; but her marriage was not her only peculiarity, or the only one which impartial relations might dislike.

The pair appear to have been for a little while tolerably happy. Lady Mary was excitable, and wanted letters when absent, and attention when present: Mr. Wortley was heavy and slow; could not write letters when away, and seemed torpid in her society when at home.

Still, these are common troubles. Common, too, is the matrimonial correspondence upon baby's deficiency in health, and on Mrs. Behn's opinion that 'the cold bath is the best medicine for weak children.' It seems an odd end to a deferential perusal of Latin authors in girlhood, and to a spirited elopement with the preceptor in after years; but the transition is only part of the usual irony of human life.

The world, both social and political, into which Lady Mary was introduced by her marriage was singularly calculated to awaken the faculties, to stimulate the intellect, to sharpen the wit, and to harden the heart of an intelligent, witty, and hard-headed woman. The world of London—even the higher world—is now too large to be easily seen, or to be pithily described. The elements are so many, their position is so confused, the display of their mutual counteraction is so involved, that many years must pass away before even a very clever woman can thoroughly comprehend it all. She will cease to be young and handsome long ere she does comprehend it. And when she at last understands it, it does not seem a fit subject for concise and summary wit. Its evident complexity refuses to be condensed into pithy sayings and brilliant *bon-mots*. It has fallen into the hands of philosophers, with less brains perhaps than the satirists of our fathers, but with more anxiety to tell the whole truth, more toleration for the many-sidedness of the world, with less of sharp conciseness, but, perhaps, with more of useful completeness. As are the books, so are the readers. People do not wish to read satire nowadays. The epigrams even of Pope would fall dull and dead upon this serious and investigating time. The folly of the last age affected levity; the folly of this, as we all know, encases itself in ponderous volumes which defy refutation, in elaborate arguments which prove nothing, in theories which confuse the uninstructed, and which irritate the well-informed. The folly of a hundred years since was at least the folly of Vivien, but ours is the folly of Merlin:

> *You* read the book, my pretty Vivien,
>
> . . . . . .
>
> And none can read the text, not even I;
> And none can read the comment but myself;
>
> . . . . . .
>
> O, the results are simple;

Perhaps people did not know then as much as they know now: indisputably they knew nothing like so much in a superficial way *about*

so many things; but they knew far more correctly where their knowledge began and where it stopped; what they thought and why they
thought it: they had readier illustrations and more summary phrases;
they could say at once what it *came to*, and to what action it should
lead. The London of 1700 was an aristocratic world,[8] which lived to itself,
which displayed the virtues and developed the vices of an aristocracy
which was under little fear of external control or check; which had
emancipated itself from the control of the crown; which had not fallen
under the control of the *bourgeoisie*; which saw its own life, and saw
that, according to its own maxims, it was good. Public opinion now
rules, and it is an opinion which constrains the conduct, and narrows
the experience, and dwarfs the violence, and *minimises* the frankness
of the highest classes, while it diminishes their vices, supports their
conscience, and precludes their grossness. There was nothing like this
in the last century, especially in the early part of it. The aristocracy came
to town from their remote estates—where they were uncontrolled by
any opinion or by any equal society, and where the eccentricities and
personalities of each character were fostered and exaggerated—to a
London which was like a large county town, in which everybody of
rank knew everybody of rank, where the eccentricities of each rural
potentate came into picturesque collision with the eccentricities of
other rural potentates, where the most minute allusions to the peculiarities and the career of the principal persons were instantly understood, where squibs were on every table, and where satire was in the
air. No finer field of social observation could be found for an intelligent
and witty woman. Lady Mary understood it at once.

Nor was the political life of the last century so unfavourable to the
influence and so opposed to the characteristic comprehension of women
as our present life. We are now ruled by political discussion and by a
popular assembly, by leading articles, and by the House of Commons.
But women can scarcely ever compose leaders, and no woman sits in
our representative chamber. The whole tide of abstract discussion
which fills our mouths and deafens our ears, the whole complex
accumulation of facts and figures to which we refer every thing, and
which we apply to every thing, is quite unfemale. A lady has an in-

---

[8] Both Morgan and Hutton have 'The London of the eighteenth century' instead of
'The London of 1700' but there does not seem sufficient justification for departing from
the original and I have followed it here.

sight into what she sees; but how will this help her with the case of the *Trent*, with the proper structure of a representative chamber, with Indian finance or parliamentary reform? Women are clever, but cleverness of itself is nothing at present. A sharp Irish writer described himself 'as bothered intirely by the want of preliminary information;' women are in the same difficulty now. Their nature may hereafter change, as some sanguine advocates suggest. But the visible species certainly have not the intellectual providence to acquire the vast stores of dry information which alone can enable them to judge adequately of our present controversies. We are ruled by a machinery of oratory and discussion, in which women have no share, and which they hardly comprehend: we are engaged on subjects which need an arduous learning, to which they have no pretensions.

In the last century much of this was very different. The Court still counted for much in English politics. The House of Commons was the strongest power in the State machine, but it was not so immeasurably the strongest power as now. It was absolutely supreme within its sphere, but that sphere was limited. It could absolutely control the money, and thereby the policy, of the State. Whether there should be peace or war, excise or no excise, it could and did despotically determine. It was supreme in its choice of *measures*. But, on the other hand, it had only a secondary influence in the choice of *persons*. Who the Prime Minister was to be, was a question not only theoretically determinable, but in fact determined by the Sovereign. The House of Commons could despotically impose two conditions: first, that the Prime Minister should be a man of sufficient natural ability, and sufficient parliamentary experience, to conduct the business of his age; secondly, that he should adopt the policy which the nation wished. But, subject to a conformity with these prerequisites, the selection of the King was nearly uncontrolled. Sir Robert Walpole was the greatest master of parliamentary tactics and political business in his generation; he was a statesman of wide views and consummate dexterity; but these intellectual gifts, even joined to immense parliamentary experience, were not alone sufficient to make him and to keep him Prime Minister of England. He also maintained, during two reigns, a complete system of court-strategy. During the reign of George II. he kept a *queen-watcher*. Lord Hervey, one of the cleverest men in England, the keenest observer, perhaps, in England, was induced, by very dexterous management, to remain at court during many years—to observe the queen, to hint to the queen, to remove wrong impressions from the queen, to confirm the Walpolese pre-dilections of the queen, to report every incident to Sir Robert. The records of politics tell us few stranger tales than that it should have been necessary for the Sir Robert Peel of the age to hire a subordinate as safe as Eldon, and as witty as Canning, fcr the sole purpose of managing a clever German woman, to whom the selection of a Prime Minister was practically intrusted. Nor was this the only court-cam-paign which Sir Robert had to conduct, or in which he was successful. Lady Mary, who hated him much, has satirically described the founda-tion upon which his court-favour rested during the reign of George I.

The new court with all their train was arrived before I left the country. The Duke of Marlborough was returned in a sort of triumph, with the ap-parent merit of having suffered for his fidelity to the succession, and was reinstated in his office of general, &c. In short, all people who had suffered any hardship or disgrace during the late ministry, would have it believed that it was occasioned by their attachment to the House of Hanover. Even Mr. Walpole, who had been sent to the Tower for a piece of bribery proved upon him, was called a confessor to the cause. But he had another piece of good luck that yet more contributed to his advancement; he had a very handsome sister, whose folly had lost her reputation in London; but the yet greater folly of Lord Townshend, who happened to be a neighbour in Norfolk to Mr. Walpole, had occasioned his being drawn in to marry her some months before the queen died.

Lord Townshend had that sort of understanding which commonly makes men honest in the first part of their lives; they follow the instruction of their tutor, and, till somebody thinks it worth their while to show them a new path, go regularly on in the road where they are set. Lord Townshend had then been many years an excellent husband to a sober wife, a kind master to all his servants and dependents, a serviceable relation wherever it was in his power, and followed the instinct of nature in being fond of his children. Such a sort of behaviour, without any glaring absurdity either in prodigality or avarice, always gains a man the reputation of reasonable and honest; and this was his character when the Earl of Godolphin sent him envoy to the States, not doubting but he would be faithful to his orders, without giving himself the trouble of criticising on them, which is what all ministers wish in an envoy. Robotun, a French refugee (secretary to Bernstoff, one of the Elector of Hanover's ministers), happened then to be at the Hague, and was civilly received at Lord Townshend's, who treated him at his table with the English hospitality, and he was charmed with a reception which his birth and education did not entitle him to. Lord Townshend was recalled when the queen changed her ministry; his wife died, and he retired into the country, where (as I have said before) Walpole had art enough to make him marry his sister Dolly. At that time, I believe, he did not propose much more advantage by the match than to get rid of a girl that lay heavy on his hands.

When King George ascended the throne, he was surrounded by all his German ministers and playfellows male and female. Baron Goritz was the most considerable among them both for birth and fortune. He had managed the king's treasury thirty years with the utmost fidelity and economy; and had the true German honesty, being a plain, sincere, and unambitious man. Bernstoff the secretary was of a different turn. He was avaricious, artful, and designing; and had got his share in the king's councils by bribing his women. Robotun was employed in these matters, and had the sanguine ambition of a Frenchman. He resolved there should be an English ministry of his choosing: and, knowing none of them personally but Townshend, he had not failed to recommend him to his master, and his master to the king, as the only proper person for the important post of Secretary of State; and he entered upon that office with universal applause, having at that time a very popular character, which he might possibly have retained for ever if he had not been entirely governed by his wife and her brother R. Walpole, whom he immediately advanced to be paymaster, esteemed a post of exceeding profit, and very necessary for his indebted estate.

And it is indisputable that Lord Townshend, who thought he was a very great statesman, and who began as the patron of Sir Robert Walpole, nevertheless was only his Court-agent—the manager on his behalf of the king and of the king's mistresses.

We need not point out at length, for the passage we have cited of itself indicates, how well suited this sort of politics is to the comprehension and to the pen of a keen-sighted and witty woman.

Nor was the Court the principal improver of the London society of the age. The House of Commons was then a part of society. This separate, isolated, aristocratic world, of which we have spoken, had an almost undisputed command of both Houses in the Legislature. The letter of the constitution did not give it them, and no law appointed that it should be so. But the aristocratic class were by far the most educated, by far the most respected, by far the most *eligible* part of the nation. Even in the boroughs, where there was universal suffrage, or something near it, they were the favourites. Accordingly, they gave the tone to the House of Commons; they required the small community of members who did not belong to their order to conform as far as they could to their usages, and to guide themselves by their code of morality and of taste. In the main the House of Commons obeyed these injunctions, and it was repaid by being incorporated within the aristocratic world: it became not only the council of the nation, but the debating-club of fashion. That which was 'received' modified the recipient. The remains of the aristocratic society, wherever we find them, are penetrated not only with an aristocratic but with a political spirit. They breathe a sort of atmosphere of politics. In the London of the present day, the vast miscellaneous *bourgeois* London, we all know that this is not so. 'In the country,' said a splenetic observer, 'people talk politics; at London dinners you talk nothing; between two pillars of crinoline you eat and are resigned.' A hundred and fifty years ago, as far as our rather ample materials inform us, people in London talked politics just as they now talk politics in Worcestershire; and being on the spot, and cooped up with politicians in a small social world, their talk was commonly better. They knew the people of whom they spoke, even if they did not know the subjects with which they were concerned.

No element is better fitted to counteract the characteristic evil of an aristocratic society. The defect of such societies in all times has been frivolity. All talk has tended to become gossip; it has ceased to deal with important subjects, and has devoted itself entirely to unimportant incidents. Whether the Duc de —— has more or less prevailed with the Marquise de —— is a sort of common form into which any details may be fitted, and any names inserted. The frivolities of gallantry— never very important save to some woman who has long been dead— fill the records of all aristocracies who lived under a despotism, who had no political authority, no daily political cares. The aristocracy of England in the last century were, at any rate, exempt from *this* reproach. There is in the records of it not only an intellectuality, which would prove little, for every clever describer, by the subtleties of his language and the arrangement of his composition, gives a sort of intellectuality even to matters which have no pretension to it in themselves, but likewise a pervading medium of political discussion. The very language in which they are written is the language of political business. Horace Walpole was certainly by nature no politician and no orator; yet no discerning critic can read a page of his voluminous remains without feeling that the writer has through life lived with politicians and talked with politicians. A keen observant mind, not naturally political, but capable of comprehending and viewing any subject which was brought before it, has chanced to have this particular subject—politics—presented to it for a lifetime; and all its delineations, all its efforts, all its thoughts, reflect it, and are coloured by it. In all the records of the eighteenth century the tonic of business is seen to combat the relaxing effect of habitual luxury.

This element, too, is favourable to a clever woman. The more you can put before such a person, the greater she will be; the less her world, the less she is. If you place the most keen-sighted lady in the midst of the pure futilities and unmitigated flirtations of an aristocracy, she will sink to the level of those elements, and will scarcely seem to wish for any thing more, or to be competent for any thing higher. But if she is placed in an intellectual atmosphere, in which political or other important subjects are currently passing, you will probably find that she can talk better upon them than you can, without your being able to explain whence she derived either her information or her talent.

The subjects, too, which were discussed in the political society of the last age were not so inscrutable to women as our present subjects; and even when there were great difficulties, they were more on a level with men in the discussion of them than they now are. It was no disgrace to be destitute of preliminary information at a time in which there were no accumulated stores from which such information could be derived. A lightening element of female influence is therefore to be found through much of the politics of the eighteenth century.

Lady Mary entered easily into all this world, both social and political. She had beauty for the fashionable, satire for the witty, knowledge for the learned, and intelligence for the politician. She was not too refined to shrink from what we now consider the coarseness of that time. Many of her verses themselves are scarcely adapted for our decorous pages. Perhaps the following give no unfair idea of her ordinary state of mind;

TOWN ECLOGUES.

ROXANA; OR, THE DRAWING-ROOM.

Roxana from the court retiring late,
Sigh'd her soft sorrows at St. James's gate.
Such heavy thoughts lay brooding in her breast,
Not her own chairmen with more weight oppress'd;
They groan the cruel load they're doom'd to bear;
She in these gentle sounds express'd her care.

'Was it for this that I these roses wear,
For this new-set the jewels for my hair?
Ah! princess! with what zeal have I pursue'd!
Almost forgot the duty of a prude.
Thinking I never could attend too soon,
I've miss'd my prayers, to get me dress'd by noon.
For thee, ah! what for thee did I resign?
My pleasures, passions, all that e'er was mine.
I sacrific'd both modesty and ease,
Left operas and went to filthy plays;
Double-entendres shock'd my tender ear,
Yet even this for thee I choose to bear.
In glowing youth, when nature bids be gay,
And every joy of life before me lay,
By honour prompted, and by pride restrain'd,
The pleasures of the young my soul disdain'd:
Sermons I sought, and with a mien severe
Censur'd my neighbours, and said daily prayer.

Alas! how chang'd!—with the same sermon-mien
That once I pray'd, the *What d'ye call 't* I've seen.
Ah! cruel princess, for thy sake I've lost
That reputation which so dear had cost:
I, who avoided every public place,
When bloom and beauty bade me show my face;
Now near thee constant every night abide
With never-failing duty by thy side,
Myself and daughters standing on a row,
To all the foreigners a goodly show!
Oft had your drawing room been sadly thin,
And merchants' wives close by the chair been seen;
Had not I amply fill'd the empty space,
And saved your highness from the dire disgrace.

Yet Coquetilla's artifice prevails,
When all my merit and my duty fails:
That Coquetilla, whose deluding airs
Corrupt our virgins, still our youth ensnares;
So sunk her character, so lost her fame,
Scarce visited before your highness came:
Yet for the bed-chamber 'tis her you choose,
When Zeal and Fame and Virtue you refuse.
Ah! worthy choice! not one of all your train
Whom censure blasts not, and dishonours stain:

Let the nice hind now suckle dirty pigs,
And the proud pea-hen hatch the cuckoo's eggs!
Let Iris leave her paint and own her age,
And grave Suffolka wed a giddy page!
A greater miracle is daily view'd,
A virtuous princess with a court so lewd.

 I know thee, Court! with all thy treach'rous wiles,
Thy false caresses and undoing smiles!
Ah! princess, learn'd in all the courtly arts
To cheat our hopes, and yet to gain our hearts!

 Large lovely bribes are the great statesman's aim;
And the neglected patriot follows fame.
The prince is ogled; some the king pursue;
But your Roxana only follows You.
Despis'd Roxana, cease, and try to find
Some other, since the princess proves unkind:
Perhaps it is not hard to find at court,
If not a greater, a more firm support?' [9]

There was every kind of rumour as to Lady Mary's own conduct, and we have no means of saying whether any of these rumours were true. There is no evidence against her which is worthy of the name. So far as can be proved, she was simply a gay, witty, bold-spoken, handsome woman, who made many enemies by unscrupulous speech, and many friends by unscrupulous flirtation. We may believe, but we cannot prove, that she found her husband tedious, and was dissatisfied that his slow, methodical, *borné* mind made so little progress in the political world, and understood so little of what really passed there. Unquestionably she must have much preferred talking to Lord Hervey to talking with Mr. Montagu. But we must not credit the idle scandals of a hundred years since, because they may have been true, or because they appear not inconsistent with the characters of those to whom they relate. There were legends against every attractive and fashionable woman in that age, and most of the legends were doubtless exaggerations and inventions. We cannot know the truth of such matters now, and it would hardly be worth searching into if we could; but the important fact is certain, Lady Mary lived in a world in which the worst rumours were greedily told, and often believed, about her and others;

[9] Quoted from Volume II of Lady Mary Wortley Montagu's *Letters and Works*, 1861 —Ed.

and the moral refinement of a woman must always be impaired by such a contact.

Lady Mary was so unfortunate as to incur the partial dislike of one of the great recorders of that age, and the bitter hostility of the other. She was no favourite with Horace Walpole, and the bitter enemy of Pope. The first is easily explicable. Horace Walpole never loved his father, but recompensed himself by hating his father's enemies. No one connected with the opposition to Sir Robert is spared by his son if there be a fair opportunity for unfavourable insinuation. Mr. Wortley was the very man for a grave mistake. He made the very worst which could be made in that age. He joined the party of constitutional exiles on the Opposition bench, who had no real objection to the policy of Sir Robert Walpole; who, when they had a chance, adopted that policy themselves; who were discontented because they had no power, and he had all the power. Probably, too, being a man eminently respectable, Mr. Montagu was frightened at Sir Robert's unscrupulous talk and not very scrupulous actions. At any rate, he opposed Sir Robert; and thence many a little observation of Horace Walpole's against Lady Mary.

Why Pope and Lady Mary quarrelled is a question on which much discussion has been expended, and on which a judicious German professor might even now compose an interesting and exhaustive monograph. A curt English critic will be more apt to ask, 'Why they should *not* have quarrelled?' We know that Pope quarrelled with almost every one; we know that Lady Mary quarrelled or half quarrelled with most of her acquaintances. Why, then, should they not have quarrelled with one another?

It is certain that they were very intimate at one time; for Pope wrote to her some of the most pompous letters of compliment in the language. And the more intimate they were to begin with, the more sure they were to be enemies in the end. Human nature will not endure that sort of proximity. An irritable vain poet, who always fancies that people are trying to hurt him, whom no argument could convince that every one is not perpetually thinking about him, cannot long be friendly with a witty woman of unscrupulous tongue, who spares no one, who could sacrifice a good friend for a bad *bon-mot*, who thinks of the person whom she is addressing, not of those about whom she is speaking. The natural relation of the two is that of victim and torturer, and no other will long continue. There appear also to have been

229

some money matters (of all things in the world) between the two. Lady Mary was intrusted by Pope with some money to use in specula- tion during the highly fashionable panic which derives its name from the South-Sea Bubble,—and as of course it was lost, Pope was very angry. Another story goes, that Pope made serious love to Lady Mary, and that she laughed at him; upon which a very personal, and not always very correct, controversy has arisen as to the probability or improbability of Pope's exciting a lady's feelings. Lord Byron took part in it with his usual acuteness and incisiveness, and did not leave the discussion more decent than he found it. Pope doubtless was deformed, and had not the large red health that uncivilised women admire; yet a clever lady might have taken a fancy to him, for the little creature knew what he was saying. There is, however, no evidence that Lady Mary did so. We only know that there was a sudden cool- ness or quarrel between them, and that it was the beginning of a long and bitter hatred.

In their own times Pope's sensitive disposition probably gave Lady Mary a great advantage. Her tongue perhaps gave him more pain than his pen gave her. But in later times she has fared the worse. What between Pope's sarcasms and Horace Walpole's anecdotes, Lady Mary's reputation has suffered very considerably. As we have said, her offences are *non proven*; there is no evidence to convict her; but she is likely to be condemned upon the general doctrine that a person who is accused of much is probably guilty of something.

During many years Lady Mary continued to live a distinguished fashionable and social life, with a single remarkable break. This in- terval was her journey to Constantinople. The powers that then were, thought fit to send Mr. Wortley as ambassador to Constantinople, and his wife accompanied him. During that visit she kept a journal, and wrote sundry real letters, out of which, after her return, she composed a series of unreal letters as to all she saw and did in Turkey, and on the journey there and back, which were published, and which are still amusing, if not always select, reading. The Sultan was not then the 'dying man;' he was the 'Grand Turk.' He was not simply a potentate to be counted with, but a power to be feared. The appearance of a Turkish army on the Danube had in that age much the same effect as the appearance of a Russian army now. It was an object of terror and dread. A mission at Constantinople was not then a *bureau* for interference in Turkey; but a serious office for transacting business with a great European power. A European ambassador at Constantinople now presses on the Government there impracticable reforms; he then asked for useful aid. Lady Mary was evidently impressed by the power of the country in which she sojourned; and we observe in her letters evident traces of the notion that the Turk was the dread of Christendom,—which is singular now, when the Turk is its *protégé*.

Lady Mary had another advantage too. Many sorts of books make steady progress; a scientific treatise published now is sure to be fuller and better than one on the same subject written long ago. But with books of travels in a stationary country the presumption is the contrary. In that case the old book is probably the better book. The first traveller writes out a plain straightforward description of the most striking objects with which he meets; he believes that his readers know nothing of the country of which he is writing, for till he visited it he probably knew nothing himself; and, if he is sensible, he describes simply and clearly all which most impresses him. He has no motive for not dwelling upon the principal things, and most likely will do so, as they are probably the most conspicuous. The second traveller is not so fortunate. He is always in terror of the traveller who went before. He fears the criticism,—'This is all very well, *but* we knew the whole of it before. No. 1 said that at page 103.' In consequence he is timid. He picks and skips. He fancies that you are acquainted with all which is great and important, and he dwells, for your good and to your pain, upon that which is small and unimportant. For ordinary readers no result can be more fatal. They perhaps never read—they certainly do not remember—any thing upon the subject. The curious *minutiæ*, so elaborately set forth, are quite useless, for they have not the general framework in which to store them. Not knowing much of the first traveller's work, that of the second is a supplement to a treatise with which they are unacquainted. In consequence they do not read it. Lady Mary made good use of her position in the front of the herd of tourists. She told us what she saw in Turkey—all the best of what she saw, and all the most remarkable things—and told it very well.

Nor was this work the only fruit of her Turkish travels; she brought home the notion of inoculation. Like most improvers, she was roughly spoken to. Medical men were angry because the practice was not in their books, and conservative men were cross at the agony of a new idea. Religious people considered it wicked to have a disease which Providence did not think fit to send you; and simple people 'did not like to make themselves ill of their own accord.' She triumphed, however, over all obstacles; inoculation, being really found to lengthen life and save complexions, before long became general.

One of the first patients upon whom Lady Mary tried the novelty was her own son, and many considerate people thought it 'worthy of observation' that he turned out a scamp. When he ran away from school, the mark of inoculation, then rare, was used to describe him, and after he was recovered, he never did any thing which was good. His case seems to have been the common one in which nature (as we speak) requites herself for the strongheadedness of several generations by the weakness of one. His father's and his mother's family had been rather able for some generations; the latter remarkably so. But this boy had always a sort of practical imbecility. He was not stupid, but he never did any thing right. He exemplified another curious trait of nature's practice. Mr. Montagu was obstinate, though sensible; Lady Mary was flighty, though clever. Nature combined the defects. Young Edward Montagu was both obstinate and flighty. The only pleasure he can ever have given his parents was the pleasure of *feeling* their own wisdom. He showed that they were right before marriage in not settling the paternal property upon him, for he ran through every shilling he possessed. He was not sensible enough to keep his property, and just not fool enough for the law to take it from him.

After her return from Constantinople, Lady Mary continued to lead the same half-gay and half-literary life as before; but at last she did not like it. Various ingenious inquirers into antiquated *minutiæ* have endeavoured, without success, to discover reasons of detail which might explain her dissatisfaction. They have suggested that some irregular love-affair was unprosperous, and hinted that she and her husband were not on good terms. The love-affair, however, when looked for, cannot be found; and though she and her husband would appear to have been but distantly related, they never had any great quarrel which we know of. Neither seems to have been fitted to give the other much pleasure, and each had the fault of which the other was most impatient. Before marriage Lady Mary had charmed Mr. Montagu, but she had also frightened him; after marriage she frightened, but did not charm him. He was formal and composed; she was flighty and *outrée*. 'What *will* she do next?' was doubtless the poor man's daily feeling; and 'Will he ever do any thing?' was probably also hers. Torpid business, which is always going on, but which never seems to come to anything, is simply aggravating to a clever woman. Even the least impatient lady can hardly endure a perpetual process for which there is little visible and nothing theatrical to show; and Lady Mary was by no means the least impatient. But there was no abrupt quarrel between the two; and a husband and wife who have lived together more than twenty years can generally manage to continue to live together during a second twenty years. These reasons of detail are scarcely the reasons for Lady Mary's wishing to break away from the life to which she had so long been used. Yet there was clearly some reason, for Lady Mary went abroad, and stayed there during many years.

We believe that the cause was not special and peculiar to the case, but general, and due to the invariable principles of human nature, at all times and everywhere. If historical experience proves any thing, it proves that the earth is not adapted for a life of mere intellectual pleasure. The life of a brute on earth, though bad, is possible. It is not even difficult to many persons to destroy the higher part of their nature by a continual excess in sensual pleasure. It is even more easy and possible to dull all the soul and most of the mind by a rapid accumulation of torpid comfort. Many of the middle classes spend their whole lives in a constant series of petty pleasures, and an undeviating pursuit of small material objects. The gross pursuit of pleasure, and the tiresome pursuit of petty comfort, are quite suitable to such 'a being as man in such a world as the present one.' What is not possible, is to combine the pursuit of pleasure and the enjoyment of comfort with the characteristic pleasures of a strong mind. If you wish for luxury, you must not nourish the inquisitive instinct. The great problems of human life are in the air; they are without us in the life we see, within us in the life we feel. A quick intellect feels them in a moment. It says, 'Why am I here? What is pleasure, that I desire it? What is comfort, that I seek it? What are carpets and tables? What is the lust of the eye? What is the pride of life, that they should satisfy *me*? I was not made for such things. I hate them, because I have liked them; I loathe them, because it seems that there is nothing else for me.' An impatient woman's intellect comes to this point in a moment; it says, 'Society is good, but I have seen society. What is the use of talking, or hearing *bon-mots*? I have done both till I am tired of doing either.[10] I have laughed

---

[10] The *National Review* has 'with both' but the sense requires 'both' and 'with' has been omitted.

till I have no wish to laugh again, and made others laugh till I have hated them for being such fools. As for instruction, I have seen the men of genius of my time; and they tell me nothing,—nothing of what I want to know. They are choked with intellectual frivolities. They cannot say "whence I came, and whither I go." What do they know of themselves? It is not from literary people that we can learn any thing; more likely, they will copy, or try to copy, the manners of lords, and make ugly love, in bad imitation of those who despise them.' Lady Mary felt this, as we believe. She had seen all the world of England, and it did not *satisfy*. She turned abroad, not in pursuit of definite good, nor from fear of particular evil, but from a vague wish for some great change—from a wish to escape from a life which harassed the soul, but did not calm it; which awakened the intellect without answering its questions.

She lived abroad for more than twenty years, at Avignon and Venice and elsewhere; and, during that absence, she wrote the letters which compose the greater part of her works. And there is no denying that they are good letters. The art of note-writing may become classical—it is for the present age to provide models of that sort of composition—but letters have perished. Nobody but a bore now takes pains enough to make them pleasant; and the only result of a bore's pains is to make them unpleasant. The correspondence of the present day is a continual labour without any visible achievement. The dying penny-a-liner said with emphasis, 'That which I have written has perished.' We might all say so of the mass of petty letters we write. They are a heap of small atoms, each with some interest individually, but with no interest as a whole; all the items concern us, but they all add up to nothing. In the last century, cultivated people who sat down to write a letter took pains to have something to say, and took pains to say it. The postage was perhaps ninepence; and it would be impudent to make a correspondent pay ninepence for nothing. Still more impudent was it, *after* having made him pay ninepence, to give him the additional pain of making out what was half expressed. People, too, wrote to one another then, not unfrequently, who had long been separated, and who required much explanation and many details to make the life of each intelligible to the other. The correspondence of the nineteenth century is like a series of telegrams with amplified headings. There is not more than one idea; and that idea comes soon, and is soon over. The best correspondence of the last age is rather like a good light article,—in which the points are studiously made,—in which the effort to make them is studiously concealed, —in which a series of selected circumstances is set forth,—in which you feel, but are not told, that the principle of the writer's selection was to make his composition pleasant.

In letter-writing of this kind Lady Mary was very skilful. She has the highest merit of letter-writing,—she is concise without being affected. Fluency, which a great orator pronounced to be the curse of orators, is at least equally the curse of writers. There are many people, many ladies especially, who can write letters at any length, in any number, and at any time. We may be quite sure that the letters so written are not good letters. Composition of any sort implies consideration; you must see where you are going before you can go straight, or can pick your steps as you go. On the other hand, too much consideration is unfavourable to the ease of letter-writing, and perhaps of all writing. A letter too much studied wants flow; it is a museum of hoarded sentences. Each sentence sounds effective, but the whole composition wants vitality. It was written with the memory instead of the mind; and every reader feels the effect, though only the critical reader can detect the cause. Lady Mary understood all this. She said what she had to say in words that were always graphic and always sufficiently good, but she avoided curious felicity. Her expressions seem choice, but not chosen.

At the end of her life Lady Mary pointed a subordinate but not a useless moral. The masters of mundane ethics observe 'that you should stay in the world, or stay out of the world.' Lady Mary did neither. She went out, and tried to return. Horace Walpole thus describes the result:

Lady Mary Wortley is arrived; I have seen her; I think her avarice, her art, and her vivacity are all increased. Her dress, like her language, is a *galimatias* of several countries; the groundwork rags, and the embroidery nastiness. She needs no cap, no handkerchief, no gown, no petticoat, and no shoes. An old black laced hood represents the first; the fur of a horseman's coat, which replaces the third, serves for the second; a dimity petticoat is deputy and officiates for the fourth; and slippers act the part of the last. When I was at Florence, and she was expected there, we were drawing *sortes Virgilianas* for her; we literally drew
'Insanam vatem aspicies.'
It would have been a stranger prophecy now even than it was then.

There is a description of what the favourite of society becomes after leaving it for years, and after indulging eccentricities for years! There is a commentary on the blunder of exposing yourself in your old age to young people, to whom you have always been a tradition and a name! Horace Walpole doubtless painted up a few trivialities a little. But one of the traits is true. Lady Mary lived before the age in which people waste half their lives in washing the whole of their persons.

Lady Mary did not live long after her return to England. Horace Walpole's letter is written on the 2nd February 1762,[11] and she died on the 21st August in the same year. Her husband had died just before her return, and perhaps, after so many years, she would not have returned unless he had done so. *Requiescat in pace*, for she quarrelled all her life.

[11] The *National Review* has 1809 but the correct date is 1762 which has been substituted.

Arthur Hugh Clough
Introductory note

Arthur Hugh Clough was born in 1819, the second son of James Clough, a Liverpool cotton merchant, and Anne Perfect. In 1823 the family moved to South Carolina, where they lived until 1836. Clough was sent to school at Rugby when Dr. Arnold was headmaster, and was described as 'the only boy in the history of the school to win all the honours Rugby had to offer.' In 1837 he went to Balliol College, Oxford. His friendship with Matthew Arnold, which began there, is commemorated in Arnold's *Thyrsis*. He resigned from an Oriel fellowship in 1848 after a dispute over supporting the Thirty-nine Articles. In 1849 he became head of University Hall, a residence for students of London University. After a year in America he returned to a post as examiner in the Education Office. He married in 1854; in 1859 he began to travel as his health was failing. He died at Florence in 1861. In 1836 he had published *The Longest Day*; in 1848 *The Bothie of Tober-na-Vuolich*; *Amours de Voyage* in 1858, and his *Poems* were published in 1862.

R. H. Hutton in his memoir of Bagehot describes Clough as '... the man who had, I think, a greater intellectual fascination for Bagehot than any of his contemporaries ... Bagehot had subscribed for the erection of University Hall and took an active part at one time on its council. Thus he saw a good deal of Clough and did what he could to mediate between that enigma to Presbyterian parents—a college-head who held himself serenely neutral on almost all moral and educational subjects interesting to parents and pupils, except the observance of disciplinary rules—and the managing body who bewildered him and were by him bewildered. ... He at least gained in Clough a cordial friend, and a theme of profound intellectual and moral interest to himself which lasted him his life, and never failed to draw him into animated discussion, long after Clough's own premature death; and I think I can trace the effect which some of Clough's writings had on Bagehot's mind to the very end of his career ...' Clough offered a warning '. . . to withhold judgement and not cheat ourselves into beliefs which our own imperious desire to believe had alone engendered . . .' He insists on ' "the *ruinous* force of the will" to persuade us of illusions which please us, of the tendency of practical life to give us beliefs which suit that practical life, but are none the truer for that . . . This practical teaching which Clough urges, in season and out of season, met an answering chord in Bagehot's mind, not so much in relation to religious belief as in relation to the over-haste and over-eagerness of human conduct, and I can trace the effect of it in all his writings, political and otherwise, to the end of his life.'

Mr. Clough's Poems[1]

No one can be more rigid than we are in our rules as to the publication of remains and memoirs. It is very natural that the friends of a cultivated man who seemed about to do something, but who died before he did it, should desire to publish to the world the grounds of their faith, and the little symptoms of his immature excellence. But though they act very naturally, they act very unwisely. In the present state of the world there are too many half-excellent people: there is a superfluity of persons who have all the knowledge, all the culture, all the requisite taste,—all the tools, in short, of achievement, but who are deficient in the latent impulse and secret vigour which alone can turn such instruments to account. They have all the outward and visible signs of future success; they want the invisible spirit, which can only be demonstrated by trial and victory. Nothing, therefore, is more tedious or more worthless than the posthumous delineation of the possible successes of one who did not succeed. The dreadful remains of nice young persons which abound among us prove almost nothing as to the future fate of those persons, if they had survived. We can only tell that any one is a man of genius by his having produced some work of genius. Young men must practise themselves in youthful essays; and to some of their friends these may seem works not only of fair promise, but of achieved excellence. The cold world of critics and readers will not, however, think so; that world well understands the distinction between promise and performance, and sees that these laudable *juvenilia* differ from good books as much as legitimate bills of exchange differ from actual cash.

If we did not believe that Mr. Clough's poems, or at least several of them, had real merit, not as promissory germs, but as completed performances, it would not seem to us to be within our province to notice them. Nor if Mr. Clough were now living among us, would he

[1] *Poems.* By Arthur Hugh Clough, sometime Fellow of Oriel College, Oxford. With a Memoir. Macmillan. This essay was first published in the *National Review*, October 1862, Volume XV, pp. 310–26.

wish us to do so. The marked peculiarity, and, so to say, the *flavour* of his mind, was a sort of truthful scepticism, which made him anxious never to overstate his own assurance of anything; disinclined him to overrate the doings of his friends; and absolutely compelled him to underrate his own past writings, as well as his capability for future literary success. He could not have borne to have his poems reviewed with 'nice remarks' and sentimental epithets of insincere praise. He was equal to his precept:

> Where are the great, whom thou would'st wish to praise thee?
> Where are the pure, whom thou would'st choose to love thee?
> Where are the brave, to stand supreme above thee,
> Whose high commands, would cheer, whose chiding raise thee?
> Seek, seeker, in thyself; submit to find
> In the stones bread; and life in the blank mind.

To offer petty praise and posthumous compliments to a stoic of this temper is like buying sugar-plums for St. Simon Stylites. We venture to write an article on Mr. Clough, because we believe that his poems depict an intellect in a state which is always natural 'to such a being as man in such a world as the present,' which is peculiarly natural to us just now; and because we believe that many of these poems are very remarkable for true vigour and artistic excellence, although they certainly have several defects and shortcomings, which would have been lessened, if not removed, if their author had lived longer and had written more.

In a certain sense there are two[2] great opinions about everything. There are two about the universe itself. The world as we know it is this. There is a vast, visible, indisputable sphere, of which we never lose the consciousness, of which no one seriously denies the existence, about the most important part of which most people agree tolerably and fairly. On the other hand, there is the invisible world, about which men are not agreed at all, which all but the faintest minority admit to exist somehow and somewhere, but as to the nature or locality of which there is no efficient popular demonstration; there is no such compulsory argument as will *force* the unwilling conviction of any one disposed to denial. As our minds rise, as our knowledge enlarges, as our wisdom grows, as our instincts deepen, our conviction of this invisible world is daily strengthened, and our estimate of its nature is

[2] The *National Review* has 'so' but the sense requires 'two' and this has been substituted.

continually improved. But—and this is the most striking peculiarity of the whole subject—the more we improve, the higher we rise, the nobler we conceive the unseen world which is in us and about us, in which we live and move, the more unlike that world becomes to the world which we *do* see. The divinities of Olympus were in a very plain and intelligible sense part and parcel of this earth; they were better specimens than could be found below, but they belonged to extant species; they were better editions of visible existences; they were like the heroines whom young men imagine after the young ladies of their vicinity—they were better and handsomer, but they were of the same sort; they had never been seen, but they might have been seen any day. So too of the God with whom the Patriarch wrestled: he might have been wrestled with even if he was not; he was that sort of person. If we contrast with these the God of whom Christ speaks—the God, who has not been seen at any time, whom no man hath seen or can see, who is infinite in nature, whose ways are past finding out—the transition is palpable. We have passed from gods—from an invisible world which is similar to, which is a *natural appendix* to, the world in which we live,—and we have come to believe in an invisible world which is altogether unlike that which we see, which is certainly not opposed to our experience, but is altogether beyond and unlike our experience; which belongs to another set of things altogether; which is, as we speak, transcendental. The 'possible' of early barbarism is like the reality of early barbarism; the 'may be,' the 'great perhaps,' of late civilisation is most unlike the earth, whether barbaric or civilised.

Two opinions as to the universe naturally result from this fundamental contrast. There are plenty of minds, like that of Voltaire, who have simply no sense or perception of the invisible world whatever, who have no ear for religion, who are in the technical sense unconverted, whom no conceivable process could convert without altering what to bystanders and ordinary observers is their identity. They are, as a rule, acute, sensible, discerning and humane; but the first observation which the most ordinary person would make as to them is that they are 'limited;' they understand palpable existence; they elaborate it, and beautify and improve it; but an admiring bystander who can do none of these things, who can beautify nothing, who, if he tried, would only make what is ugly uglier, is conscious of a latent superiority which he can hardly help connecting with his apparent inferiority. We cannot write Voltaire's sentences; we cannot make things as clear as he made them; but we do not much care for our deficiency. Perhaps we think 'things ought not to be so plain as all that.' There is a hidden, secret, unknown side to this universe, which these picturesque painters of the visible, these many-handed manipulators of the palpable, are not aware of, which would spoil their dexterity if it were displayed to them. Sleep-walkers can tread safely on the very edge of any precipice; but those who see, cannot. On the other hand, there are those whose minds have not only been converted, but in some sense *inverted*. They are so occupied with the invisible world as to be absorbed in it entirely; they have no true conception of that which stands plainly before them; they never look coolly at it, and are cross with those who do; they are wrapt up in their own faith as to an unseen existence; they rush upon mankind with 'Ah, there it is! there it is!—don't you see it?' and so incur the ridicule of an age.

The best of us try to avoid both fates. We strive, more or less, to 'make the best of both worlds.' We know that the invisible world cannot be duly discerned, or perfectly appreciated. We know that we see as in a glass darkly; but still we look on the glass. We frame to ourselves some image which we know to be incomplete, which probably is in part untrue, which we try to improve day by day, of which we do not deny the defects,—but which nevertheless is our 'all;' which we hope, when the accounts are taken, may be found not utterly *unlike* the unknown reality. This is, as it seems, the best religion for finite beings, living, if we may say so, on the very edge of two dissimilar worlds, on the very line on which the infinite, unfathomable sea surges up, and just where the queer little bay of this world ends. We count the pebbles on the shore, and image to ourselves as best we may the secrets of the great deep.

There are, however, some minds (and of these Mr. Clough's was one) which will not accept what appears to be an intellectual destiny. They struggle against the limitations of mortality, and will not condescend to use the natural and needful aids of human thought. They will not *make their image*. They struggle after an 'actual abstract.' They feel, and they rightly feel, that every image, every translation, every mode of conception by which the human mind tries to place before itself the Divine mind, is imperfect, halting, changing. They feel, from their own experience, that there is no one such mode of representation which will suit their own minds at all times, and they smile with bitterness at the notion that they could contrive an image

244

which will suit all other minds. They could not become fanatics or missionaries, or even common preachers, without forfeiting their natural dignity, and foregoing their very essence. To cry in the streets, to uplift their voice in Israel, to be 'pained with hot thoughts,' to be 'preachers of a dream,' would reverse their whole cast of mind. It would metamorphose them into something which omits every striking trait for which they were remarked, and which contains every trait for which they were not remarked. On the other hand, it would be quite as opposite to their whole nature to become followers of Voltaire. No one knows more certainly and feels more surely that there is an invisible world, than those very persons who decline to make an image or representation of it, who shrink with a nervous horror from every such attempt when it is made by any others. All this inevitably leads to what common practical people term a 'curious' sort of mind. You do not know how to describe these 'universal negatives,' as they seem to be. They will not fall into place in the ordinary intellectual world anyhow. If you offer them any known religion, they 'won't have that;' if you offer them no religion, they will not have that either; if you ask them to accept a new and as yet unrecognised religion, they altogether refuse to do so. They seem not only to believe in an 'unknown God,' but in a God whom no man can ever know. Mr. Clough has expressed, in a sort of lyric, what may be called their essential religion:

> O Thou whose image in the shrine
> Of human spirits dwells divine;
> Which from that precinct once conveyed,
> To be to outer day displayed,
> Doth vanish, part, and leave behind
> Mere blank and void of empty mind,
> Which wilful fancy seeks in vain
> With casual shapes to fill again—
>
> O thou that in our bosoms' shrine
> Dost dwell, because unknown divine!
> I thought to speak, I thought to say,
> 'The light is here,' 'behold the way,'
> 'The voice was thus,' and 'thus the word,'
> And 'thus I saw,' and 'that I heard,'—
> But from the lips but half essayed
> The imperfect utterance fell unmade.

O thou, in that mysterious shrine
Enthroned, as we must say, divine!
I will not frame one thought of what
Thou mayest either be or not.
I will not prate of 'thus' and 'so,'
And be profane with 'yes' and 'no.'
Enough that in our soul and heart
Thou, whatsoe'er thou may'st be, art.

It was exceedingly natural that Mr. Clough should incline to some such creed as this, with his character and in his circumstances. He had by nature, probably, an exceedingly real mind, in the good sense of that expression and the bad sense. The actual visible world, as it was and he saw it, exercised over him a compulsory influence. The hills among which he had wandered, the cities he had visited, the friends whom he knew,—these were his world. Many minds of the poetic sort easily melt down these palpable facts into some impalpable ether of their own. To such a mind as Shelley's the 'solid earth' is an immaterial fact; it is not even a cumbersome difficulty—it is a preposterous imposture. Whatever may exist, all that *clay* does not exist; it would be too absurd to think so. Common persons can make nothing of this dreaminess; and Mr. Clough, though superficial observers set him down as a dreamer, could not make much either. To him, as to the mass of men, the vulgar outward world was a primitive fact. 'Taxes *is* true,'[3] as the miser said. Reconcile what you have to say with green peas, for green peas are certain; such was Mr. Clough's idea. He could not dissolve the world into credible ideas and then believe those ideas, as many poets have done. He could not catch up a creed, as ordinary men do. He had a *straining*, inquisitive, critical mind; he scrutinised every idea before he took it in; he did not allow the moral forces of life to act as they should; he was not content to gain a belief 'by going on living.' He said,

> *Action will furnish belief*, but will that belief be the true one?
> This is the point, you know.[4]

He felt the coarse facts of the plain world so thoroughly that he could not readily take in anything which did not seem in accordance with

---

[3] Forrest Morgan has made the curious substitution 'Texas is true'.
[4] *Amours de Voyage*, Volume II—Ed.

them and like them. And what common idea of the invisible world seems in the least in accordance with them or like them?

A journal-writer, in one of his poems, has expressed this:

Comfort has come to me here in the dreary streets of the city,
Comfort—how do you think?—with a barrel-organ to bring it.
Moping along the streets, and cursing my day, as I wandered,
All of a sudden my ear met the sound of an English psalm-tune.
Comfort me it did, till indeed I was very near crying.
Ah, there is some great truth, partial, very likely, but needful,
Lodged, I am strangely sure, in the tones of the English psalm-tune.
Comfort it was at least; and I must take without question
Comfort, however it come, in the dreary streets of the city.

What with trusting myself, and seeking support from within me,
Almost I could believe I had gained a religious assurance,
Found in my own poor soul a great moral basis to rest on.
Ah, but indeed I see, I feel it factitious entirely;
I refuse, reject, and put it utterly from me;
I will look straight out, see things, not try to evade them;
Fact shall be fact for me, and the Truth the Truth as ever,
Flexible, changeable, vague, and multiform, and doubtful.—
Off, and depart to the void, thou subtle, fanatical tempter![5]

Mr. Clough's fate in life had been such as to exaggerate this naturally peculiar temper. He was a pupil of Arnold's; one of his best, most susceptible, and favourite pupils. Some years since, there was much doubt and interest as to the effect of Arnold's teaching. His sudden death, so to say, cut his life in the middle, and opened a tempting discussion as to the effect of his teaching when those taught by him should have become men and not boys. The interest which his own character then awakened, and must always awaken, stimulated the discussion, and there was much doubt about it. But now we need doubt no longer. The Rugby 'men' are *real* men, and the world can pronounce its judgment. Perhaps that part of the world which cares for such things has pronounced it. Dr. Arnold was almost indisputably an admirable master for a common English boy,—the small, apple-eating animal whom we know. He worked, he pounded, if the phrase may be used, into the boy a belief, or at any rate a floating, confused conception, that there are great subjects, that there are strange problems, that knowledge has an indefinite value, that life is a serious and

[5] Ibid., Volume V—Ed.

solemn thing. The influence of Arnold's teaching upon the majority of his pupils was probably very vague, but very good. To impress on the ordinary Englishman a general notion of the importance of what is intellectual and the reality of what is supernatural, is the greatest benefit which can be conferred upon him. The common English mind is too coarse, sluggish, and worldly to take such lessons too much to heart. It is improved by them in many ways, and is not harmed by them at all. But there are a few minds which are very likely to think too much of such things. A susceptible, serious, intellectual boy may be injured by the incessant inculcation of the awfulness of life and the magnitude of great problems. It is not desirable to take this world too much *au sérieux*; most persons will not; and the one in a thousand who will, should not. Mr. Clough was one of those who will. He was one of Arnold's favourite pupils, because he gave heed so much to Arnold's teaching; and exactly because he gave heed to it was it bad for him. He required quite another sort of teaching: to be told to take things easily; not to try to be wise overmuch; to be 'something beside critical;' to go on living quietly and obviously, and see what truth would come to him. Mr. Clough had to his latest years what may be noticed in others of Arnold's disciples,—a fatigued way of looking at great subjects. It seemed as if he had been put into them before his time, had seen through them, heard all which could be said about them, had been bored by them, and had come to want something else.

A still worse consequence was that the faith, the doctrinal teaching, which Arnold impressed on the youths about him was one personal to Arnold himself, which arose out of the peculiarities of his own character, which can only be explained by them. As soon as an inquisitive mind was thrown into a new intellectual atmosphere, and was obliged to naturalise itself in it, to consider the creed it had learned with reference to the facts which it encountered and met, much of that creed must fade away. There were inevitable difficulties in it, which only the personal peculiarities of Arnold prevented his perceiving, and which every one else must soon perceive. The new intellectual atmosphere into which Mr. Clough was thrown was peculiarly likely to have this disenchanting effect. It was the Oxford of Father Newman; an Oxford utterly different from Oxford as it is, or from the same place as it had been twenty years before. A complete estimate of that remarkable thinker cannot be given here; it would be no easy task even now, many years after his influence has declined, nor is it necessary

for the present purpose. Two points are quite certain of Father Newman, and they are the only two which are at present material. He was
undeniably a consummate master of the difficulties in the creeds of
other men. With a profoundly religious organisation which was hard
to satisfy, with an imagination which could not help setting before
itself simply and exactly what different creeds would come to and mean
in life, with an analysing and most subtle intellect which was sure to
detect the weak point in an argument if a weak point there was, with
a manner at once grave and fascinating,—he was a nearly perfect
religious disputant, whatever may be his deficiencies as a religious
teacher. The most accomplished theologian of another faith would
have looked anxiously to the joints of his harness before entering the
lists with an adversary so prompt and keen. To suppose that a youth
fresh from Arnold's teaching, with a hasty faith in a scheme of thought
radically inconsistent, should be able to endure such an encounter was
absurd. Arnold flattered himself that he was a principal opponent of
Mr. Newman; but he was rather a principal fellow-labourer. There
was but one quality in a common English boy which would have
enabled him to resist such a reasoner as Mr. Newman. We have a heavy
apathy on exciting topics, which enables us to leave dilemmas un-
solved, to forget difficulties, to go about our pleasure or our business,
and to leave the reasoner to pursue his logic: 'anyhow he is very
long'—*that* we comprehend. But it was exactly this happy apathy,
this commonplace indifference, that Arnold prided himself on removing. He objected most strenuously to Mr. Newman's creed, but he
prepared most anxiously the very soil in which that creed was sure to
grow. A multitude of such minds as Mr. Clough's, from being Ar-
noldites, became Newmanites.

A second quality in Mr. Newman is at least equally clear. He was
much better skilled in finding out the difficulties of other men's creeds
than in discovering and stating a distinct basis for his own. In most of
his characteristic works he does not even attempt it. His argument is
essentially an argument *ad hominem*; an argument addressed to the
present creed of the person with whom he is reasoning. He says:
'Give up what you hold already, or accept what I now say; for that
which you already hold involves it.' Even in books where he is especially called on to deal with matters of first principle, the result is
unsatisfactory. We have heard it said that he has in later life accounted
for the argumentative vehemence of his book *against* the Church of

Rome by saying: 'I did it as a duty; I *put* myself into a state of mind to write that book.' And this is just the impression which his arguments give. His elementary principles seem *made*, not born. Very likely he would admit the fact, and yet defend his practice. He would say: 'Such a being as man is, in such a world as this is, *must* do so; he must make a venture for his religion; he may see a greater probability that the doctrine of the Church is true than that it is false; he may see before he believes in her that she has greater evidence than any other creed; but he must do the rest for himself. *By means of his will* he must put himself into a new state of mind; he must cast in his lot with the Church here and hereafter; *then* his belief will gradually strengthen; he will in time become sure of what she says.' He undoubtedly, in the time of his power, persuaded many young men to try some such process as this. The weaker, the more credulous, and the more fervent, were able to persevere; those who had not distinct perceptions of real truth, who were dreamy and fanciful by nature, persevered without difficulty. But Mr. Clough could not do so; he felt it was 'something factitious.' He began to speak of the 'ruinous force of the will,' and 'our terrible notions of duty.' He ceased to be a Newmanite.

Thus Mr. Clough's career and life were exactly those most likely to develop and foster a morbid peculiarity of his intellect. He had, as we have explained, by nature an unusual difficulty in forming a creed as to the unseen world; he could not get the visible world out of his head; his strong grasp of plain facts and obvious matters was a difficulty to him. Too easily one great teacher inculcated a remarkable creed; then another great teacher took it away; then this second teacher made him believe for a time some of his own artificial faith; then it would not do. He fell back on that vague, impalpable, unembodied religion which we have attempted to describe.

He has himself given in a poem,[6] now first published, a very remarkable description of this curious state of mind. He has prefixed to it the characteristic motto, '*Il doutait de tout, même de l'amour.*' It is the delineation of a certain love-passage in the life of a hesitating young gentleman, who was in Rome at the time of the revolution of 1848; who could not make up his mind about the revolution, who could not make up his mind whether he liked Rome, who could not make up his mind whether he liked the young lady, who let her go away with-

[6] *Amours de Voyage.*—Ed.

out him, who went in pursuit of her, and could not make out which
way to look for her,—who, in fine, has some sort of religion, but cannot himself tell what it is. The poem was not published in the author's
lifetime, and there are some lines which we are persuaded he would
have further polished, and some parts which he would have improved,
if he had seen them in print. It is written in conversational hexameters,
in a tone of semi-satire and half-belief. Part of the commencement is a
good example of them:

Rome disappoints me much; I hardly as yet understand, but
Rubbishy seems the word that most exactly would suit it.
All the foolish destructions, and all the sillier savings,
All the incongruous things of past incompatible ages,
Seem to be treasured up here to make fools of present and future.
Would to Heaven the old Goths had made a cleaner sweep of it!
Would to Heaven some new ones would come and destroy these churches!
However, one can live in Rome as also in London.
Rome is better than London, because it is other than London.
It is a blessing, no doubt, to be rid, at least for a time, of
All one's friends and relations,—yourself (forgive me!) included,—
All the *assujettissement* of having been what one has been,
What one thinks one is, or thinks that others suppose one;
Yet, in despite of all, we turn like fools to the English.
Vernon has been my fate; who is here the same that you knew him,—
Making the tour, it seems, with friends of the name of Trevellyn.

Rome disappoints me still; but I shrink and adapt myself to it.
Somehow a tyrannous sense of a superincumbent oppression
Still, wherever I go, accompanies ever, and makes me
Feel like a tree (shall I say?) buried under a ruin of brick work.
Rome, believe me, my friend, is like its own Monte Testaceo,
Merely a marvellous mass of broken and castaway wine-pots.
Ye Gods! what do I want with this rubbish of ages departed,
Things that nature abhors, the experiments that she has failed in?
What do I find in the Forum? An archway and two or three pillars.
Well, but St. Peter's? Alas, Bernini has filled it with sculpture!
No one can cavil, I grant, at the size of the great Coliseum.
Doubtless the notion of grand and capacious and massive amusement,
This the old Romans had; but tell me, is this an idea?
Yet of solidity much, but of splendour little is extant:
'Brick-work I found thee, and marble I left thee!' their Emperor vaunted;
'Marble I thought thee, and brick-work I find thee!' the Tourist may
    answer.

251

As he goes on, he likes Rome rather better, but hazards the following imprecation on the Jesuits:

Luther, they say, was unwise; he didn't see how things were going;
Luther was foolish,—but, O great God! what call you Ignatius?
O my tolerant soul, be still! but you talk of barbarians,
Alaric, Attila, Genseric;—why, they came, they killed, they
Ravaged, and went on their way; but these vile, tyrannous Spaniards,
These are here still,—how long, O ye heavens, in the country of Dante?
These, that fanaticised Europe, which now can forget them, release not
This, their choicest of prey, this Italy; here you see them,—
Here, with emasculate pupils and gimcrack churches of Gesu,
Pseudo-learning and lies, confessional-boxes and postures,—
Here, with metallic beliefs and regimental devotions,—
Here, overcrusting with slime, perverting, defacing, debasing,
Michael Angelo's dome, that had hung the Pantheon in heaven,
Raphael's Joys and Graces, and thy clear stars, Galileo!

The plot of the poem is very simple, and certainly is not very exciting. The moving force, as in most novels of verse or prose, is the love of the hero for the heroine; but this love assuredly is not of a very impetuous and overpowering character. The interest of this story is precisely that it is not overpowering. The over-intellectual hero, over-anxious to be composed, will not submit himself to his love; over-fearful of what is voluntary and factitious, he will not make an effort and cast in his lot with it. He states his view of the subject better than we can state it:

I am in love, meantime, you think; no doubt you would think so.
I am in love, you say, with those letters, of course, you would say so.
I am in love, you declare. I think not so; yet I grant you
It is a pleasure indeed to converse with this girl. Oh, rare gift,
Rare felicity, this! she can talk in a rational way, can
Speak upon subjects that really are matters of mind and of thinking,
Yet in perfection retain her simplicity; never, one moment,
Never, however you urge it, however you tempt her, consents to
Step from ideas and fancies and loving sensations to those vain
Conscious understandings that vex the minds of mankind.
No, though she talk, it is music; her fingers desert not the keys; 'tis
Song, though you hear in the song the articulate vocables sounded,
Syllabled singly and sweetly the words of melodious meaning.

I am in love, you say; I do not think so, exactly.
There are two different kinds, I believe, of human attraction:

One which simply disturbs, unsettles, and makes you uneasy,
And another that poises, retains, and fixes and holds you.
I have no doubt, for myself, in giving my voice for the latter.
I do not wish to be moved, but growing where I was growing,
There more truly to grow, to live where as yet I had languished.
I do not like being moved: for the will is excited; and action
Is a most dangerous thing; I tremble for something factitious,
Some malpractice of heart and illegitimate process;
We are so prone to these things, with our terrible notions of duty.

Ah, let me look, let me watch, let me wait, unhurried, unprompted!
Bid me not venture on aught that could alter or end what is present!
Say not, Time flies, and Occasion, that never returns, is departing!
Drive me not out, ye ill angels with fiery swords, from my Eden,
Waiting, and watching, and looking! Let love be its own inspiration!
Shall not a voice, if a voice there must be, from the airs that environ,
Yea, from the conscious heavens, without our knowledge or effort,
Break into audible words? And love be its own inspiration?

It appears, however, that even this hesitating hero would have come
to the point at last. In a book, at least, the hero has nothing else to do.
The inevitable restrictions of a pretty story hem him in; to wind up
the plot, he must either propose or die, and usually he prefers proposing. Mr. Claude,—for such is the name of Mr. Clough's hero,—is
evidently on his road towards the inevitable alternative, when his
fate intercepts him by the help of a person who meant nothing less.
There is a sister of the heroine, who is herself engaged to a rather quick
person, and who cannot make out any one's conducting himself
differently to her George Vernon. She writes:

Mr. Claude, you must know, is behaving a little bit better;
He and Papa are great friends; but he really is too *shilly-shally,*—
So unlike George! Yet I hope that the matter is going on fairly.
I shall, however, get George, before he goes, to say something.
Dearest Louise, how delightful to bring young people together!

As the heroine says, 'dear Georgina' wishes for nothing so much as
to show her adroitness. George Vernon does interfere, and Mr.
Claude may describe for himself the change it makes in his fate:

Tibur is beautiful, too, and the orchard slopes, and the Anio
Falling, falling yet, to the ancient lyrical cadence;
Tibur and Anio's tide; and cool from Lucretilis ever,

With the Digentian stream, and with the Bandusian fountain,
Folded in Sabine recesses, the valley and villa of Horace:—
So not seeing I sang; so seeing and listening say I,
Here as I sit by the stream, as I gaze at the cell of the Sibyl,
Here with Albuncea's home and the grove of Tiburnus beside me;*
Tivoli beautiful is, and musical, O Teverone,
Dashing from mountain to plain, thy parted impetuous waters!
Tivoli's waters and rocks; and fair under Monte Gennaro
(Haunt even yet, I must think, as I wander and gaze, of the shadows,
Faded and pale, yet immortal, of Faunus, the Nymphs, and the Graces),
Fair in itself, and yet fairer with human completing creations,
Folded in Sabine recesses the valley and villa of Horace:—
So not seeing I sang; so now—Nor seeing, nor hearing,
Neither by waterfall lulled, nor folded in sylvan embraces,
Neither by cell of the Sibyl, nor stepping the Monte Gennaro,
Seated on Anio's bank, nor sipping Bandusian waters,
But on Montorio's height, looking down on the tile-clad streets, the
Cupolas, crosses, and domes, the bushes and kitchen-gardens,
Which, by the grace of the Tiber, proclaim themselves Rome of the
    Romans,—
But on Montorio's height, looking forth to the vapoury mountains,
Cheating the prisoner Hope with illusions of vision and fancy,—
But on Montorio's height, with these weary soldiers by me,
Waiting till Oudinot enter, to reinstate Pope and Tourist.

.   .   .   .   .

Yes, on Montorio's height for a last farewell of the city,—
So it appears; though then I was quite uncertain about it.
So, however, it was. And now to explain the proceeding.
    I was to go, as I told you, I think, with the people to Florence.
Only the day before, the foolish family Vernon
Made some uneasy remarks, as we walked to our lodging together,
As to intentions, forsooth, and so forth. I was astounded,
Horrified quite; and obtaining just then, as it happened, an offer
(No common favour) of seeing the great Ludovisi collection,
Why, I made this a pretence, and wrote that they must excuse me.
How could I go? Great Heavens! to conduct a permitted flirtation
Under those vulgar eyes, the observed of such observers!
Well, but I now by a series of fine diplomatic inquiries,
Find from a sort of relation, a good and sensible woman,
Who is remaining at Rome with a brother too ill for removal,

* '——domus Albuneæ resonantis,
    Et præceps Anio, et Tiburni lucus, et uda
    Mobilibus pomaria rivis.'

254

That it was wholly unsanctioned, unknown,—not, I think, by Georgina:
She, however, ere this,—and that is the best of the story,—
She and the Vernon, thank Heaven, are wedded and gone—
　　honey-mooning.
So—on Montorio's height for a last farewell of the city.
Tibur I have not seen, nor the lakes that of old I had dreamt of;
Tibur I shall not see, nor Anio's waters, nor deep en-
Folded in Sabine recesses the valley and villa of Horace;
Tibur I shall not see;—but something better I shall see.
Twice I have tried before, and failed in getting the horses;
Twice I have tried and failed: this time it shall not be a failure.

But, of course, he does not reach Florence till the heroine and her family are gone; and he hunts after them through North Italy, not very skilfully, and then he returns to Rome; and he reflects, certainly not in a very dignified or heroic manner:

I cannot stay at Florence, not even to wait for a letter.
Galleries only oppress me. Remembrance of hope I had cherished
(Almost more than as hope, when I passed through Florence the first time)
Lies like a sword in my soul. I am more a coward than ever,
Chicken-hearted, past thought. The *caffés* and waiters distress me.
All is unkind, and, alas! I am ready for any one's kindness.
Oh, I knew it of old, and knew it, I thought, to perfection,
If there is any one thing in the world to preclude all kindness,
It is the need of it,—it is this sad, self-defeating dependence.
Why is this, Eustace? Myself, were I stronger, I think I could tell you.
But it is odd when it comes. So plumb I the deeps of depression,
Daily in deeper, and find no support, no will, no purpose.
All my old strengths are gone. And yet I shall have to do something.
Ah, the key of our life, that passes all wards, opens all locks,
Is not *I will*, but *I must*. I must,—I must,—and I do it.

After all, do I know that I really cared so about her?
Do whatever I will, I cannot call up her image;
For when I close my eyes, I see, very likely, St. Peter's,
Or the Pantheon façade, or Michel Angelo's figures,
Or at a wish, when I please, the Alban hills and the Forum,—
But that face, those eyes,—ah no, never anything like them;
Only, try as I will, a sort of featureless outline,
And a pale blank orb, which no recollection will add to.
After all, perhaps there was something factitious about it;
I have had pain, it is true: have wept; and so have the actors.

At the last moment I have your letter, for which I was waiting;
I have taken my place, and see no good in inquiries.
Do nothing more, good Eustace, I pray you. It only will vex me.
Take no measures. Indeed, should we meet, I could not be certain;
All might be changed, you know. Or perhaps there was nothing to be
    changed.
It is a curious history, this; and yet I foresaw it;
I could have told it before. The Fates, it is clear, are against us;
For it is certain enough I met with the people you mention;
They were at Florence the day I returned there, and spoke to me even;
Stayed a week, saw me often; departed, and whither I know not.
Great is Fate, and is best. I believe in Providence partly.
What is ordained is right, and all that happens is ordered.
Ah, no, that isn't it. But yet I retain my conclusion.
I will go where I am led, and will not dictate to the chances.
Do nothing more, I beg. If you love me, forbear interfering.

And the heroine, like a sensible, quiet girl, sums up:

You have heard nothing; of course, I know you can have heard nothing.
Ah, well, more than once I have broken my purpose, and sometimes,
Only too often, have looked for the little lake-steamer to bring him.
But it is only fancy,—I do not really expect it.
Oh, and you see I know so exactly how he would take it:
Finding the chances prevail against meeting again, he would banish
Forthwith every thought of the poor little possible hope, which
I myself could not help, perhaps, thinking only too much of;
He would resign himself, and go. I see it exactly.
So I also submit, although in a different manner.
Can you not really come? We go very shortly to England.

And there let us hope she found a more satisfactory lover and husband.

The same defect which prevented Mr. Claude from obtaining his bride will prevent this poem from obtaining universal popularity. The public like stories which come to something; Mr. Arnold teaches that a great poem must be founded on a great action, and this one is founded on a long inaction. But Art has many mansions. Many poets, whose cast of thought unfits them for very diffused popularity, have yet a concentrated popularity which suits them and which lasts. Henry Taylor has wisely said that 'a poet does not deserve the name who would not rather be read a thousand times by one man than a single time by a thousand.' This repeated perusal, this testing by continual repetition and close contact, is the very test of intellectual poetry; unless such poetry can identify itself with our nature, and dissolve itself into our constant thought, it is nothing, or less than nothing; it is an ineffectual attempt to confer a rare pleasure; it teazes by reminding us of that pleasure, and tires by the effort which it demands from us. But if a poem really possess this capacity of intellectual absorption—if it really is in matter of fact accepted, apprehended, delighted in, and retained by a large number of cultivated and thoughtful minds,—its non-recognition by what is called the public is no more against it than its non-recognition by the coal-heavers. The half-educated and busy crowd, whom we call the public, have no more right to impose their limitations on highly-educated and meditative thinkers, than the uneducated and yet more numerous crowd have to impose their still narrower limitations on the half-educated. The coal-heaver will not read any books whatever; the mass of men will not read an intellectual poem: it can hardly ever be otherwise. But timid thinkers must not dread to have a secret and rare faith. Little deep poetry is very popular, and *no* severe art. Such poetry as Mr. Clough's especially, can never be so; its subjects would forbid it, even if its treatment were perfect: but it may have a better fate; it may have a tenacious hold on the solitary, the meditative, and the calm. It is this which Mr. Clough would have wished; he did not desire to be liked by 'inferior people'—at least he would have much distrusted any poem of his own which they did like.

The artistic skill of these poems, especially of the poem from which we have extracted so much, and of a long-vacation pastoral published in the Highlands, is often excellent, and occasionally fails when you least expect it. There was an odd peculiarity in Mr. Clough's mind; you never could tell whether it was that he would not show himself to the best advantage, or whether he *could* not; it is certain that he very often did not, whether in life or in books. His intellect moved with a great difficulty, and it had a larger inertia than any other which we have ever known. Probably there was an awkwardness born with him and his shyness and pride prevented him from curing that awkwardness as most men would have done. He felt he might fail, and he knew that he hated to fail. He neglected, therefore, many of the thousand petty trials which fashion and form the accomplished man of the world. Accordingly, when at last he wanted to do something, or was obliged to attempt something, he had occasionally a singular difficulty. He could not get his matter out of him.

In poetry he had a further difficulty, arising from perhaps an over-cultivated taste. He was so good a disciple of Wordsworth, he hated so thoroughly the common sing-song metres of Moore and Byron, that he was apt to try to write what will seem to many persons to have scarcely a metre at all. It is quite true that the metre of intellectual poetry should not be so pretty as that of songs, or so plain and impressive as that of vigorous passion. The rhythm should pervade it and animate it, but should not protrude itself upon the surface, or intrude itself upon the attention. It should be a latent charm, though a real one. Yet though this doctrine is true, it is nevertheless a dangerous doctrine. Most writers need the strict fetters of familiar metre; as soon as they are emancipated from this, they fancy that *any* words of theirs are metrical. If a man will read any expressive and favourite words of his own often enough, he will come to believe that they are rhythmical; probably they have a rhythm as he reads them; but no notation of pauses and accents could tell the reader how to read them in that manner; and when read in any other mode they may be prose itself. Some of Mr. Clough's early poems, which are placed at the beginning of this volume, are perhaps examples of more or less of this natural self-delusion. Their writer could read them as verse, but that was scarcely his business; and the common reader fails.

Of one metre, however, the hexameter, we believe the most accomplished judges, and also common readers, agree that Mr. Clough possessed a very peculiar mastery. Perhaps he first showed in English its *flexibility*. Whether any consummate poem of great length and sustained dignity can be written in this metre, and in our language, we do not know. Until a great poet has written his poem, there are commonly no lack of plausible arguments that seem to prove he cannot write it; but Mr. Clough has certainly shown that in the hands of a skilful and animated artist it is capable of adapting itself to varied descriptions of life and manners, to noble sentiments, and to changing thoughts. It is perhaps the most flexible of English metres. Better than any others it changes from grave to gay without desecrating what should be solemn, or disenchanting that which should be graceful. And Mr. Clough was the first to prove this, by writing a noble poem, in which it was done.

In one principal respect Mr. Clough's two poems in hexameters, and especially the Roman one, from which we made so many extracts, are very excellent. Somehow or other he makes you understand what the people of whom he is writing precisely were. You may object to the means, but you cannot deny the result. By fate he was thrown into a vortex of theological and metaphysical speculation, but his genius was better suited to be the spectator of a more active and moving scene. The play of mind upon mind; the contrasted view which contrasted minds take of great subjects; the odd irony of life which so often thrusts into conspicuous places exactly what no one would expect to find in those places,—these were his subjects. Under happy circumstances, he might have produced on such themes something which the mass of readers would have greatly liked; as it is, he has produced a little which meditative readers will much value, and which they will long remember.

Of Mr. Clough's character it would be out of place to say anything, except in so far as it elucidates his poems. The sort of conversation for which he was most remarkable rises again in the *Amours de Voyage*, and gives them, to those who knew him in life, a very peculiar charm. It would not be exact to call its best lines a pleasant cynicism; for cynicism has a bad name, and the ill-nature and other offensive qualities which have given it that name were utterly out of Mr. Clough's way. Though without much fame, he had no envy. But he had a strong realism. He saw what it is considered cynical to see—the absurdities of many persons, the pomposities of many creeds, the splendid zeal with which missionaries rush on to teach what they do not know, the wonderful earnestness with which most incomplete solutions of the universe are thrust upon us as complete and satisfying. '*Le fond de la Providence,*' says the French novelist, '*c'est l'ironie.*' Mr. Clough would not have said that; but he knew what it meant, and what was the portion of truth contained in it. Undeniably this *is* an *odd* world, whether it should have been so or no; and all our speculations upon it should begin with some admission of its strangeness and singularity. The habit of dwelling on such thoughts as these will not of itself make a man happy, and may make unhappy one who is inclined to be so. Mr. Clough in his time felt more than most men the weight of the unintelligible world; but such thoughts make an instructive man. Several survivors may think they owe much to Mr. Clough's quiet question, 'Ah, then you think—?' Many pretending creeds, and many wonderful demonstrations, passed away before that calm inquiry. He had a habit of putting your own doctrine concisely before you, so that you might see what it came to, and that you did not like it. Even now that he is gone, some may feel the recollection of his society a check on unreal theories and half-mastered thoughts. Let us part from him in his own words:

Some future day when what is now is not,
When all old faults and follies are forgot,
And thoughts of difference passed like dreams away,
We'll meet again, upon some future day.

When all that hindered, all that vexed our love
As tall rank weeds will climb the blade above,
When all but it has yielded to decay,
We'll meet again upon some future day.

When we have proved, each on his course alone,
The wider world, and learnt what's now unknown,
Have made life clear, and worked out each a way,
We'll meet again,—we shall have much to say.

With happier mood, and feelings born anew,
Our boyhood's bygone fancies we'll review,
Talk o'er old talks, play as we used to play,
And meet again, on many a future day.

Some day, which oft our hearts shall yearn to see,
In some far year, though distant yet to be,
Shall we indeed,—ye winds and waters, say!—
Meet yet again, upon some future day?

Armand Renaud
Introductory note

Armand Renaud (1836–1884) was a chief inspector 'de beaux arts et travaux historiques á la prefecture de la Seine'. *La Griffe Rose* was his only novel; otherwise he published three books of poems between 1860–65.

La Griffe Rose[1]

THE state of French fiction has at length become such that it is scarcely possible to give in the English language and within the settled conventions of English writing an accurate account of any of its more characteristic productions. The plot not only abounds in incidents, but essentially depends on relations between men and women which English books never mention, which Englishmen call *en masse* immoral, which none of us, without Continental assistance, would have the patience or the wish to pursue into their natural complexities. An English writer would consider he was advancing into debateable if not forbidden ground, if he treated of the events with which Sir Cresswell Cresswell is specially concerned. Divorce and adultery are, perhaps, within the present limits of English art, if treated with rapidity and delicacy, and if admitted to be immoral. Not one in twenty even of our most popular novelists could handle such topics graphically and dramatically, and yet not overstep the prescribed boundaries. Almost every one would hazard some expression or venture on some dangerous scene, which would exclude his book from 'family' perusal, and thereby deprive it of saleability, and him of his remuneration. We pay our writers to be moral, and they are moral. But the French have no such custom; on the contrary, a French novelist is rather expected to be immoral. Among the purchasers of such works, probably the

[1] *La Griffe Rose.* Par Armand Renaud. Paris. *The Spectator*, 13 September 1862, Volume 35, pp. 1029–30.
    This article was first attributed to Bagehot by Professor W. D. Paden of Kansas University in 'Swinburne, The Spectator in 1862 and Walter Bagehot', printed in 'Six Studies in Nineteenth Century English Literature and Thought', edited by Harold Orel and George J. Worth. University of Kansas Humanistic Studies No. 35.
    I agree with the attribution for which three main reasons can be advanced. In the first place the argument in *La Griffe Rose* that because young ladies were readers of literature in England, writers were restricted in their subject matter and its treatment, is taken up in very similar terms in Bagehot's essay on Sterne and Thackeray published in the *National Review* in April 1864. Thackeray is quoted in *La Griffe Rose* and Bagehot had just been reviewing 'The Adventures of Philip' in the *Spectator*. Thirdly there is an anecdote about a Somerset woman. Somerset was Bagehot's county and he was fond of telling stories about it. None of these reasons is conclusive but the piece as a whole has the feel of Bagehot and the impress of his style and I have therefore included it in the collected edition.

majority would feel *hurt* if they contained no scenes which English morals would forbid, and which English women would shrink from. A mere infraction of the marriage vow is too trifling a peccadillo, if indeed it is even a peccadillo, to be the subject of an exciting narrative. Dumas *fils* has indeed contrived to render it proper for modern art. His '*Roman d'une Femme*' entirely turns on such an event; but he escaped the vice of commonplace by making the wife love her husband, and *not* love her lover all the while that she is guilty of adultery with her lover; and thus contrived to make the situation sufficiently *piquant*. The author of 'Fanny' went over to the side of the lover, showed what he considered to be a wife, his duties, and described his natural and suitable jealousy of the husband. His book is intended for an inventory of the duties of a married woman towards the admirer whom she does love. In the novel before us, M. Renaud has undertaken to delineate a phase yet more curious. *La Griffe Rose* is an account of the evil consequences which ensued from a married lady's not yielding sufficiently *soon* to the addresses of an admirer whom she does not love. She did yield at last, but it was too late. He committed suicide and she went into a convent.

If the plot of the novel is not English, its reflections and its fundamental view of life are more un-English still, if possible. Who can translate such sentiments as the following?—'O grandes courtisanes de tous les temps! ils sont aveugles les philosophes qui vous insultent. Qu'ils amassent déclamations sur déclamations! ils n'empêcheront pas que le culte rendu par vous au luxe, á l'élégance, à tous les rayonnements de la forme, n'ait sa bonne influence, qu'en faisant de vos chambres une féerie, de vos toilettes un rêve; que vous ne developpiez le sens artistique; qu'il ne s'exhale de vos dentelles et de vos parfums un certain idéal élevant l'âme á sa manière, car tout chemin mène à Rome, et *toute beauté mene à Dieu?*' Perhaps no one attained to God that way before, with whomever *else* they may have connected themselves. A whole volume, too, of utterly un-English reflection may be summed up in the following description of a woman's marriage, 'Son esclavage de fille est fini; elle est femme, c'est-á-dire, en bon français, *elle peut se laisser aimer*.'

Very many persons will say that such books ought not to be written; that, if written, they ought not to be read, that they express thoughts which it is unwise to think and delineate scenes which it is objectionable to imagine. As for the writing of such books, *we* have no call to say anything; the clever writers of them, if it is ever needful, will say all which can be said on that head much better than we can. It may not be much after all;—still it will be much more than anything we could say. But as to the reading of them, we think there are reasons why persons of sufficient age and sufficient moral stability should not eschew the practice.

In the first place, it is a rare advantage to find in a highly civilised age a really *frank* literature. Books seem at first to have been written for men only. They now scarcely seem to be written for men at all; they are written for every part of the species *except* men. The mode in which the change has happened is certainly very natural; the change itself was nearly inevitable, and, perhaps, upon the whole, by no means undesirable. So long as hard-headed men were, as in Greece and Rome, the principal part of the great literary public, all subjects could be discussed with the freedom of exclusively masculine conversation. No man at a club is afraid of hurting other men by explaining his meaning; he believes that they have encountered much before, and therefore will probably be able to bear what he wishes to say; he is sure that if his conversation will hurt them, their moral state must be so delicate that something else will impair it before the day is out, even if he hold his tongue. The old writers must have had much the same feeling. They wrote for men whose minds were seasoned, or were being seasoned; they wrote nearly as they talked, without much fear and with very little reticence. We cannot write so now. We have taken young ladies into the club. Every remarkable work of fiction is certain at present to be read by many immature minds of the feebler sex before it has been many days published. On such minds an outspoken literature might easily produce very pernicious effects. A large experience proves that the moral constitution of the female mind loses its tone far more easily than the masculine; it is in the good sense and the bad a more delicate constitution. It is both more easily destroyed, and is finer and gentler while it lasts. There is a light bloom upon it which man's nature has not, but if that bloom is rubbed off,—and it is rubbed off very easily,—woman's nature becomes inferior to man's. We teach our boys to read novels, too, now-a-days, and we must be careful that there is not anything in them which we do not wish them to read. As civilisation grows, literature is cramped; the fetters of a propriety are laid upon it, which our fathers had not to bear, and which hamper half its movements.

French literature is exempt from this defect, at any rate. Young ladies are not allowed to read novels in France, and do not read them. They marry earlier than here, and before marriage they are permitted very little liberty,—are prevented from knowing much, and are sedulously taught to seem to know less than they do. Writers in France, therefore, still retain much of the liberty of ancient writers. And though France is unquestionably injured by her habit in this matter, other nations may be benefited. Hardly any part of life can be well comprehended until it is imaginatively delineated. Even common persons who pass through it learn its facts, but do not learn its spirit; they are as superficial travellers, who see the mile-stones and the hedges, and the bats, but who know little of the broad country and rural population on either side of them. Those who have not themselves experienced any sort of life,—and there are many sorts of life which it is very undesirable to experience—are dependent on description of necessity. The *demi-monde* in London thrusts itself in our very faces; we see it in the parks and at the opera; but how are those who are too moral to associate with it to learn anything about it? Some people may come to think too much about it if it is always unknown, mysterious, and good-looking. They may, however, learn something from M. Dumas *fils* and his imaginative delineation of it. They may learn, at least, this—that it consists of human beings 'like unto us,' who are in part evil, but yet not all evil.

Secondly, and this is, perhaps, the more material consideration of the two, an observing student of French novels may easily learn from them the real consequences of several decent vices which exist among ourselves, but which are here too decent, are too much involved in the complexities of life, and too intermingled with other more innocent elements, to display their latent deformity. In France some of these vices are practised on a great scale, as well as more openly, and their novelists who are cunning in the artistic development of immorality, display all their bad consequences without glozing over any and even with a sort of ardour. Take, for instance, the vice of immoral marriage, which is always one of the characteristic sins of a highly civilised society. It certainly is not unknown in England. Mr. Thackeray has proposed to call a 'midnight meeting' in Belgravia of all the ladies in that quarter who have, as he phrases it, '*sold* themselves in marriage.' He has pointed out what a respectable, genteel, fashionable, and multitudinous assembly it would be; in what 'diamonds and Chantilly

266

lace' its company would be clothed; what bishops went to their weddings; what a big room would be required to hold them. Nor is this vice confined to the highest class; it goes down to the lowest steps of the social scale. Not long ago a woman in Somersetshire, who had married a most unpromising brute, and had been very ill-used by him, was asked, 'However came you to marry this man?' 'Oh, ma'am,' she replied, with sobs, 'he had a dresser *and that.*' Yet although the existence of this vice is well known and obvious with us, its effects are disguised and latent. It is commonly the only considerable sin which a young lady has a chance of committing, and she very frequently commits it without reluctance. Still she hurts herself rather than us. She leads in appearance an unexceptionable life; society cannot discover the interior of women's minds, and cannot discriminate which of them love their husbands when they marry them and which do not. The acutest of us would probably be often deceived if we attempted to decide in particular cases where there was real affection and where there was none. And as we cannot be sure where the original fault has been committed, we cannot say what ill consequences it has or has not produced. Very often, as far as we can judge, it produces no bad public results whatever.

If a young lady sells herself to an old fool and does it decently, she is a discreditable young person leading a discreditable life, and that is the whole story. Such marriages being the exception, and not the rule, she goes to and fro among innocent women; she does some harm, of course; she lowers the tone of modesty as she passes; she thinks all men 'much the same,' and regards a decorous and regular vice as the ineradicable habit of the human race. Still the state of these ladies, though despicable, is not intolerable; they suffer little and they have nice dresses; it will not do to 'point a moral.' But French society is different. Marriages of affection are there the exception—the rare exception. Marriages of *convenance* and arrangement are the common rule. The writers of fiction trade upon this social fact; it is the central idea of their works, the staple out of which most of them are manufactured. We see in them clearly delineated—depicted, we may say, *ad nauseam*—the whole results of a social system in which a principal engine of moral good is turned into a principal engine of moral evil. 'If water chokes a man,' says the Greek proverb, 'what shall he take after it?' If marriage itself leads men and women into sin; if, being contracted from base motives or bad feelings, it is itself a sin, what is to be done, how can the social evil be cured? The true salt has lost its savour, and where shall we seek a substitute? The inevitable consequences of such a sort of marriage are to be found in *Fanny* and *La Griffe Rose*. When a woman's relation to her husband becomes sinful, moralists or *quasi* moralists endeavour to inquire what should be her relation to her lover, and it cannot be said that they arrive at any very satisfactory result.

Joseph-Ernest Renan
Introductory note

Joseph-Ernest Renan was born in 1823 at Tréguier, the son of a naval officer. He went to Paris in 1836 and began to be educated for the priesthood, but his philological and critical study of the semitic languages led him to question the divine inspiration of the Bible, and thence the fundamental doctrines of revealed religion. After working as an officer of the manuscript department of the Bibliothèque Nationale, he became in 1862 a Professor of Hebrew at the Collège de France. He was suspended from this post by government order, when his lectures on Jews in the history of civilisation were considered unorthodox. In 1863 his *Vie de Jésus* appeared, and his chair was suppressed. The book was the first volume of *Les Origines Du Christianisme*, a study of the gradual emergence of a monotheistic doctrine from the beliefs of a small Jewish sect, and the founding of the Church. Renan's approach was through the figures of the founders of Christianity. He was reinstated at the Collège in 1870, and became its head in 1883. Renan died in 1892.

French Religiousness and M. Renan[1]

THE popularity of M. Renan's *Vie de Jésus* in France is very great and very sudden. Already four large editions have been exhausted, and everywhere the fifth is on sale. In the common country town, far from the influence of Paris, in places such as Abbeville and Lisieux, there are copies in the meanest bookshop. Crowds of answers, most of them by the Roman Catholic clergy are advertised. The 'Evangile selon Renan,' as one of them calls it, is the most frequent topic of intellectual conversation. When men talk of theology they talk of M. Renan. Dr. Johnson would have said:—'Sir, this is fame;' we may say, 'at least this is influence.' If the *Vie de Jésus* had nothing in it which was remarkable, and we have shown that it has much, the eagerness with which it has been received at the centre of European thought would in itself demand attention.

The first cause of this remarkable popularity is unquestionably the perfection of M. Renan's style. A Frenchman, above all things, demands good prose, and he will not read bad prose. As an Englishman of business will not look at an account of figures unless it is stated in what he considers the business-like shape, so a Frenchman will not read a piece of intellectual writing unless it is what he calls *bien redigé*, unless it is reduced into a simple, lucid, and attractive style. A badly written book in France is of necessity a stillborn book. A writer who wrote in France, like Bishop Butler or like the late Mr. Austin in England, could never hope for real influence; *we* pardon unattractive expression for the sake of solid thought; perhaps we are not sufficiently sensitive to the merits of style; but a Frenchman in this particular is exacting and rigid. It is true that this eagerness after good writing creates much writing which has good words and no thought; it is true that the popular style in France has considerable defects; it is true that it is too

<hr>

[1] *The Spectator*, September 12 1863, Volume 36, pp. 2483-4. This article was first ascribed to Bagehot by Dr. Tener and I agree with the attribution on the grounds that the article has the full impress of Bagehot's style. The allusion to Dr. Johnson is characteristic of Bagehot and the description of the Frenchman's religion as 'floating' recalls his words in his essay on Clough '. . . a belief, or at any rate a floating, confused conception.'

epigrammatic and cuts up large facts into little sentences; it is true that a French writer avoids complexities which are real, and do not admit of easy explanation; it is certain that he cares to be brilliant more than he cares to be just. But after every allowance is made it will remain true that more good prose is written in France than is written anywhere else; that every year sends forth some specimens of a fine style which it would not be easy to rival in any other literature; that the ordinary Frenchman has a tact in, and a taste for, nicely fitting words that no other modern people claim or share. A book which has a great run in France must have, with whatever defects, many literary merits. These M. Renan's book undoubtedly has. Much of them will evaporate in translation, for there is a delicacy of statement, and especially a delicacy of ambiguity, which no translator will ever preserve. But even in a disenchanting translation the magic of the composition will be a little felt, and in the original the unwilling are bound by it as if by a spell. M. Renan has the first requisite of a French writer—*he can write*.

But it would be literary pedantry to suppose that mere excellence of style, however great, would give to any book that quick and potent popularity which the *Vie de Jésus* possesses. Unless a writer have something fascinating to say, no charm of words will carry the reader through a volume. We may read one page for expression merely, as we eat a bonbon or two; but we soon tire. It is impossible to doubt that M. Renan's treatise is suited to the sentiments, opinions, and habits of many Frenchmen.

The present state of French belief is, as M. Comte remarked, disorganised. A Frenchman has generally some vague, some floating, some unsolidified religion of his own, but the only point on which he has a very definite and precise conviction is that priests are not to be listened to. 'I do not, Sir, believe as my wife believes,' a great English poet once said; and most Frenchmen would say so, and have little else very exact upon religion to say. Catholicism they reject, as it were, from experience; a sort of religiosity they preserve;—but a precise new creed to substitute for the precise old creed they have not, and scarcely hope to have. Mr. Arnold, in his report on French education, illustrates this remark by an anecdote which would give even an undue idea of the disorganised state of French thought. 'In what condition is the moral and religious instruction in your school?' one of M. Guizot's inspectors asked a schoolmaster; '*Je n'enseigne pas ces bêtises là!'* That such a phrase could be used by a recognised teacher of little children is a significant indication of the loose state of ordinary thought. As far, indeed, as this anecdote gives an impression of formed irreligion or immorality it is a libel on Frenchmen; but as far as it indicates the vague laxity of their creed it is not a libel. They have religious feelings; but as far as precise propositions go their intellects are *to let.*

For minds such as these a book such as M. Renan's has, and must have, a singular interest. They wish, above most things, to adjust their mental position as respects Christianity; they consider Catholicism to be an incredible legend, but they have no substitute to offer for it. They have no theory; they cannot say what Christianity is, whence it comes, and whither it goes. They want, too, a theory in some sense suitable to the age. In the eighteenth century men could be satisfied to impute the great religions of the world to craft, fraud, and imposture; but they cannot be so now. In France especially history has been studied, and its results have become generally known. It is understood that fraud did not create faith, though it may sometimes modify and determine the embodiments of faith. Such a mode of studying history as M. Guizot's, though it may not be familiar to the mass of men at first hand,—though M. Guizot's books may be too stately and too dull for universal perusal,—yet at second hand has generated a reverential treatment of history. Frenchmen now desire a *religious disbelief*; and it is this which M. Renan gives them. He is sceptical in history, but he is religious in feeling.

The solution, too, of the problem which M. Renan proposes seems to be an easy one. A little study would show that it contains insuperable difficulties; but a casual reader may take it as it comes. He can glide upon the limpid stream, and not see the rocks below. The French are not hard readers; they have no taste for research, they accumulate particular facts neither on old history nor on foreign countries at present. They are a people of intellectual curiosity, but there is no work in them. There is no diffused taste in France for a student's life; England is not more practical in her way than France in hers. Ordinary persons in France wish to read a pleasant summary of German criticism, and this M. Renan gives them. In England such a treatise excites among ordinary persons at once a bitter repugnance. It proposes to destroy the Book which we know better than any book. But the French do not feel so. One of M. Renan's adversaries—one among the most bitter of them—observes naïvely, 'After all this book may have a good effect, it may make us read the Scriptures.' The difference between the familiarity with the Bible in France and the familiarity with it in England is written on the face of the two literatures. Every allusion to it in England is pointed, correct, and popular; in France, not long ago, a distinguished writer spoke of the 'beautiful *mot* of *Châteaubriand*,' 'Thou shall not live by bread alone.' We must remember that M. Renan's book was written for and that it is read by a clever nation, which knows the *Génie de Christianisme* better than it knows the Gospels.

For the same reason, the French are not sensitive to one of M. Renan's peculiarities—his sentimentality. M. Renan holds that if St. John wrote the Gospel which bears his name, it must have been when he was old, and did not remember what happened. His mode of expressing that opinion is, 'If the son of Zebedee really traced these pages, he had certainly forgotten the Lake of Genesareth, and the *charming conversations* (*les charmants entretiens*) which he had heard upon its banks.' He speaks as if of a flirtation.

But it is not only in these secondary aspects that M. Renan's book is congenial to the tastes and to the habits of many Frenchmen; not only are they sensitive to its accessory merits and insensible to its accessory defects, but the back-bone of it, the very essence of M. Renan's conception, is suitable to such minds as theirs in such circumstances as theirs. We cannot hope to bring home to Protestant Englishmen the exclusiveness with which Frenchmen associate Christianity and Catholicism, but a curious instance of it has lately occurred in reference to a person whose writings have attracted much attention among literary persons in England. M. Sainte-Beuve, after describing a life of letters at Paris, certainly not extremely sceptical, not exceedingly different from the life of literary men in all countries, says of Maurice de Guérin that his family had the satisfaction of seeing him again become a Christian. He means that he again became a Catholic. He, like most Frenchmen, scarcely thinks of an intermediate state. It never occurs to him that there is any other form of Christianity, any real variety of it effectually competing for human belief except Catholicism. French Protestantism is, in a great degree like English dissent. It has no influence on people of the world. You know that Lord Palmerston—you know that a Belgravian lady, may either of them be subject to change; but you know that neither of them will become an Independent dissenter. That form of religion is made for people who do not belong to the world, who are ignorant of the things of the world. Just so with French Protestantism. It is a thing apart, a creed for worthy and wanton persons, a creed not competing for intellects which the world has enlivened. And if it is natural for most Frenchmen to judge so it is even more natural for M. Renan. He was a *seminarist*, he was to have been a Catholic priest. As Catholicism is a form of religion to which he was born, and which he tried to adhere, he naturally thinks it the principal form.

If we examine M. Renan's view of the origin of Christianity we shall find that it has a close analogy to the present working of Catholicism. Like most other writers, he takes into the remote past which he has not seen, the familiar present which he has seen. It is not, indeed, easy to reduce M. Renan's conception of the first Christianity to a sentence or two without either seeming vague or seeming blasphemous. His opinions are so different from those of most Englishmen, that when tangibly and precisely presented most Englishmen are revolted by them. Still, their essence is this. He believes that Christianity was first disseminated by the undefinable attraction of Jesus, by his winning and subduing personality; but he believes also that this personality was aided by an unfounded belief in the approaching end of the world, and by an unfounded belief that He himself was in some special sense a king and prophet. The announcement that the world would break up enabled Him to preach a life apart, to found a separate sect with an impracticable morality; His announcement of His own place in the future kingdom enabled Him to govern that sect, to speak with authority as to that morality. The charm of His person was, says M. Renan, aided by the power of His errors. He advertised Himself by mistake and exaggeration, and He ruled by a magic of fascination. Now, if this is a very bad description of the first Christianity, it is a very good description of one aspect of existing Catholicism. It advertises itself by its bold pretension; it says it is a king, a prophet, a supernatural agency; it can bind and loose; it has authority to speak; it has a lesson to teach; it teaches an unearthly morality; it tells men not to form ties in the world, not to go out of the world, not to be comfortable and rich, but to be poor and holy; to live as saints in convents, not to live as men in the world. This is a lesson which eager men learn readily, which imaginative men love to hear. It gets rid of the tameness of life, of the poorness of human duties, of the petty definiteness of ordinary existence. A superhuman morality will always be acceptable to aspiring youth; they will run to hear it, they will long to obey and practise it. Catholicism advertises for men with spiritual ambition, and she bids higher than any other creed. We need not show at length her imaginative attraction; all the world knows that, and has known it for ages. She rules many men and innumerable women by a magic attraction which is scarcely applicable to those who do not feel it. She, too, advertises by her errors and charms by her undefinable essence. M. Renan's Christ, if we look into it, is only a reduced copy of the Christianity of the Catholicism of the church of his boyhood. He fancies that Jesus ruled as he saw her rule, that He erred as she erred, that He charmed as she charmed.

Frenchmen who, like M. Renan, in fact, identify Christianity with Catholicism are not, therefore, unlikely to be attracted by his theory. It rests on the facts which they know and it neglects all the facts which they do not know. It says, in substance, 'Jesus charmed the women of his time as the priests charm the women of your time,' and this is the very theory which Frenchmen would most readily appreciate and most easily believe.

Introductory note

Laurence Sterne

Laurence Sterne (1713–1768) was the son of Roger Sterne, an army ensign. He went with his family from barracks to barracks until in 1723 he was sent to school in Halifax, and in 1733 to Cambridge. He was ordained in 1738, but regarded the priesthood as a living rather than a vocation; he received through his uncle a Yorkshire living, and then a series of court sinecures with incomes. The first part of *Tristram Shandy* appeared in 1760, four more volumes in 1761, two in 1765 and the last in 1767. He was denounced by Dr. Johnson, Horace Walpole, Goldsmith and others, and many pamphlets were issued against him. His *Sentimental Journey* appeared in 1768 and he died in London in the same year.

William Makepeace Thackeray

William Makepeace Thackeray (1811–1863) was born in Calcutta, the only child of Richmond Thackeray, of the East India Company, and of Anne Becher. He was educated at Charterhouse, and then went to Cambridge which he left in 1830 without taking a degree. In 1831 he entered the Middle Temple, but gave up the legal profession as soon as he came of age. In 1837 he became proprietor of *The National Standard*, for which he wrote and drew. When it failed he settled in Paris for a while, but returned to London in 1837. He was associated with *Punch* from its earliest years, contributing to it from 1842, but the beginning of his popularity was the publication of *The Snobs Papers* which appeared in *Punch* in 1847. Before the *Snobs* was completed, *Vanity Fair* had begun to appear in serial numbers, followed by *Pendennis* in 1848, *Esmond* in 1852, and *The Newcomes* in 1853–5. *The English Humourists of The Eighteenth Century* was published in 1853, and a sequel to *Esmond*, *The Virginians* appeared in serial numbers between 1857–9. Thackeray died in London in 1863.

Sterne and Thackeray[1]

MR. PERCY FITZGERALD has expressed his surprise that no one before him has narrated the life of Sterne in two volumes. We are much more suprised that he has done so. The life of Sterne was of the very simplest sort. He was a Yorkshire clergyman, and lived for the most part a sentimental, questionable, jovial life in the country. He was a queer parson, according to our notions; but in those days there were many queer parsons. Late in life he wrote a book or two, which gave him access to London society; and then he led a still more questionable and unclerical life at the edge of the great world. After that he died in something like distress, and leaving his family in something like misery. A simpler life, as far as facts go, never was known; and simple as it is, the story has been well told by Sir Walter Scott, and has been well commented on by Mr. Thackeray. It should have occurred to Mr. Fitzgerald that a subject may only have been briefly treated because it is a limited and simple subject, which suggests but few remarks, and does not require an elaborate and copious description.

There are but few materials, too, for a long life of Sterne. Mr. Fitzgerald has stuffed his volumes with needless facts about Sterne's distant relations, his great-uncles and ninth cousins, in which no one now can take the least interest. Sterne's daughter, who was left ill-off, did indeed publish two little volumes of odd letters, which no clergyman's daughter would certainly have published now. But even these are too small in size and thin in matter to be spun into a copious narrative. We should in this Review have hardly given even a brief sketch of Sterne's life, if we did not think that his artistic character presented one fundamental resemblance and many superficial contrasts to that of a great man whom we have lately lost. We wish to point these out; and a few interspersed remarks on the life of Sterne will

1 *The Life of Laurence Sterne.* By Percy Fitzgerald, M.A., M.R.I.A. In two volumes. Chapman and Hall. *Thackeray the Humourist and the Man of Letters.* By Theodore Taylor, Esq. London: John Camden Hotten. This essay first appeared in the *National Review*, April 1864, Volume XVIII, pp. 523–53.

enable us to enliven the tedium of criticism with a little interest from human life.

Sterne's father was a shiftless roving Irish officer in the early part of the last century. He served in Marlborough's wars, and was cast adrift, like many greater people, by the caprice of Queen Anne and the sudden peace of Utrecht. Of him only one anecdote remains. He was, his son tells us, 'a little smart man, somewhat rapid and hasty' in his temper; and during some fighting at Gibraltar he got into a squabble with another young officer, a Captain Phillips. The subject, it seems, was a goose; but that is not now material. It ended in a duel, which was fought with swords in a room. Captain Phillips pinned Ensign Sterne to a plaster-wall behind; upon which he quietly asked, or is said to have asked, 'Do wipe the plaster off your sword before you pull it out of me;' which, if true, showed at least presence of mind. Mr. Fitzgerald, in his famine of matter, discusses who this Captain Phillips was; but into this we shall not follow him.

A smart, humorous, shiftless father of this sort is not perhaps a bad father for a novelist. Sterne was dragged here and there, through scenes of life where no correct and thriving parent would ever have taken him. Years afterwards, with all their harshness softened and half their pains dissembled, Sterne dashed them upon pages which will live for ever. Of money and respectability Sterne inherited from his father little or none; but he inherited two main elements of his intellectual capital— a great store of odd scenes, and the sensitive Irish nature which appreciates odd scenes.

Sterne was born in the year 1713, the year of the peace of Utrecht, which cast his father adrift upon the world. Of his mother we know nothing. Years afterwards, it was said that he behaved ill to her; at least neglected her in misery[2] when he had the means of placing her in comfort. His enemies neatly said that he preferred 'whining over a dead ass to relieving a living mother.' But these accusations have never been proved. Sterne was not remarkable for active benevolence, and certainly may have neglected an old and uninteresting woman, even though that woman was his mother; he was a bad hand at dull duties, and did not like elderly females; but we must not condemn him on simple probabilities, or upon a neat epigram and loose tradition. 'The regiment,' says Sterne, 'in which my father served being broke, he

[2] Morgan and Hutton have 'neglected and left her in misery' but there is insufficient justification for such a change and the original has been followed.

left Ireland as soon as I[3] was able to be carried, and came to the family seat at Elvington, near York, where his mother lived.' After this he was carried about for some years, as his father led the rambling life of a poor ensign, who was one of very many engaged during a very great war, and discarded at a hasty peace. Then, perhaps luckily, his father died, and 'my cousin Sterne of Elvington,' as he calls him, took charge of him, and sent him to school and college. At neither of these was he very eminent. He told one story late in life which may be true, but seems very unlike the usual school-life. 'My schoolmaster,' he says, 'had the ceiling of the schoolroom new whitewashed: the ladder remained there. I one unlucky day mounted it, and wrote with a brush in large capital LAU. STERNE, for which the usher severely punished me. My master was much hurt at this, and said before me that never should that name be effaced, for I was a boy of genius, and he was sure I should come to preferment.' But 'genius' is rarely popular in places of education; and it is, to say the least, remarkable that so sentimental a man as Sterne should have chanced upon so sentimental an instructor. It is wise to be suspicious of aged reminiscents; they are like persons entrusted with 'untold gold:' there is no check on what they tell us.

Sterne went to Cambridge, and though he did not acquire elaborate learning, he thoroughly learned a gentlemanly stock of elementary knowledge. There is even something scholarlike about his style. It bears the indefinable traces which an exact study of words will always leave upon the use of words. He was accused of stealing learning, and it is likely enough that a great many needless quotations which were stuck into *Tristram Shandy* were abstracted from second-hand store-houses where such things are to be found. But what he stole was worth very little, and his theft may now at least be pardoned, for it injures the popularity of his works. Our present novel-readers do not at all care for an elaborate caricature of the scholastic learning; it is so obsolete that we do not care to have it mimicked. Much of *Tristram Shandy* is a sort of antediluvian fun, in which uncouth Saurian jokes play idly in an unintelligible world.

When he left college, Sterne had a piece of good fortune which in fact ruined him. He had an uncle with much influence in the church, and he was thereby seduced to enter the church. There could not have been a greater error. He had no special vice; he was notorious for no

[3] The *National Review* has 'he' but the sense clearly requires 'I' and this has been substituted.

281

wild dissipation or unpardonable folly; he had done nothing which even in this more discreet age would be considered imprudent. He had even a refinement which must save him from gross vice, and a nicety of nature which must save him from coarse associations. But for all that he was as little fit for a Christian priest as if he had been a drunkard and a profligate. Perhaps even he was less fit.

There are certain persons whom taste guides, much as morality and conscience guide ordinary persons. They are 'gentlemen.' They revolt from what is coarse; are sickened by that which is gross; hate what is ugly. They have no temptation to what we may call ordinary vices; they have no inclination for such raw food; on the contrary, they are repelled by it, and loathe it. The law in their members does *not* war against the law of their mind; on the contrary, the *taste* of their bodily nature is mainly in harmony with what conscience would prescribe or religion direct. They may not have heard the saying that the 'beautiful is higher than the good, for it includes the good.' But when they do hear it, it comes upon them as a revelation of their instinctive creed, of the guidance under which they have been living all their lives. They are pure because it is ugly to be impure; innocent because it is out of taste to be otherwise; they live within the hedge-rows of polished society; they do not wish to go beyond them into the great deep of human life; they have a horror of that 'impious ocean,' yet not of the impiety, but of the miscellaneous noise, the disordered confusion of the whole. These are the men whom it is hardest to make Christian,—for the simplest reason: paganism is sufficient for them. Their pride of the eye is a good pride; their love of the flesh is a delicate and directing love. They keep 'within the path-ways' because they dislike the gross, the uncultured, and the untrodden. Thus they reject the primitive precept which comes before Christianity. Repent! repent! says a voice in the wilderness; but the delicate pagan feels superior to the voice in the wilderness. Why should he attend to this uncouth person? He has nice clothes and well-chosen food, the treasures of exact knowledge, the delicate results of the highest civilisa-tion. Is he to be directed by a person of savage habits, with a distorted countenance, who lives on wild honey, who does not wear decent clothes? To the pure worshipper of beauty, to the naturally refined pagan, conscience and the religion of conscience are not merely in-truders, but barbarous intruders. At least so it is in youth, when life is simple and temptations, if strong, are distinct. Years afterwards, probably, the purest pagan will be taught by a constant accession of indistinct temptations, and by a gradual declension of his nature, that taste at the best, and sentiment of the very purest, are insufficient guides in the perplexing labyrinth of the world.

Sterne was a pagan. He went into the Church; but Mr. Thackeray, no bad judge, said most justly that his sermons 'have not a single Christian sentiment.' They are well-expressed, vigorous, moral essays; but they are no more. Much more was not expected by many congregations in the last age. The secular feeling of the English people, though always strong,—though strong in Chaucer's time, and though strong now,—was never so all-powerful as in the last century. It was in those days that the poet Crabbe was remonstrated with for introducing heaven and hell into his sermons; such extravagances, he was told, were very well for the Methodists, but a *clergyman* should confine himself to sober matters of this world, and show the prudence and the reasonableness of virtue during this life. There is not much of heaven and hell in Sterne's sermons, and what there is seems a rhetorical emphasis which is not essential to the argument, and which might perhaps as well be left out. Auguste Comte might have admitted most of these sermons; they are healthy statements of earthly truths, but they would be just as true if there was no religion at all. Religion helps the argument, because foolish people might be perplexed with this world, and they yield readily to another; religion enables you—such is the real doctrine of these divines, when you examine it—to coax and persuade those whom you cannot rationally convince; but it does not alter the matter in hand—it does not affect that of which you wish to persuade men, for you are but inculcating a course of conduct *in this life*. Sterne's sermons would be just as true if the secularists should succeed in their argument, and the 'valuable illusion' of a deity were omitted from the belief of mankind.

However, in fact, Sterne took orders, and by the aid of his uncle, who was a church politician, and who knew the powers that were, he obtained several small livings. Being a pluralist was a trifle in those easy times; nobody then thought that the parishioners of a parson had a right to his daily presence; if some provision were made for the performance of a Sunday service, he had done his duty, and he could spend the surplus income where he liked. He might perhaps be bound to reside, if health permitted, on one of his livings, but the law allowed him to have many, and he could not be compelled to reside on them all. Sterne preached well-written sermons on Sundays, and led an easy pagan life on other days, and no one blamed him.

He fell in love too, and after he was dead, his daughter found two or three of his love-letters to her mother, which she rashly published. They have been the unfeeling sport of persons not in love up to the present time. Years ago Mr. Thackeray used to make audiences laugh till they cried by reading one or two of them, and contrasting them with certain other letters, also about his wife, but written many years later. This is the sort of thing.

Yes! I will steal from the world, and not a babbling tongue shall tell where I am—Echo shall not so much as whisper my hiding-place—suffer thy imagination to paint it as a little sun-gilt cottage, on the side of a romantic hill—dost thou think I will leave love and friendship behind me? No! they shall be my companions in solitude, for they will sit down and rise up with me in the amiable form of my L.—We will be as merry and as innocent as our first parents in Paradise, before the arch fiend entered that undescribable scene.

The kindest affections will have room to shoot and expand in our retirement, and produce such fruit as madness, and envy, and ambition have always killed in the bud.—Let the human tempest and hurricane rage at a distance, the desolation is beyond the horizon of peace. My L. has seen a polyanthus blow in December—some friendly wall has sheltered it from the biting wind.—No planetary influence shall reach us, but that which presides and cherishes the sweetest flowers.—God preserve us! How delightful this prospect in idea! We will build, and we will plant, in our own way—simplicity shall not be tortured by art—we will learn of nature how to live—she shall be our alchymist, to mingle all the good of life into one salubrious draught.—The gloomy family of care and distrust shall be banished from our dwelling, guarded by thy kind and tutelar deity—we will sing our choral songs of gratitude, and rejoice to the end of our pilgrimage.

Adieu, my L. Return to one who languishes for thy society.

L. STERNE.

The beautiful language with which young ladies were wooed a century ago is a characteristic of that extinct age; at least, we fear that no such beautiful English will be discovered when our secret repositories are ransacked. The age of ridicule has come in, and the age of good words has gone out.

There is no reason to doubt, however, that Sterne was really in love with Mrs. Sterne. People have doubted it because of these beautiful words; but, in fact, Sterne was just the sort of man to be subject to this kind of feeling. He took—and to this he owes his fame—the *sensitive* view of life. He regarded it not from the point of view of intellect, or conscience, or religion, but in the plain way in which natural feeling impresses, and will always impress, a natural person. He is a great author; certainly not because of great thoughts, for there is scarcely a sentence in his writings which can be called a thought; nor from sublime conceptions which enlarge the limits of our imagination, for he never leaves the sensuous,—but because of his wonderful sympathy with, and wonderful power of representing, simple human nature. The best passages in Sterne are those which every one knows, like this:

Thou has left this matter short, said my uncle Toby to the corporal, as he was putting him to bed,—and I will tell thee in what, Trim.—In the first place, when thou madest an offer of my services to Le Fever,—as sickness and travelling are both expensive, and thou knowest he was but a poor lieutenant, with a son to subsist as well as himself, out of his pay,—that thou didst not make an offer to him of my purse; because, had he stood indeed, thou knowest, Trim, he had been as welcome to it as myself.——Your honour knows, said the corporal, I had no orders;——True, quoth my uncle Toby,—thou didst very right, Trim, as a soldier,—but certainly very wrong as a man.

In the second place, for which, indeed, thou hast the same excuse, continued my uncle Toby,——when thou offeredst him whatever was in my house,—thou shouldst have offered him my house too:——A sick brother officer should have the best quarters, Trim, and if we had him with us,— we could tend and look to him:——Thou art an excellent nurse thyself, Trim,—and what with thy care of him, and the old woman's, and his boy's, and mine together, we might recruit him again at once, and set him upon his legs.

——In a fortnight or three weeks, added my uncle Toby, smiling,—he might march.——He will never march, an' please your honour, in this world, said the corporal:——He will march, said my uncle Toby, rising up from the side of the bed, with one shoe off.—— An' please your honour, said the corporal, he will never march, but to his grave:——He shall march, cried my uncle Toby, marching the foot which had a shoe on, though without advancing an inch,—he shall march to his regiment.——He cannot stand it, said the corporal:——He shall be supported, said my uncle Toby:——He'll drop at last, said the corporal, and what will become of his boy?——He shall not drop, said my uncle Toby, firmly.——A-well-o'day,—do what we can for him, said Trim, maintaining his point,—the poor soul will die: ——He shall not die, by G—, cried my uncle Toby.

—The ACCUSING SPIRIT, which flew up to heaven's chancery with the oath, blush'd as he gave it in;—and the RECORDING ANGEL, as he wrote it down, dropp'd a tear upon the word, and blotted it out for ever.

—My uncle Toby went to his bureau,—put his purse into his breeches pocket, and having ordered the corporal to go early in the morning for a physician,—he went to bed, and fell asleep.

The sun looked bright the morning after, to every eye in the village but Le Fever's and his afflicted son's; the hand of death press'd heavy upon his eye-lids,——and hardly could the wheel at the cistern turn round its circle, —when my uncle Toby, who had rose up an hour before his wonted time, entered the lieutenant's room, and without preface or apology, sat himself down upon the chair by the bed-side and, independently of all modes and customs, opened the curtain in the manner an old friend and brother officer would have done it, and asked him how he did,—how he had rested in the night,—what was his complaint,—where was his pain,—and what he could do to help him:——and without giving him time to answer any one of the enquiries, went on and told him of the little plan which he had been con-certing with the corporal the night before for him.——

——You shall go home directly, Le Fever, said my uncle Toby, to my house,—and we'll send for a doctor to see what's the matter,—and we'll have an apothecary,—and the corporal shall be your nurse;——and I'll be your servant, Le Fever.

There was a frankness in my uncle Toby,—not the *effect* of familiarity,— but the *cause* of it,—which let you at once into his soul, and shewed you the goodness of his nature; to this there was something in his looks, and voice, and manner, super-added, which eternally beckoned to the unfortunate to come and take shelter under him; so that before my uncle Toby had half finished the kind offers he was making to the father, had the son insensibly pressed up close to his knees, and had taken hold of the breast of his coat, and was pulling it towards him.——The blood and spirits of Le Fever, which were waxing cold and slow within him, and were retreating to their last citadel, the heart,—rallied back,—the film forsook his eyes for a moment,— he looked up wishfully in my uncle Toby's face,—then cast a look upon his boy,——and that *ligament*, fine as it was,—was never broken.——

Nature instantly ebb'd again,—the film returned to its place,——the pulse fluttered——stopp'd——went on——throbb'd——stopp'd again ——moved——stopp'd——shall I go on?——No.

In one of the 'Roundabout Papers' Mr. Thackeray introduces a literary man complaining of his 'sensibility.' 'Ah,' he replies, 'my good friend, your sensibility is your livelihood: if you did not feel the events and occurrences of life more acutely than others, you could not describe them better; and it is the excellence of your description by which you live.' This is precisely true of Sterne. He is a great author because he felt acutely. He is the most pathetic of writers because he had—when writing, at least—the most pity. He was, too, we believe, pretty sharply in love with Mrs. Sterne, because he was sensitive to that sort of feeling likewise.

The difficulty of this sort of character is the difficulty of keeping it. It does not last. There is a certain bloom of sensibility and feeling about it which, in the course of nature, is apt to fade soon, and which, when it has faded, there is nothing to replace. A character with the binding elements—with a firm will, a masculine understanding, and a persistent conscience—may retain, and perhaps improve, the early and original freshness. But a loose-set, though pure character, the moment it is thrown into temptation, sacrifices its purity, loses its gloss, and gets, so to speak, out of form entirely.

We do not know with great accuracy what Sterne's temptations were, but there was one, which we can trace with some degree of precision, which has left ineffaceable traces on his works,—which probably left some traces upon his character and conduct. There was in that part of Yorkshire a certain John Hall Stevenson, a country gentleman of some fortune, and possessed of a castle, which he called Crazy Castle. Thence he wrote tales, which he named 'Crazy Tales,' but which certainly are not entitled to any such innocent name. The licence of that age was unquestionably wonderful. A man of good property could write any evil. There was no legal check, or ecclesiastical check, and hardly any check of public opinion. These 'Crazy Tales' have licence without humour, and vice without amusement. They are the writing of a man with some wit, but only enough wit for light conversation, which becomes overworked and dull when it is reduced to regular composition and made to write long tales. The author, feeling his wit jaded, perpetually becomes immoral, in the vain hope that he will cease to be dull. He has attained his reward; he will be remembered for nauseous tiresomeness by all who have read him.

But though the 'Crazy Tales' are now tedious, Crazy Castle was a pleasant place, at least to men like Sterne. He was an idle young parson, with much sensibility, much love of life and variety, and not a bit of grave goodness. The dull duties of a country parson, as we now understand them, would never have been to his taste; and the sinecure idleness then permitted to parsons left him open to every temptation. The frail texture of merely natural purity, the soft fibre of the instinctive pagan, yield to the first casualty. Exactly what sort of life they led at Crazy Castle we do not know, but vaguely we do know, and we may be sure *Mrs.* Sterne was against it.

One part of Crazy Castle has had effects which will last as long as English literature. It had a library richly stored in old folio learning, and also in the amatory reading of other days. Every page of *Tristram Shandy* bears traces of both elements. Sterne, when he wrote it, had filled his head and his mind, not with the literature of his own age, but with the literature of past ages. He was thinking of Rabelais rather than of Fielding; of forgotten romances rather than of Richardson. He wrote, indeed, of his own times and of men he had seen, because his sensitive vivid nature would only endure to write of present things. But the *mode* in which he wrote was largely coloured by literary habits and literary fashions that had long passed away. The oddity of the book was a kind of advertisement to its genius, and that oddity consisted in the use of old manners upon new things. No analysis or account of *Tristram Shandy* could be given which would suit the present generation; being, indeed, a book without plan or order, it is in every generation unfit for analysis. This age would not endure a statement of the most telling points, as the writer thought them, and no age would like an elaborate plan of a book in which there is no plan, in which the detached remarks and separate scenes were really meant to be the whole. The notion that 'a plot was to hang plums upon' was Sterne's notion exactly.

The real excellence of Sterne is single and simple; the defects are numberless and complicated. He excels, perhaps, all other writers in mere simple description of common sensitive human action. He places before you in their simplest form the elemental facts of human life; he does not view them through the intellect, he scarcely views them through the imagination; he does but reflect the unimpaired impression which the facts of life, which does not change from age to age, make on the deep basis of human feeling, which changes as little though years go on. The example we quoted just now is as good as any other, though not better than any other. Our readers should go back to it again, or our praise may seem overcharged. It is the portrait-painting of the heart. It is as pure a reflection of mere natural feeling as literature has ever given, or will ever give. The delineation is nearly perfect. Sterne's feeling in his higher moments so much overpowered his intellect, and so directed his imagination, that no intrusive thought blemishes, no distorting fancy mars, the perfection of the representation. The disenchanting facts which deface, the low circumstances which debase, the simpler feelings oftener than any other feelings, his art excludes. The feeling which would probably be coarse in the reality is refined in the picture. The unconscious tact of the nice artist heightens and chastens reality, but yet it is reality still. His mind was like a pure lake of delicate water: it reflects the ordinary landscape, the rugged hills, the loose pebbles, the knotted and the distorted firs perfectly and as they are, yet with a charm and fascination that they have not in themselves. This is the highest attainment of art: to be at the same time nature and something more than nature.

But here the great excellence of Sterne ends as well as begins. In *Tristram Shandy* especially there are several defects which, while we are reading it, tease and disgust so much that we are scarcely willing even to admire as we ought to admire the nice pictures of human emotion. The first of these, and perhaps the worst, is the fantastic disorder of the form. It is an imperative law of the writing art that a book should go straight on. A great writer should be able to tell a great meaning as coherently as a small writer tells a small meaning. The magnitude of the thought to be conveyed, the delicacy of the emotion to be painted, render the introductory touches of consummate art not of less importance, but of more importance. A great writer should train the mind of the reader for his greatest things; that is, by first strokes and fitting preliminaries he should form and prepare his mind for the due appreciation and the perfect enjoyment of high creations. He should not blunder upon a beauty, nor, after a great imaginative creation, should he at once fall back to bare prose. The high-wrought feeling which a poet excites should not be turned out at once and without warning into the discomposing world. It is one of the greatest merits of the greatest living writer of fiction—of the authoress of *Adam Bede*—that she never brings you to anything without preparing you for it; she has no loose lumps of beauty; she puts in nothing at random; after her greatest scenes, too, a natural sequence of subordinate realities again tones down the mind to this sublunary world. Her logical style—the most logical, probably, which a woman ever wrote—aids in this matter her natural sense of due proportion.

There is not a space of incoherency—not a gap. It is not natural to begin with the point of a story, and she does not begin with it. When some great marvel has been told, we all wish to know what came of it, and she tells us. Her natural way, as it seems to those who do not know its rarity, of telling what happened produces the consummate effect of gradual enchantment and as gradual disenchantment. But Sterne's style is *un*natural. He never begins at the beginning and goes straight through to the end. He shies in a beauty suddenly; and just when you are affected he turns round and grins at it. 'Ah,' he says, 'is it not fine?' And then he makes jokes which at that place and that time are out of place, or passes away in scholastic or other irrelevant matter, which simply disgusts and disheartens those whom he has just delighted. People excuse all this iregularity of form by saying that it was imitated from Rabelais. But this is nonsense. Rabelais, perhaps, could not in his day venture to tell his meaning straight out; at any rate, he did not tell it. Sterne should not have chosen a model so monstrous. Incoherency is not less a defect because an imperfect foreign writer once made use of it. 'You may have, sir, a reason,' said Dr. Johnson, 'for saying that two and two make five, but they will still make four.' Just so, a writer may have a reason for selecting the defect of incoherency, but it is a defect still. Sterne's best things read best out of his books—in Enfield's *Speaker* and other places—and you can say no worse of any one as a continuous artist.

Another most palpable defect—especially palpable nowadays—in *Tristram Shandy* is its indecency. It is quite true that the customary conventions of writing are much altered during the last century, and much which would formerly have been deemed blameless would now be censured and disliked. The audience has changed; and decency is of course in part dependent on who is within hearing. A divorce case may be talked over across a club-table with a plainness of speech and development of expression which would be indecent in a mixed party, and scandalous before young ladies. Now, a large part of old novels may very fairly be called club-books; they speak out plainly and simply the notorious facts of the world, as men speak of them to men. Much excellent and proper masculine conversation is wholly unfit for repetition to young girls; and just in the same way books written— as was almost all old literature,—for men only, or nearly only, seem coarse enough when contrasted with novels written by young ladies upon the subjects and in the tone of the drawing-room. The change is inevitable; as soon as works of fiction are addressed to boys and girls, they must be fit for boys and girls; they must deal with a life which is real so far as it goes, but which is yet most limited; which deals with the most passionate part of life, and yet omits the errors of the passions; which aims at describing men in their relations to women, and yet omits an all but universal influence which more or less distorts and modifies all these relations.

As we have said, the change cannot be helped. A young ladies' literature must be a limited and truncated literature. The indiscriminate study of human life is not desirable for them, either in fiction or in reality. But the habitual formation of a scheme of thought and a code of morality upon incomplete materials is a very serious evil. The readers for whose sake the omissions are made cannot fancy what is left out. Many a girl of the present day reads novels, and nothing but novels; she forms her mind by them, as far as she forms it by reading at all; even if she reads a few dull books, she soon forgets all about them, and remembers the novels only; she is more influenced by them than by sermons. They form her idea of the world, they define her taste, and modify her morality; not so much in explicit thought and direct act as unconsciously and in her floating fancy. How is it possible to convince such a girl, especially if she is clever, that on most points she is all wrong? She has been reading most excellent descriptions of mere society; she comprehends those descriptions perfectly, for her own experience elucidates and confirms them. She has a vivid picture of a *patch* of life. Even if she admits in words that there is something beyond, something of which she has no idea, she will not admit it really and in practice. What she has mastered and realised will incurably and inevitably overpower the unknown something of which she knows nothing, can imagine nothing, and can make nothing. 'I am not sure,' said an old lady, 'but I think it's the novels that make my girls so *heady*.' It is the novels. A very intelligent acquaintance with limited life makes them think that the world is far simpler than it is, that men are easy to understand, 'that mamma is *so* foolish.'

The novels of the last age have certainly not this fault. They do not err on the side of reticence. A girl may learn from them more than it is desirable for her to know. But, as we have explained, they were meant for men and not for girls; and if *Tristram Shandy* had simply given a plain exposition of necessary facts—necessary, that is, to the development of the writer's view of the world, and to the telling of the story in hand—we should not have complained; we should have regarded it as the natural product of a now extinct society. But there are most unmistakable traces of 'Crazy Castle' in *Tristram Shandy*. There is indecency for indecency's sake. It is made a sort of recurring and even permeating joke to mention things which are not generally mentioned. Sterne himself made a sort of defence, or rather denial, of this. He once asked a lady if she had read *Tristram*. 'I have not, Mr. Sterne,' was the answer; 'and, to be plain with you, I am informed it is not proper for female perusal.' 'My dear good lady,' said Sterne, 'do not be gulled by such stories; the book is like your young heir there' (pointing to a child of three years old who was rolling on the carpet in white tunics): 'he shows at times a good deal that is usually concealed, but it is all in perfect innocence.' But a perusal of *Tristram* would not make good the plea. The unusual publicity of what is ordinarily imperceptible is not the thoughtless accident of amusing play; it is deliberately sought after as a nice joke; it is treated as a good in itself.

The indecency of *Tristram Shandy*—at least of the early part, which was written before Sterne had been to France—is especially an offence against taste, because of its ugliness. *Moral* indecency is always disgusting. There certainly is a sort of writing which cannot be called decent, and which describes a society to the core immoral, which nevertheless is no offence against art; it violates a higher code than that of taste, but it does not violate the code of taste. The *Mémoires de Grammont*—hundreds of French memoirs about France—are of this kind, more or less. They describe the refined, witty, elegant immorality of an idle aristocracy. They describe a life 'unsuitable to such a being as man in such a world as the present one,' in which there are no high aims, no severe duties, where some precepts of morals seem not so much to be sometimes broken as to be generally suspended and forgotten; such a life, in short, as God has never suffered men to lead on this earth long, which He has always crushed out by calamity and revolution. This life, though an offence in morals, was not an offence in taste. It was an elegant, a *pretty* thing while it lasted. Especially in enhancing description, where the alloy of life may be omitted, where nothing vulgar need be noticed, where everything elegant may be neatly painted,—such a world is elegant enough. Morals and policy must decide how far such delineations are permissible or expedient;

but the art of beauty—art criticism[4],—has no objection to them. They are pretty paintings of pretty objects, and that is all it has to say. They may very easily do harm; if generally read among the young of the middle class, they would be sure to do harm: they would teach not a few to aim at a sort of refinement denied them by circumstances, and to neglect the duties allotted them; it would make shopmen 'bad imitations of polished ungodliness,' and also bad shopmen. But still, though it would in such places be noxious literature, in itself it would be pretty literature. The critic must praise it, though the moralist must condemn it, and perhaps the politician forbid it.

But *Tristram's* indecency is the very opposite to this refined sort. It consists in allusions to certain inseparable accompaniments of actual life which are not beautiful, which can never be made interesting, which would, *if* they were decent, be dull and uninteresting. There is, it appears, a certain excitement in putting such matters into a book: there is a minor exhilaration even in petty crime. At first such things look so odd in print that you go on reading them to see what they look like; but you soon give up. What is disenchanting or even disgusting in reality does not become enchanting or endurable in delineation. You are more angry at it in literature than in life; there is much which is barbarous and animal in reality that we could wish away; we endure it because we cannot help it, because we did not make it and cannot alter it, because it is an inseparable part of this inexplicable world. But why we should put this coarse alloy, this dross of life, into the *optional* world of literature, which we can make as we please, it is impossible to say. The needless introduction of accessory ugliness is always a sin in art, and is not at all less so when such ugliness is disgusting and improper. *Tristram Shandy* is incurably tainted with a pervading vice; it dwells at length on, it seeks after, it returns to, it gloats over, the most unattractive part of the world.

There is another defect in *Tristram Shandy* which would of itself remove it from the list of first-rate books, even if those which we have mentioned did not do so. It contains eccentric characters only. Some part of this defect may be perhaps explained by one peculiarity of its origin. Sterne was so sensitive to the picturesque parts of life, that he wished to paint the picturesque parts of the people he hated. Country-

[4] The *National Review* has '—but criticism' which seems unlikely especially in view of the 'it' in the following sentence which indicates a singular subject. I have substituted 'art' for 'but', following Morgan and Hutton.

towns in those days abounded in odd character. They were out of the way of the great opinion of the world, and shaped themselves to little opinions of their own. They regarded the customs which the place had inherited as the customs which were proper for it, and which it would be foolish, if not wicked, to try to change. This gave English country-life a motley picturesqueness then, which it wants now, when London ideas shoot out every morning, and carry on the wings of the railway a uniform creed to each cranny of the kingdom, north and south, east and west. These little public opinions of little places wanted, too, the crushing power of the great public opinion of our own day; at the worst, a man could escape from them into some different place which had customs and doctrines that suited him better. We now may fly into another 'city,' but it is all the same Roman empire; the same uniform justice, the one code of heavy laws, press us down and make us—the sensible part of us at least—as like other people as we can make ourselves. The public opinion of county-towns yielded soon to individual exceptions; it had not the confidence in itself which the opinion of each place now receives from the accordant and simultaneous echo of a hundred places. If a man chose to be queer, he was bullied for a year or two, then it was settled that he was 'queer;' that was the fact about him,[5] and must be accepted. In a year or so he became an 'institution' of the place, and the local pride would have been grieved if he had amended the oddity which suggested their legends and added a flavour to their life. Of course, if a man was rich and influential, he might soon disregard the mere opinion of the petty locality. Every place has wonderful traditions of old rich men who did exactly as they pleased, because they could set at naught the opinions of the neighbours, by whom they were feared; and who did not, as now, dread the unanimous conscience which does not fear even a squire of £2000 a year, or a banker of £800, because it is backed by the wealth of London and the magnitude of all the country. There is little oddity in county-towns now; they are detached scraps of great places; but in Sterne's time there was much, and he used it unsparingly.

Much of the delineation is of the highest merit. Sterne knew how to describe eccentricity, for he showed its relation to our common human nature: he showed how we were related to it, how in some sort and in some circumstances we might ourselves become it. He

---

[5] The *National Review* has 'fact to him' which does not make sense and I have substituted 'the fact about him'. Morgan and Hutton have made similar emendations.

reduced the abnormal formation to the normal rules. Except upon this condition, eccentricity is no fit subject for literary art. Every one must have known characters which, if they were put down in books, barely and as he sees them, would seem monstrous and disproportioned, which would disgust all readers, which every critic would term unnatural. While characters are monstrous, they should be kept out of books; they are ugly unintelligibilities, foreign to the realm of true art. But as soon as they can be explained to us, as soon as they are shown in their union with, in their outgrowth from, common human nature, they are the best subjects for great art—for they are new subjects. They teach us, not the old lesson which our fathers knew, but a new lesson which will please us and make us better than them. Hamlet is an eccentric character, one of the most eccentric in literature; but because, by the art of the poet, we are made to understand that he is a possible, a *vividly* possible man, he enlarges our conceptions of human nature; he takes us out of the bounds of commonplace. He 'instructs us by means of delight.' Sterne does this too. Mr. Shandy, Uncle Toby, Corporal Trim, Mrs. Shandy,—for in strictness she too is eccentric from her abnormal commonplaceness,—are beings of which the possibility is brought home to us, which we feel we could under circumstances and by influences become, which, though contorted and twisted, are yet spun out of the same elementary nature, the same thread, as we are. Considering how odd these characters are, the success of Sterne is marvellous, and his art in this respect consummate. But yet on a point most nearly allied it is very faulty. Though each individual character is shaded off into human nature, the whole is not shaded off into the world. This society of originals and oddities is left to stand by itself, as if it were a natural and ordinary society,—a society easily conceivable and needing no explanation. Such is not the manner of the great masters; in their best works a constant atmosphere of half commonplace personages surrounds and shades off, illustrates and explains, every central group of singular persons.

On the whole, therefore, the judgment of criticism on *Tristram Shandy* is concise and easy. It is immortal because of certain scenes suggested by Sterne's curious experience, detected by his singular sensibility, and heightened by his delineative and discriminative imagination. It is defective because its style is fantastic, its method illogical and provoking; because its indecency is of the worst sort, as far as in such matters an artistic judgment can speak of worst and best; because its world of characters forms an incongruous group of singular persons utterly dissimilar to, and irreconcilable with, the world in which we live. It is a great work of art, but of barbarous art. Its mirth is boisterous. It is *provincial*. It is redolent of an inferior society; for those who think crude animal spirits in themselves delightful, who do not know that, without wit to point them or humour to convey them, they are disagreeable to others; who like disturbing transitions, blank pages, and tricks of style; who do not know that a simple and logical form of expression is the most effective, if not the easiest,—the least laborious to readers, if not always the most easily attained by writers.

The oddity of *Tristram Shandy* was, however, a great aid to its immediate popularity. If an author were to stand on his head now and then in Cheapside, his eccentricity would bring him into contact with the police, but it would advertise his writings; they would sell better: people would like to see what was said by a great author who was so odd as to stand so. Sterne put his eccentricity into his writings, and therefore came into collision with the critics; but he attained the same end. His book sold capitally. As with all popular authors, he went to London; he was *fêted*. 'The *man* Sterne,' growled Dr. Johnson, 'has dinner engagements for three months.' The upper world,—ever desirous of novelty, ever tired of itself, ever anxious to be amused,—was in hopes of a new wit. It naturally hoped that the author of *Tristram* would talk well, and it sent for him to talk.

He did talk well, it appears, though not always very correctly, and never very clerically. His appearance was curious, but yet refined. Eager eyes, a wild look, a long lean frame, and what he called a cadaverous bale of goods[6] for a body, made up an odd exterior, which attracted notice, and did not repel liking. He looked like a scarecrow with bright eyes. With a random manner, but not without a nice calculation, he discharged witticisms at London parties. His keen nerves told him which were fit witticisms; *they* took, and *he* was applauded.

He published some sermons too. That tolerant age liked, it is instructive as well as amusing to think, sermons by the author of *Tristram Shandy*. People wonder at the rise of Methodism; but ought they to wonder? If a clergyman publishes his sermons *because* he has

[6] Morgan has 'bale of cadaverous goods'.

written an indecent novel—a novel which is purely pagan—which is outside the ideas of Christianity, whose author can scarcely have been inside of them,—if a man so made and so circumstanced is *as such* to publish Christian sermons, surely Christianity is a joke and a dream. Wesley was right in this at least; if Christianity be true, the upper life of the last century was based on rotten falsehood. A world which is really secular—which professes to be Christian, is the worst of worlds.

The only point in which Sterne resembles a clergyman of our own time is that he lost his voice. That peculiar affection of the chest and throat, which is hardly known among barristers, but which inflicts such suffering upon parsons, attacked him also. Sterne too, as might be expected, went abroad for it. He 'spluttered French,' he tells us, with success in Paris; the accuracy of the grammar some phrases in his letters would lead us to doubt; but few, very few Yorkshire parsons could then talk French at all, and there was doubtless a fine tact and sensibility in what he said. A literary phenomenon wishing to enjoy society, and able to amuse society, has ever been welcome in the Parisian world. After Paris, Sterne went to the south of France, and on to Italy, lounging easily in pretty places, and living comfortably, as far as one can see, upon the profits of *Tristram Shandy*. Literary success has seldom changed more suddenly and completely the course of a man's life. For years Sterne resided in a country parsonage, and the sources of his highest excitement were a country-town full of provincial oddities, and a 'Crazy Castle' full of the license and the whims of a country squire. On a sudden London, Paris, and Italy were opened to him. From a few familiar things he was suddenly transferred to many unfamiliar things. He was equal to them, though the change came so suddenly in middle life; though the change from a secluded English district to the great and interesting scenes was far greater, far fuller of unexpected sights and unforeseen phenomena, than it can be now, when travelling is common, when the newspaper is 'abroad,' when every one has in his head some feeble image of Europe and the world. Sterne showed the delicate docility which belongs to a sensitive and experiencing nature. He understood and enjoyed very much of this new and strange life, if not the whole.

The proof of this remains written in the *Sentimental Journey*. There is no better painting of first and easy impressions than that book. After all which has been written on the *ancien régime*, an Englishman at least will feel a fresh instruction on reading these simple observations. They are instructive *because of* their simplicity. The old world at heart was not like that; there were depths and realities, latent forces and concealed results, which were hidden from Sterne's eye, which it would have been quite out of his way to think of or observe. But the old world *seemed* like that. This was the spectacle of it as it was seen by an observing stranger; and we take it up, not to know what was the truth, but to know what we should have thought to be the truth if we had lived in those times. People say *Eöthen* is not like the real East; very likely it is not, but it is like what an imaginative young Englishman would *think* the East. Just so the *Sentimental Journey* is not the true France of the old monarchy, but it is exactly what an observant quick-eyed Englishman might fancy that France to be. This has given it popularity; this still makes it a valuable relic of the past. It is not true to the outward nature of real life, but it is true to the reflected image of that life in an imaginative and sensitive man.

Here is the actual description of the old chivalry of France; the 'cheap defence of nations,' as Mr. Burke called it a little while afterwards.

When states and empires have their periods of declension, and feel in their turns what distress and poverty is—I stop not to tell the causes which gradually brought the house d'E—— in Brittany into decay. The Marquis d'E—— had fought up against his condition with great firmness; wishing to preserve, and still show to the world, some little fragments of what his ancestors had been—their indiscretions had put it out of his power. There was enough left for the little exigencies of *obscurity.*—But he had two boys who look'd up to him for *light*—he thought they deserved it. He had tried his sword—it could not open the way—the *mounting* was too expensive— and simple economy was not a match for it—there was no resource but commerce.

In any other province in France, save Brittany, this was smiting the root for ever of the little tree his pride and affection wish'd to see reblossom. But in Brittany, there being a provision for this, he avail'd himself of it; and taking an occasion when the states were assembled at Rennes, the Marquis, attended with his two boys, entered the court; and having pleaded the right of an ancient law of the duchy, which, though seldom claim'd, he said, was no less in force, he took his sword from his side—Here, said he, take it; and be trusty guardians of it, till better times put me in condition to reclaim it.

The president accepted the Marquis's sword—he staid a few minutes to see it deposited in the archives of his house—and departed.

The Marquis and his whole family embarked the next day for Martinico, and in about nineteen or twenty years of successful application to business, with some unlook'd-for bequests from distant branches of his house, return'd home to reclaim his nobility and to support it.

It was an incident of good fortune which will never happen to any traveller but a sentimental one, that I should be at Rennes at the very time of this solemn requisition: I call it solemn—it was so to me.

The Marquis enter'd the court with his whole family: he supported his lady—his eldest son supported his sister, and his youngest was at the other extreme of the line next his mother—he put his handkerchief to his face twice—

—There was a dead silence. When the Marquis had approach'd within six paces of the tribunal, he gave the Marchioness to his youngest son, and advancing three steps before his family—he reclaim'd his sword. His sword was given him; and the moment he got it into his hand, he drew it almost out of the scabbard—'twas the shining face of a friend he had once given up—he look'd attentively along it, beginning at the hilt, as if to see whether it was the same— when observing a little rust which it had contracted near the point, he brought it near his eye, and bending his head down over it—I think I saw a tear fall upon the place: I could not be deceived by what followed.

'I shall find,' said he, 'some *other way* to get it off.'

When the Marquis had said this, he return'd his sword into its scabbard, made a bow to the guardians of it—and with his wife and daughter, and his two sons following him, walk'd out.

O how I envied him his feelings!

It shows a touching innocence of the imagination to believe,—for probably Sterne did believe,—or to expect his readers to believe, in a *noblesse* at once so honourable and so theatrical.

In two points the *Sentimental Journey*, viewed with the critic's eye and as a mere work of art, is a great improvement upon *Tristram Shandy*. The style is simpler and better; it is far more connected; it does not jump about, or leave a topic *because* it is interesting; it does not worry the reader with fantastic transitions, with childish contrivances and rhetorical intricacies. Highly elaborate the style certainly is, and in a certain sense artificial; it is full of nice touches, which must have come only upon reflexion,—a careful polish and judicious enhancement, in which the critic sees many a trace of time and toil. But a style delicately adjusted and exquisitely polished belongs to such a subject. Sterne undertook to write, *not* of the coarse business of life,—very strong common sort of words are best for that,—*not* even of interesting outward realities, which may be best described in a nice and simple style; but of the passing moods of human nature, of the impressions which a sensitive nature receives from the world without; and it is only the nicest art and the most dexterous care which can fit an obtuse language to such fine employment. How language was first invented and made we may not know; but beyond doubt it was shaped and fashioned into its present state by common ordinary men and women using it for common and ordinary purposes. They wanted a carving-knife, not a razor or lancet. And those great artists who have to use language for more exquisite purposes, who employ it to describe changing sentiments and momentary fancies and the fluctuating and indefinite inner world, must use curious nicety and hidden but effectual artifice, else they cannot duly punctuate their thoughts and slice the fine edges of their reflexions. A hair's-breadth is as important to them as a yard's-breadth to a common workman. Sterne's style has been criticised as artificial; but it is justly and rightly artificial, because language used in its natural and common mode was not framed to delineate, cannot delineate, the delicate subjects with which he occupies himself.

That contact with the world, and with the French world especially, should teach Sterne to abandon the arbitrary and fantastic structure of *Tristram Shandy* is most natural. French prose may be unreasonable in its meaning, but is ever rational in its structure; it is logic itself. It will not endure that the reader's mind should be jarred by rough transitions, or distracted by irrelevant oddities. *Antics* in style are prohibited by its severe code, just as eccentricities in manner are kept down by the critical tone of a fastidious society. In a barbarous country oddity may be attractive; in the great world it never is, except for a moment; it is on trial to see whether it is really oddity, to see if it does not contain elements which may be useful to, which may be naturalised in, society at large. But inherent eccentricity, oddity *pur et simple*, is *immiscible* in the great ocean of universal thought; it is apart from it, even when it floats in and is contained in it; very, very soon it is cast out from the busy waters, and left alone upon the beach. Sterne had the sense to be taught by the sharp touch of the world; he threw aside the 'player's garb' which he had been tempted to assume. He discarded too, as was equally natural, the ugly indecency of *Tristram Shandy*. We will not undertake to defend the morality of certain scenes in the *Sentimental Journey*; there are several which might easily do much harm; but there is nothing displeasing to the natural man in them. They are nice enough; to those whose æesthetic nature has not been laid waste by their moral nature, they are attractive. They have a dangerous prettiness, which may easily incite to practical evil; but in itself, and separated from its censurable consequences, such prettiness is an artistic perfection. It was natural that the aristocratic world should easily teach Sterne that separation between the laws of beauty and the laws of morality which has been familiar to it during many ages—which makes so much of its essence.

Mrs. Sterne did not prosper all this time. She went abroad and stayed at Montpellier with her husband; but it is not wonderful that a mere 'wife,' taken out of Yorkshire, should be unfit for the great world. The domestic appendices of men who rise much hardly ever suit the high places at which they arrive. Mrs. Sterne was no exception. She seems to have been sensible, but it was *domestic* sense. It was of the small world, small; it was fit to regulate the Yorkshire parsonage, it was suitable to a small *ménage* even at Montpellier. But there was a deficiency in general mind. She did not, we apprehend, comprehend or appreciate the new thoughts and feelings which a new and great experience had awakened in her husband's mind. His mind moved, but hers could not; she was anchored, but he was at sea.

To fastidious writers who will only use very dignified words, there is much difficulty in describing Sterne's life in his celebrity. But to humbler persons, who can only describe the things of society in the words of society, the case is simple. Sterne was 'an old flirt.' These are short and expressive words, and they tell the whole truth. There is no good reason to suspect his morals, but he dawdled about pretty women. He talked at fifty with the admiring tone of twenty; pretended to 'freshness' of feeling; though he had become mature, did not put away immature things. That he had any real influence over women is very unlikely; he was a celebrity, and they liked to exhibit him; he was amusing, and they liked him to amuse them. But they doubtless felt that he too was himself a joke. Women much respect real virtue; they much admire strong and successful immorality; but they neither admire nor respect the timid age which affects the forms of vice without its substance; which preserves the exterior of youth, though the reality is departed; which is insidious but not dangerous, sentimental but not passionate. Of this sort was Sterne, and he had his reward.

Women of the world are willing to accept any admiration, but this sort they accept with suppressed and latent sarcasm. They ridiculed his imbecility while they accepted his attentions and enjoyed his society.

Many men have lived this life with but minor penalties, and justly; for though perhaps a feeble and contemptible, it is not a bad or immoral life. But Sterne has suffered a very severe though a delayed and posthumous penalty. He was foolish enough to write letters to some of his friends, and after his death, to get money, his family published them. This is the sort of thing:

Eliza will receive my books with this. The sermons came all hot from the heart: I wish that I could give them any title to be offered to yours.—The others came from the head—I am more indifferent about their reception.

I know not how it comes about, but I am half in love with you—I ought to be wholly so; for I never valued (or saw more good qualities to value) or thought more of one of your sex than of you; so adieu.

Yours faithfully,
if not affectionately,
L. STERNE.

I cannot rest, Eliza, though I shall call on you at half-past twelve, till I know how you do.—May thy dear face smile, as thou risest, like the sun of this morning. I was much grieved to hear of your alarming indisposition yesterday; and disappointed too, at not being let in. Remember, my dear, that a friend has the same right as a physician. The etiquettes of this town (you'll say) say otherwise.—No matter! Delicacy and propriety do not always consist in observing their frigid doctrines.

I am going out to breakfast, but shall be at my lodgings by eleven, when I hope to read a single line under thy own hand, that thou art better, and wilt be glad to see thy Bramin.

This Eliza was a Mrs. Draper, the wife of a judge in India, 'much respected in that part of the world.'[7] We know little of Eliza, except that there is a stone in Bristol cathedral

SACRED

TO THE MEMORY

OF

MRS. ELIZABETH DRAPER

IN WHOM

GENIUS AND BENEVOLENCE

WERE UNITED.

She died August 3, 1778, aged 35.

[7] Morgan has substituted 'quarter of the globe' for 'part of the world'.

Let us hope she possessed, in addition to genius and benevolence, the good sense to laugh at Sterne's letters.

In truth, much of the gloss and delicacy of Sterne's pagan instinct had faded away by this time. He still retained his fine sensibility, his exquisite power of entering into and of delineating plain human nature. But the world had produced its inevitable effect on that soft and voluptuous disposition. It is not, as we have said, that he was guilty of grave offences or misdeeds; he made what he would have called a 'splutter of vice,' but he would seem to have committed very little. Yet, as with most minds which have exempted themselves from rigid principle, there was a diffused texture of general laxity. The fibre had become imperfect; the moral constitution was impaired; the high colour of rottenness had come at last out, and replaced the delicate bloom and softness of the early fruit. There is no need to write commonplace sermons on an ancient text. The beauty and charm of natural paganism will not endure the stress and destruction of this rough and complicated world. An instinctive purity will preserve men for a brief time, but hardly through a long and varied life of threescore and ten years.

Sterne, however, did not live so long. In 1768 he came to London for the last time, and enjoyed himself much. He dined with literary friends and supped with fast friends. He liked both. But the end was at hand. His chest had long been delicate; he got a bad cold which became a pleurisy, and died in a London lodging—a footman sent by 'some gentlemen who were dining,' and a hired nurse, being the only persons present. His family were away; and he had devoted himself to intellectual and luxurious enjoyments, which are at least as sure to make a lonely deathbed as a refined and cultivated life. 'Self-school'd, self-scann'd, self-honour'd, self-secure,' a man may perhaps live, but even so *by himself* he will be sure to die. For self-absorbed men the world at large cares little; as soon as they cease to amuse, or to be useful, it flings them aside, and they die alone. Even Sterne's grave, they say, was so obscure and neglected that the corpse-stealers ventured to open it, and his body was dissected without being recognised. The life of literary men is often a kind of sermon in itself; for the pursuit of fame, when it is contrasted with the grave realities of life, seems more absurd and trifling than most pursuits, and to leave less behind it. Mere *amusers* are never respected. It would be harsh to call Sterne a mere amuser, he is much more; but so the contemporary world regarded him. They laughed at his jests, disregarded his deathbed, and neglected his grave.

What, it may be asked, is there in such a career, or such a character as this, to remind us of the great writer whom we have just lost?[8] In externals there seems little resemblance, or rather there seems to be great contrast. On the one side a respected manhood, a long industry, an honoured memory; on the other hand a life lax, if not dissolute, little labour, and a dishonoured grave. Mr. Thackeray, too, has written a most severe criticism on Sterne's character. Can we, then, venture to compare the two? We do so venture; and we allege, and that in spite of many superficial differences, there was one fundamental and ineradicable resemblance between the two.

Thackeray, like Sterne, looked at every thing—at nature, at life, at art—from a *sensitive* aspect, His mind was, to some considerable extent, like a woman's mind. It could comprehend abstractions when they were unrolled and explained before it but it never naturally created them; never of itself, and without external obligation, devoted itself to them. The visible scene of life—the streets, the servants, the clubs, the gossip, the West End—fastened on his brain. These were to him reality. They burnt in upon his brain; they pained his nerves; their influence reached him through many avenues which ordinary men do not feel much, or to which they are altogether impervious. He had distinct and rather painful sensations where most men have but confused and blurred ones. Most men have felt the *instructive* headache, during which they are more acutely conscious than usual of all which goes on around them,—during which every thing seems to pain them, and in which they understand it because it pains them, and they cannot get their imagination away from it. Thackeray had a nerve-ache of this sort always. He acutely felt every possible passing fact, every trivial interlude in society. Hazlitt used to say of himself, and used to say truly, that he could not enjoy the society in a drawing-room for thinking of the opinion which the footman formed of his odd appearance as he went upstairs. Thackeray had too healthy and stable a nature to be thrown so wholly off his balance; but the footman's view of life was never out of his head. The obvious facts which suggest it to the footman poured it in upon him; he could not exempt himself from them. As most men say that the earth *may* go round the sun, but in fact, when we look at the sun, we cannot help believing it goes round

[8] Thackeray who died in 1863.—Ed.

the earth,—just so this most impressible, susceptible genius could not help half accepting, half believing the common ordinary sensitive view of life, although he perfectly knew in his inner mind and deeper nature that this apparent and superficial view of life was misleading, inadequate, and deceptive. He could not help seeing everything, and what he saw made so near and keen an impression upon him that he could not again exclude it from his understanding; it stayed there, and disturbed his thoughts.

If, he often says, 'people could write about that of which they are really thinking, how interesting books would be!' More than most writers of fiction, he felt the difficulty of abstracting his thoughts and imagination from near facts which *would* make themselves felt. The sick wife in the next room, the unpaid baker's bill, the lodging-house keeper who doubts your solvency; these, and such as these,—the usual accompaniments of an early literary life,—are constantly alluded to in his writings. Perhaps he could never take a grand enough view of literature, or accept the truth of 'high art,' because of his natural tendency to this stern and humble realism. He knew that he was writing a tale which would appear in a green magazine (with others) on the 1st of March, and would be paid for perhaps on the 11th, by which time, probably, 'Mr. Smith' would have to 'make up a sum,' and would again present his *little account*.[9] There are many minds besides his who feel an interest in these realities, though they yawn over 'high art' and elaborate judgments.

A painfulness certainly clings like an atmosphere round Mr. Thackeray's writings, in consequence of his inseparable and ever-present realism. We hardly know where it is, yet we are all conscious of it less or more. A free and bold writer, Sir Walter Scott, throws himself far away into fictitious worlds, and roars there without effort, without pain, and with unceasing enjoyment. You see, as it were, between the lines of Mr. Thackeray's writing, that his thoughts were never long away from the close proximate scene. His writings might be better if it had been otherwise; but they would have been less peculiar, less individual; they would have wanted their character, their flavour, if he had been able, while writing them, to forget for many moments the ever-attending, the ever-painful sense of himself.

Hence have arisen most of the censures upon him, both as he seemed

[9] 'little account' is not in italics in the *National Review* but seems to require them. Morgan and Hutton have italics.

to be in society and as he was in his writings. He was certainly uneasy in the common and general world, and it was natural that he should be so. The world poured in upon him, and *inflicted* upon his delicate sensibility a number of petty pains and impressions which others do not feel at all, or which they feel but very indistinctly. As he sat he seemed to read off the passing thoughts—the base, common, ordinary impressions—of every one else. Could such a man be at ease? Could even a quick intellect be asked to set in order with such velocity so many data? Could any temper, however excellent, be asked to bear the contemporaneous influx of innumerable minute annoyances? Men of ordinary nerves, who feel a little of the pains of society, who perceive what really passes, who are not absorbed in the petty pleasures of sociability, could well observe how keen was Thackeray's *sensation* of common events, could easily understand how difficult it must have been for him to keep mind and temper undisturbed by a miscellaneous tide at once so incessant and so forcible.

He could not emancipate himself from such impressions even in a case where most men hardly feel them. Many people have—it is not difficult to have—some vague sensitive perception of what is passing in the minds of the guests, of the ideas of such as sit at meat; but who remembers that there are also nervous apprehensions, also a latent mental life among those who 'stand and wait'—among the floating figures which pass and carve? But there was no impression to which Mr. Thackeray was more constantly alive, or which he was more apt in his writings to express. He observes:

Between me and those fellow-creatures of mine who are sitting in the room below, how strange and wonderful is the partition! We meet at every hour of the daylight, and are indebted to each other for a hundred offices of duty and comfort of life; and we live together for years, and don't know each other. John's voice to me is quite different from John's voice when it addresses his mates below. If I met Hannah in the street with a bonnet on, I doubt whether I should know her. And all these good people, with whom I may live for years and years, have cares, interests, dear friends and relatives, mayhap schemes, passions, longing hopes, tragedies of their own, from which a carpet and a few planks and beams utterly separate me. When we were at the sea-side, and poor Ellen used to look so pale, and run after the postman's bell, and seize a letter in a great scrawling hand, and read it, and cry in a corner, how should we know that the poor little thing's heart was breaking? She fetched the water, and she smoothed the ribbons, and she laid out the dresses, and brought the early cup of tea in the morning, just as if she had

had no cares to keep her awake. Henry (who lived out of the house) was the servant of a friend of mine who lived in chambers. There was a dinner one day, and Henry waited all through the dinner. The champagne was properly iced, the dinner was excellently served; every guest was attended to; the dinner disappeared; the dessert was set; the claret was in perfect order, carefully decanted, and more ready. And then Henry said, 'If you please, sir, may I go home?' He had received word that his house was on fire; and, having seen through his dinner, he wished to go and look after his children and little sticks of furniture. Why, such a man's livery is a uniform of honour. The crest on his button is a badge of bravery.

Nothing in itself could be more admirable than this instinctive sympathy with humble persons; not many things are rarer than this nervous apprehension of what humble persons think. Nevertheless it cannot, we think, be effectually denied that it coloured Mr. Thackeray's writings and the more superficial part of his character—that part which was most obvious in common and current society—with very considerable defects. The pervading idea of the 'Snob Papers' is too frequent, too recurring, too often insisted on, even in his highest writings; there was a slight shade of similar feeling even in his occasional society, and though it was certainly unworthy of him, it was exceedingly natural that it should be so, with such a mind as his and in a society such as ours.

There are three methods in which a society may be constituted. There is the equal system, which, with more or less of variation, prevails in France and in the United States. The social presumption in these countries always is that every one is on a level with every one else. In America, the porter at the station, the shopman at the counter, the boots at the hotel, when neither a Negro nor an Irishman, is your equal. In France égalité is a political first principle. The whole of Louis Napoleon's régime depends upon it: remove that feeling, and the whole fabric of the Empire will pass away. We once heard a great French statesman illustrate this. He was giving a dinner to the clergy of his neighbourhood, and was observing that he had now no longer the power to help or hurt them, when an eager curé said, with simple-minded joy, 'Oui, monsieur, maintenant personne ne peut rien, ni le comte, ni le prolétaire.' The democratic priest so rejoiced at the universal levelling which had passed over his nation, that he could not help boasting of it when silence would have been much better manners. We are not now able—we have no room and no inclination—to discuss the advantages of democratic society; but we think in England we may venture to assume that it is neither the best nor the highest form which a society can adopt, and that it is certainly fatal to that development of individual originality and greatness by which the past progress of the human race has been achieved, and from which alone, it would seem, all future progress is to be anticipated. If it be said that people are all alike, that the world is a plain with no natural valleys and no natural hills, the picturesqueness of existence is destroyed, and, what is worse, the instinctive emulation by which the dweller in the valley is stimulated to climb the hill is annihilated and becomes impossible.

On the other hand, there is the opposite system, which prevails in the East,—the system of irremovable inequalities, of hedged-in castes which no one can enter but by birth, and from which no born member can issue forth. This system likewise, in this age and country, needs no attack, for it has no defenders. Every one is ready to admit that it cramps originality by defining our work irrespective of our qualities and before we were born; that it retards progress by restraining the wholesome competition between class and class, and the wholesome migration from class to class, which are the best and strongest instruments of social improvement.

And if both these systems be condemned as undesirable and prejudicial, there is no third system except that which we have,—the system of *removable inequalities*, where many people are inferior to and worse off than others, but in which each may *in theory* hope to be on a level with the highest below the throne, and in which each may reasonably, and without sanguine impracticability, hope to gain one step in social elevation, to be at last on a level with those who at first were just above them. But, from the mere description of such a society, it is evident that, taking man as he is, with the faults which we know he has, and the tendencies which he invariably displays, some poison of 'snobbishness' is inevitable. Let us define it as the habit of 'pretending to be higher in the social scale than you really are.' Everybody will admit that such pretension is a fault and a vice, yet every observant man of the world would also admit that, considering what other misdemeanours men commit, this offence is not inconceivably heinous; and that, if people never did any thing worse, they might be let off with a far less punitive judgment than in the actual state of human conduct would be just or conceivable. How are we to hope men will pass their lives in putting their best foot foremost, and yet will never boast that their better foot is farther advanced and more perfect than in fact it is? Is boasting to be made a capital crime? Given social ambition as a propensity of human nature; given a state of society like ours, in which there are prizes which every man may seek, degradations which every one may erase, inequalities which every one may remove,—it is idle to suppose that there will not be all sorts or striving to cease to be last and to begin to be first, and it is equally idle to imagine that all such strivings will be of the highest kind. This effort will be, like all the efforts of our mixed and imperfect human nature, partly good and partly bad, with much that is excellent and beneficial in it, and much also which is debasing and pernicious. The bad striving after unpossessed distinction is snobbishness, which from the mere definition cannot be defended, but which may be excused as a natural frailty in an emulous man who is not distinguished, who hopes to be distinguished, and who perceives that a valuable means of gaining distinction is a judicious though false pretension that it has already been obtained.

Mr. Thackeray, as we think, committed two errors in this matter. He lacerates 'snobs' in his books as if they had committed an unpardonable outrage and inexpiable crime. That man, he says, is anxious 'to know lords; and he pretends to know more of lords than he really does know. What a villain! what a disgrace to our common nature! what an irreparable reproach to human reason!' Not at all; it is a fault which satirists should laugh at, and which moralists condemn and disapprove, but which yet does not destroy the whole vital excellence of him who possesses it,—which may leave him a good citizen, a pleasant husband, a warm friend; 'a fellow,' as the under graduate said, 'up in his morals.'

In transient society it is possible, we think, that Mr. Thackeray thought too much of social inequalities. They belonged to that common, plain, perceptible world which filled his mind, and which left him at times, and at casual moments, no room for a purely intellectual and just estimate of men as they really are in themselves and apart from social perfection or defects. He could gauge a man's reality as well as any observer, and far better than most: his attainments were great, his perception of men instinctive, his knowledge of casual matters enormous; but he had a greater difficulty than other men in relying only upon his own judgment. 'What the footman—what Mr.

Yellowplush Jeames would think and say,' could not but occur to his mind, and would modify, not his settled judgment, but his transient and casual opinion of the poet or philosopher. By the constitution of his mind he thought much of social distinctions, and yet he was in his writings too severe on those who, in cruder and baser ways, showed that they also were thinking much.

Those who perceive that this irritable sensibility was the basis of Thackeray's artistic character, that it gave him his materials, his implanted knowledge of things and men, and gave him also that keen and precise style which hit in description the nice edges of all objects, —those who trace these great qualities back to their real source in a somewhat painful organisation, must have been vexed or amused, according to their temperament, at the common criticism which associates him with Fielding. Fielding's essence was the very reverse; it was a bold spirit of bounding happiness. No just observer could talk to Mr. Thackeray, or look at him, without seeing that he had deeply felt many sorrows,—perhaps that he was a man *likely* to feel sorrows,— that he was of an anxious temperament. Fielding was a reckless enjoyer. He saw the world,—wealth and glory, the best dinner and the worst dinner, the gilded *salon* and the low sponging-house,—and he saw that they were good. Down every line of his characteristic writings there runs this elemental energy of keen delight. There is no trace of such a thing in Thackeray. A musing fancifulness is far more characteristic of him than a joyful energy.

Sterne had all this sensibility also, but—and this is the cardinal discrepancy—it did not make him irritable. He was not hurried away, like Fielding, by buoyant delight; he stayed and mused on painful scenes. But they did not make him angry. He was not irritated at the 'foolish fat scullion.' He did not vex himself because of the vulgar. He did not amass petty details to prove that tenth-rate people were ever striving to be ninth-rate people. He had no tendency to rub the bloom off life. He accepted pretty-looking things, even the French aristocracy, and he owes his immortality to his making them prettier than they are. Thackeray was pained by things, and exaggerated their imperfections; Sterne brooded over things with joy or sorrow, and he idealised their sentiment—their pathetic or joyful characteristics. This is why the old lady said, 'Mr. Thackeray was an uncomfortable writer,'—and an uncomfortable writer he is.

Nor had Sterne a trace of Mr. Thackeray's peculiar and characteristic scepticism. He accepted simply the pains and pleasures, the sorrows and the joys, of the world; he was not perplexed by them, nor did he seek to explain them, or account for them. There is a tinge—a mitigated but perceptible tinge—of Swift's philosophy in Thackeray. 'Why is all this? Surely this is very strange? Am I right in sympathising with such stupid feelings, such petty sensations? Why are these things? Am I not a fool to care about or think of them? The world is dark, and the great curtain hides from us all.' This is not a steady or an habitual feeling, but it is never quite absent for many pages. It was inevitable, perhaps, that, in a sceptical and inquisitive age like this, some vestiges of puzzle and perplexity should pass into the writings o our great sentimentalist. He would not have fairly represented the moods of his time if he omitted that pervading one.

We had a little more to say of these great men, but our limits are exhausted, and we must pause. Of Thackeray it is too early to speak at length. A certain distance is needful for a just criticism. The present generation have learned too much from him to be able to judge him rightly. We do not know the merit of those great pictures which have sunk into our minds, and which have coloured our thoughts, which are become habitual memories. In the books we know best, as in the people we know best, small points, sometimes minor merits, sometimes small faults, have an undue prominence. When the young critics of this year have gray hairs, their children will tell them what is the judgment of posterity upon Mr. Thackeray.

The Adventures of Philip on His Way Through the World[1]

MR. THACKERAY has arrived at a peculiar distinction in the world of art. When we look at a new picture of any recognised school—suppose the Dutch School of Art—we do not expect to receive any entirely novel idea. We look at the pictures of Wouvermans' and we ask where is the White Horse; we look at Teniers or Ostade, and we expect to see our old friends, the old clay jug, the old merry boors, the old natural bourgeois life. Of each new picture, we judge, or attempt to judge, whether that new specimen of the familiar class is of the first excellence in that class. If a person says, 'Teniers is occupied with low subjects,' we answer, 'Of course he is! how young *you* are !' In the same way, when we read a new book of Mr. Thackeray's, we know precisely that which we have to anticipate. We are well aware that human life will be delineated in a certain characteristic way, and according to certain very peculiar and characteristic conventions. *That* is Thackeray, we say; we know what he is, and we do not expect him to change; we compare himself with himself; we only ask whether he is good today in comparison to what he was yesterday.

Mr. Thackeray is a writer to whom this peculiar sort of fame is especially natural and appropriate. His most obvious merit is an artistic expression. His words have a felicity in conveying what he means, which no other words would have. His delineation is inexplicably, but somehow certainly, better than any other sort of delineation of the same kind. You say those sentiments are low; they are, at any rate, not the highest; but if you try to express those sentiments yourself, you will find that you come to nothing, or that you become unendurable. The author of 'Vanity Fair' can describe the world as if it were a vanity fair, and all men read him, and those who study the art of expression study him for that art; but we should laugh at a baby imitator. We should say, 'My dear young sir, it takes years of

[1] This review first appeared in *The Spectator* for August 9 1862, Volume 35: pp. 885–6.

worldly study and years of deep feeling, at once worldly and unworldly to know how to use these worldly words so spiritually and so nicely. You can hardly talk as yet. Do not try to imitate the delicate *finesse* of the practised *raconteur*, or the melancholy mirth of the Belgravian novelist. It is not for young enthusiasts, it is not for patient-thinking men so to dress thought or a near approach to thought, that the unthinking world will read and reread it.'

In this book, 'Philip,' Mr. Thackeray is evidently trying to baffle his critics. They have said very often that he could never make a plot. He is now trying to show that he can. He has accumulated all the best traditional material. An eager, impetuous hero, who is skilful in getting into scrapes, and unskilful in extricating himself from them; a nice little heroine, gentle on all other matters, but biting like a tigress when her lover is attacked; a bad father, who commits forgery and seduction; a bad mother, who wishes to induce her daughter to abandon her lover, partly from a just belief that the match is a bad one, but partly also from a maternal impulse to bully and tyrannize; a professional nurse who is still not very old, and who was seduced in her youth, and who passes her life in doing good actions to a son of her seducer by a different woman; an old lord of diabolical principles and conversation to match; a marriage perhaps valid, perhaps invalid; a long period, during which the hero is interestingly poor; a sudden discovery of a lost will by which he is reinstated in comfort and opulence; these are good materials. They are the best part of the recognised stock in hand of narrative artists. If a writer could accomplish nothing with this capital apparatus, it is not likely that he will accomplish much with any other. He has as good a chance with this machinery as he is ever likely to have with any. Nevertheless as far as 'plot' is concerned, 'Philip' is a failure. No one of all its most numerous readers has probably read it with eager interest as a story. You no more care what becomes of any of Mr. Thackeray's celebrated characters than you want a biography of a Dutch boor or a Dutch utensil in Teniers' pictures. There the characters are in 'Thackeray;' you contemplate them with pleasure and indulgence and satisfaction; and you watch them as you watch your companions at a party only that you feel that you understand them better. Thackeray is like the edited and illustrated edition of a great dinner; but as for caring what becomes of those people, of the adjacent crinolines and opposite white ties, no, you cannot do that. You see what they are but you cannot be interested in their future. Mr. Thackeray, as we know well, cares for the people in the book, and Providence (we suppose) will care for the people at the dinner, but we cannot in either case concern ourselves with the subject.

Mr. Thackeray evidently feels this himself. He has no great impulse to tell us what happened to his characters. He must have a story, he knows, to tell us, and, therefore, he concocts or adapts a story, and involves his characters in it as best he may, but he can do no more. His feeling is the opposite of Mr. Canning's knife-grinder; the latter had nothing to relate, and was sorry for it: Mr. Thackeray must relate something, and is sorry for that also. His characteristic exclamation is, 'Story! God bless you, I have one to tell you, Sir; but do not ask me to tell it, Sir; it *is* such a bore, Sir.'

Mr. Thackeray likes to have a characteristic particular in every book, and he has one here. It is the relation of children to their parents. We do not mean the sentimental relation in which each is fond of the other, or the pecuniary relation in which one inherits from the other, but a more complex relation in which one of them is contrasted with the other. With a very peculiar watchfulness Nature has provided us with an instinctive aversion to what our parents do. '*I* won't do *that*, at any rate,' says the eager vanity, the improving conceit of youth. From the faults and vanities of our fathers we rush, angry and ardent, to follies of our own. Even with the very best children of the best parents it is so. The religious daughter of a Puritan mother has very early a latent weakness for the Virgin Mary. In the early self-will that accompanies second teeth, she peruses the 'Christian Year' as a secret study, not being quite sure whether she enjoys most the overt excellence of the pure book or the latent flavour of her slight dis obedience. All the Wilberforces are anti-Evangelical, and the Bishop of Oxford has very little anti-slavery fanaticism. The good children of good parents are sure to have, at any rate, a very different sort of goodness from that of their parents. And the good children of bad parents feel the reaction too, and make a much better use of it. They are excellent with the very virtues which their progenitors missed, and loath all the offences in which those progenitors especially indulged. Philip is bold, outspoken, and unworldly, because his father is mean, cringing, and parasitical. Nature won't have a monotonous world at any rate. With an impatience of what it has always seen, an antipathy to what it has always heard, and a frantic wish to be original

315

an eager youth flounders into life. 'May I be delivered from father and mother!' so begins his litany. And his prayer is granted. The world strikes him hard enough and often enough, but it has an insidious pleasure in exiling him far from his paternal home and driving him far from his ancestral creed.

We do not mean that Mr. Thackeray resembles Sir Archibald Alison. His books are not sermons with narratives between them. Mr. Thackeray's favourite art is a sort of annotated picture. He describes to you Philip and Charlotte, the mother-in-law and the aunt-in-law, and then he likes to pause to analyse, to assure you that Philip was very impetuous and eager, which was a disadvantage to him generally in life; but an advantage to him in this case, for else he would never have been bold enough to seize that pretty little girl; and as to Charlotte, he tells you that she is a weak little thing, which is also a difficulty for her in the general course of life, but an advantage now, for if she had had any mind, she might have obtruded it during the courtship, and so disconcerted and startled her admirer. Any particular intellect in either party would rather, the commentator says, disenchant than enchant the other. And so he goes on volume after volume painting for us pretty scenes, and covering them with worldly remarks.

It is for these sort of half cynical, half true delineations that Mr. Thackeray's pen was meant. He looks at the spectacle of society, the *play* which is going on in the miscellaneous theatre of the world. He rather yawns at the great passions, and but torpidly wonders at its great efforts and troublesome events. The 'grand style' may be grand, but it is a little tiresome; it is rather a young notion to be taken in by all that. Some divines earnestly counsel us not to be busy about 'public matters which concern us not;' the true philosophy of this world is of the same mind. 'If you bore yourself, my son,' it says, 'you will become a bore; leave the great tasks of life to the few who are intrusted with them and paid for them; it is *ridiculous* to be an amateur statesman; if you have an opinion on such subjects secrete it; sooner or later it will bring you into trouble, and you will be laughed at for it.' Such is Mr. Thackeray's evident belief. He won't encumber himself with big ideas. If he should encounter a serious discussion, as will happen to the lightest writers, he will lounge through it if he can. He is great in minute anatomy. The subsoil of life—not the very surface, but just the next layer, which one little painful scratch will bring up—this is his region, and it is an immense one. The great passions are few

316

and simple; lists of the best situations might well be drawn up, and categories of the highest characters even more easily. The peaks of great mountains are much like one another, and an artist who was celebrated only for painting them would have but few pictures to sell. Various art is, in its essence, sublunary. Do not be exaggerated, do not aim too low; do not take the worst of the world; extreme badness is a monotonous and of as few species as the best excellence. Live on the ordinary common follies of the ordinary common world; analyse most men as they stand before you, interested in most things and practising most things. By natural tact and studious pains Mr. Thackeray does so inimitably well, and therefore his art is copious as well as excellent.

Introductory note
William Wordsworth

William Wordsworth (1770–1850) was the son of John Wordsworth, an attorney. Born at Cockermouth, Cumberland, he was educated at Hawleshead grammar school, Cumberland, and at Cambridge. A visit to France in 1791, where the revolutionary movement was at its height, exercised a great influence on him. His friendship with Samuel Taylor Coleridge began in 1785, and in 1798 the two poets published *Lyrical Ballads*. An enlarged edition of this work, published in 1800, was prefaced by an essay expounding Wordsworth's poetic theories, proposing 'a selection of language really used by men' as opposed to the mannered language of contemporary poets. This edition was received with extreme hostility by the critics. Wordsworth completed in 1805 *The Prelude*, which was not published until after his death. His *Poems* were published in 1807, containing much of his best work, including the odes *To Duty* and *Intimations of Immortality*. *The Excursion* appeared in 1814, and *Ecclesiastical Sonnets* in 1822. Wordsworth succeeded Southey as Poet Laureate in 1843. He had settled in Grasmere, Cumberland, in 1799 ,where he remained until his death in 1850.

Robert Browning

Robert Browning (1812–1889) was born in Camberwell, the only son of Robert Browning, a clerk in the Bank of England, and of Sarah Wiedemann. His first poem, *Pauline*, appeared in 1833. It was followed by *Paracelcus* in 1835, which won him the friendship of Carlyle, Wordsworth, Dickens and Leigh Hunt. In 1840 he published *Sordello*, which public and critics alike found mystifyingly obscure. He married Elizabeth Barrett in 1846 and lived with her in Italy until her death in

1861, after which he settled in London. In 1855 he published *Men and Women*, and in 1864 *Dramatis Personæ*, which met with greater success than any of his previous work. A second edition was soon in the press, but it was not until four year's after Bagehot's article that Browning's reputation began to mount with the general public. After the publication of *The Ring and the Book* in 1868, he came to be, with Tennyson, the most noted of English poets. *Dramatic Idylls* appeared in 1879, *Parleyings with Certain People* in 1887, and his last volume *Asolando* in 1889. Browning died in Venice in 1889.

824 B14C
824 B14l
824 B14 L2

Wordsworth, Tennyson, and Browning; or, Pure, Ornate, and Grotesque Art in English Poetry[1]

WE couple these two books together, not because of their likeness, for they are as dissimilar as books can be; nor on account of the eminence of their authors, for in general two great authors are too much for one essay; but because they are the best possible illustration of something we have to say upon poetical art—because they may give to it life and freshness. The accident of contemporaneous publication has here brought together two books very characteristic of modern art, and we want to show how they are characteristic.

Neither English poetry nor English criticism have ever recovered the *eruption* which they both made at the beginning of this century into the fashionable world. The poems of Lord Byron were received with an avidity that resembles our present avidity for sensation novels, and were read by a class which at present reads little but such novels. Old men who remember those days may be heard to say, 'We hear nothing of poetry now-a-days; it seems quite down.' And 'down' it certainly is, if for poetry it be a descent to be no longer the favourite excitement of the more frivolous part of the 'upper' world. That stimulating poetry is now little read. A stray schoolboy may still be detected in a wild admiration for the *Giaour* or the *Corsair* (and it is suitable to his age, and he should not be reproached for it), but the *real* posterity—the quiet students of a past literature—never read them or think of them. A line or two linger on the memory; a few telling strokes of occasional and felicitous energy are quoted, but this is all. As wholes, these exaggerated stories were worthless; they taught nothing, and, therefore, they are forgotten. If now-a-days a dismal poet were, like Byron, to lament the fact of his birth, and to

[1] *Enoch Arden, &c.* By Alfred Tennyson, D.C.L., Poet Laureate. *Dramatis Personæ.* By Robert Browning. This essay first appeared in the *National Review*, November 1864. Volume I (New Series), pp. 27–66.

hint that he was too good for the world, the *Saturday Review*[2] would say that 'they doubted if he *was* too good; that a sulky poet was a questionable addition to a tolerable world; that he need not have been born, as far as they were concerned.' Doubtless, there is much in Byron besides his dismal exaggeration, but it was that exaggeration which made 'the sensation,' which gave him a wild moment of dangerous fame. As so often happens, the cause of his momentary fashion is the cause also of his lasting oblivion. Moore's former reputation was less excessive, yet it has not been more permanent. The prettiness of a few songs preserves the memory of his name, but as a poet to *read* he is forgotten. There is nothing to read in him; no exquisite thought, no sublime feeling, no consummate description of true character. Almost the sole result of the poetry of that time is the harm which it has done. It degraded for a time the whole character of the art. It said by practice, by a most efficient and successful practice, that it was the aim, the *duty* of poets, to catch the attention of the passing, the fashionable, the busy world. If a poem 'fell dead,' it was nothing; it was composed to please the 'London' of the year, and if that London did not like it, why, it had failed. It fixed upon the minds of a whole generation, it engraved in popular memory and tradition, a vague conviction that poetry is but one of the many *amusements* for the light[3] classes, for the lighter hours of all classes. The mere notion, the bare idea, that poetry is a deep thing, a teaching thing, the most surely and wisely elevating of human things, is even now to the coarse public mind nearly unknown.

As was the fate of poetry, so inevitably was that of criticism. The science that expounds which poetry is good and which is bad is dependent for its popular reputation on the popular estimate of poetry itself. The critics of that day had *a* day, which is more than can be said for some since; they professed to tell the fashionable world in what books it would find new pleasure, and therefore they were read by the fashionable world. Byron counted the critic and poet equal. The *Edinburgh Review* penetrated among the young, and into places of female resort where it does not go now. As people ask, 'Have you read *Henry Dunbar*? and what do you think of it?' so they then asked, 'Have you read the *Giaour*? and what do you think of it?' Lord Jeffrey,

[2] Both Morgan and Hutton have *Saturday Reviewers* but there is no justification for this change and the original *Saturday Review* has been preferred.
[3] Both Morgan and Hutton have 'enjoying' classes instead of 'light' classes but the original 'light' makes perfectly good sense and has been preferred.

a shrewd judge of the world, employed himself in telling it what to think; not so much what it ought to think, as what at bottom it did think; and so by dexterous sympathy with current society he gained contemporary fame and power. Such fame no critic must hope for now. His articles will not penetrate where the poems themselves do not penetrate. When poetry was noisy, criticism was loud; now poetry is a still small voice, and criticism must be smaller and stiller. As the function of such criticism was limited, so was its subject. For the great and (as time now proves) the *permanent* part of the poetry of his time—for Shelley and for Wordsworth—Lord Jeffrey had but one word. He said* 'It won't do.' And it will not do to amuse a drawing-room.

The doctrine that poetry is a light amusement for idle hours, a metrical species of sensational novel, has not indeed been without gainsayers wildly popular.[4] Thirty years ago, Mr. Carlyle most rudely contradicted it. But perhaps this is about all that he has done. He has denied, but he has not disproved. He has contradicted the floating paganism, but he has not founded the deep religion. All about and around us a *faith* in poetry struggles to be extricated, but it is not extricated. Some day, at the touch of the true word, the whole confusion will by magic cease; the broken and shapeless notions cohere[5] and crystallise into a bright and true theory. But this cannot be yet.

But though no complete theory of the poetic art as yet be possible for us, though perhaps only our children's children will be able to speak on this subject with the assured confidence which belongs to accepted truth, yet something of some certainty may be stated on[6] the easier elements, and something that will throw light on these two new books. But it will be necessary to assign reasons, and the assigning of reasons is a dry task. Years ago, when criticism only tried to show

* The first words in Lord Jeffrey's celebrated review of the 'Excursion' were 'This will never do.'

[4] This sentence is a little obscure. Morgan and Hutton have 'did not indeed become popular without gainsayers', but the original does not make nonsense. It could mean that the 'gainsayers' such as Carlyle were wildly popular. A simpler correction and probably the best would be to transpose the end of the sentence to read 'has not indeed been wildly popular without gainsayers'. There is insufficient justification for changing 'been' to 'become'.

[5] Morgan and Hutton have 'will cohere' instead of 'cohere', but the insertion of a second 'will' is not necessary since the first 'will' governs all the verbs in the sentence. The original has been preferred.

[6] The original *National Review* version has 'in' instead of 'on', but the sense requires 'on' which has been preferred. Both Morgan and Hutton have 'on'.

how poetry could be made a *good* amusement, it was not impossible that criticism itself should be amusing. But now it must at least be serious, for we believe that poetry is a serious and a deep thing.

There should be a word in the language of literary art to express what the word 'picturesque' expresses for the fine arts. *Picturesque* means fit to be put into a picture; we want a word *literatesque*, 'fit to be put into a book.' An artist goes through a hundred different country scenes, rich with beauties, charms and merits, but he does not paint any of them. He leaves them alone; he idles on till he finds the hundred-and-first—a scene which many observers would not think much of, but which *he* knows by virtue of his art will look well on canvas,—and this he paints and preserves. Susceptible observers, though not artists, feel this quality too; they say of a scene, 'How picturesque!' meaning by this a quality distinct from that of beauty, or sublimity, or grandeur—meaning to speak not only of the scene as it is in itself, but also of its fitness for imitation by art; meaning not only that it is good, but that its goodness is such as ought to be transferred to paper; meaning not simply that it fascinates, but also that its fascination is such as ought to be copied by man. A fine and insensible instinct has put language to this subtle use; it expresses an idea without which fine 'art' criticism could not go on, and it is very natural that the language of pictorial art[7] should be better supplied with words than that of literary criticism, for the eye was used before the mind, and language embodies primitive sensuous ideas, long ere it expresses, or need express, abstract and literary ones.

The reason why a landscape is 'picturesque' is often said to be that such landscape represents an 'idea.' But this explanation, though in the minds of some who use it, it is near akin to the truth, fails to explain that truth to those who did not know it before; the word 'idea' is so often used in these subjects when people do not know anything else to say; it represents so often a kind of intellectual insolvency, when philosophers are at their wit's end, that shrewd people will never readily on any occasion give it credit for meaning anything. A wise explainer must, therefore, look out for other words to convey what he has to say. *Landscapes*, like everything else in nature, divide themselves as we look at them into a sort of rude classification. We go down a river, for example, and we see a hundred landscapes on both sides of

---

[7] The *National Review* omits the word 'art' but the sense requires it and it has been inserted. Both Morgan and Hutton have inserted 'art'.

it, resembling one another in much, yet differing in something; with trees here, and a farmhouse there, and shadows on one side, and a deep pool far on; a collection of circumstances most familiar in themselves, but making a perpetual novelty by the magic of their various combinations. We travel so for miles and hours, and then we come to a scene which also has these various circumstances and adjuncts, but which combines them best, which makes the best whole of them, which shows them in their best proportion at a single glance before the eye. Then we say, 'This is the place to paint the river; this is the picturesque point!' Or, if not artists or critics of art, we feel without analysis or examination that somehow this bend or sweep of the river shall in future *be the river to us*: that it is the image of it which we will retain in our mind's eye, by which we will remember it, which we will call up when we want to describe or think of it. Some fine countries, some beautiful rivers, have not this picturesque quality: they give us elements of beauty, but they do not combine them together; we go on for a time delighted, but *after a time* somehow we get wearied; we feel that we are taking in nothing and learning nothing; we get no collected image before our mind; we see the accidents and circumstances of that sort of scenery, but the summary scene we do not see; we have[8] *disjecta membra*, but no form; various and many and faulty approximations are displayed in succession; but the absolute perfection in that country or river's scenery—its *type*—is withheld. We go away from such places in part delighted, but in part baffled; we have been puzzled by pretty things; we have beheld a hundred different inconsistent specimens of the same sort of beauty; but the rememberable idea, the full development, the characteristic individuality of it, we have not seen.

We find the same sort of quality in all parts of painting. We see a portrait of a person we know, and we say, 'It is like—yes, like, of course, but it is not *the man;*' we feel it could not be anyone else, but still, somehow it fails to bring home to us the individual as we know him to be. *He* is not there. An accumulation of features like his are painted, but his essence is not painted; an approximation more or less excellent is given, but the characteristic expression, the *typical* form, of the man is withheld.

Literature—the painting of words—has the same quality, but

---

[8] Morgan and Hutton both have 'find' instead of 'have' but there seems no need for this substitution and the original 'have' has been preferred.

wants the analogous word. The word *'literatesque,'* would mean, if we possessed it, that perfect combination in the *subject-matter* of literature, which suits the *art* of literature. We often meet people, and say of them, sometimes meaning well and sometimes ill, 'How well so-and-so would do in a book!' Such people are by no means the best people; but they are the most effective people—the most rememberable people. Frequently, when we first know them, we like them because they explain to us so much of our experience; we have known many people 'like that,' in one way or another, but we did not seem to understand them; they were nothing to us, for their traits were indistinct; we forgot them, for they *hitched* on to nothing, and we could not classify them; but when we see the *type* of the genus, at once we seem to comprehend its character; the inferior specimens are explained by the perfect embodiment; the approximations are definable when we know the ideal to which they draw near. There are an infinite number of classes of human brings, but in each of these classes there is a distinctive type which, if we could expand it out in words, would define the class. We cannot expand it in formal terms any more than a landscape, or a species of landscapes; but we have an art, an art of words, which can draw it. Travellers and others often bring home, in addition to their long journals—which, though so living to them, are so dead, so inanimate, so undescriptive to all else—a pen-and-ink sketch, rudely done very likely, but which, perhaps, even the more for the blots and strokes, gives a distinct notion, an emphatic image, to all who see it. They[9] say at once, *now* we know the sort of thing. The sketch has *hit* the mind. True literature does the same. It describes sorts, varieties, and permutations, by delineating the type of each sort, the ideal of each variety, the central, the marking trait of each permutation.

On this account, the greatest artists of the world have ever shown an enthusiasm for reality. To care for notions and abstractions; to philosophise; to reason out conclusions; to care for schemes of thought, are signs in the artistic mind of secondary excellence. A Schiller, an Euripides, a Ben Jonson cares for *ideas*—for the parings of the intellect, and the distillation of the mind; a Shakespeare, a Homer, a Goethe finds his mental occupation, the true home of his natural thoughts, in the real world—'which is the world of all of us'—

[9] Morgan and Hutton have 'We' for 'They' but 'They' is perfectly adequate and the original has been preferred.

where the face of nature, the moving masses of men and women, are ever changing, ever multiplying, ever mixing one with the other. The reason is plain—the business of the poet, of the artist, is with *types*; and those types are mirrored in reality. As a painter must not only have a hand to execute, but an eye to distinguish—as he must go here and then[10] there through the real world to catch the picturesque man, the picturesque scene, which are[11] to live on his canvas—so the poet must find in that reality, the *literatesque* man, the *literatesque* scene which nature intends for him, and which will live in his page. Even in reality he will not find this type complete, or the characteristics perfect; but there,[12] he will find at least *something*, some hint, some intimation, some suggestion; whereas, in the stagnant home of his own thoughts he will find nothing pure, nothing *as it is*, nothing which does not bear his own mark, which is not somehow altered by a mixture with himself.

The first conversation of Goethe and Schiller illustrates this conception of the poet's art. Goethe was at that time prejudiced against Schiller, we must remember, partly from what he considered the *outrages* of the *Robbers*, partly because of the philosophy of Kant. Schiller's 'Essay on Grace and Dignity,' he tells us,

was yet less of a kind to reconcile me. The philosophy of Kant, which exalts the dignity of mind so highly, while appearing to restrict it, Schiller had joyfully embraced: it unfolded the extraordinary qualities which Nature had implanted in him; and in the lively feeling of freedom and self-direction, he showed himself unthankful to the Great Mother, who surely had not acted like a step-dame towards him. Instead of viewing her as self-subsisting, as producing, with a living force and according to appointed laws, alike the highest and the lowest of her works, he took her up under the aspect of some empirical native qualities of the human mind. Certain harsh passages I could even directly apply to myself: they exhibited my confession of faith in a false light; and I felt that if written without particular attention to me, they were still worse; for, in that case, the vast chasm which lay between us gaped but so much the more distinctly.

After a casual meeting at a Society for Natural History, they walked home, and Goethe proceeds:

---

[10] 'Then' is omitted by Morgan and Hutton.
[11] Morgan and Hutton have substituted 'is' for 'are'.
[12] The *National Review* has 'at least' after the word 'there' but I have omitted it in view of the 'at least' immediately following.

We reached his house; the talk induced me to go in. I then expounded to him, with as much vivacity as possible, the *Metamorphosis of Plants*,† drawing out on paper, with many characteristic strokes, a symbolic plant for him, as I proceeded. He heard and saw all this, with much interest and distinct comprehension; but when I had done, he shook his head and said: 'This is no experiment, this is an idea.' I stopped with some degree of irritation; for the point which separated us was most luminously marked by this expression. The opinions in *Dignity and Grace* again occurred to me; the old grudge was just awakening; but I smothered it, and merely said: 'I was happy to find that I had got ideas without knowing it, nay, that I saw them before my eyes.'

Schiller had much more prudence and dexterity of management that I; he was also thinking of his periodical the *Horen*, about this time, and of course rather wished to attract than repel me. Accordingly, he answered me like an accomplished Kantite; and as my stiff-necked Realism gave occasion to many contradictions, much battling took place between us, and at last a truce, in which neither party would consent to yield the victory, but each held himself invincible. Positions like the following grieved me to the very soul: *How can there ever be an experiment that shall correspond with an idea? The specific quality of an idea is that no experiment can reach it or agree with it.* Yet if he held as an idea the same thing which I looked upon as an experiment, there must certainly, I thought, be some community between us, some ground whereon both of us might meet!

With Goethe's natural history, or with Kant's philosophy, we have here no concern, but we can combine the expressions of the two great poets into a nearly complete description of poetry. The 'symbolic plant' is the *type* of which we speak, the ideal at which inferior specimens aim, the class-characteristic in which they all share, but which none shows forth fully. Goethe was right in searching for this in reality and nature; Schiller was right in saying that it was an 'idea,' a transcending notion to which approximations could be found in experience, but only approximations—which could not be found there itself. Goethe, as a poet, rightly felt the primary necessity of outward suggestion and experience; Schiller, as a philosopher, rightly felt its imperfection.

But in these delicate matters, it is easy to misapprehend. There is,

† A curious physiologico-botanical theory by Goethe, which appears to be entirely unknown in this country: though several eminent continental botanists have noticed it with commendation. It is explained at considerable length in this same *Morphologie*. [Note by Carlyle, from whose life of Schiller these extracts are taken.—Ed.]

undoubtedly, a sort of poetry which is produced as it were out of the author's mind. The description of the poet's own moods and feelings is a common sort of poetry—perhaps the commonest sort. But the peculiarity of such cases is that the poet does not describe himself *as himself*: autobiography is not his subject; he takes himself as a specimen of human nature; he describes, not himself, but a distillation of himself: he takes such of his moods as are most characteristic, as most typify certain moods of certain men, or certain moods of all men; he chooses preponderant feelings of special sorts of men, or occasional feelings of men of all sorts; but with whatever other difference and diversity, the essence is that such self-describing poets describe what is *in* them, but not *peculiar* to them,—what is generic, not what is special and individual. Gray's *Elegy* describes a mood which Gray felt more than other men, but which most others, perhaps all others, feel too. It is more popular, perhaps, than any English poem, because that sort of feeling is the most diffused of high feelings, and because Gray added to a singular nicety of fancy an habitual proneness to a *contemplative*—a discerning but unbiased—meditation on death and on life. Other poets cannot hope for such success: a subject, so popular, so grave, so wise, and yet so suitable to the writer's nature, is hardly to be found. But the same ideal, the same unautobiographical character, is to be found in the writings of meaner men. Take sonnets of Hartley Coleridge, for example:—

I.

TO A FRIEND.

When we were idlers with the loitering rills,
The need of human love we little noted:
Our love was nature; and the peace that floated
On the white mist, and dwelt upon the hills,
To sweet accord subdued our wayward wills:
One soul was ours, one mind, one heart devoted,
That, wisely doating, ask'd not why it doated,
And ours the unknown joy, which knowing kills.
But now I find, how dear thou wert to me;
That man is more than half of nature's treasure,
Of that fair Beauty which no eye can see,
Of that sweet music which no ear can measure;
And now the streams may sing for others' pleasure,
The hills sleep on in their eternity.

II.
TO THE SAME.

In the great city we are met again,
Where many souls there are, that breathe and die,
Scarce knowing more of nature's potency,
Than what they learn from heat, or cold, or rain,
The sad vicissitude of weary pain:
For busy man is lord of ear and eye,
And what hath nature, but the vast, void sky,
And the throng'd river toiling to the main?
Oh! say not so, for she shall have her part
In every smile, in every tear that falls;
And she shall hide her in the secret heart,
Where love persuades, and sterner duty calls:
But worse it were than death, or sorrow's smart
To live without a friend within these walls.

III.
TO THE SAME.

We part'd on the mountains, as two streams
From one clear spring pursue their several ways;
And thy fleet course hath been through many a maze
In foreign lands, where silvery Padus gleams
To that delicious sky, whose glowing beams
Brighten'd the tresses that old Poets praise;
Where Petrarch's patient love, and artful lays,
And Ariosto's song of many themes,
Moved the soft air. But I, a lazy brook,
As close pent up within my native dell,
Have crept along from nook to shady nook,
Where flowrets blow, and whispering Naiads dwell.
Yet now we meet, that parted were so wide,
O'er rough and smooth to travel side by side.

The contrast of instructive and enviable locomotion with refining but instructive meditation is not special and peculiar to these two, but general and universal. It was set down by Hartley Coleridge because he was the most meditative and refining of men.

What sort of literatesque types are fit to be described in the sort of literature called poetry, is a matter on which much might be written. Mr. Arnold, some years since, put forth a theory that the art of poetry could only delineate *great actions*. But though, rightly interpreted and understood—using the word action so as to include high and sound activity in contemplation—this definition may suit the highest poetry, it certainly cannot be stretched to include many inferior sorts and even many good sorts. Nobody in their senses would describe Gray's *Elegy* as the delineation of a 'great action;' some kinds of mental contemplation may be energetic enough to deserve this name, but Gray would have been frightened at the very word. He loved scholar-like calm and quiet inaction; his very greatness depended on his *not* acting, on his 'wise passiveness,' on his indulging the grave idleness which so well appreciates so much of human life. But the best answer —the *reductio ad absurdum*—of Mr. Arnold's doctrine, is the mutilation which it has caused him to make of his own writings. It has forbidden him, he tells us, to reprint *Empedocles*—a poem undoubtedly containing defects and even excesses, but containing also these lines:—

> And yet what days were those, Parmenides!
> When we were young, when we could number friends
> In all the Italian cities like ourselves,
> When with elated hearts we join'd your train,
> Ye Sun-born virgins! on the road of truth.
> Then we could still enjoy, then neither thought
> Nor outward things were clos'd and dead to us,
> But we received the shock of mighty thoughts
> On simple minds with a pure natural joy;
> And if the sacred load oppress'd our brain,
> We had the power to feel the pressure eased,
> The brow unbound, the thoughts flow free again,
> In the delightful commerce of the world.
> We had not lost our balance then, nor grown
> Thought's slaves, and dead to every natural joy.
> The smallest thing could give us pleasure then—
> The sports of the country—people,
> A flute note from the woods,
> Sunset over the sea;
> Seed-time and harvest,
> The reapers in the corn,
> The vinedresser in his vineyard,
> The village-girl at her wheel.
> Fullness of life and power of feeling, ye
> Are for the happy, for the souls at ease,
> Who dwell on a firm basis of content!

331

> But he, who has outlived his prosperous days—
> But he, whose youth fell on a different world
> From that on which his exiled age is thrown—
> Whose mind was fed on other food, was train'd
> By other rules than are in vogue to-day—
> Whose habit of thought is fix'd, who will not change,
> But in a world he loves not, must subsist
> In ceaseless opposition, be the guard
> Of his own breast, fetter'd to what he guards,
> That the world win no mastery over him—
> Who has no friend, no fellow left, not one;
> Who has no minute's breathing space allow'd
> To nurse his dwindling faculty of joy—
> Joy and the outward world must die to him,
> As they are dead to me.

What freak of criticism can induce a man who has written such poetry as this, to discard it, and say it is not poetry? Mr. Arnold is privileged to speak of his own poems, but no other critic could speak so and not be laughed at.

We are disposed to believe that no very sharp definition can be given—at least in the present state of the critical art—of the boundary line between poetry and other sorts of imaginative delineation. Between the undoubted dominions of the two kinds there is a debateable land; everybody is agreed that the *Œdipus at Colonus is* poetry: everyone is agreed that the wonderful appearance of Mrs. Veal is *not* poetry. But the exact line which separates grave novels in verse, like *Aylmer's Field* or *Enoch Arden*, from grave novels not in verse, like *Silas Marner* or *Adam Bede*, we own we cannot draw with any confidence. Nor, perhaps, is it very important; whether a narrative is thrown into verse or not certainly depends in part on the taste of the age, and in part on its mechanical helps. Verse is the only mechanical help to the memory in rude times, and there is little writing till a cheap something is found to write upon, and a cheap something to write with. Poetry—verse, at least—is the literature of *all work* in early ages; it is only later ages which write in what *they* think a natural and simple prose. There are other casual influences in the matter too; but they are not material now. We need only say here that poetry, because it has a more marked rhythm than prose, must be more intense in meaning and more concise in style than prose. People expect a 'marked rhythm' to imply something worth marking; if it fails to do so they are disappointed. They are displeased at the visible waste of a powerful instrument; they call it 'doggerel,' and rightly call it, for the metrical expression of full thought and eager feeling—the burst of metre—incident to high imagination, should not be wasted on petty matters which prose does as well,—which it does better—which it suits by its very limpness and weakness, whose small changes it follows more easily, and to whose lowest details it can fully and without effort degrade itself. Verse, too, should be *more concise*, for long continued rhythm tends to jade the mind, just as brief rhythm tends to attract the attention. Poetry should be memorable and emphatic, intense, and *soon over.*

The great divisions of poetry, and of all other literary art, arise from the different modes in which these *types*—these characteristic men, these characteristic feelings—may be variously described. There are three principal modes which we shall attempt to describe—the *pure*, which is sometimes, but not very wisely, called the classical; the *ornate*, which is also unwisely called romantic; and the *grotesque*, which might be called the mediæval. We will describe the nature of these a little. Criticism, we know, must be brief—not, like poetry, because its charm is too intense to be sustained—but on the contrary, because its interest is too weak to be prolonged; but elementary criticism, if an evil, is a necessary evil; a little while spent among the simple principles of art is the first condition, the absolute pre-requisite, for surely apprehending and wisely judging the complete embodiments and miscellaneous forms of actual literature.

The definition of *pure* literature is that it describes the type in its simplicity; we mean, with the exact amount of accessory circumstance which is necessary to bring it before the mind in finished perfection, and *no more* than that amount. The *type* needs some accessories from its nature—a picturesque landscape does not consist wholly of picturesque features. There is a setting of surroundings—as the Americans would say, of *fixings*—without which the reality is not itself. By a traditional mode of speech, as soon as we see a picture in which a complete effect is produced by detail so rare and so harmonised as to escape us, we say how 'classical.'[13] The whole which is to be seen appears at once and through the detail, but the detail itself is not seen: we do not

---

[13] Morgan has 'How classical!' and Hutton has 'How "classical."' There is no necessity for altering Bagehot's original 'classical'.

think of that which gives us the idea; we are absorbed in the idea itself. Just so in literature, the pure art is that which works with the fewest strokes; the fewest, that is, for its purpose, for its aim is to call up and bring home to men an idea, a form, a character; and if that idea be twisted, that form be involved, that character perplexed, many strokes of literary art will be needful. Pure art does not mutilate its object: it represents it as fully as is possible with the slightest effort which is possible: it shrinks from no needful circumstances, as little as it inserts any which are needless. The precise peculiarity is not merely that no incidental circumstance is inserted which does not tell on the main design:—no art is fit to be called *art* which permits a stroke to be put in without an object;—but that only the minimum of such circumstance is inserted at all. The form is sometimes said to be bare, the accessories are sometimes said to be invisible, because the appendages are so choice that the shape only is perceived.

The English literature undoubtedly contains much impure literature; impure in its style, if not in its meaning: but it also contains one great, one nearly perfect, model of the pure style in the literary expression of typical *sentiment*; and one not perfect, but gigantic and close approximation to perfection, in the pure delineation of objective character. Wordsworth, perhaps, comes as near to choice purity of style in sentiment as is possible; Milton, with exceptions and conditions to be explained, approaches perfection by the strenuous purity with which he depicts character.

A wit once said that '*pretty* women had more features than *beautiful* women,' and though the expression may be criticised, the meaning is correct. Pretty women seem to have a great number of attractive points, each of which attracts your attention, and each one of which you remember afterwards; yet these points have not *grown together*, their features have not linked themselves into a single inseparable whole. But a beautiful woman is a whole as she is; you no more take her to pieces than a Greek statue; she is not an aggregate of divisible charms, she is a charm in herself. Such ever is the dividing test of pure art; if you catch yourself admiring its details, it is defective; you ought to think of it as a single whole which you must remember, which you must admire, which somehow subdues you while you admire it, which is a 'possession' to you 'for ever.'

Of course, no individual poem embodies this ideal perfectly; of course, every human word and phrase has its imperfections, and if we choose an instance to illustrate that ideal, the instance has scarcely a fair chance. By contrasting it with the ideal we suggest its imperfections; by protruding it as an example, we turn on its defectiveness the microscope of criticism. Yet these two sonnets of Wordsworth may be fitly read in this place, not because they are quite without faults, or because they are the very best examples of their kind of style; but because they are *luminous* examples; the compactness of the sonnet and the gravity of the sentiment, hedging in the thoughts, restraining the fancy, and helping to maintain a singleness of expression.

THE TROSSACHS.

There's not a nook within this solemn Pass
But were an apt confessional for One
Taught by his summer spent, his autumn gone,
That Life is but a tale of morning grass
Withered at eve. From scenes of art which chase
That thought away, turn, and with watchful eyes
Feed it 'mid Nature's old felicities,
Rocks, rivers, and smooth lakes more clear than glass
Untouched, unbreathed upon. Thrice happy quest,
If from a golden perch of aspen spray
(October's workmanship to rival May)
The pensive warbler of the ruddy breast
That moral sweeten by a heaven-taught lay,
Lulling the year, with all its cares, to rest!

COMPOSED UPON WESTMINSTER BRIDGE, SEPT. 3, 1802.

Earth has not anything to show more fair;
Dull would he be of soul who could pass by
A sight so touching in its majesty:
This City now doth, like a garment, wear
The beauty of the morning; silent, bare,
Ships, towers, domes, theatres, and temples lie
Open unto the fields and to the sky;
All bright and glittering in the smokeless air.
Never did sun more beautifully steep
In his first splendour, valley, rock, or hill;
Ne'er saw I, never felt, a calm so deep!
The river glideth at his own sweet will:
Dear God! The very houses seem asleep;
And all that mighty heart is lying still!

Instances of barer style than this may easily be found, instances of colder style—few better instances of purer style. Not a single expression (the invocation in the concluding couplet of the second sonnet perhaps excepted) can be spared, yet not a single expression rivets the attention. If, indeed, we take out the phrase—

> The city now doth like a garment wear
> The beauty of the morning.

and the description of the brilliant yellow of autumn—

> October's workmanship to rival May,

they have independent value, but they are not noticed in the sonnet when we read it through; they fall into place there, and being in their place, are not seen. The great subjects of the two sonnets,—the religious aspect of beautiful but grave nature, the religious aspect of a city about to awaken and be alive,—are the only ideas left in our mind. To Wordsworth has been vouchsafed the last grace of the self-denying artist; you think neither of him nor his style, but you cannot help thinking of—you *must* recall—the exact phrase, the *very* sentiment he wished.

Milton's purity is more eager. In the most exciting parts of Wordsworth—and these sonnets are not very exciting—you always feel, you never forget, that what you have before you is the excitement of a recluse. There is nothing of the stir of life; nothing of the *brawl* of the world. But Milton, though always a scholar by trade, though solitary in old age, was through life intent on great affairs, lived close to great scenes, watched a revolution, and if not an actor in it, was at least secretary to the actors. He was familiar—by daily experience and habitual sympathy—with the earnest debate of arduous questions, on which the life and death of the speakers certainly depended, on which the weal or woe of the country perhaps depended. He knew how profoundly the individual character of the speakers—their inner and real nature—modifies their opinion on such questions; he knew how surely that nature will appear in the expression of them. This great experience, fashioned by a fine imagination, gives to the debate of Satanic Council in Pandæmonium its reality and its life. It is a debate in the Long Parliament, and though the *theme* of *Paradise Lost* obliged Milton to side with the monarchical element in the universe, his old habits are often too much for him: and his real sympathy—the

336

impetus and energy of his nature—side with the rebellious element. For the purposes of art this is much better—of a court a poet can make but little; of a heaven he can make very little, but of a courtly heaven, such as Milton conceived, he can make nothing at all. The idea of a court and the idea of a heaven are so radically different, that a distinct combination of them is always grotesque and often ludicrous. *Paradise Lost*, as a whole, is radically tainted by a vicious principle. It professes to justify the ways of God to man, to account for sin and death; and it tells you that the whole originated in a *political event*, in a court squabble as to a particular act of patronage and the due or undue promotion of an eldest son. Satan may have been wrong, but on Milton's theory he had an *arguable* case at least. There was something arbitrary in the promotion; there were little symptoms of a job; in *Paradise Lost* it is always clear that the devils are the weaker, but it is never clear that the angels are the better. Milton's sympathy and his imagination slip back to the Puritan rebels whom he loved, and desert the courtly angels whom he could not love, although he praised. There is no wonder that Milton's hell is better than his heaven, for he hated officials and he loved rebels,[14] for he employs his genius below, and accumulates his pedantry above. On the great debate in Pandæmonium all his genius is concentrated. The question is very practical; it is, 'What are we devils to do, now we have lost heaven?' Satan, who presides over and manipulates the assembly; Moloch,

> the fiercest spirit
> That fought in Heaven, now fiercer by despair,

who wants to fight again; Belial, 'the man of the world,' who does not want to fight any more; Mammon, who is for commencing an industrial career; Beelzebub, the official statesman,

> deep on his front engraven,
> Deliberation sat and Public care,

who, at Satan's instance, proposes the invasion of earth—are as distinct as so many statues. Even Belial, 'the man of the world,' the sort of man with whom Milton had least sympathy, is perfectly painted. An inferior artist would have made the actor, who 'counselled ignoble

---

[14] The *National Review* has 'for he employs his genius below', but this 'for' was rejected by both Morgan and Hutton. Although the double 'for' may be clumsy this is not sufficient reason for removing it and it is left as written.

ease and peaceful sloth,' a degraded and ugly creature; but Milton knew better. He knew that low notions require a better garb than high notions. Human nature is not a high thing, but at least it has a high idea of itself; it will not accept mean maxims, unless they are gilded and made beautiful. A prophet in goatskin may cry, 'Repent, repent,' but it takes 'purple and fine linen' to be able to say 'Continue in your sins.' The world vanquishes with its speciousness and its show, and the orator who is to persuade men to worldliness must have a share in them. Milton well knew this; after the warlike speech of the fierce Moloch, he introduces a brighter and a more graceful spirit.

> He ended frowning, and his look denounc'd
> Desp'rate revenge, and Battel dangerous
> To less than Gods. On th' other side up rose
> *Belial*, in act more graceful and humane;
> A fairer person lost not Heav'n; he seem'd
> For dignity compos'd and high exploit:
> But all was false and hollow; though his Tongue
> Dropt Manna, and could make the worse appear
> The better reason, to perplex and dash
> Maturest Counsels: for his thoughts were low;
> To vice industrious, but to Nobler deeds
> Timorous and slothful: yet he pleas'd the eare,
> And with perswasive accent thus began.

He does not begin like a man with a strong case, but like a man with a weak case; he knows that the pride of human nature is irritated by mean advice, and though he may probably persuade men to *take* it, he must carefully apologise for *giving* it. Here, as elsewhere, though the formal address is to devils, the real address is to men: to the human nature which we know, not to the fictitious demonic[15] nature we do not know.

> I should be much for open Warr, O Peers,
> As not behind in hate; if what was urg'd
> Main reason to perswade immediate Warr,
> Did not disswade me most, and seem to cast
> Ominous conjecture on the whole success:
> When he who most excels in fact of Arms,
> In what he counsels and in what excels

---

[15] Morgan, followed by Hutton, substituted 'diabolic' for the perfectly correct and acceptable 'demonic' of the original. The original has been followed here.

338

Mistrustful, grounds his courage on despair
And utter dissolution, as the scope
Of all his aim, after some dire revenge.
First, what Revenge? the Towrs of Heav'n are fill'd
With Armed watch, that render all access
Impregnable; oft on the bordering Deep
Encamp thir Legions, or with obscure wing
Scout far and wide into the Realm of night,
Scorning surprise. Or could we break our way
By force, and at our heels all Hell should rise
With blackest Insurrection, to confound
Heav'n's purest Light, yet our Great Enemie
All incorruptible, would on his Throne
Sit unpolluted, and th' ethereal mould
Incapable of stain would soon expel
Her mischief, and purge off the baser fire
Victorious. Thus repuls'd, our final hope
Is flat despair; we must exasperate
Th' Almighty Victor to spend all his rage,
And that must end us, that must be our cure,
To be no more; sad cure; for who would loose,
Though full of pain, this intellectual being,
Those thoughts that wander through Eternity,
To perish rather, swallow'd up and lost
In the wide womb of uncreated night,
Devoid of sense and motion? and who knows,
Let this be good, whether our angry Foe
Can give it, or will ever? how he can
Is doubtful; that he never will is sure.
Will he, so wise, let loose at once his ire,
Belike through impotence, or unaware,
To give his Enemies thir wish, and end
Them in his anger, whom his anger saves
To punish endless? wherefore cease we then?
Say they who counsel Warr, We are decreed,
Reserv'd, and destin'd, to Eternal woe;
Whatever doing, what can we suffer more,
What can we suffer worse? is this then worst,
Thus sitting, thus consulting, thus in Arms?

And so on.

Mr. Pitt knew this speech by heart, and Lord Macaulay has called it incomparable; and these judges of the oratorical art have well decided.

A mean foreign policy cannot be better defended. Its sensibleness is effectually explained, and its tameness as much as possible disguised. But we have not here to do with the excellence of Belial's policy, but with the excellence of his speech; and with that speech in a peculiar manner. This speech, taken with the few lines of description with which Milton introduces them, embody, in as short a space as possible, with as much perfection as possible, the delineation of the type of character common at all times, dangerous in many times; sure to come to the surface in moments of difficulty, and never more dangerous than then. As Milton describes it,[16] it is one among several *typical* characters which will ever have their place in great councils, which will ever be heard at important decisions, which are part of the characteristic and inalienable whole of this statesmanlike world. The debate in Pandæmonium is a debate among these typical characters at the greatest conceivable crisis, and with adjuncts of solemnity which no other situation could rival. It is the greatest *classical* triumph, the highest achievement of the *pure* style, in English literature; it is the greatest description of the highest and most typical characters with the most choice circumstances and in the fewest words.

It is not unremarkable that we should find in Milton and in *Paradise Lost* the best specimen of pure style. He was a[17] schoolmaster in a pedantic age, and there is nothing so unclassical—nothing so impure in style—as pedantry. The out-of-door conversational life of Athens was as opposed to bookish scholasticism as a life can be. The most perfect books have been written not by those who thought much of books, but by those who thought little; by those who were under the restraint of a sensitive talking world, to which books had contributed something, and a various eager life the rest. Milton is generally unclassical in spirit where he is learned, and naturally, because the purest poets do not overlay their conceptions with book knowledge, and the classical poets, having in comparison no books, were under little temptation to impair the purity of their style by the accumulation of their research. Over and above this, there is in Milton, and a little in Wordsworth also, one defect which is in the highest degree faulty and unclassical, which mars the effect and impairs the perfection of the pure style. There is a want of *spontaneity*, and a sense of effort. It has been happily said that Plato's words must have *grown* into their

16 I have added an additional 'it' here as the sense requires it.
17 The *National Review* has no 'a' here but the sense requires it and I have put it in.

places. No one would say so of Milton, or even of Wordsworth. About both of them there is a taint of duty; a vicious sense of the good man's task. Things seem right where they are, but they seem to be put where they are. *Flexibility* is essential to the consummate perfection of the pure style, because the sensation of the poet's efforts carries away our thoughts from his achievements. We are admiring his labours when we should be enjoying his words. But this is a defect in those two writers, not a defect in pure art. Of course it *is* more difficult to write in few words than to write in many; to take the best adjuncts, and those only, for what you have to say, instead of using all which comes to hand; it *is* an additional labour, if you write verses in a morning, to spend the rest of the day in *choosing*, or making those verses fewer. But a perfect artist in the pure style is as effortless and as natural as in any style, perhaps is more so. Take the well-known lines:—

> There was a little lawny islet
> By anemone and violet,
>   Like mosaic, paven:
> And its roof was flowers and leaves
> Which the summer's breath enweaves,
> Where nor sun, nor showers, nor breeze,
> Pierce the pines and tallest trees,
>   Each a gem engraven;—
> Girt by many an azure wave
> With which the clouds and mountains pave
>   A lake's blue chasm.

Shelley had many merits and many defects. This is not the place for a complete, or indeed for *any*, estimate of him. But one excellence is most evident. His words are as flexible as any words; the rhythm of some modulating air seems to move them into their place without a struggle by the poet, and almost without his knowledge. This is the perfection of pure art: to embody typical conceptions in the choicest, the fewest, accidents, to embody them so that each of these accidents may produce its full effect, and so to embody them without effort.

The extreme opposite to this pure art is what may be called ornate art. This species of art aims also at giving a delineation of the typical idea in its perfection and its fulness, but it aims at so doing in a manner most different. It wishes to surround the type with the greatest number of circumstances which it will *bear*. It works not by choice and selec-

WORDSWORTH, TENNYSON, AND BROWNING

tion, but by accumulation and aggregation. The idea is not, as in the pure style, presented with the least clothing which it will endure, but with the richest and most involved clothing that it will admit.

We are fortunate in not having to hunt out of past literature an illustrative specimen of the ornate style. Mr. Tennyson has just given one, admirable in itself, and most characteristic of the defects and the merits of this style. The story of *Enoch Arden*, as he has enhanced and presented it, is a rich and splendid composite of imagery and illustration. Yet how simple that story is in itself. A sailor who sells fish, breaks his leg, gets dismal, gives up selling fish, goes to sea, is wrecked on a desert island, stays there some years, on his return finds his wife married to a miller, speaks to a landlady on the subject, and dies. Told in the pure and simple, the unadorned and classical style, this story would not have taken three pages, but Mr. Tennyson has been able to make it the principal, the largest, tale in his new volume. He has done so only by giving to every event and incident in the volume an accompanying commentary. He tells a great deal about the torrid zone which a rough sailor like Enoch Arden certainly would not have perceived; and he gives to the fishing village, to which all the characters belong, a softness and a fascination which such villages scarcely possess in reality.

The description of the tropical island, on which the sailor is thrown, is an absolute model of adorned art:—

> The mountain wooded to the peak, the lawns
> And winding glades high up like ways to Heaven,
> The slender coco's drooping crown of plumes,
> The lightning flash of insect and of bird,
> The lustre of the long convolvuluses
> That coil'd around the stately stems, and ran
> Ev'n to the limit of the land, the glows
> And glories of the broad belt of the world,
> All these he saw; but what he fain had seen
> He could not see, the kindly human face,
> Nor ever hear a kindly voice, but heard
> The myriad shriek of wheeling ocean-fowl,
> The league-long roller thundering on the reef,
> The moving whisper of huge trees that branch'd
> And blossom'd in the zenith, or the sweep
> Of some precipitous rivulet to the wave,
> As down the shore he ranged, or all day long

> Sat often in the seaward-gazing gorge,
> A shipwreck'd sailor, waiting for a sail:
> No sail from day to day, but every day
> The sunrise broken into scarlet shafts
> Among the palms and ferns and precipices;
> The blaze upon the waters to the east;
> The blaze upon his island overhead;
> The blaze upon the waters to the west;
> Then the great stars that globed themselves in Heaven,
> The hollower-bellowing ocean, and again
> The scarlet shafts of sunrise—but no sail.

No expressive circumstance can be added to this description, no enhancing detail suggested. A much less happy instance is the description of Enoch's life before he sailed:—

> While Enoch was abroad on wrathful seas,
> Or often journeying landward; for in truth
> Enoch's white horse, and Enoch's ocean spoil
> In ocean-smelling osier, and his face,
> Rough-redden'd with a thousand winter gales,
> Not only to the market-cross were known,
> But in the leafy lanes behind the down,
> Far as the portal-warding lion-whelp,
> And peacock yew-tree of the lonely Hall,
> Whose Friday fare was Enoch's ministering.

So much has not often been made of selling fish.

The essence of ornate art is in this manner to accumulate round the typical object, everything which can be said about it, every associated thought that can be connected with it, without impairing the essence of the delineation.

The first defect which strikes a student of ornate art—the first which arrests the mere reader of it—is what is called a want of simplicity. Nothing is described as it is, everything has about it an atmosphere of *something else*. The combined and associated thoughts, though they set off and heighten particular ideas and aspects of the central and typical conception, yet complicate it: a simple thing—'a daisy[18] by the river's brim'—is never left by itself, something else is put with it; something not more connected with it than 'lion-whelp' and the 'peacock yew-tree' are with the 'fresh fish for sale' that Enoch carries

[18] Morgan has 'primrose' instead of 'daisy'.

past them. Even in the highest cases, ornate art leaves upon a cultured and delicate taste the conviction that it is not the highest art, that is is somehow excessive and overrich, that it is not chaste in itself or chastening to the mind that sees it—that it is in an unexplained[19] manner unsatisfactory, 'a thing in which we feel there is some hidden want!'

That want is a want of 'definition.' We must all know landscapes, river landscapes especially, which are in the highest sense beautiful, which when we first see them give us a delicate pleasure; which in some—and these the best cases—give even a gentle sense of surprise that such things should be so beautiful, and yet when we come to live in them, to spend even a few hours in them, we seem stifled and oppressed. On the other hand, there are people to whom the sea-shore is a companion, an exhilaration; and not so much for the brawl of the shore as for the *limited* vastness, the finite infinite, of the ocean as they see it. Such people often come home braced and nerved, and if they spoke out the truth, would have only to say 'We have seen the horizon line;' if they were let alone, indeed, they would gaze on it hour after hour, so great to them is the fascination, so full the sustaining calm, which they gain from that union of form and greatness. To a very inferior extent, but still, perhaps, to an extent which most people understand better, a common arch will have the same effect. A bridge completes a river landscape; if of the old and many-arched sort, it regulates by a long series of defined forms the vague outline of wood and river which before had nothing to measure it; if of the new scientific sort, it introduces still more strictly a geometrical element; it stiffens the scenery which was before too soft, too delicate, too vegetable. Just such is the effect of pure style in literary art. It calms by conciseness; while the ornate style leaves on the mind a mist of beauty, an excess of fascination, a complication of charm, the pure style leaves behind it the simple, defined, measured idea, as it is, and by itself. That which is chaste chastens; there is a poised energy—a state half thrill, and half tranquillity—which pure art gives; which no other can give; a pleasure justified as well as felt; an ennobled satisfaction at what ought to satisfy us, and must ennoble us.

Ornate art is to pure art what a painted statue is to an unpainted. It is impossible to deny that a touch of colour *does* bring out certain

[19] Morgan rather curiously has 'an [un]explained' and Hutton has 'an explained'. The sense indicates that the original 'unexplained' is correct.

344

parts, does convey certain expressions, does heighten certain features, but it leaves on the work as a whole, a want, as we say, 'of something;' a want of that inseparable chasteness which clings to simple sculpture, an impairing predominance of alluring details which impairs our satisfaction with our own satisfaction; which makes us doubt whether a higher being than ourselves will be satisfied even though we are so. In the very same manner, though the *rouge* of ornate literature excites our eye, it also impairs our confidence.

Mr. Arnold has justly observed that this self-justifying, self-*proving* purity of style is commoner in ancient literature than in modern literature, and also that Shakespeare is not a great or an unmixed example of it. No one can say that he is. His works are full of undergrowth, are full of complexity, are not models of style; except by a miracle nothing in the Elizabethan[20] could be a model of style; the restraining taste of that age was feebler and more mistaken than that of any other equally great age. Shakespeare's mind so teemed with creation that he required the most just, most forcible, most constant restraint from without. Of poets he most needed to be guided,[21] and he was the least and worst guided. As a whole, no one can call his works finished models of the pure style, or of any style. But he has many passages of the most pure style, passages which could be easily cited if space served. And we must remember that the task which Shakespeare undertook was the most difficult which any poet has ever attempted, and that it is a task in which after a million efforts every other poet has failed. The Elizabethan drama—as Shakespeare has immortalised it—undertakes to delineate in five acts, under stage restrictions, and in mere dialogue, a whole list of *dramatis personæ*, a set of characters enough for a modern novel, and with the distinctness of a modern novel. Shakespeare is not content to give two or three great characters in solitude and in dignity, like the classical dramatists; he wishes to give a whole *party* of characters in the play of life, and according to the nature of each. He would 'hold the mirror up to nature,' not to catch a monarch in a tragic posture, but a whole group of characters engaged in many actions, intent on many purposes, thinking many thoughts. There is life enough, there is action enough,

---

[20] Morgan and Hutton have added 'age' after 'Elizabethan'. This is not necessary as 'the Elizabethan' may well be referring to 'style'.

[21] I have transposed 'He most needed to be guided' and 'of poets'. Morgan and Hutton have substituted 'among poets' for 'of poets'.

in single plays of Shakespeare to set up an ancient dramatist for a long career. And Shakespeare succeeded. His characters, taken *en masse*, and as a whole, are as well known as any novelist's characters; cultivated men known all about them, as young ladies know all about Mr. Trollope's novels. But no other dramatist has succeeded in such an aim. No one else's characters are staple people in English literature, hereditary people whom everyone knows all about in every generation. The contemporary dramatists, Beaumont and Fletcher, Ben Jonson, Marlowe, &c., had many merits, some of them were great men. But a critic must say of them the worst thing he has to say: 'They were men who failed in their characteristic aim;' they attempted to describe numerous sets of complicated characters, and they failed. No one of such characters, or hardly one, lives in common memory; the 'Faustus' of Marlowe, a really great idea, is not remembered. They undertook to write what they could not write, five acts full of real characters, and in consequence, the fine individual things they conceived are forgotten by the mixed multitude, and known only to a few of the few. Of the Spanish theatre we cannot speak; but there are no such characters in any French tragedy: the whole aim of that tragedy forbad it. Goethe has added to literature a few great characters; he may be said almost to have added to literature the idea of 'intellectual creation,'—the idea of describing great characters through the intellect; but he has not added to the common stock what Shakespeare added, a new *multitude* of men and women; and these not in simple attitudes, but amid the most complex parts of life, with all their various natures roused, mixed, and strained. The severest art must have allowed many details, much overflowing circumstance, to a poet who undertook to describe what almost defies description. Pure art would have *commanded* him to use details lavishly, for only by a multiplicity of such could the required effect have been at all produced. Shakespeare could accomplish it, for his mind was a *spring*, an inexhaustible fountain of human nature; and it is no wonder that being compelled by the task of his time to let the fulness of his nature overflow, he sometimes let it overflow too much, and covered with erroneous conceits and superfluous images characters and conceptions which would have been far more justly, far more effectually, delineated with conciseness and simplicity. But there is an infinity of pure art *in* Shakespeare although there is a great deal else also.

It will be said, if ornate art be, as you say, an inferior species of art, why should it ever be used? If pure art be the best sort of art, why should it not always be used? The reason is this: literary art, as we just now explained, is concerned with literatesque characters in literatesque situations; and the *best* art is concerned with the *most* literatesque characters in the *most* literatesque situations. Such are the subjects of pure art; it embodies with the fewest touches, and under the most select and choice circumstances, the highest conceptions; but it does not follow that only the best subjects are to be treated by art, and then only in the very best way. Human nature could not endure such a critical commandment as that, and it would be an erroneous criticism which gave it. *Any* literatesque character may be described in literature under *any* circumstances which exhibit its literatesqueness.

The essence of pure art consists in its describing what is as it is, and this is very well for what can bear it; but there are many inferior things which will not bear it, and which nevertheless ought to be described in books. A certain kind of literature deals with illusions, and this kind of literature has given a colouring to the name romantic. A man of rare genius, and even of poetical genius, has gone so far as to make these illusions the true subject of poetry—almost the sole subject.

'Without,' says Father Newman, of one of his characters, 'being himself a poet, he was in the season of poetry, in the sweet spring-time, when the year is most beautiful, because it is new. Novelty was beauty to a heart so open and cheerful as his; not only because it was novelty, and had its proper charm as such, but because when we first see things, we see them in a gay confusion, which is a principal element of the poetical. As time goes on, and we number and sort and measure things,—as we gain views, we advance towards philosophy and truth, but we recede from poetry.

'When we ourselves were young, we once on a time walked on a hot summer-day from Oxford to Newington—a dull road, as any one who has gone it knows; yet it was new to us; and we protest to you, reader, believe it or not, laugh or not, as you will, to us it seemed on that occasion quite touchingly beautiful; and a soft melancholy came over us, of which the shadows fall even now, when we look back upon that dusty, weary journey. And why? because every object which met us was unknown and full of mystery. A tree or two in the distance seemed the beginning of a great wood, or park, stretching endlessly; a hill implied a vale beyond, with that vale's history; the bye-lanes, with their green hedges, wound on and vanished, yet were not lost to the imagination. Such was our first journey; but when we had gone it several times, the mind refused to act, the scene ceased to en-

347

chant, stern reality alone remained; and we thought it one of the most tire-some, odious roads we ever had occasion to traverse.'

That is to say, that the function of the poet is to introduce a 'gay confusion,' a rich medley which does not exist in the actual world—which perhaps could not exist in any world—but which would seem pretty if it did exist. Everyone who reads *Enoch Arden* will perceive that this notion of all poetry is exactly applicable to this one poem. Whatever be made of Enoch's, 'Ocean spoil in ocean-smelling osier,' of the 'portal-warding lion-whelp,' and the 'peacock yew-tree,' everyone knows that in himself Enoch could not have been charming. People who sell fish about the country (and this is what he did, though Mr. Tennyson won't speak out, and wraps it up) never are beautiful. As Enoch was and must be coarse, in itself the poem must depend for its charm on a 'gay confusion'—on a splendid accumulation of impossible accessories.

Mr. Tennyson knows this better than many of us—he knows the country world; he has proved it that no one living knows it better; he has painted with pure art—with art which describes what is a race perhaps more refined, more delicate, more conscientious, than the sailor—the 'Northern Farmer,' and we all know what a splendid, what a living thing, he has made of it. He could, if he only would, have given us the ideal sailor in like manner—the ideal of the natural sailor, we mean—the characteristic present man as he lives and is. But this he has not chosen. He has endeavoured to describe an exceptional sailor, at an exceptionally refined port, performing a graceful act, an act of relinquishment. And with this task before him, his profound taste taught him that ornate art was a necessary medium—was the sole effectual instrument—for his purpose. It was necessary for him, if possible, to abstract the mind from reality, to induce it *not* to conceive or think of sailors as they are while they are reading of his sailors, but to think of what a person who did not know might fancy sailors to be. A casual traveller on the seashore, with the sensitive mood and the romantic imagination Mr. Newman has described, might fancy, would fancy, a seafaring village to be like that. Accordingly, Mr. Tennyson has made it his aim to call off the stress of fancy from real life, to occupy it otherwise, to bury it with pretty accessories; to engage it on the 'peacock yew-tree,' and the 'portal-warding lion-whelp.' Nothing, too, can be more splendid than the description of the tropics as Mr. Tennyson delineates them, but a sailor would not have

348

felt the tropics in that manner. The beauties of nature would not have so much occupied him. He would have known little of the scarlet shafts of sunrise and nothing of the long convolvuluses. As in *Robinson Crusoe*, his own petty contrivances and his small ailments would have been the principal subject to him. 'For three years,' he might have said, 'my back was bad, and then I put two pegs into a piece of drift-wood and so made a chair, and after that it pleased God to send me a chill.' In real life his piety would scarcely have gone beyond that.

It will indeed be said, that though the sailor had no words for, and even no explicit consciousness of, the splendid details of the torrid zone, yet that he had, notwithstanding, a dim latent inexpressible conception of them: though he could not speak of them or describe them, yet they were much to him. And doubtless such is the case. Rude people are impressed by what is beautiful—deeply impressed—though they could not describe what they see, or what they feel. But what is absurd in Mr. Tennyson's description—absurd when we abstract it from the gorgeous additions and ornaments with which Mr. Tennyson distracts us—is that his hero feels nothing else but these great splendours. We hear nothing of the physical ailments, the rough devices, the low superstitions, which really would have been the *first* things, the favourite and principal occupations of his mind. Just so, when he gets home he *may* have had such fine sentiments, though it is odd, and he *may* have spoken of them to his landlady, though that is odder still,—but it is incredible that his whole mind should be made up of fine sentiment. Beside those sweet feelings, if he had them, there must have been many more obvious, more prosaic, and some perhaps more healthy. Mr. Tennyson has shown a profound judgment in distracting us as he does. He has given us a classic delineation of the 'Northern Farmer' with no ornament at all—as bare a thing as can be because he then wanted to describe a true type of real men: he has given us a sailor crowded all over with ornament and illustration, because he then wanted to describe an unreal type of fancied men,— not sailors as they are, but sailors as they might be wished.

Another prominent element in *Enoch Arden* is yet more suitable to, yet more requires the aid of, ornate art. Mr. Tennyson undertook to deal with *half belief*. The presentiments which Annie feels are exactly of that sort which everybody has felt, and which everyone has half believed—which hardly anyone has more than half believed. Almost everyone, it has been said, would be angry if anyone else reported that he believed in ghosts; yet hardly anyone, when thinking by himself, wholly disbelieves them. Just so, such presentiments as Mr. Tennyson depicts, impress the inner mind so much that the outer mind—the rational understanding—hardly likes to consider them nicely or to discuss them sceptically. For these dubious themes an ornate or complex style is needful. Classical art speaks out what it has to say plainly and simply. Pure style cannot hesitate; it describes in concisest outline what is, as it is. If a poet really believes in presentiments, he can speak out in pure style. One who could have been a poet[22]—one of the few in any age of whom one can say certainly that they could have been, and have not been—has spoken thus:—

> When Heaven sends sorrow,
>   Warnings go first,
>   Lest it should burst
>   With stunning might
>   On souls too bright
> To fear the morrow.
>
> Can science bear us
>   To the hid springs
>   Of human things?
>   Why may not dream,
>   Or thought's day—gleam,
>   Startle, yet cheer us?
>
> Are such thoughts fetters,
>   While Faith disowns
>   Dread of earth's tones,
>   Recks but Heaven's call,
>   And on the wall
> Reads but Heaven's letters?

But if a poet is not sure whether presentiments are true or not true; if he wishes to leave his readers in doubt; if he wishes an atmosphere of indistinct illusion and of moving shadow, he must use the romantic style, the style of miscellaneous adjunct, the style 'which shirks, not meets' your intellect, the style, which as you are scrutinising, disappears.

Nor is this all, or even the principal lesson, which *Enoch Arden* may suggest to us of the use of ornate art. That art is the appropriate

[22] John Henry Newman—the poem is *Warnings*.—Ed.

art for an *unpleasing type*. Many of the characters of real life, if brought distinctly, prominently, and plainly before the mind as they really are, if shown in their inner nature, their actual essence, are doubtless very unpleasant. They would be horrid to meet and horrid to think of. We fear it must be owned that Enoch Arden is this kind of person. A dirty sailor who did *not* go home to his wife is not an agreeable being: a varnish must be put on him to make him shine. It is true that he acts rightly; that he is very good. But such is human nature that it finds a little tameness in mere morality. Mere virtue belongs to a charity school-girl, and has a taint of the catechism. All of us feel this, though most of us are too timid, too scrupulous, too anxious about the virtue of others, to speak out. We are ashamed of our nature in this respect, but it is not the less our nature. And if we look deeper into the matter, there are many reasons why we should not be ashamed of it. The soul of man, and as we necessarily believe, of beings greater than man, has many parts beside its moral part. It has an intellectual part, an artistic part, even a religious part, in which mere morals have no share. In Shakespeare or Goethe, even in Newton or Archimedes, there is much which will not be cut down to the shape of the commandments. They have thoughts, feelings, hopes—immortal thoughts and hopes— which have influenced the life of men, and the souls of men, ever since their age, but which the 'whole duty of man,' the ethical compendium, does not recognise. Nothing is more unpleasant than a virtuous person with a mean mind. A highly developed moral nature joined to an undeveloped intellectual nature, an undeveloped artistic nature, and a very limited religious nature, is of necessity repulsive. It represents a bit of human nature—a good bit, of course, but a bit only—in disproportionate, unnatural, and revolting prominence; and therefore, unless an artist use delicate care, we are offended. The dismal act of a squalid man needed many condiments to make it pleasant, and therefore Mr. Tennyson was right to mix them subtly and to use them freely.

A mere act of self-denial can indeed scarcely be pleasant upon paper. An heroic struggle with an external adversary, even though it end in a defeat, may easily be made attractive. Human nature likes to see itself look grand, and it looks grand when it is making a brave struggle with foreign foes. But it does not look grand when it is divided against itself. An excellent person striving with temptation is a very admirable being in reality, but he is not a pleasant being in description.

We hope he will win and overcome his temptation, but we feel that he would be a more interesting being, a higher being, if he had not felt that temptation so much. The poet must make the struggle great in order to make the self-denial virtuous, and if the struggle be too great, we are apt to feel some mixture of contempt. The internal metaphysics of a divided nature are but an inferior subject for art, and if they are to be made attractive, much else must be combined with them. If the excellence of *Hamlet* had depended on the ethical qualities of Hamlet, it would not have been the masterpiece of our literature. He acts virtuously of course, and kills the people he ought to kill, but Shakespeare knew that such goodness would not much interest the pit. He made him a handsome prince, and a puzzling meditative character; these secular qualities relieve his moral excellence, and so he becomes 'nice.' In proportion as an artist has to deal with types essentially imperfect, he must disguise their imperfections; he must accumulate around them as many first-rate accessories as may make his readers forget that they are themselves second-rate. The sudden millionaires[23] of the present day hope to disguise their social defects by buying old places, and hiding among aristocratic furniture; just so, a great artist who has to deal with characters artistically imperfect, will use an ornate style, will fit them into a scene where there is much else to look at.

For these reasons ornate art is within the limits as legitimate as pure art. It does what pure art could not do. The very excellence of pure art confines its employment. Precisely because it gives the best things by themselves and exactly as they are, it fails when it is necessary to describe inferior things among other things, with a list of enhancements and a crowd of accompaniments that in reality do not belong to it. Illusion, half belief, unpleasant types, imperfect types, are as much the proper sphere of ornate art, as an inferior landscape is the proper sphere for the true efficacy of moonlight. A really great landscape needs sunlight and bears sunlight; but moonlight is an equaliser of beauties; it gives a romantic unreality to what will not stand the bare truth. And just so does romantic art.

There is, however, a third kind of art which differs from these on the point in which they most resemble one another. Ornate art and pure art have this in common, that they paint the types of literature in as

---

[23] 'Millionaires' in the *National Review* was printed in italics but this hardly seems appropriate today and I have used roman lettering.

good perfection as they can.[24] Ornate art, indeed, uses undue disguises and unreal enhancements; it does not confine itself to the best types; on the contrary it is its office to make the best of imperfect types and lame approximations; but ornate art, as much as pure art, catches its subject in the best light it can, takes the most developed aspect of it which it can find, and throws upon it the most congruous colours it can use. But grotesque art does just the contrary. It takes the type, so to say, *in difficulties*. It gives a representation of it in its minimum development, amid the circumstances least favourable to it, just while it is struggling with obstacles, just where it is encumbered with incongruities. It deals, to use the language of science, not with normal types but with abnormal specimens; to use the language of old philosophy, not with what nature is striving to be, but with what by some lapse she has happened to become.

This art works by contrast. It enables you to see, it makes you see, the perfect type by painting the opposite deviation. It shows you what ought to be by what ought not to be; when complete, it reminds you of the perfect image by showing you the distorted and imperfect image. Of this art we possess in the present generation one prolific master. Mr. Browning is an artist working by incongruity. Possibly hardly one of his most considerable efforts can be found which is not great because of its odd mixture. He puts together things which no one else would have put together, and produces on our minds a result which no one else would have produced, or tried to produce. His admirers may not like all we may have to say of him. But in our way we too are among his admirers. No one ever read him without seeing not only his great ability but his great *mind*. He not only possesses superficial useable talents, but the strong something, the inner secret something, which uses them and controls them; he is great, not in mere accomplishments, but in himself. He has applied a hard strong intellect to real life; he has applied the same intellect to the problems of his age. He has striven to know what *is*: he has endeavoured not to be cheated by counterfeits, not[25] to be infatuated with illusions. His heart is in what he says. He has battered his brain against his creed till he believes it. He has accomplishments too, the more effective because they are mixed. He is at once a student of mysticism and a citizen of

<hr>

[24] Morgan and Hutton have substituted 'in a form as perfect' for 'as good perfection' but there is no justification for this and the original version has been retained.

[25] I have inserted a 'not' here as the sense requires it.

the world. He brings to the club sofa distinct visions of old creeds, intense images of strange thoughts: he takes to the bookish student tidings of wild Bohemia, and little traces of the *demi-monde*. He puts down what is good for the naughty and what is naughty for the good. Over women his easier writings exercise that imperious power which belongs to the writings of a great man of the world upon such matters. He knows women, and therefore they wish to know him. If we blame many of Browning's efforts, it is in the interest of art, and not from a wish to hurt or degrade him.

If we wanted to illustrate the nature of grotesque art by an exaggerated instance, we should have selected a poem which the chance of late publication brings us in this new volume. Mr. Browning has undertaken to describe what may be called *mind in difficulties*—mind set to make out the universe under the worst and hardest circumstances. He takes 'Caliban,' not perhaps exactly Shakespeare's Caliban, but an analogous and worse creature; a strong thinking power, but a nasty creature—a gross animal, uncontrolled and unelevated by any feeling of religion or duty. The delineation of him will show that Mr. Browning does not wish to take undue advantage of his readers by a choice of nice subjects.

> 'Will sprawl, now that the heat of day is best,
> Flat on his belly in the pit's much mire,
> With elbows wide, fists clenched to prop his chin.
> And, while he kicks both feet in the cool slush,
> And feels about his spine small eft-things course,
> Run in and out each arm, and make him laugh;
> And while above his head a pompion-plant,
> Coating the cave-top as a brow its eye,
> Creeps down to touch and tickle hair and beard,
> And now a flower drops with a bee inside,
> And now a fruit to snap at, catch and crunch,—

This pleasant creature proceeds to give his idea of the origin of the universe, and it is as follows. Caliban speaks in the third person, and is of opinion that the maker of the universe took to making it on account of his personal discomfort:—

> Setebos, Setebos, and Setebos!
> 'Thinketh, He dwelleth i' the cold o' the moon.

'Thinketh He made it, with the sun to match,
But not the stars; the stars came otherwise;
Only made clouds, winds, meteors, such as that;
Also this isle, what lives and grows thereon,
And snaky sea which rounds and ends the same.

'Thinketh, it came of being ill at ease:
He hated that He cannot change His cold,
Nor cure its ache. 'Hath spied an icy fish
That longed to 'scape the rock-stream where she lived,
And thaw herself within the lukewarm brine
O' the lazy sea her stream thrusts far amid,
A crystal spike 'twixt two warm walls of wave;
Only she ever sickened, found repulse
At the other kind of water, not her life,
(Green-dense and dim-delicious, bred o' the sun)
Flounced back from bliss she was not born to breathe,
And in her old bounds buried her despair,
Hating and loving warmth alike: so He.

'Thinketh, He made thereat the sun, this isle,
Trees and the fowls here, beast and creeping thing.
Yon otter, sleek-wet, black, lithe as a leech;
Yon auk, one fire-eye, in a ball of foam,
That floats and feeds; a certain badger brown
He hath watched hunt with that slant white-wedge eye
By moonlight; and the pie with the long tongue
That pricks deep into oakwarts for a worm,
And says a plain word when she finds her prize,
But will not eat the ants; the ants themselves
That build a wall of seeds and settled stalks
About their hole—He made all these and more,
Made all we see, and us, in spite: how else?

It may seem perhaps to most readers that these lines are very difficult, and that they are unpleasant. And so they are. We quote them to illustrate, not the *success* of grotesque art, but the *nature* of grotesque art. It shows the end at which this species of art aims, and if it fails it is from over-boldness in the choice of a subject by the artist, or from the defects of its execution. A thinking faculty more in difficulties—a great type—an inquisitive, searching intellect under more disagreeable conditions, with worse helps, more likely to find falsehood, less likely

to find truth, can scarcely be imagined. Nor is the mere description
of the thought at all bad: on the contrary, if we closely examine it, it
is very clever. Hardly anyone could have amassed so many ideas at
once nasty and suitable. But scarcely any readers—any casual readers
—who are not of the sect of Mr. Browning's admirers will be able to
examine it enough to appreciate it. From a defect, partly of subject, and
partly of style, many of Mr. Browning's works make a demand upon
the reader's zeal and sense of duty to which the nature of most readers
is unequal. They have on the turf the convenient expression 'staying
power': some horses can hold on and others cannot. But hardly any
reader not of especial and peculiar nature can hold on through such
composition. There is not enough of 'staying power' in human nature.
One of his greatest admirers once owned to us that he seldom or never
began a new poem without looking on in advance, and foreseeing
with caution what length of intellectual adventure he was about to
commence. Whoever will work hard at such poems will find much
mind in them: they are a sort of quarry of ideas, but whoever goes there
will find these ideas in such a jagged, ugly, useless shape that he can
hardly bear them.

We are not judging Mr. Browning simply from a hasty recent
production. All poets are liable to misconceptions, and if such a piece
as 'Caliban upon Setebos' were an isolated error, a venial and particular
exception, we should have given it no prominence. We have put it
forward because it just elucidates both our subject and the characteristics of Mr. Browning. But many other of his best known pieces
do so almost equally; what several of his devotees think his best piece
is quite enough illustrative for anything we want. It appears that on
Holy Cross day at Rome the Jews were obliged to listen to a Christian
sermon in the hope of their conversion, though this is, according to
Mr. Browning, what they really said when they came away:—

> Fee, faw, fum! bubble and squeak!
> Blessedest Thursday's the fat of the week.
> Rumble and tumble, sleek and rough,
> Stinking and savoury, smug and gruff,
> Take the church-road, for the bell's due chime
> Gives us the summons—'tis sermon-time.
>
> Boh, here's Barnabas! Job, that's you?
> Up stumps Solomon—bustling too?

356

Shame, man! greedy beyond your years
To handsel the bishop's shaving-shears?
Fair play 's a jewel! leave friends in the lurch?
Stand on a line ere you start for the church.

Higgledy, piggledy, packed we lie,
Rats in a hamper, swine in a stye,
Wasps in a bottle, frogs in a sieve,
Worms in a carcase, fleas in a sleeve.
Hist! square shoulders, settle your thumbs
And buzz for the bishop—here he comes.

And after similar nice remarks for a church, the edified congregation
concludes:—

But now, while the scapegoats leave our flock,
And the rest sit silent and count the clock,
Since forced to muse the appointed time
On these precious facts and truths sublime,—
Let us fitly employ it, under our breath,
In saying Ben Ezra's Song of Death.

For Rabbi Ben Ezra, the night he died,
Called sons and son's sons to his side,
And spoke, 'This world has been harsh and strange;
Something is wrong: there needeth a change.
But what, or where? at the last, or first?
In one point only we sinned, at worst.

The Lord will have mercy on Jacob yet,
And again in his border see Israel set.
When Judah beholds Jerusalem,
The stranger-seed shall be joined to them:
To Jacob's House shall the Gentiles cleave,
So the Prophet saith and his sons believe.

Ay, the children of the chosen race
Shall carry and bring them to their place:
In the land of the Lord shall lead the same,
Bondsmen and handmaids. Who shall blame,
When the slaves enslave, the oppressed ones o'er
The oppressor triumph for evermore?

God spoke, and gave us the word to keep,
Bade never fold the hands nor sleep
'Mid a faithless world,—at watch and ward,
Till Christ at the end relieve our guard.
By His servant Moses the watch was set:
Though near upon cock-crow, we keep it yet.

Thou! if Thou wast He, who at mid-watch came,
By the starlight, naming a dubious name!
And if, too heavy with sleep—too rash
With fear—O Thou, if that martyr-gash
Fell on Thee coming to take thine own,
And we gave the Cross, when we owed the Throne—

Thou art the Judge. We are bruised thus.
But, the Judgment over, join sides with us!
Thine too is the cause! and not more thine
Than ours, is the work of these dogs and swine,
Whose life laughs through and spits at their creed!
Who maintain Thee in word, and defy Thee in deed!

We withstood Christ then? Be mindful how
At least we withstand Barabbas now!
Was our outrage sore? But the worst we spared,
To have called these—Christians, had we dared!
Let defiance to them pay mistrust of Thee,
And Rome make amends for Calvary!

By the torture, prolonged from age to age,
By the infamy, Israel's heritage,
By the Ghetto's plague, by the garb's disgrace,
By the badge of shame, by the felon's place,
By the branding-tool, the bloody whip,
And the summons to Christian fellowship,—

We boast our proof that at least the Jew
Would wrest Christ's name from the Devil's crew
Thy face took never so deep a shade
But we fought them in it, God our aid!
A trophy to bear, as we march, thy band
South, East, and on to the Pleasant Land!'

358

It is very natural that a poet whose wishes incline, or whose genius conducts him, to a grotesque art, should be attracted towards mediæval subjects. There is no age whose legends are so full of grotesque subjects, and no age where real life was so fit to suggest them. Then, more than at any other time, good principles have been under great hardships. The vestiges of ancient civilisation, the germs of modern civilisation, the little remains of what had been, the small beginnings of what is, were buried under a cumbrous mass of barbarism and cruelty. Good elements hidden in horrid accompaniments are the special theme of grotesque art, and these mediæval life and legends afford more copiously than could have been furnished before Christianity gave its new elements of good, or since modern civilisation has removed some few at least of the old elements of destruction. A *buried* life like the spiritual mediæval was Mr. Browning's natural element, and he was right to be attracted by it. His mistake has been, that he has not made it pleasant; that he has forced his art to topics on which no one could charm, or on which he, at any rate, could not; that on these occasions and in these poems he has failed in fascinating men and women of sane taste.

We say 'sane' because there is a most formidable and estimable *insane* taste. The will has great though indirect power over the taste, just as it has over the belief. There are some horrid beliefs from which human nature revolts, from which at first it shrinks, to which, at first, no effort can force it. But if we fix the mind upon them they have a power over us just because of their natural offensiveness. They are like the sight of human blood: experienced soldiers tell us that at first men are sickened by the smell and newness of blood almost to death and fainting, but that as soon as they harden their hearts and stiffen their minds, as soon as they *will* bear it, then comes an appetite for slaughter, a tendency to gloat on carnage, to love blood, at least for the moment, with a deep, eager love. It is a principle that if we put down a healthy instinctive aversion, nature avenges herself by creating an unhealthy insane attraction. For this reason, the most earnest truth-seeking men fall into the worst delusions; they will not let their mind alone; they force it towards some ugly thing, which a crotchet of argument, a conceit of intellect recommends, and nature punishes their disregard of her warning by subjection to the ugly[26] one, by

26 The *National Review* has 'holy' for 'ugly' but the sense requires 'ugly' and I have substituted it. Both Morgan and Hutton have 'ugly'.

belief in it. Just so, the most industrious critics get the most admiration. They think it unjust to rest in their instinctive natural horror: they overcome it, and angry nature gives them over to ugly poems and marries them to detestable stanzas.

Mr. Browning possibly, and some of the worst of Mr. Browning's admirers certainly, will say that these grotesque objects exist in real life, and therefore they ought to be, at least may be, described in art. But though pleasure is not the end of poetry, pleasing is a condition of poetry. An exceptional monstrosity of horrid ugliness cannot be made pleasing, except it be made to suggest—to recall—the perfection, the beauty, from which it is a deviation. Perhaps in extreme cases no art is equal to this; but then such self-imposed problems should not be worked by the artist; these out-of-the-way and detestable subjects should be let alone by him. It is rather characteristic of Mr. Browning to neglect this rule. He is the most of a realist, and the least of an idealist, of any poet we know. He evidently sympathises with some part at least of Bishop Blougram's apology. Anyhow this world exists. 'There *is* good wine—there *are* pretty women—there *are* comfortable benefices—there *is* money, and it is pleasant to spend it. Accept the creed of your age and you get these, reject that creed and you lose them. And for what do you lose them? For a fancy creed of your own, which no one else will accept, which hardly anyone will call a "creed," which most people will consider a sort of unbelief.' Again, Mr. Browning evidently loves what we may call the realism, the grotesque realism, of Orthodox Christianity. Many parts of it in which great divines have felt keen difficulties are quite pleasant to him. He must *see* his religion, he must have an 'object-lesson' in believing. He must have a creed that will *take*, which wins and holds the miscellaneous world, which stout men will heed, which nice women will adore. The spare moments of solitary religion—the 'obstinate questionings,' the 'high instincts,' the 'first affections,' the 'shadowy recollections,'

> Which, be they what they may,
> Are yet the fountain light of all our day,
> Are yet a master light of all our seeing;

the great but vague faith—the unutterable tenets—seem to him worthless, visionary; they are not enough 'immersed in matter;' they move about 'in worlds not realised.' We wish he could be tried like the prophet once; he would have found God in the earthquake and the storm; he would[27] have deciphered from them a bracing and a rough religion: he would have known that crude men and ignorant women felt them too, and he would accordingly have trusted them; but he would have distrusted and disregarded the 'still small voice;' he would have said it was 'fancy'—a thing you thought you heard to-day, but were not sure you had heard to-morrow: he would call it a nice illusion, an immaterial prettiness; he would ask triumphantly, 'How are you to get the mass of men to heed this little thing?' he would have persevered and insisted, '*My wife* does not hear it.'

But although a suspicion of beauty, and a taste for ugly reality, have led Mr. Browning to exaggerate the functions, and to caricature the nature of grotesque art, we own, or rather, we maintain, that he has given many excellent specimens of that art within its proper boundaries and limits. Take an example, his picture of what we may call the *bourgeois* nature in *difficulties*; in the utmost difficulty, in contact with magic and the supernatural. He has made of it something homely, comic, true; reminding us of what *bourgeois* nature really is. By showing us the type under abnormal conditions, he reminds us of the type under its best and most satisfactory conditions:—

> Hamelin Town's in Brunswick,
> By famous Hanover city;
> The river Weser, deep and wide,
> Washes its walls on the southern side;
> A pleasanter spot you never spied;
> But, when begins my ditty,
> Almost five hundred years ago,
> To see the townsfolk suffer so
> From vermin, was a pity.

> Rats!
> They fought the dogs, and killed the cats,
> And bit the babies in the cradles,
> And ate the cheeses out of the vats,
> And licked the soup from the cook's own ladles
> Split open the kegs of salted sprats,
> Made nests inside men's Sunday hats,
> And even spoiled the women's chats,

---

[27] The *National Review* has 'could' but the sense needs 'would' and this has been substituted. Both Morgan and Hutton have 'would'.

By drowning their speaking
With shrieking and squeaking
In fifty different sharps and flats.

At last the people in a body
To the Town Hall came flocking:
"'Tis clear,' cried they, 'our Mayor's a noddy;
And as for our Corporation—shocking
To think we buy gowns lined with ermine
For dolts that can't or won't determine
What's best to rid us of our vermin!
You hope, because you're old and obese,
To find in the furry civic robe ease?
Rouse up, sirs! Give your brains a racking
To find the remedy we're lacking,
Or, sure as fate, we'll send you packing!'
At this the Mayor and Corporation
Quaked with a mighty consternation.

A person of musical abilities proposes to extricate the civic dig-
nitaries from the difficulty, and they promise him a thousand guilders
if he does.

Into the street the Piper stept,
Smiling first a little smile,
As if he knew what magic slept
In his quiet pipe the while;
Then, like a musical adept,
To blow the pipe his lips he wrinkled,
And green and blue his sharp eye twinkled
Like a candle-flame where salt is sprinkled;
And ere three shrill notes the pipe uttered,
You heard as if an army muttered;
And the muttering grew to a grumbling;
And the grumbling grew to a mighty rumbling:
And out of the houses the rats came tumbling.
Great rats, small rats, lean rats, brawny rats,
Brown rats, black rats, grey rats, tawny rats,
Grave old plodders, gay young friskers,
Fathers, mothers, uncles, cousins,
Cocking tails and pricking whiskers,
Families by tens and dozens,

362

Brothers, sisters, husbands, wives—
Followed the Piper for their lives.
From street to street he piped advancing,
And step for step they followed dancing,
Until they came to the river Weser
Wherein all plunged and perished!
—Save one who, stout as Julius Cæsar,
Swam across and lived to carry
    (As he, the manuscript he cherished)
To Rat-land home his commentary:
Which was, 'At the first shrill notes of the pipe,
I heard a sound as of scraping tripe,
And putting apples, wondrous ripe,
Into a cider-press's gripe:
And a moving away of pickle-tub boards,
And a leaving ajar of conserve-cupboards,
And a drawing the corks of train-oil-flasks,
And a breaking the hoops of butter-casks:
And it seemed as if a voice
    (Sweeter far than by harp or by psaltery
Is breathed) called out, "Oh rats, rejoice!
The world is grown to one vast drysaltery!
So munch on, crunch on, take your nuncheon,
Breakfast, supper, dinner, luncheon!"
And just as a bulky sugar-puncheon,
All ready staved, like a great sun shone
Glorious scarce an inch before me,
Just as methought it said, "Come, bore me!"
—I found the Weser rolling o'er me.'
You should have heard the Hamelin people
Ringing the bells till they rocked the steeple
'Go,' cried the Mayor, 'and get long poles,
Poke out the nests and block up the holes!
Consult with carpenters and builders,
And leave in our town not even a trace
Of the rats!'—when suddenly, up the face
Of the Piper perked in the market-place,
With a, 'First, if you please, my thousand guilders!'

A thousand guilders! The Mayor looked blue;
So did the Corporation too.
For council dinners made rare havoc

With Claret, Moselle, Vin-de-Grave, Hock;
And half the money would replenish
Their cellar's biggest butt with Rhenish.
To pay this sum to a wandering fellow
With a gipsy coat of red and yellow!
'Beside,' quoth the Mayor with a knowing wink,
'Our business was done at the river's brink;
We saw with our eyes the vermin sink,
And what's dead can't come to life, I think.
So, friend, we're not the folks to shrink
From the duty of giving you something for drink,
And a matter of money to put in your poke;
But as for the guilders, what we spoke
Of them, as you very well know, was in joke.
Beside, our losses have made us thrifty.
A thousand guilders! Come, take fifty!'

The piper's face fell, and he cried,
'No trifling! I can't wait, beside!
I've promised to visit by dinnertime
Bagdat, and accept the prime
Of the Head-Cook's pottage, all he's rich in,
For having left, in the Caliph's kitchen,
Of a nest of scorpions no survivor:
With him I proved no bargain-driver,
With you, don't think I'll bate a stiver!
And folks who put me in a passion
May find me pipe after another fashion.'

'How?' cried the Mayor, 'd'ye think I'll brook
Being worse treated than a Cook?
Insulted by a lazy ribald
With idle pipe and vesture piebald?
You threaten us, fellow? Do your worst,
Blow your pipe there till you burst!'

Once more he stept into the street
    And to his lips again
    Laid his long pipe of smooth straight cane;
And ere he blew three notes (such sweet
Soft notes as yet musician's cunning
    Never gave the enraptured air)

364

There was a rustling that seemed like a bustling
Of merry crowds justling at pitching and hustling,
Small feet were pattering, wooden shoes clattering,
Little hands clapping and little tongues chattering,
And, like fowls in a farm-yard when barley is scattering,
Out came the children running.
All the little boys and girls,
With rosy cheeks and flaxen curls,
And sparkling eyes and teeth like pearls,
Tripping and skipping, ran merrily after
The wonderful music with shouting and laughter.

    .   .   .   .   .

And I must not omit to say
That in Transylvania there's a tribe
Of alien people who ascribe
The outlandish ways and dress
On which their neighbours lay such stress,
To their fathers and mothers having risen,
Out of some subterraneous prison
Into which they were trepanned
Long time ago in a mighty band
Out of Hamelin town in Brunswick land,
But how or why, they don't understand.

Something more we had to say of Mr. Browning, but we must stop. It is singularly characteristic of this age that the poems which rise to the surface should be examples of ornate art and grotesque art, not of pure art. We live in the realm of the *half* educated. The number of readers grows daily, but the quality of readers does not improve rapidly. The middle class is scattered, headless; it is well-meaning, but aimless; wishing to be wise, but ignorant how to be wise. The aristocracy of England never was a literary aristocracy, never even in the days of its full power, of its unquestioned predominance, did it guide—did it even seriously try to guide—the taste of England. Without guidance young men, and tired men, are thrown amongst a mass of books; they have to choose which they like; many of them would much like to improve their culture, to chasten their taste, if they knew how. But left to themselves they take, not pure art, but showy art; not that which permanently relieves the eye and makes it happy whenever it looks, and as long as it looks, but *glaring* art which catches and arrests the eye for a moment, but which in the end fatigues it.

But before the wholesome remedy of nature—the fatigue—arrives, the hasty reader has passed on to some new excitement, which in its turn stimulates for an instant, and then is passed by for ever. These conditions are not favourable to the due appreciation of pure art— of that art which must be known before it is admired—which must have fastened irrevocably on the brain before you appreciate it—which you must love ere it will seem worthy of your love. Women, too, whose voice in literature counts as well as that of men—and in a light literature counts for more than that of men—women, such as we know them, such as they are likely to be, ever prefer a delicate unreality to a true or firm art. A dressy literature, an exaggerated literature, seem to be fated to us. These are our curses, as other times had theirs.

> And yet
> Think not the living times forget.
> Ages of heroes fought and fell
> That Homer in the end might tell;
> O'er grovelling generations past
> Upstood the Doric fane at last;
> And countless hearts in countless years
> Had wasted thoughts, and hopes, and fears,
> Rude laughter and unmeaning tears,
> Ere England Shakespeare saw, or Rome
> The pure perfection of her dome.
> Others, I doubt not, if not we,
> The issue of our toils shall see;
> And (they forgotten and unknown)
> Young children gather as their own
> The harvest that the dead had sown,
> The dead forgotten and unknown.

George Grote
Introductory note

George Grote (1794–1871) was the son of George Grote, a banker. He was educated at Charterhouse, and entered his father's bank at sixteen, where he worked until 1843, meanwhile privately studying philosophy, classics and political economics. He began to plan his history of Greece in 1832, there being no other such work then existing in England. The twelve volumes of the *History* appeared between 1845–56. Grote was a friend of Ricardo, James Mill and Jeremy Bentham. He was deeply interested in the establishment of London University and in parliamentary reform, and was also active in the founding of Mechanic's Institutes for the education of working men. From 1832–41 he was a Liberal M.P. and a rigorous advocate of the ballot vote. He died in London in 1871.

Mr. Grote[1]

'MR. GROTE, a merchant who reads German,' writes Mr. Crabb Robinson, in an early entry of his diary, and this is perhaps the earliest mention in print or in literature of the great historian whom we have this week lost. And though in detail the entry is wrong, though Mr. Grote never was exactly a merchant, yet in an essential point it indicates his characteristic excellence. Mr. Grote was not a mere literary man, and no mere literary man could have written his history. He was essentially a practical man of business, a banker trained in the City, a politician trained in Parliament, and every page in his writings bears witness that he was so. Just as in every sentence of Thucydides there lurks some trace of exercised sagacity fit for the considerate decision of weighty affairs, though by fate excluded from them, so in every page of Grote there is a flavour not exactly of this quality, but yet others only to be learned in the complex practical life of modern times, and equally necessary for it. At the beginning he impressed the shrewd diarist as pre-eminently a man of business, and pre-eminently a man of business he remained to the end.

Since 1842 he devoted himself so exclusively to literature that his powers in action were little known to younger men. Only a few now remember what he was as a banker and what he was as a politician. But for many years he has been Vice Chancellor of the University of London and Vice-President and President of University College, and those who have seen him in those capacities well know that he had all the faculties of a great administrator and many of the faculties of a great ruler. Almost all the important measures of these bodies wear the almost personal mark of his wide knowledge and strenuous decision, and it was difficult in both to carry much in opposition to them.

The style of the 'History of Greece' shows the practical taste of its author in its most marked quality,—its *reality*. As it is twelve thick volumes long, it cannot be called a short book, but there is not a

[1] This article was first published in *The Spectator* for June 24 1871, Volume 44, pp. 762-3.

word added for the sake of effect. Every word was written because it was wanted to express the full meaning of the writer, and because the writer would be content with nothing less than his full meaning. Most writers on ancient subjects leave their readers to suppose something, require of them to fill in some links in the chain of reasoning. But Mr. Grote argues everything out. He tries historical questions as if he were a judge expounding them to a jury. He states every probability, weighs each witness, discusses every reason. It never strikes him that his readers may not wish to go through these processes, that they may not have as much interest in the subject as he has himself. He evidently thinks they ought to wish to know it all, even if they do not. They are impanelled to try the issue, and they are bound in conscience not to relax their attention till they have heard all which can be said about it. The conscientious historian will not let them off a single reason or permit them to omit the minutest authority. The whole style says, from the author to the reader, 'Now I want to explain this to you, and I know you want to have it explained to you, therefore let us go all through it.' How different this is from most historians we all know. Most of them never give their readers credit for a sustained interest in the matter in hand; they think that their style must be ornamental or no one will read them; that they must hurry on quick or no one will have patience with them. Probably at times Mr. Grote is needlessly full, and certainly on many occasions he argues the same point too often; the case of the 'Sophists' is argued in his 'Plato' at least a hundred times, still, on the whole, a reader wanting to understand Greek history will be refreshed by a writer 'who has no style,' who at least does not think of his style, who pours all his ideas plainly forth, who assumes his readers to be as really interested in the events as if they were his own money matters.

The views of evidence in Mr. Grote's history are as practical as the style. 'Why do I believe events in common life,' he asks, 'because I have the evidence of honest eye-witnesses for them, either given to me at first hand, or communicated through trustworthy channels, and under the same circumstances and no other, will I accept events in history'? Tried by this rigid rule, the Argonautic expedition, the Trojan war, the legends of Thebes vanish alike, and vanish wholly. Sir G. Lewis upon Niebuhr is not more contemptuous than Mr. Grote on the constructive critics—on those who try to make bricks without straw—who think they can evolve 'certified fact' from 'uncertified fiction,' who have canons of probability, or, what is more convenient, an internal tact by which they learn which is truth and which is legend. Mr. Grote's questions in all cases are,—who saw this, and how do you know that he saw it? He will listen to nothing else. We need not, indeed we cannot, discuss here whether this is a good theory of evidence or a bad, a complete one or an incomplete, we cite it only as showing the practical bent and bearing of Mr. Grote's mind. He brings historical evidence 'out of the clouds;' he reduces it to the same sort of evidence as that upon which a banker discounts a bill, a politician believes a contemporary conversation.

Practical men have always an object in what they do; and strange as it seems to those who 'think other thoughts and live in other days,' Mr. Grote's object was to refute Mitford. That clever writer is now unread and forgotten, but in his day he was a keen Tory and discussed the affairs of Athens in the spirit of a Tory. The contest between oligarchy and democracy, between the rule of the many and the rule of the few, was as vigorous in the time of the Peloponnesian war as in that of the first French Revolution, when Mitford lived. Being a Tory, he fell upon the Liberals of Athens as vigorously, as keenly, as unscrupulously as he would have fallen on Mr. Fox and Lord Grey. If there could have been a bill of Pains and Penalties against Cleon, Mr. Mitford would have produced a bill of Pains and Penalties. As he could not do this, he amassed every prejudice and accumulated every innuendo. In Mr. Grote's youth, more than forty years since, this party pamphlet was in orthodox England received history, and he determined to reply to it. The original design of the twelve volumes, which begin at Troy and end with the death of Alexander, was to refute the accusations of Mitford against Greek Liberals, and expose the false panegyrics of Mitford upon Greek aristocrats. There is much else, of course, in Grote's history, much else far more valuable. This was the first thought, the young man's dream of what it was to be.

Mr. Grote was peculiarly likely to write such a reply, for he belonged to a remarkable class of most vigorous Liberals. They were called the 'Philosophic Radicals' forty years ago, and had a curious, hard, compact, consistent creed. They were in the most anomalous position possible as politicians. They were unpopular Democrats; they liked the people, but the people did not like them or their ideas; they said that the mass of the nation ought to have direct conclusive power, but the mass of the nation said they would not on any account have such power. To preach that the numerical majority ought to rule to a numerical majority which does not wish to rule is painful. A barbarous demagogue, no doubt, will shout till the people hears. But the 'Philosophic Radicals' were not barbarous demagogues, but grave, careful reasoners. They might defend Cleon in theory, but they had no tinge of the Cleon in practice. Some, Mr. Grote even perhaps, would not have borne at all easily the liberties which Cleon would have taken with him. The philosophic Radicals had a lesson to teach the people which the people did not wish to learn, and they were decidedly the last sort of people to make them learn it. It was natural that a man like Mr. Grote, with ample leisure and conscious of great literary power, should turn to a more congenial occupation.

Around the original anti-Mitford thesis Mr. Grote accumulated the most enormous store of miscellaneous knowledge. There was perhaps no subject that he could possibly bring into his theme which he did not bring in, and on which he did not write as fully as it was decent to write. Nor does the trumpet ever give an uncertain sound. Sir George Lewis justly said that Dr. Thirlwall was like Lord Eldon; 'he even used his acuteness in order to avoid coming to a decision.' But no one would say this of Mr. Grote. Perhaps he discusses a million subjects or more, and has expressed more than a million distinct opinions. No doubt this omnivorous discussion and this universal copiousness have impaired the merits of the 'History.' The main subject is buried under the collateral, and only a very careful reader can always bear in mind whence he came or perceive why he is going where he seems to be taken. Nor has Mr. Grote, as a mere narrator, any peculiar charm; he tells his story plainly and fairly, but he does not make you read for the sake of the story. In ancient history, however, mere narrative is almost a secondary element. So many cardinal facts are omitted, and so many important inferences denied, that a perpetual disquisition must be mixed with the regular narrative, and in disquisition Mr. Grote has been very rarely equalled, and never surpassed. That Macaulay's famous criticism, 'too many plums and no suet,' is applicable to Grote's history is certain, but Greek history is of necessity almost entirely 'plums.'

That the political part of Grote's history is much better than most of the other parts everyone will admit. Scarcely any one will now think the treatment of the mythology sufficient. 'Prehistoric' speculation, as we now call it, might be made to elucidate the opening part of Greek history. But comparative mythology and prehistoric speculation are subjects which have been quite elaborated afresh since Mr. Grote dealt with the earliest Greece. If they had been known in 1846, we should have had an ample dissertation on them; probably many dissertations. There are defects of omission, and there are other (as most people will think) defects of commission. To estimate Grote's great work, the greatest philosophical problems and the deepest religious questions must be discussed; on almost every one of them he has expressly given his opinion, or not obscurely hinted it. But wecannot deal with these great subjects now. Gibbon said he was sustained by the hope that 'a hundred years hence I might still continue to be abused.' Abuse is not the word for Mr. Grote, but a hundred years hence his writings will still continue to be the ground of controversy and the basis of discussion. The scholarship and the mode of teaching grave history in our time will be judged of hereafter by the 'History of Greece' more than by any other work. 'Those who go down to posterity,' said Mr. Disraeli, both wittily and wisely, 'are about as rare as planets,' and Mr. Grote will be one of the few in this generation.

Nassau William Senior

Introductory note

Nassau William Senior (1790–1864) was the son of the Rev. John Senior of Berkshire. He was educated at Eton and Oxford, and was called to the bar in 1819, but as he suffered from a delicate throat and a weak voice he continued as a conveyancer in which profession he had qualified earlier. His observation of the inadequate working of the poor law in his father's parish had first interested him in the study of economics, and his first publication on an economic question was an article on agriculture in the *Quarterly Review*, 1821. He was Professor of Economics at Oxford from 1825–30, and 1847–52, and was the first to hold the post. As a member of the poor law commission, he wrote the report on which the poor law of 1834 was based. He became well known in literary and official circles, and published political articles in the *Edinburgh Review* and literary articles in the *Quarterly* and *London* Reviews. He made many continental journeys, and was in Paris at the time of the attack on the National Assembly in 1848. From this time he kept a detailed journal of conversations, often revised by the original speakers, which reveal the opinions of statesmen and others on contemporary affairs. In general Senior was in sympathy with the Whigs, but his records are not partisan. As an economist he belonged mainly to the school of Ricardo, but being concerned with the practical application of principles, he did not express them in James Mill's absolute terms. Senior was responsible for the *Economist's* views on foreign affairs under Wilson, and for a time under Bagehot. Senior published *Outline of the Science of Political Economy*, 1836, and a volume of the *Journals*, 1851; another volume of journals appeared in 1871, and the *Conversations*, between 1871–8. He died in London in 1864.

Senior's Journals[1]

MR. GLADSTONE—at least every one alleges it to be Mr. Gladstone— said in the *Edinburgh Review*, that unhappily we scarcely possessed in England the kind of writer who abroad is called a publicist. Indeed it is not very easy to give an Englishman only familiar with English discussions and English ways of thought, an exact idea of the word. But probably the late Mr. Senior, in the last years of his life, came very near to it. He lived among politicians; he spent the main stress of his speculative mind upon politics; he wrote largely upon them. But he had none of the ties to them usual in England. He was neither a practical politician, engaged in real affairs, nor the editor of a political periodical, nor even a stirring writer addressing a large audience. He devoted much of his time to temporary politics, but he always dealt with them in an abstract and philosophical manner. He always endeavoured to deal with the permanent aspects of them, he addressed only thoughtful men, he was a 'didactic member' of the republic of letters; and this we suppose is the idea of a publicist.

Many persons may regret it as Mr. Gladstone did, but the fact certainly is that we have very few such writers in this country, and that the tendency of present times is rather to diminish than to increase their number. There is something artificial about the species. That a man of ability should spend a great part of his mind on political affairs, but that he should neither have a practical share in them nor an effective say to a large audience, is not natural. Such a type can exist only in periods of transition, as in despotic countries where the government though absolute will allow discussion, perhaps is moved by discussion, where there are many cultivated men who wish to read good and long reasonings on political subjects, but where there is as yet no people, no vast numerous class, who wish to read and who will only read short sharp arguments on present issues. As soon as 'leading articles' come in, publicists and pamphlets die out. Those who could

[1] This essay first appeared in the *Fortnightly Review* for August 1 1871, Volume X (New Series), pp. 156–65.

best write pamphlets are drawn off to the more lucrative trade of writing 'leaders.' And readers, especially the most important readers whose time is valuable, have so many leaders to read, and are so sickened of the subject, that they will not read a word beside. Mr. Disraeli once compared the great Quarterly Reviews, whose political articles are pamphlets in disguise, to the old mail coaches, which were capital things in their way, but when they tried to start in the present day found that all the travellers had gone on by the train. A quicker mode of travelling has come in, a hastier mode of reading, and a scrappier mode of writing. Fifty years ago, when Mr. Senior began to write, all this had not happened. The English Government was then predominantly ruled by aristocratic politicians, some of whom were reading men, more of whom respected reading though they did not practise it, and beneath whom there was a still larger body of educated men who cared for political discussion, who already possessed some public power, and who were eagerly desirous of more. At that time the grave political essayist could speak to the few, without being shouted down by the many.

That political writing has in consequence declined in this country is certain, at least it has been *minced*. No practical subject can be discussed thoroughly at sufficient length, and with all the arguments set in one view. No observant person could write such things on a pressing practical point, and think they would have any influence on events. On the politics of the hour the great penny papers of the North have infinitely more effect than all the reviews in London. These rule the constituencies, and on great pressing issues rule Parliament too. In time to come they will prevent the existence of publicists, or at least take care that they shall be few, and those few not powerful.

At first it might seem that the change was bad, but I am not sure that it is so. On the contrary, it has one good effect. It prevents the highest class of philosophical minds from worrying themselves with momentary affairs. This is not their characteristic function. They have by nature in a rare degree that in which most men are most deficient— the faculty of abstraction. It is given them steadily to see not only a particular instance, or a few instances, but that which all such instances have in common. They can keep their attention fixed on this common element, and so fashion a doctrine common to all like cases. But when they have made their doctrine, their work is done: when that doctrine comes to be applied in real life a different class of faculties are wanted, and a most opposite set of powers become necessary. A philosopher having a particularly fine vision of the common elements in all cases is apt to be particularly blind to the uncommon qualities of individual instances. As objectors say, he is *doctrinaire*—that is, his doctrine telling him that 'C will happen because A and B are present, if A and B are unresisted'—he is apt to be very fond of his theory, and some time or other to overlook some unknown and uncatalogued resisting agency, and which modifies or overpowers A and B, and changes C altogether. We need for practice a more pliable class of mind, which though not able perhaps to invent a good abstract doctrine, is able to use it when made; and is able, too, to see the resisting agencies or modifying media, which the originator of the theory neither could nor would. The best applier is seldom the real discoverer, and still more seldom is the man who discovers the best man, or at all a good man to persuade others to use his discoveries. The difference between the patentee of an invention, and the capitalist who uses it, is not greater than that between the discoverer of an abstract political doctrine, and the practical politicians, active or rhetorical, who use it.

Mr. Mill is, of course, the standing instance of a philosopher spoiled by sending him into Parliament and the world. But in a very different way I think Mr. Senior, our last 'publicist,' was in some sense a spoiled philosopher. And I hope none of his friends will be offended at my saying so, for I intend it in no bad sense. What I mean is, that he scattered and wasted in a semi-abstract discussion of practical topics, powers which were fit to have produced a lasting and considerable work of philosophy. And I cannot think the practical discussion, as a discussion, very good. Take, for instance, the essay on Ireland, which is republished as a preface to his 'Irish Conversations.' It is certainly very dull, and dull in the most teasing way, for you feel that the subject is most interesting, and that the writer is a man of ability, but there is no corresponding result. Your mind is not engrossed as it ought to be, or instructed as it ought to be. In truth, the essay is too abstract for a work on a living subject like Ireland. You always feel that you are reading about an economical island in the air; you are always pausing to think whether something that is not said may not affect and overthrow that which is said. You are never presented, as a writer on real politics should present you, with a living image which impresses itself rightly or wrongly on your imagination as a picture of the subject, and interests and persuades you even more by what it

377

suggests to your own imagination than by the bare words on the paper. If, on the other hand, any one wishes to see what Mr. Senior was really capable of, I should refer him to the collection of Mr. Senior's philosophical essays lately published—say to the review of Sir George Lewis's essay on 'Authority in Matters of Opinion'—and unless I am much mistaken, he will find there clear proofs of a speculative intellect of singular clearness and of high force, which it is a pity should have left no equal memory of itself, and which for the want of such is even already fading as time passes and the generations change.

One reason why Mr. Senior's name is sooner passing away than it ought is that he was best known as a political economist, and that it must be owned that of late years abstract political economy—and it was with the abstract part that Mr. Senior dealt—has fallen somehow in public confidence, and that people's minds are a little in doubt about it. One principal cause of this is the set—the most mischievous set in my judgment—which is being made against abstract reasoning in general. This is due to the rise of an immense class of readers who find, as everybody ought to find, abstractions difficult, and who being incessantly told that they are the great reading public, and the judge of everything, instantly begin to judge that what is unpleasant to them cannot be very valuable. The great rise of 'Physics' ought, of course, to have prevented this. Our railways were made, so to say, out of abstract geometry, abstract algebra, abstract mechanics. Even in the kinds of science now most talked of those who can pass a good examination in Darwin's 'Origin of Species' must have had some practice in gaining a familiarity with abstract knowledge. But, in fact, 'Physics' have had a contrary effect. The thousands of popular students only know the results at second-hand; they have no conception of the processes by which they were discovered. They see brilliant experiments on optics, and because there is so much to see they think there is nothing hard or abstract in the subject; yet if they would try and master the undulatory theory of light, which very likely is the basis of these experiments, and that for which they were tried, they would find many and grave difficulties—exactly the same sort of difficulties which there are in mastering abstract political economy and applying it to the moving facts of trade and life. A very rapid diffusion of popular knowledge necessarily brings with it a certain dislike and distrust of that abstract reasoning which never can be popular, and which people are only too glad to think unnecessary.

378

And, besides this, political economy has fallen into some difficulty from causes peculiar to itself, and heresies, or what Mr. Senior and other economists of the old school would have thought to be especially such, are daily propounded. I was myself examined by him years ago, in the time of the strict school, at the London University, and I am sure he would have plucked various present examiners and professors. If it could have been revealed to him that persons of authority would dare to teach that profit had no tendency to become equal in different trades,—that the Ricardo theory of rent was a blunder and a misconception,—that it was unnecessary for bankers to keep a stock of gold or silver to meet their liabilities, but that they should buy the gold in the market when they wanted it, I think Mr. Senior would have been aghast. Yet such is the present state of the science, and naturally the rise of the heresiarchs has diminished the dignity of the orthodox heads. Now that the fame of Ricardo (one of the greatest and most consecutive of English thinkers) is a little dimmed, no wonder that the fame of an able follower of his, and such was Mr. Senior in the main, is much diminished. Secondary fame of that sort, if once lost, is scarcely to be recovered; and, therefore, I fear Mr. Senior's economical writings, or his philosophical essays (very able as several of the latter seem to me to be), will not long keep alive in the world the recollection of what in his own generation was justly thought to be his ability.

Possibly Mr. Senior, who was a shrewd observer of the world, had no confidence in the endurance of his philosophical fame; at all events, he took singular and sedulous pains to provide himself with a substitute in case of a failure. There has been, as we all know, a great deal of discussion, modern and ancient, about posthumous fame, and some species of it have been catalogued. The 'immortality of quotation' is one of these. There are many writers really known by some few sentences or some half-dozen stanzas, which everyone knows, but all the rest of their works are dead, and no one knows anything about them. And it has been argued whether this kind of immortality of 'extract' is or is not desirable or worth having. I believe the better opinion to be that it is worth having; always assuming that any posthumous fame is so. After all, your best words—your most characteristic words—are quoted continually, and have the chance of making a good impression of you year after year if anything of yours can make a good impression. But Mr. Senior has invented, or almost invented a new and different sort of immortality. He aspired to immortality as a *referee*. He went about Europe, indeed, beyond Europe, for he visited Egypt, talking carefully to the best known, the best informed, and most influential people on the affairs of each country, and on general intellectual affairs, and he wrote down the answers. There was no breach of confidence in this, for he told everybody—at least, everybody of importance—what he was doing; and if they liked, and if there were opportunity, he submitted that part of his journal which concerned them to their revision. His idea, of course, was that by preserving valuable thoughts, setting down on the instant fresh and characteristic remarks, he should earn permanent repute for himself. And if that sort of repute be desirable he will earn it. He will appear at the bottom of pages in many books for many years, as, 'See Senior's "Journals," vol. ii. p. 293.' And occasionally, according to the convenience of writers, his name will creep into the text, 'according to a good observation reported by Mr. Senior,' X Y was true; or, 'if we may rely on an assertion made to Mr. Senior, A B was not true.' And this will be the reward for years of endless pains and labour. It will not be like the common 'immortality of quotation,' in which your characteristic words are kept alive; it will be in the slightest sense a name only that will live; no image of Mr. Senior will then be preserved. The reader of after years will know only that a person called Mr. Senior, and about whom he has no other knowledge, was told so and so, true or false, by a Pasha of Egypt, or by such and such a French statesman, and *this* is all the immortality.

A certain peculiar power of asking questions is necessary in this mode. M. Léon Faucher was Prime Minister of France, and Mr. Senior steps up to him with—'Now that I have you for ten minutes, will you tell me what is your plan for a campaign?'—that is, for the policy of his government. No doubt it is a weakness, but there are many men thick-skinned enough in most ways, who could not ask such a question for any money or any fame. And the notoriety that Mr. Senior, as a professed journalist, might ask such questions, led people to be prepared to answer them. As years went on, it used to be said that the value of his journal was impaired, because persons of eminence prepared for their interviews, and corrected (as he was kind enough to let them) their sayings into what they would wish to have said rather than that which they did really say. The conversations thus became minor manifestos, not unguarded utterances, and so lost their greatest interest.

And independently of having to ask as a habit questions too direct to be pleasant, most people would rather go to the galleys than be bound to put down at the end of a party what was said in the course of it. The pang of the coming task would poison most men's social pleasure. And Mr. Senior often looked as if it spoiled his pleasure. His face had a care down it, as if he was keeping up the recollection of what *had* been said, rather than enjoying what was *being* said. And, at times, not quite gratifying to the speaker, the interest for what you were saying seemed to cease on a sudden (as does that of a reporter when he puts down his pen), as if he thought what was being said was no way remarkable, and that he would rest himself by not attending to it. To gain an immortality of referential citation, Mr. Senior certainly sacrificed much social enjoyment and some social popularity.

It should be seen, however, that most people could not gain that immortality by any sacrifice. First of all you must be something or somebody before the first people in foreign countries will speak to you freely, or indeed at all. Mr. Senior went abroad as a celebrated English economist, and with strenuous introductions from the most powerful and best people in England whom he had the gift of knowing. And what is more, he had the rarer gift of being able to use those introductions well. There was nothing in his daily pursuits to give him that knowledge; on the contrary, by profession he was an equity barrister, and he has himself described how difficult, how almost impossible it is, to get any foreigner to comprehend what 'equity' in England means; and with much exaggeration, yet not without some truth, Political Economy, as Mr. Senior understood it, has been called an 'insular science,' of which the authors were Englishmen, which assumed in the beings so treated of conditions and qualities hardly to be met with out of England. But Mr. Senior was an 'International Man,' well able, as many volumes of 'conversations' prove, to enter into the thoughts and report the words, not only of one sort of foreigners, but of various sorts. And the number of Masters in Chancery of whom this can be said is very small indeed.

Certainly, however, as was perhaps inevitable, the conversations are reported a little drily, and scarcely at all dramatically. Everybody speaks the same language—a French lady, a Pyrenean peasant, an Italian statesman, all use the same grave and cultivated words; all shape their sentences in the same clear, but rather formal, fashion. Nor is there much play of dialogue. In the best cases Mr. Senior's object was to get at the thoughts of some one eminent man, and that he has given us, but he left inferior speakers to shift for themselves. And in all cases the thoughts appear in their driest—we might say in their most algebraic form; it might be all about A, B, C, S, and E, F for any life there is. Mr. Senior gives us what a man said, but not how he said it; he does not make us know them better for having said it; and this because he either did not notice, or disdained to set down, the little traits and intricacies which distinguish one man's conversation from another. He rarely tells us whether a great statesman is tall or short; never mentions what sort of a coat any one wore; he shows no man 'in his habit as he was.'

In the substance of the two volumes of Journals now before us, Mr. Senior was very fortunate, for they turn on the two most prominent parts of foreign politics—the condition of the Pope, who, if he be not restored to temporal sovereignty, is sure to be in 'continual claim' for that sovereignty much longer than the lives of any of us; and the state of France, which is 'always with us,' an unequalled source of care, and an everlasting subject for excellent writing. At this instant almost everyone will turn to the French journals, but this extract from the Roman journal of 1851 is worth reading:—

Dr. T. came to take leave of us. He is going to England, and describes the formalities which attend the grant of a passport to a Roman. First, he must have the consent of his wife; secondly, of the curate of his parish; and thirdly, a certificate from two persons in the confidence of the Government that he behaved well during the Revolution. 'But,' I said, 'if the wife or the curate refuse to consent, what is the remedy?' 'In respect of the curate,' he said, 'there is none. He is the sole judge of what is favourable or unfavourable to the spiritual health of his parishioners: and if he thinks that foreign travel is likely to disagree with your soul, you must stay at home. As to your wife, you may summon her before the tribunal to give her reasons, and if the Court thinks them insufficient, you are allowed to go; but there is no saying how long the suit may last.'

And this observation from the Duc de Sermoneta, 'considered then as now,' the editor tells us, 'the cleverest man in Rome, is not ungratifying to English vanity:—

'Assassination,' he added, 'is almost the only classical custom which we have preserved; in other things we are more Turkish than European. Our system of government is eminently Turkish. It consists of a central despotism and provincial despots, whom *they* call pashas and cadis, and *we* call cardinals and prelates, in the provinces. The real successors of the ancient Romans are the English. You have inherited the Roman respect for law and authority, the Roman love for what is established, the Roman fidelity to engagements, the Roman pertinacity of purpose, and the Roman contempt for foreigners. When you commit follies they are all of your own invention. We add to our own absurdities those of every other country. Like the Romans, wherever you go you take all your immunities. An Englishman, or even a Jew who calls himself an Englishman, is *civis Romanus*. He is not bound to put up with the institutions of other countries. He carries abroad with him his amusements, his comforts, his habits, and even his hours. Wherever you go the *Galignani* follows you. No foreign post-office ventures to intercept it. When I read Cicero's 'Letters' I fancy myself reading the correspondence of one of your statesmen. All the thoughts, all the feelings, almost all the expressions are English.'

I cannot help thinking that this saying of the 'cleverest man in Rome' might be coupled with Professor Huxley's dictum that the 'English and the Italian are the best brains now extant;' and that Mr. Arnold might fitly append both to the next reprint of 'My Countrymen.'

The conversations of Mr. Senior on France in 1848, 1850, and 1851, in several parts, are very curious, and would afford easy matter for an article if it were desirable to add another to the innumerable ones already written in England on French politics. But at present I need not do this, nor is there room. I will only take two salient points which these conversations illustrate, make a quotation from them, and then stop.

First, and this is the greatest point of all, no one of Mr. Senior's interlocutors seems to have had the secret gift of correct anticipation. In May, 1848, Michel Chevalier predicted the days of June of the same year; but this, though a very sensible remark, was no miraculous prophecy. It was certain to everybody that the struggle between the *rouge* party and the party of order had not yet been fought out, and that it must be fought out, and few close judges probably could doubt that at last the party of order would win; at last they always *have* won. But this is almost the only instance in these volumes of tolerable prediction. One instance of bad prophecy is very curious. Naturally very many if not most of Mr. Senior's friends were, if not professed economists, at least men of an economical and financial turn. After the *coup d'état* of the late Emperor, the question continually is not so much what is coming to the French nation, as what will happen to French trade—the French exchequer. And it is very remarkable that though these experienced and close observers might and did in some degree differ as to the intensity of the economical disaster which was impending in 1851, everyone expected economical disaster more or less severe. The following, from an unknown converser V., is a fair specimen:—

'What do you mean,' I asked, 'by ruin? How can such a country as France be ruined?'

'By ruin,' he answered, 'I mean progressive decline. I mean deterioration of agriculture, of manufactures, and of commerce. I mean capital exported, railroads unfinished, rents unpaid, increasing pauperism, a growing deficit; in short, the continuance of our present state of insecurity, and therefore of semi-paralysis.'

But neither V. nor any other 'authority' dreamed that the next twenty years would be years of incomparably the greatest economical prosperity which France had ever seen; that the railway system would be developed with a rapidity far greater than in the time of Louis Philippe; that commerce would grow with unknown celerity; that agriculture would thrive; that the deficit in the finances would be caused not by the deficiency of the revenue, for that augmented faster than ever, but by the prodigality of the Government; and that this prodigality, though there seemed no end to it, and though financiers were always exposing it, would in no way exhaust France, but leave her able at her need to raise suddenly an immense sum of ready money far greater than she ever raised before, than former Governments would have dreamed of demanding, or than in 1851 would have been thought possible. At this moment, when so many predictions are in the air as to *future* France, it is useful to see how wrong the most sure predictions, and those of the best authorities, have been as to *past* France.

And in addition to this general difficulty of prediction, there are also the clearest warnings in these volumes, how difficult the French then found it (and now find it, for the circumstances are not really altered) to establish what to a common Englishman seems the most obvious form of government in their case: parliamentary government and constitutional royalty. 'France,' says one of Mr. Senior's interlocutors, an Imperialist, it is fair to say,—

Is unfit for Parliamentary government. It wants two things, both elements of that form of government. One is moderation. Every French party, if it gets the upper hand, pushes its victory to the utmost, alters the policy and displaces the administration of its predecessors, and carries out its own views to the utmost extreme, until it disgusts the country, and the Opposition comes in, and acts with equal intemperance. Another deficiency is an aristocracy. We have indeed an aristocracy of birth and an aristocracy of wealth; but the former is poor, ignorant, and presumptuous, the latter ignoble and servile. The great object of our rich *roturiers* is to connect themselves with noble families. They succeed more easily for their daughters, but even that success is a miserable one. An Englishman can scarcely conceive the stupidity, ignorance, and frivolity of the young men of our ancient families. They disdain the learned professions and trade, there is room for only a portion of them in the army, and what is the army in a long peace? Then we have no political bodies with any inherent strength or traditionary influence. In short, there is nothing powerful but the Government and the army.

And a much higher authority, Gustave de Beaumont, the friend and the biographer of Tocqueville, spoke still more clearly and still more strongly on the incompatibility to France of our English constitutional king.

'I objected,' said Mr. Senior, 'to his calling the government of Louis-Philippe constitutional, since Louis-Philippe was his own prime minister—a most unconstitutional proceeding, according to our notions.'

'Yes,' he said, 'according to your notions, but not according to ours. We have not yet adopted the true faith, the faith of the *cochon à l'engrais*. To preserve our respect our sovereign must act. And this, perhaps, makes us incapable at present of your constitutional government. If our sovereign, whether you call him president or king, merely takes the members whom the Assembly points out to him, keeps them so long as they can keep their majority, follows their advice implicitly, and dismisses them as soon as they lose their majority, he becomes King Log, and we despise him. If he acts he must sometimes make mistakes, and still oftener be thought to do so. He will sometimes offend the good sense of the nation, and oftener its susceptibilities, and we shall hate him. This is the objection to a president for life; he would inevitably in time become hated or despised, or both, and then we should go into the streets and depose him. For in France,' he added, 'we are not good balancers of inconveniences. "Nous sommes trop logiques." As soon as we see the faults of an institution, *nous la brisons*. In England you calculate; we act on impulse. We should never have tolerated your Hanoverian kings, with their German favourites and their German policy. We should have turned them out in a year. You kept them until they were acclimatised, and gradually became the best royal stock in Europe. Unless we greatly improve, we never shall have any permanent institutions; for as we destroy every institution as soon as we discover its faults and no one is free from them, nothing can last.'

Enough has been quoted to show the amount of curious information in these volumes. But it ought to be added that there is a great difficulty in using them. Archbishop Whately used to say that he had often heard the words of Eliphaz, the Temanite, quoted in good pulpits as 'on conclusive authority;' the preacher found them in the Book of Job in the very centre of the Bible, and did not see why he should not quote them. The fact that they were dramatically put in the mouth of an ill-natured and mistaken friend did not occur to him. Just so in Mr. Senior's journals, there are interlocutors of every sort, and any one who seeks a text on any side or anything for France or Italy may find it here. This will contribute much to their 'immortality of reference,' but it will also make a wise critic suspicious of their authority. He will want to see not only what was said, but who said it, lest the words may be those of some nameless fool or grave charlatan, instead of those of Faucher or Tocqueville.

End of Volume II

INDEX*

I—Editorial Sections

Note: All page references in this index are to volume I unless preceded by figure II

* The index is divided into three parts:
Part I Editorial Sections (p. 387), Part II Texts (p. 392),
Part III Bagehot's Epigrams (p. 399).

II—Texts

INDEX

Scott, Sir Walter—*cont.*
ignorance of abstract intellect,
II 66–8, 73–4
ignorance of women, *II* 68–70
imaginative use of detail,
I 414–15
literary style, *II* 74–5
natural scenery, descriptions,
I 178–80
political economy, ideas,
II 58–60
political sense, *II* 52–3
religious sense, *II* 71–4
retribution, concept of, *II* 60–2
sentiment, fact mingled, *II* 48–50,
62–6
works: *Ivanhoe, II* 63–4, 186
works: *Old Mortality, I* 327
Senior, Nassau William:
'publicist', *II* 375–6
'referee', current affairs,
II 380–6
Sensitivity, insensitivity, *I* 409–10
Shakespeare, William, *I* 474, *II* 79–80,
181, 198
ability to know people, *I* 188–92,
338
character, *I* 173–4, 176
commercial success, *I* 212–14
cultivated intellect lacking, *II* 206
fanciful poet, *I* 198–202
introspective qualities, *I* 195–8
learning, book knowledge,
I 209–10
liveliness of mind, *I* 192–5
malevolence, *I* 204–5
natural scenery, observation,
I 180–1, 182–3
ornate, romantic writer, *II* 345–6
political views, *I* 202–4
religion, *I* 210–12
sportsman, *I* 176–7, 182–3
theory of drama, *I* 139
universal writer, *I* 212
visual memory, *I* 176–8
women, observation, *I* 205–7,
208–9

works:
Hamlet, II 352
King Lear, I 114, 161, 471
Othello, I 161
Shelley, Percy Bysshe, *I* 131, 137,
138, 139, 159
comparison with Tennyson,
II 200–2, 205, 206–7
conscience, lack of, *I* 446–8
education, Oxford, *I* 444–6
Harriett Westbrook, marriage and
death, *I* 456–62
Hazlitt on, quoted, *I* 436–7, 474
impulse, purity of, *I* 434–6, 446,
454, 462, 472
impulse to reform, *I* 436–7, 438–9,
445, 454–5
literary style, *I* 475–6
mythological Epicurean tendency
I 448–51
nihilistic, Hume tendency, *I* 451–2
on love, *I* 437–8
on poetry, *I* 290, 463–4
Platonian tendency, *I* 452–3,
II 341
poetry of, *I* 464–8, 471–6, *II* 27
search for truth, *I* 439–41
self-delineative, *I* 433–4, 455–6
sensibility, nature of, *I* 474–5
works: *The Cenci, I* 441–4, *II* 181
young men's poet, *II* 180–1
Sheridan, Richard Brinsley, on
Gibbon, *I* 377
Smith, Adam, *I* 418, *II* 58
Smith, Sydney, *I* 323, 333–9, *II* 33
humanity, *I* 334–6
humour, *I* 336–8
literary style, *I* 333–4
Snobbishness, *II* 307–9
Society, structure of, *II* 307–9
Society, worldliness, *II* 14–16
Soliloquy, literary, *II* 197–8
Somers, Lord, *I* 325
Sophocles:
decorum of, *I* 470–1
influence on Shelley, *I* 475–6
South Sea Bubble, *I* 352–3

397

III—Bagehot's Epigrams

Note: References to volume numbers are shown by figures I and II